# OPTIMIZING HUMAN RESOURCES:
## Readings in Individual and Organization Development

Edited by
**GORDON L. LIPPITT** – The George Washington University
**LESLIE E. THIS** – Project Associates, Inc.
**ROBERT G. BIDWELL, JR.** – U.S. Department of the Interior

**ADDISON-WESLEY PUBLISHING COMPANY**
Reading, Massachusetts · Menlo Park, California · London · Don Mills, Ontario

# PREFACE

This book has been compiled to meet the needs of persons concerned with the application of human resource development in organizations. Although its basic aim is one of practicality, we have tried to bridge the gap between theory and practice whenever possible. We feel that this is particularly important today since both theory and practice in this area are expanding at an incredible rate.

A book of readings has both advantages and disadvantages when it is compared with a publication written by one author. In reaching our decision to prepare a book on human resource development, we concluded that here the advantages clearly outweigh any limitations; the different authors represented in this book offer a total enrichment that could not be provided by one writer. Many persons from a number of disciplines and backgrounds are using new concepts, methods, and approaches to develop human resources in organizations. So many are doing so much, in fact, that we found excellent material far in excess of what any one book could include.

Our choice of the term *human resource development* is intended to focus on the broad developmental process of people as resources to themselves, groups, organizations, communities, and larger cultures. We have not tried to cover the traditional field of training and development. Instead, we have tried to identify the key impact areas that have come to the fore in organizations during the last several years. In this context we have attempted to show the change in orientation of developmental activities in today's organizations.

It is important for the reader to understand the objectives of the editors in putting together this collection of readings:

First, we recognized the extensive changes in the human resource development field since 1965 and observed that reports of these applications were greatly diffused. This led us to feel that we could make a contribution by assembling some of this recent literature in an organized manner.

Second, we felt that there was a need to put the developing trends, methods, and activities into a single frame of reference, so that some "linkage" (old and future) could be established between such disparate areas as laboratory training, systems concepts, and minority-group programs. We have tried to provide that linkage by the format of the book—in which we start with an examination of the changing nature of society, move into learning concepts and practices, treat a number of approaches to human resource development, and conclude with implications for the future role of those who are responsible for developing human resources in organizations.

Our third objective was to choose areas that are on the "cutting edge" of human resource development. We want this book to be something more than another of the so-called handbooks that attempt to cover the basic elements in assessing training needs, designing programs, choosing methods, implementing the programs, and training administration. Times have been changing dramatically in the field, and we have attempted to be "future oriented" in our scope. Consequently the book is largely devoted to newer methods of developing human resources, newer methods that have already been successful or promise a high potential for success.

Our fourth aim was to present different points of view about the key areas. We want the reader to feel that we have fairly presented both points of view in the treatment of controversial areas such as laboratory training and organization development. In complex areas such as learning theory and motivation to work, we have presented multiple views; thus no one advocate dominates the selections. If in some instances the differences are not evident, it is due to a lack of balance in the literature and not to a designed "slanting."

If our objectives are clear, the reader may wonder why we organized the book as we did.

The first chapter's focus on trends in society sets a backdrop for the whole field of human resource development. Following this introduction, we felt it appropriate in Chapter 2 to cover briefly the research, theory, and guidelines on how people learn and change. A systems approach to developing human resources became the focus of Chapter 3, because it was seen as the proper conceptual frame of reference for many of the processes of human resource development covered throughout the book. Although the systems approach is a topic of increasing concern, even of belief, no earlier collection of significant writings on systems of human resources has been assembled. In Chapter 4, we discuss the field of organization development or renewal, one of the most recent and most rapidly expanding areas of human resource development. Numerous opinions and methods are growing in geometric proportion in this field, and they needed to be pulled together. Especially in this area there are a large number of excellent readings we were unable to include because of space limitations.

Chapter 5 deals with laboratory training in developing human potential. A section on this controversial area is a must in any current look at evolving practices. Strong opinions about this field range from those who feel it is the most valuable method of developing human resources to those who feel it is either dangerous or inappropriate, if not both.

In Chapter 6, we focus on a new area of training and development in which there is limited but exciting experience—developing specialized groups. The editors selected three key examples through which to examine our practices: the disadvantaged, the young, and women. These three populations have been underutilized, their human potential far from optimized, and there is a great need to learn more about how they can best be developed.

The inclusion of a chapter entitled, "Restructuring Work for Developing People," may be a surprise to some training and development specialists. We felt, however, that while a great deal of attention has been given to various theories of motivation, the potential benefits to be found in changing the structure, nature, and expectations of one's job have often been overlooked. The focus on "work itself" as an enrichment factor requires us to take such an examination. While differing views exist in this area, a great deal of future emphasis will be placed here.

Our eighth chapter deals with one of the true dilemmas of the field: How do you evaluate the results of human resource development? While numerous attempts have been made to evaluate and follow up learning experiences, theory and practice in these areas has long been inadequate. It is our hope that this chapter may stimulate additional research and experimentation.

Chapter 9 attempts to put into perspective the emerging needs, roles, and qualifications of specialists in human resource development. We try to help the reader define his role and appreciate the skills he will need.

Some readers may be curious about how we selected the writings included in this book.

First, we developed our outline and agreed that, with rare exceptions, we would not use material that had been written prior to 1965. (Of the 39 articles in the book only 4 were published before 1965.) The exceptions are considered "classics" in their particular areas.

Second, we reviewed countless appropriate journals, recent books, and numerous bibliographies or materials published since 1965. From this extensive review we selected over 500 articles for evaluation and reading by the editors.

Third, we assigned the preliminary screened articles to chapter headings and made selections for quality, uniqueness, and duplication. This brought us to 102 selections.

Fourth, in developing the chapter sequence, balancing chapter lengths, and in the process of securing permissions, we arrived at our final collection of 39 articles, excerpts, or papers. This was by far the most difficult part of the process and entailed numerous meetings and discussions.

It might be worthwhile to note that the editors do represent a wide range of interests including university, private enterprise, consulting, and program leadership of governmental training in a number of agencies. We feel this aided the eclectic nature of selections and improved the quality of our coverage.

We wish to express our appreciation to a number of persons who have made this volume possible. Most important are the authors and publishers who so kindly gave us permission to reprint their works. While a total of 14 different publications are represented in these selections, we want to express our particular appreciation to the *Training and Development Journal, the Journal of Applied Behavioral Science,* and the *Harvard Business Review,* in which many of the articles originally appeared. We wish to acknowledge permission to reprint copyrighted material from Leadership Resources, to Mrs. Edith Stivers, without whose manuscript work and securing of permissions we could not have brought this project to fruition; and we want to thank our publishers for their assistance.

We hope you, the reader, find this book a helpful resource in developing others. The process of bringing it to you has furthered our appreciation of this field of human resource development.

*May 1971*                                                                G.L.L.
                                                                            L.E.T.
                                                                         R.G.B., Jr.

# CONTENTS

*ix*

x    *Contents*

# 1.
# HUMAN RESOURCE DEVELOPMENT IN A CHANGING WORLD

Too frequently the training and development of human resources has been considered an expendable luxury during trying financial times, a specific tool of management to develop individual skills, or a means of developing people for promotion to the next level of organizational leadership. While these views carry some validity, it is rapidly becoming apparent that the development of human resources should be regarded in the larger context of trends in society and the needs of changing organizations.

In this chapter, the editors attempt to capture not only the changes in modern society, but also the implications of these changes for human resource training and development.

Some people might feel that the "revolutions" of our time are beyond the concern of a human resource specialist or a training professional. The words of Ted Sorensen, in the first selection of this chapter, present a strong case to the contrary: The key revolutions that we face today will require "peaceful revolutions" in the human resource development field if we are to cope effectively with the rapid changes in man's institutions. The distinction between peaceful and violent revolution should be clear to those who observe the militant destruction of property, violation of the rights of others, and acts of force. The relevant human resource development person will see his role as one of dissatisfaction with part of the status quo. As a concerned individual he will be prepared to work within organizations, communities, or groups to improve and change their functioning.

In the second article, Warren Bennis examines some of the ways in which man's institutions are experiencing change. He looks at the limitations of bureaucracy, but indicates a number of alternatives that might not be any more satisfactory. He proceeds to enunciate his idea of colleaguality in organizational functioning.

The final paper, written by Gordon Lippitt, relates the revolutions and new patterns of organizational functioning to the nature of training and development. His twelve projected trends seem likely guidelines for the future of manpower development.

In such a setting it appears that human resource development is by no means a "luxury"; it is the key with which to unlock creative helping and problem-solving processes that can move a changing society constructively forward.

## THE REVOLUTIONS OF OUR TIME AND THEIR IMPLICATIONS FOR TRAINING AND DEVELOPMENT

*Theodore C. Sorensen*

I've been asked to put into perspective the "Revolutions of Our Time". We first ought to ask ourselves whether "revolutions" is the right word. It's not a word to be used loosely, it's not a word to be used lightly, and the imprecise use of words, I have found, as both a writer and a lawyer can cause more trouble than silence itself.

A revolution is a rare occurrence. I realize that it is a word that is popularly used—people talk about a revolution in plastics or a revolution in clothespins or a revolution in one phase of life or another. But, I think before we use that as it's used here today and will be used this week we should examine what revolutions we're talking about and make certain they are revolutions. If it's something that's temporary, if it's something that's common, if it's something that's modest in proportions, I would not call it a revolution.

The four areas we're talking about primarily are four overlapping revolutions—if indeed they are revolutions. The first is taking place on our college campuses where the outbreaks of student disorder, demonstrations, violence, threats, and coercion have spread from a handful to dozens of college campuses not only in the East, but in all parts of the country.

There are no doubt some who would say: "this is not a revolution—this is a fad. We've had these before. College students at one time were swallowing goldfish. At another time they were overcrowding into telephone booths. Every spring we have panty raids or parking riots on college campuses. Boys will be boys and soon they will be brokers and bankers and lawyers and we shouldn't worry about it very much."

I think we make a great mistake if we dismiss the present unrest on campus in those ways. I think we are faced with a revolution. We are faced with a deep-seated, long-lasting scale of disorder and unrest that will be with us for some time.

Those who are committed to a course of violence, I agree, are very few. They do not represent the majority opinion on campus; they do not have a legitimate program of goals, of their own; they do not have any hesitance about shutting down and wrecking universities instead of trying to improve them; and, in my opinion, they have no business being on a college campus. But they are the small—very small—minority.

There is a much larger group of students who from time to time join with that small group either because they sympathize with the treatment they have received from university authorities or from outside police (outside police rarely know how to deal effectively and discriminately with student behavior)—or because they sympathize

From *Selected Papers* of the 1969 national convention of the American Society for Training and Development. Reprinted by permission of the American Society for Training and Development.

not with the means used by the violent few but with the grievances which they hold. For that majority of students is dissatisfied with the society they are about to inherit, with the institutions that are preparing them for that society, and with the whole spectrum of morality, value-judgment and decision-making that faces them as young Americans.

Black students are in a special category, concerned not so much with the sickening aspects of too much affluence, but with the sickening aspects of not enough affluence for themselves and for their people, concerned with the fact that they feel resented and used in a white man's environment while they are trying to find their own identity.

These disorders will remain with us—they will spread to high schools, they will spread to some of the sleepier campuses that have not yet been affected, until we learn how to cope with what I regard as a serious revolution.

Secondly, we are faced with disorders and unrest in our black communities. Some people would say that this is not a revolution that's taking place in the ghetto today—that this is a form of evolution, that we had unrest over the years among our minority populations that is understandable in view of the treatment to which they have been subjected, that disorders will break out from time to time but that there is nothing sufficiently unusual about what is going on now to deserve the label "revolution".

There again, I must disagree. What is taking place in the black community today is too far-reaching, too long-lasting, and too unlikely to be turned back or repressed under any circumstances to be categorized with incidents of similar unrest that have happened before. This is a revolution. It has many different leaders. It has many different labels.

Blacks having listened for a long time to white liberals as to how they should run their lives, how they should improve their lot, are now starting out on their own. They are talking about black power or black studies or black capitalism or black culture or one plan after another.

There are a variety of leaders—sometimes competing with each other to see who can make the most exaggerated attacks on the white establishment—partly to gain publicity and following in the black community, partly to antagonize and frighten the whites who have antagonized and frightened them and their people for so long.

But, in the final analysis, their goals are not really so different from one another or so different from what this country has stood for for a long time. A decent education for their children that is equal to the education received by any other American, a decent place to live, to grow up, to play that will give them the same opportunity as any other American; a decent job that has some dignity as well as a reasonable means of income; an equal opportunity to stand up in life, to stand up in American society and be treated and regarded as anyone else.

Unfortunately since this revolution began some six or seven years ago the gap between the average white man's affluence and the average black man's affluence has grown larger instead of less. This revolution is with us until we can reverse that trend and narrow that gap until there is no gap at all between the way peoples of different races live and are treated in this country.

Both the revolution of the young and the revolution of the blacks are reflected in the third area of unrest and change that confronts us today and that is in the area of politics. Some would say: this is not a revolution that we are seeing now, only a new form of factionalism, with new splinter groups arising, abrogating unto themselves the right to say that they have all the wisdom and are going to have their own way about politics in this country (or else).

We thereby mistake the New Politics as it is called for the New Left as they like to call themselves, and the two are very different indeed.

The New Left—with their militants, and their high ideological tests that admit no one but a few of their friends, and their willingness resort to demonstrations and profanity, and their willingness to factionalize our existing political parties do not represent the New Politics.

The key word to the New Politics is participation. It's encouraging rank and file members of political parties, amateurs and students and housewives, to take part not only in the envelope licking and the doorbell ringing but in the real decision-making that goes on in our political world. And that participatory politics, as it is called, that movement toward broadening the base of political decision-making in this country, is here to stay regardless of whether the New Left succeeds or fails.

And finally, there is a revolution—or suggested revolution—in morals in the United States. The young people have had a hand in it, the Negro population has had a hand in it, it's even related and reflected at times in the changes in the political picture. Someone said it is not a revolution—that only a few sensation seekers were trying to obtain publicity or profit by means of the exploitation of sex and immoral behavior. It is a revolution. It could be a very dangerous revolution that affects how we live, how we dress, how we drink. If affects the young people not only of college age but also of high school age. It affects their attitude toward drugs, toward tobacco, toward alcohol and toward pornography. It affects what it is we see on our television screens and on our movie screens, what we read in books, and what we see on stage. It affects what we wear and how we conduct ourselves in public. It has, as is true of all these revolutions, some positive possibilities, some liberating potentiality. We could use more frankness and more freedom in some areas of American life that have too long been restricted by inhibitions. But like each of the other revolutions, it also has grave dangers that could undermine those values from the past which will well serve us in the future.

So we have four revolutions in American life today, four overlapping revolutions that ought to be of concern to every American. Each one of these revolutions can be an opportunity or it can be a danger. Each one presents us with opportunities for enriching the lives of our students, for improving the lives of the black, for upgrading politics in America, for enlivening and enlightening our moral scene; and it presents grave dangers of wrecking our colleges, dividing black vs. white, destroying our political system and devaluating the morals that have been important to us.

To understand these revolutions, however, we have to look beyond and beneath them. Each of them, in its own way, is really a symptom. One can treat symptoms. One must treat symptoms at times just as we must treat a fever to make certain the patient does not die. But, if we treat only symptoms, if we only repress these revolutions, then we have cured nothing. We have gotten at the bottom of nothing. And we are likely to find ourselves faced with even worse diseases, repressing dissent, sapping growth and losing out on the opportunities which are presented.

For underneath those revolutions which are symptoms are other revolutions which are causes; revolutions which are taking place in this country that sometimes we don't think of in terms of revolution because they don't incite violence, they don't bring about the same kind of headline, but they are going on nevertheless.

Let me quickly mention four such underlying revolutions to you. First is one that you know better than I—the revolution of technology. Automation has moved from the farm to the plant and now to the office, to the stockbroker, to the bank, to the business office, to the retail office of every kind. It has made considerable in-roads in government. We are moving rapidly from the Nuclear Age to the Space Age, from the era of the transistor to the era of the laser.

This has given us more affluence than ever before, this has given us more leisure time than ever before, and our young people are saying "affluence for what?", "time to do what?".

It also requires us to have higher skills than ever before requiring young people to stay in school far longer than they did previously. It's requiring more high school graduates to go on to college, more college graduates to go on to post-graduate training, and this puts pressure on those who have not shared in the affluence and on those whose skin color has excluded them from those benefits, and it also puts pressure on those institutions of education and higher learning themselves.

That revolution in technology underlies each of the others. For people are asking: what kind of country is it that has the technological ability to put a man on the moon but does not have the ability to get him out of the ghetto?

Second, there is an underlying revolution in communications. This is the era of young people who were raised and weaned on the television set, whose parents placed them in front of that set as a babysitter instead of leaving them on their own, teaching them about books or sending them out to the streets to play.

The change in communication is rapidly accelerating even now. The use of satellites for television, telephone, radio and international communications is just beginning. The tremendous increase in the mass media, in the use of the printed word and its distribution has flooded us all in a sea of print that comes not only through the traditional newspapers, magazines, books and paperbacks but is now beginning to come through computers and new devices as well.

This has affected each of the symptomatic revolutions to which I've referred. The individual citizen who can sit at home and watch the candidates on television is not going to be delivered by a union or ward leader or an ethnic group chairman when he can deliver his own vote. The student who has grown up for eighteen years with television finds that he is an articulate critic of his time, aware of the imperfections as well as the graces of our society and able to talk about them sharply, succintly—sometimes lengthily. The black man has seen on television the affluence and opportunity that is available to the white man. He has heard on television and in this mass of printed words an escalation of promises and campaign rhetoric that has made each individual citizen of this country feel that he has inalienable rights, that he has opportunities that are due him, that he has reasons to be dissatisfied with his lot if he lives at a level less than that he constantly sees on television and through the other kinds of media.

The media are not only producers but in a sense consumers of information. They gobble up personalities and new stories and information as rapidly as they can be turned out because they conceive of themselves as entertainment media. They want something new, something exciting, they're tired of yesterday's stories and yesterday's heroes and each day and each week and each year they want something that is greater and more exciting. As a result, in outdoing each other and competing in that fashion they use up people and ideas and escalate the level of expectations in this country.

Thus people ask . . . young people ask . . . thoughtful citizens ask, "What kind of society is it that has the means to say so much and yet, at times, seems to be saying so little?"

That leads to the third underlying revolution I'm talking about, the revolution in expectations. We are the wealthiest country in the world today. Indeed, we are the wealthiest country in the history of mankind. The annual figures on expenditures of average Americans on boats, on yachts, on pets, on luxuries have through the mass media become known to world citizens who do not now share in that kind of luxury and affluence.

They know we have the power, we have the wealth, to do away with all economic inequality and injustice and indignity in this country. Partly because of the revolution in technology, as the voices on television and in the mass media escalate their promises, as the citizens living still in despair and degradation respond to those promises, their expectations are raised.

The young and affluent white students expect more from that society than they are seeing performed. The poor and the black expect more from that society than they are receiving.

On the weekend before Palm Sunday the New York State Legislature, because of the budget squeeze which is so familiar to most legislatures, found it necessary to cut back on the funds available for hospital care, for education, for those on welfare, and for aid to the cities. It cut back the food allowances for those on welfare to something like 15¢ a day, for example. On the same weekend, in Beverly Hills, there was a five-day party launching the premiere of a new motion picture attended by jet-setters and royalty and the high society people from this country and others; and one lady who was present said, "This is the most wonderful weekend in the history of mankind."

Think about it. Think about what kind of society it is that can spend three billion dollars a month fighting a war tens of thousands of miles away in Viet Nam but cannot find even one billion dollars a year to feed those suffering from hunger and malnutrition in our country.

Finally these three revolutions lead to a fourth, which in a sense is the one revolution that sums them all up . . . the revolution against authority. There's a feeling on the part of most citizens, rich or poor, black or white, young or old, that we live in such an age of "Bigness" that no one can do anything about it. Government has become so big, so centralized, so far away, so remote, so impersonal. The students feel that the universities have become so big that the individual student, much less his grievances, cannot be identified. The corporations have become so big, the organizations, the unions, every aspect of life seems to involve massive institutions that do not yield to change.

Thus because there is this articulateness that has developed through television, because there is this new sense of affluence, because there is a feeling of, on the one hand powerlessness, but on the other hand high expectations, we find this revolt against authority. It affects almost every aspect of our life. Children revolting against their parents, students revolting against their teachers, laymen and clerics revolting against their church. We see it overseas where small nations refuse to have super powers dictate to them. We see it at home where union members refuse to abide by the settlements worked out by their union leaders. We see it in politics where the rank and file members, on their own, insist upon overturning the decisions that have been made.

Presidents and popes and premiers and even military leaders are finding their authority challenged as never before. This is because the combination of these revolutions has convinced a large proportion of our population that they cannot accomplish change in the usual peaceful way. They are convinced that they cannot work through the system—that the system itself won't change, that those in charge of the system are unwilling or unable to change it. They have no confidence in what they call the establishment, they have no belief that those who are in power will use that power to improve society or to relieve their sense of helplessness and powerlessness.

The student wonders why a colleague of his who is opposed to an immoral war is in jail while those perpetuating immoral war are in office. The black man wonders why if he breaks through the barriers and makes the struggle and goes to college, the average black college graduate still earns less than the average white high school dropout. The political idealist wonders why it is that he can mobilize energy and talent in 1968 as he has never been mobilized before, only to find that both conventions and the national election in the long run are still controlled and settled by those who practice politics in the old way. Even the hippie who symbolizes the so-called revolution in morals wonders what kind of society it is that appears to break down on every side.

I said to one young man, who I thought was dressed disgracefully, "Why do you dress that way?" I know he came from a good family, I know that he was an intelligent, bright student. He said, "I dress the way I feel, and I don't feel so good." And, I'm not sure anyone could blame him for not feeling so good in the society which he is about to inherit.

What does all this have to do with ASTD? I think it has everything to do with ASTD, because I think that it is training and development that offer a major key to the problems that we have been talking about today.

It is through training that these young people, black and white, can achieve some hope for change, some hope for improvement in their lives in the society they are inheriting. It is through training that they can learn the techniques of organization and management and budgeting and computers that will enable them to master the system that they fear is mastering them because of its complexity. It's through training that we will develop leaders that are badly needed if this sense of powerlessness and helplessness is to be overcome.

The new movement in the country today is for decentralization and for community control—for having local leaders play a much larger role in the operation of our schools, our hospitals, our other public services and, in time, our economy. But, if we are to have decentralization and community control, we must have leaders who are able to fill those roles, who will be able to handle those problems and who will be able to instill a sense of hope in their people. It is through training that you are going to develop managers, supervisors, leaders and other trainers who will be attuned to our times, who will understand these problems, who will be responsive to the needs with which we are dealing.

In short, your task is nothing less than that of training revolutionaries. Yes, you must train peaceful revolutionaries if we are not to be taken over by violent revolutionaries. You must train those who can move this country ahead, modify and reform its system, alter our society so that it meets with onrushing stream of youth and technology and communications and economics, so that stream doesn't pour into the old narrow channels of American society. If it does then we have even deeper troubles ahead.

President Kennedy once said, "Those who make peaceful revolution impossible make violent revolution inevitable." He was talking about Latin America, but he could just as well have been talking about the United States today and tomorrow. If we do not make peaceful revolution possible, if you do not train men and women who will be peaceful revolutionaries and can lead other peaceful revolutionaries, then I'm very much afraid that violent revolution in this country is inevitable.

We need leaders who will listen to protests when they are peaceful. We need managers who will be responsive to demands that come from the rank and file. We need educators who will welcome participation by students and faculty in the decision-making process. We need administrators who are willing to move with the times and change their systems accordingly. If we don't listen, if we don't respond, if we don't move, if we don't welcome this kind of innovation, then we cannot very well protest or object when those who have been trying to move us, who have been trying to participate, who have been trying to bring about this change, give up on our system and say the only way is to confront it and attack it with violence if necessary.

We should not do this just to prevent violence. Let's don't change our system at the point of a gun. Let's don't give in to force and coercion. I'm in favor of a peaceful revolution in this country because I happen to think it is right, because I think this country has to realize the last third of the twentieth century is a completely new era. I'm asking you to train the leaders and managers and educators of tomorrow who will recognize that most of our institutions today are anachronistic, who will recognize that much of what we say in this society is hypocritical, who will treat many of the old ways of doing things as irrelevant.

Dr. Benjamin Rush, one of the founders of our country, was congratulated shortly after the last military success over Great Britain on the successful completion of the American revolution. He said, "No, we have successfully completed the American war against Britain. The American Revolution is just beginning."

The American Revolution is still continuing. The pace of that revolution is now picking up. We—each of us—have a responsibility to carry on that revolution to make certain that it is carried on peacefully. It is an enormous task. The pressures from the extreme left and the extreme right are getting larger every day. The difficulty of working with those people who are indifferent, who are still complacent, who are ignorant of these changes, is one of the most difficult tasks that we will have. We must face those people who are angered by the violence, as all of us are angered, and who refuse to change.

We must allocate resources that we have become accustomed to pouring into military hardware and other less constructive outlets, and change that stream into the development of our human resources here at home.

To change, to revolutionize a whole society, to bring a whole race of people up to a position of equality, to satisfy the urging and demands of frustrated young people, to channel into constructive means this tremendous energy that is confronting us, is a difficult and sometimes impossible job. There will be occasions when we feel like sitting and letting someone else do it. But is was all summed up centuries and centuries ago by the Hasidic Jews in the Sayings of the Fathers: "The day is short and the work is great and the laborers are sluggish and the reward is much and the matter is urgent."

# A FUNNY THING HAPPENED ON THE WAY TO THE FUTURE

*Warren G. Bennis*

Analysis of the "future," or, more precisely, inventing relevant futures, has become in recent years as respectable for the scientist as the shaman. Inspired by Bertrand de Jouvenal, Daniel Bell, Olaf Helmer, and others, there seems to be growing evidence and recognition for the need of a legitimate base of operations for the "futurologist." Writing in a recent issue of the *Antioch Review*, groping for a definition of the future I wrote:

For me, the "future" is a portmanteau word. It embraces several notions. It is an exercise of the imagination which allows us to compete with and try to outwit future events. Controlling the anticipated future is, in addition, a social invention that legitimizes the process of forward planning. There is no other way I know of to resist the "tyranny of blind forces" than by looking facts in the face (as we experience them in the present) and extrapolating to the future—nor is there any other sure way to detect compromise. Most importantly, the future is a conscious dream, a set of imaginative hypotheses groping toward whatever vivid utopias lie at the heart of our consciousness. "In dreams begin responsibilities," said Yeats, and it is to our future responsibilities as educators, researchers, and practitioners that these dreams are dedicated.[1]

Most students of the future would argue with that definition, claiming that it is "poetic" or possibly even "prescientific." The argument has validity, I believe, though it is difficult to define "futurology," let alone distinguish between and among terms such as "inventing relevant futures," scenarios, forecasts, self-fulfilling prophecies, predictions, goals, normative theories, evolutionary hypotheses, presciptions, and so on. Philosophers and sociologists, for example, are still arguing over whether Weber's theory of bureaucracy was in fact a theory, a poignant and scholarly admonition, an evolutionary hypothesis, or a descriptive statement.

However difficult it may be to identify a truly scientific study of the future, most scholars would agree that it should include a number of objectives:

1.  It should provide a survey of possible futures in terms of a spectrum of major potential alternatives.

2.  It should ascribe to the occurrence of these alternatives some estimates of relative a priori probabilities.

3.  It should, for given basic policies, identify preferred alternatives.

Reprinted from *American Psychologist*, **25**, No. 7 (July, 1970), 595-608, and reproduced by permission of the American Psychological Association and the author.

4.   It should identify those decisions which are subject to control, as well as those developments which are not, whose occurrence would be likely to have a major effect on the probabilities of these alternatives.[2]

With these objectives only dimly in mind, I wrote a paper on the future of organizations (five years ago to the day that this paper was delivered to the American Political Science Association) which was called "Organizational Developments and the Fate of Bureaucracy."[3] Essentially, it was based on an evolutionary hypothesis which asserted that every age develops a form or organization most appropriate to its genius. I then went on to forecast certain changes in a "postbureaucratic world" and how these changes would affect the structure and environment of human organizations, their leadership and motivational patterns, and their cultural and ecological values. A number of things have occurred since that first excursion into the future in September 1964 which are worth mentioning at this point, for they have served to reorient and revise substantially some of the earlier forecasts.

Perhaps only a Homer or Herodotus, or a first-rate folk-rock composer, could capture the tumult and tragedy of the five years since that paper was written and measure their impact on our lives. The bitter agony of Vietnam, the convulsive stirrings of black America, the assassinations, the bloody streets of Chicago have all left their marks. What appears is a panorama that goes in and out of focus as it is transmitted through the mass media and as it is expressed through the new, less familiar media, the strikes, injunctions, disruptions, bombings, occupations, the heart attacks of the old, and the heartaches of the young. Strolling in late August 1969 through my own campus, lush, quiet, and sensual, I was almost lulled into thinking that nothing fundamental has happened to America in the past five years. Only the residual graffiti from last spring's demonstrations ("Keep the Pigs Out!" "Be Realistic—Demand the Impossible!"), hanging all but unnoticed in the student union, remind us that something has—though what it is, as the song says, "ain't exactly clear." One continually wonders if what has happened is unique and new ("Are we in France, 1788?" as one student asked), whether what is happening at the universities will spread to other, possibly less fragile institutions, and, finally, whether the university is simply the anvil upon which the awesome problems of our entire society are being hammered out. No one really knows. Despite the proliferation of analyses attributing campus unrest to everything from Oedipal conflicts (the most comforting explanation) to the failure of the Protestant Ethic, the crises continue relentlessly.

In his *Report to Greco*, Nikos Kazantzakis tells us of an ancient Chinese imprecation: "I curse you; may you live in an important age." Thus, we are all damned, encumbered, and burdened, as well as charmed, exhilarated, and fascinated by this curse.

In the rueful words of Bob Dylan:

*Come writers and critics*
*Who prophesy with your pen*
*And keep your eyes wide*

*The chance won't come again.*
*And don't speak too soon*
*For the wheel's still in spin*
*And there's no tellin' who*
*That it's namin'*
*For the loser now*
*Will be later to win*
*For the times are a-changin'.*

Reactions to our spastic times vary. There are at least seven definable types:

1. First and most serious of all are the *militants*, composed for the most part of impotent and dependent populations who have been victimized and infantilized, and who see no way out but to mutilate and destroy the system which has decimated its group identity and pride. Excluded populations rarely define their price for belated inclusion in intellectual terms, which confuses and terrifies the incumbents who take participation for granted.

2. The *apocalyptics*, who with verbal ferocity burn everything in sight. So, in *Supergrow*, Benjamin DeMott[4] assumes the persona of a future historian and casts a saddened eye on everyone from the Beatles to James Baldwin, from the *Berkeley Barb* to Alfred Kazin, while contemplating the age of megaweapons. DeMott writes:

By the end of the sixties the entire articulate Anglo-American community . . .was transformed into a monster-chorus of damnation dealers, its single voice pitched ever at hysterical level, its prime aim to transform every form of discourse into a blast.

These voices are hot as flamethrowers, searing all that get in their way and usually fired from a vantage point several terrain features away.

3. The *regressors*, who see their world disintegrating and engage in fruitless exercises in nostalgia, keening the present and weeping for a past: orderly, humane, free, civilized, and non-existent. Someone recently recommended that the university insulate itself from outside pollutants—I suppose he meant students and the community—and set up, medieval Oxford style, a chantry for scholars, which he warmly referred to as a "speculatorium."

4. There are the *retreaters*, apathetic, withdrawn, inwardly emigrating and outwardly drugged, avoiding all environments except, at most, a communal "roll your own" or a weekend bash at Esalen, longing for a "peak experience," instant nirvana, hoping to beat out reality and consequence.

5. The *historians*, who are always capable of lulling us to sleep by returning to a virtuous past, demonstrating that the "good old days" were either far better or worse. "The good old days, the good old days," said a Negro commedienne of the 30's, "I was there; where were they?" I learned recently, for example, that the university, as a quiet placed devoted to the pursuit of learning and unaffected by the turbulence of the outside world, is of comparatively recent date, that the experience of the medieval

university made the turbulence of recent years seem like a spring zephyr. It was pointed out that a student at the University of Prague cut the throat of a Friar Bishop and was merely expelled, an expedient that may have had something to do with the fact that in dealing with student morals, university officials were constrained to write in Latin.

6. The *technocrats*, who plow heroically ahead, embracing the future and in the process usually forgetting to turn around to see if anybody is following or listening, cutting through waves of ideology like agile surfers.

7. And, finally, the rest of us, "we happy few," the *liberal-democratic reformers*, optimists believing in the perfectibility of man and his institutions, waiting for a solid scientific victory over ideology and irrationality, accepting the inevitability of technology and humanism without thoroughly examining *that* relationship as we do all others, and reckoning that the only way to preserve a democratic and scientific humanism is through inspiriting our institutions with continuous, incremental reform.

The 1964 paper I mentioned earlier was written within the liberal-democratic framework, and it contained many of the inherent problems and advantages of that perspective. The main strategy of this paper and its focus of convenience are to review briefly the main points of that paper, to indicate its shortcomings and lacunae in light of five years' experience (not the least of which has been serving as an administrator in a large, complex public bureaucracy), and then proceed to develop some new perspectives relevant to the future of public bureaucracies. I might add, parenthetically, that I feel far less certainty and closure at this time than I did five years ago. The importance of inventing relevant futures and directions is never more crucial than in a revolutionary period, exactly and paradoxically at the point in time when the radical transition blurs the shape and direction of the present. This is the dilemma of our time and most certainly the dilemma of this paper.

## THE FUTURE: 1964 VERSION

Bureaucracy, I argued, was an elegant social invention, ingeniously capable of organizing and coordinating the productive processes of the Industrial Revolution, but hopelessly out-of-joint with contemporary realities. There would be new shapes, patterns, and models emerging which promised drastic changes in the conduct of the organization and of managerial practices in general. In the next 25-50 years, I argued, we should witness and participate in the end of bureaucracy as we know it and the rise of the new social systems better suited to twentieth-century demands of industrialization.

This argument was based on a number of factors:

1. The exponential growth of science, the growth of intellectual technology, and the growth of research and development activities.

2. The growing confluence between men of knowledge and men of power or, as I put it then, "a growing affinity between those who make history and those who write it."[5]

3. A fundamental change in the basic philosophy which underlies managerial behavior, reflected most of all in the following three areas: (*a*) a new concept of man, based on increased knowledge of his complex and shifting needs, which replaces the oversimplified, innocent push-button concept of man; (*b*) a new concept of power, based on collaboration and reason, which replaces a model of power based on coercion and fear; and (*c*) a new concept of organizational values, based on humanistic-democratic ideals, which replaces the de-personalized mechanistic value system of bureaucracy.

4. A turbulent environment which would hold relative uncertainty due to the increase of research and development activities. The environment would become increasingly differentiated, interdependent, and more salient to the organization. There would be greater interpenetration of the legal policy and economic features of an oligopolistic and government—business-controlled economy. Three main features of the environment would be interdependence rather than competition, turbulence rather than a steady, predictable state, and large rather than small enterprises.

5. A population characterized by a younger, more mobile, and better educated work force.

These conditions, I believed, would lead to some significant changes:

The increased level of education and rate of mobility would bring about certain changes in values held toward work. People would tend to (*a*) be more rational, be intellectually committed, and rely more heavily on forms of social influence which correspond to their value system; (*b*) be more "other-directed" and rely on their temporary neighbors and workmates for companionships, in other words, have relationships, not relatives; and (*c*) require more involvement, participation, and autonomy in their work.

As far as organizational structure goes, given the population characteristics and features of environmental turbulence, the social structure in organizations of the future would take on some unique characteristics. I will quote from the original paper.

First of all, the key word will be temporary: Organizations will become adaptive, rapidly changing temporary systems. Second, they will be organized around problems-to-be-solved. Third, these problems will be solved by relative groups of strangers who represent a diverse set of professional skills. Fourth, given the requirements of coordinating the various projects, articulating points or "linking pin" personnel will be necessary who can speak the diverse languages of research and who relay and mediate between various project groups. Fifth, the groups will be conducted on organic rather than on mechanical lines; they will emerge and adapt to the problems, and leadership and influence will fall to those who seem most able to solve the problems rather than to programmed role expectations. People will be differentiated, not according to rank or roles, but according to skills and training.

Adaptive, temporary systems of diverse specialists solving problems, coordinated organically via articulating points, will gradually replace the theory and practice of bureaucracy. Though no catchy phrase comes to mind, it might be called an organic-adaptive structure.

(As an aside: what will happen to the rest of society, to the manual laborers, to the poorly educated, to those who desire to work in conditions of dependency, and so forth? Many such jobs will disappear; automatic jobs will be automated. However, there will be a corresponding growth in the service-type of occupation, such as organizations like the Peace Corps and AID. There will also be jobs, now being seeded, to aid in the enormous challenge of coordinating activities between groups and organizations. For certainly, consortia of various kinds are growing in number and scope and they will require careful attention. In times of change, where there is a wide discrepancy between cultures and generations, an increase in industrialization, and especially urbanization, society becomes the client for skills in human resources. Let us hypothesize that approximately 40% of the population would be involved in jobs of this nature, 40% in technological jobs, making an organic-adaptive majority with, say, a 20% bureaucratic minority.[6])

Toward the end of the paper, I wrote that

The need for instinctual renunciation decreases as man achieves rational mastery over nature. In short, organizations of the future will require fewer restrictions and repressive techniques because of the legitimization of play and fantasy, accelerated through the rise of science and intellectual achievements.[7]

To summarize the changes in emphasis of social patterns in the "postbureaucratic world" I was then describing (using Trist's[8] framework), the following paradigm may be useful:

| From | Toward |
|---|---|
| *Cultural Values* | |
| Achievement | Self-actualization |
| Self-control | Self-expression |
| Independence | Interdependence |
| Endurance of stress | Capacity for joy |
| Full employment | Full lives |
| *Organizational Values* | |
| Mechanistic forms | Organic forms |
| Competitive relations | Collaborative relations |
| Separate objectives | Linked objectives |
| Own resources regarded as owned absolutely | Own resources regarded also as society's resources |

I hope I have summarized the paper without boring you in the process. One thing is clear; looking backward, reexamining one's own work five years later is a useful exercise. Aside from the protracted decathexis from the original ideas, new experiences and other emergent factors all help to provide a new perspective which casts some doubt on a number of assumptions, only half implied in the earlier statement. For example:

1.  The organizations I had in mind then were of a single class: instrumental, large-scale, science-based, international bureaucracies, operating under rapid growth conditions. Service industries and public bureaucracies, as well as nonsalaried employees, were excluded from analysis.

2.  Practically no attention was paid to the boundary transactions of the firm or to inter-institutional linkages.

3.  The management of conflict was emphasized, while the strategy of conflict was ignored.

4.  Power of all types was underplayed, while the role of the leader as facilitator—"linking pin"—using an "agricultural model" of nurturance and climate building was stressed. Put in Gamson's[9] terms, I utilized a domesticated version of power, emphasizing the process by which the authorities attempt to achieve collective goals and to maintain legitimacy and compliance with their decisions, rather than the perspective of "potential partisans," which involves diversity of interest groups attempting to influence the choices of authorities.

5.  A theory of change was implied, based on gentle nudges from the environment coupled with a truth-love strategy; that is, with sufficient trust and collaboration along with valid data, organizations would progress monotonically along a democratic continuum.

In short, the organizations of the future I envisaged would most certainly be, along with a Bach Chorale and Chartres Cathedral, the epiphany to Western civilization.

The striking thing about truth and love is that whereas I once held them up as the answer to our institution's predicaments, they have now become the problem. And, to make matters worse, the world I envisaged as emergent in 1964 becomes, not necessarily inaccurate, but overwhelmingly problematical. It might be useful to review some of the main organizational dilemmas before going any further, both as a check on the previous forecast, as well as a preface to some new and tentative ideas about contemporary human organizations.

## SOME NEW DILEMMAS

### The Problem of Legitimacy

The key difference between the Berkeley riots of 1964 and the Columbia crisis of May 1969 is that in the pre-Columbian case the major impetus for unrest stemmed from the perceived abuse or misuse of authority ("Do not bend, fold, or mutilate"), whereas the later protest denied the legitimacy of authority. The breakdown of legitimacy in our country has many reasons and explanations, not the least of which is the increasing difficulty of converting political questions into technical-managerial ones. Or, put differently, questions of legitimacy arise whenever "expert power" becomes ineffective. Thus, black militants, drug users, draft resisters, student protestors, and liberated women all deny the legitimacy of those authorities who are not black, drug experienced, pacifists, students, or women.

The university is in an excruciating predicament with respect to the breakdown of legitimacy. Questions about admissions, grades, curriculum, and police involvement—even questions concerning rejection of journal articles—stand the chance of being converted into political-legal issues. This jeopardizes the use of universalistic-achievement criteria, upon which the very moral imperatives of our institutions are based. The problem is related, of course, to the inclusion of those minority groups in our society which have been excluded from participation in American life and tend to define their goals in particularistic and political terms.

Kelman[10] cites three major reasons for the crisis in legitimacy: (*a*) serious failings of the system in living up to its basic values and in maintaining a proper relationship between means and ends, (*b*) decreasing trust in leadership, and (*c*) dispositions of our current youth. On this last point, Flacks[11]

suggests the existence of an increasingly distinct "humanist" subculture in the middle class, consisting primarily of highly educated and urbanized families, based in professional occupations, who encourage humanist orientations in their offspring as well as questioning attitudes to traditional middle class values and to arbitrary authority and conventional politics. . . Although this humanist subculture represents a small minority of the population, many of its attributes are more widely distributed, and the great increase in the number of college graduates suggests that the ranks of this subculture will rapidly grow.

In short, as the gap between shared and new moralities and authoritative norms (i.e., the law) widens, questions of legitimacy inevitably arise.

## Populist versus Elite Functions?

Can American institutions continue to fulfill the possibly incompatible goals of their elitist and populist functions? Again, the American university is an example of this dilemma, for the same institution tries to balance both its autonomous-elite function of disinterested inquiry and criticism and an increasingly service-populist-oriented function. This has been accomplished by insulating the elite (autonomous) functions of liberal education, basic research, and scholarship from the direct impact of the larger society, whose demands for vocational training, certification, service, and the like are reflected and met in the popular functions of the university. As Trow[12] puts it:

These insulations take various forms of a division of labor within the university. There is a division of labor between departments, as for example, between a department of English or Classics, and a department of Education. There is a division of labor in the relatively unselective universities between the undergraduate and graduate schools, the former given over largely to mass higher education in the service of social mobility and occupational placement, entertainment, and custodial care, while the graduate departments in the same institutions are often able to maintain a climate in which scholarship and scientific research can be done to the highest standards. There is a familiar division of labor, though far from clear-cut, between graduate departments and professional schools. Among the faculty there is a division of labor, within many departments, between scientists and consultants, scholars and journalists, teachers and entertainers. More dangerously, there is a division of labor between regular faculty and a variety of fringe or marginal teachers—teaching assistants, visitors and lecturers—who in some schools carry a disproportionate load of the mass teaching. Within the administration there is a division of labor between the Dean of Faculty and Graduate Dean, and the Dean of Students. And among students there is a marked separation between the "collegiate" and "vocational" subcultures, on the one hand, and academically or intellectually oriented subcultures on the other [p. 2].

To a certain extent, the genius of American higher education is that it *has* fulfilled both of these functions, to the wonder of all, and especially to observers from European universities. But with the enormous expansion of American universities, proportional strains are being placed on their insulating mechanisms.

**Interdependence or Complicity in the Environment**

The environment I talked about in 1964, its interdependence and turbulence, is flourishing today. But my optimism must now be tempered, for what appeared then to be a "correlation of fates" turns out to have blocked the view of some serious problems. The university is a good example of this tension.

The relationship between the university and its environment has never been defined in more than an overly abstract way. For some, the university is a citadel, aloof, occasionally lobbing in on society the shells of social criticism. Both the radical left and the conservative right seem to agree on this model, maintaining that to yield to the claims of society will fragment and ultimately destroy the university. Others, for different reasons, prefer a somewhat similar model, that of the "speculatorium," where scholars, protected by garden walls, meditate away from society's pollutants. Still others envisage the university as an "agent of change," a catalytic institution capable of revolutionizing the nation's organizations and professions. In fact, a recent sociological study listed almost 50 viable goals for the university[13] (a reflection of our ambivalence and confusions as much as anything), and university catalogs usually list them all.

The role of the university in society might be easier to define if it were not for one unpalatable fact. Though it is not usually recognized, the truth is that the university is not self-supporting. The amount available for our educational expenditures (including funds necessary to support autonomous functions) relates directly to the valuation of the university by the general community. The extent to which the university's men, ideas, and research are valued is commensurate with the amount of economic support it receives.[14] This has always been true. During the Great Awakening, universities educated ministers; during the agricultural and industrial revolutions, the land-grant colleges and engineering schools flourished; during the rise of the service professions, the universities set up schools of social welfare, nursing, public health, and so on. And during the past 30 years or so, the universities have been increasingly geared to educate individuals to man the Galbraithean "technostructure."

Thus, the charge of "complicity" of the universities with the power structure is both valid and absurd; without this alleged complicity, there would be no universities, or only terribly poor ones. In the late 60's, the same attack comes from the New Left. The paradox can be blinding, and often leads to one of two pseudosolutions, total involvement or total withdrawal—pseudosolutions familiar enough on other fronts, for example, in foreign policy.

If I am right that the university must be valued by society in order to be supported, the question is not should the university be involved with society, but what should be the *quality* of this involvement and *with whom*? For years, there has been tacit acceptance of the idea that the university must supply industry, the professions, defense, and the technostructure with the brains necessary to carry on their work. Now there are emerging constituencies, new dependent populations, new problems, many without technical solutions, that are demanding that attention of the university. We are being called upon to direct our limited and already scattered resources to newly defined areas of concern—the quality of life, the shape and nature of our human institutions, the staggering problems of the city, legislative processes, and the management of human resources. Will it be possible for the modern university to involve itself with these problems and at the same time avoid the politicization that will threaten its autonomous functions? One thing is clear, we will never find answers to these problems if we allow rational thought to be replaced by a search for villains. To blame the establishment, or Wall Street, or the New Left for our problems is lazy, thoughtless, and frivolous. It would be comforting if we *could* isolate and personalize the problems facing the university, but we cannot.

The last two dilemmas that I have just mentioned, elitist *versus* populist strains vying within a single institution and the shifting, uncertain symbiosis between university and society, contain many of the unclear problems we face today, and I suspect that they account for much of the existential groaning we hear in practically all of our institutions, not just the university.

### The Search for the Correct Metaphor

Metaphors have tremendous power to establish new social realities, to give life and meaning to what was formerly perceived only dimly and imprecisely. What *did* students experience before Erikson's "identity crisis"? Greer[15] wrote recently:

> [But] much of our individual experience is symbolized in vague and unstandardized ways. There is, as we say, no word for it. One of the great contributions of creative scientists and artists is to make communicable what was previously moot, to sense new meanings possible in the emerging nature of human experience, giving them a form which makes communication possible. The phrase-maker is not to be despised, he may be creating the grounds for new social reality. (On the other hand, he may merely be repackaging an old product.) [p. 46]

Most of us have internalized a metaphor about organizational life, however crude that model or vivid that utopia is—or how conscious or unconscious—which governs our perceptions of our social systems. How these metaphors evolve is not clear, although I do not think Freud was far off the mark with his focus on the family, the military, and the church as the germinating institutions.

Reviewing organizational metaphors somewhat biographically, I find that my first collegiate experience, at Antioch College, emphasized a "community democracy" metaphor, obviously valid for a small, town-meeting type of political life. In strong contrast to this was the Massachusetts Institute of Technology, which employed the metaphor (not consciously, of course) of "The Club," controlled tacitly and quite democratically, but without the formal governing apparatus of political democracies, by an "old-boy network," composed of the senior tenured faculty and administration. The State University of New York at Buffalo comes close, in my view, to a "labor-relations" metaphor, where conflicts and decisions are negotiated through a series of interest groups bargaining as partisans. There are many other usable metaphors: Clark Kerr's "City," Mark Hopkins' "student and teacher on opposite ends of a log," "General Systems Analysis," "Therapeutic Community," "Scientific Management," and my own "temporary systems," and so on, that compete with the pure form of bureaucracy, but few of them seem singularly equipped to cope with the current problems facing large-scale institutions.

### Macrosystems versus Microsystems

One of the crude discoveries painfully learned during the course of recent administrative experience in a large public bureaucracy turns on the discontinuities between microsystems and macrosystems. For quite a while, I have had more than a passing *theoretical* interest in this problem, which undoubtedly many of you share, but my interest now, due to a sometimes eroding despair, has gone well beyond the purely theoretical problems involved.

My own intellectual "upbringing," to use an old-fashioned term, was steeped in the Lewinian tradition of small-group behavior, processes of social influence, and "action-research." This is not terribly exceptional, I suppose, for a social psychologist. In fact, I suppose that the major methodological and theoretical influences in the social sciences for the last two decades have concentrated on more microscopic, "manageable" topics. Also, it is not easy to define precisely where a microsocial science begins or where a macrosocial science ends. Formally, I suppose, microsystems consist of roles and actors, while macrosystems have as their constituent parts other subsystems, subcultures, and parts of society. In any case, my intellectual heritage has resulted in an erratic batting average in transferring concepts from microsystems into the macrosystem of a university.

An example of this dilemma can be seen in a letter Leonard Duhl wrote in response to an article by Carl Rogers which stressed an increased concern with human relationships as a necessary prerequisite for managing society's institutions. Duhl[16] wrote:

Though I agree with [Rogers] heartily, I have some very strong questions about whether, indeed, this kind of future is in the cards for us. I raise this primarily because out of my experiences working in the U. S. Department of Housing and Urban Development and out of experiences working in and with cities, it is clear that in the basic decision making that takes place, the values Dr. Rogers and I hold so dear have an extremely low priority. Indeed, the old-fashioned concerns with power, prestige,  money and profit so far outdistance the concerns for human warmth and love and concern that many people consider the latter extremely irrelevant in the basic decision making. Sadly, it is my feeling that they will continue to do so.

The following examples from my own recent experience tend to confirm Duhl's gloomy outlook.

The theory of consensus falters under those conditions where competing groups bring to the conference table vested interests based on group membership, what Mannhein referred to as "perspectivistic orientation." Where goals are competitive and group (or subsystem) oriented, despite the fact that a consensus might rationally create a new situation where all parties may benefit—that is, move closer to the Paretian optimal frontier—a negotiated position may be the only practical solution. There was a time when I believed that consensus was a valid operating procedure. I no longer think this is realistic, given the scale and diversity of organizations. In fact, I  have come to think that the quest for consensus, except for some microsystems where it may be feasible, is a misplaced nostalgia for a folk society as chimerical, incidentally, as the American search for "identity."

The collaborative relationship between superiors and subordinates falters as well under those conditions where "subordinates"—if that word is appropriate—are *delegates* of certain subsystems. Under this condition, collaboration may be perceived by constituents as a threat because of perceived cooption or encroachment on their formal, legal rights.

Or, to take another example, in the area of leadership, my colleagues at the State University of New York at Buffalo, Hollander and Julian,[17] have written for *Psychological Bulletin* one of the most thoughtful and penetrating articles on the leadership process. In one of their own studies,[18] reported in this article, they found that aside from the significance of task competence, the "leader's interest in group members and interest in group activity" were significantly related to the group acceptance of the leader. Yet, in macropower situations, the leader is almost always involved in boundary exchanges with salient interorganizational activities which inescapably reduce, not necessarily interest in group members or activities, but the amount of interaction he can maintain with group members. This may have more the overtones of a rationalization than an explanation, but I know of few organizations where the top leadership's commitment to internal programs and needs fully meets constituent expectations.

In short, interorganizational role set of the leader, the scale, diversity, and formal relations that ensue in a pluralistic system place heavy burdens on those managers and leaders who expect an easy transferability between the cozy gemütlichkeit of a Theory Y orientation and the realities of macropower.

### Current Sources for the Adoption or Rejection of Democratic Ideals

I wrote, not long ago, that

> While more research will help us understand the conditions under which democratic and other forms of governance will be adopted, the issue will never be fully resolved . . . . I.A. Richards once said that "language has succeeded until recently in hiding from us almost all things we talk about." This is singularly true when men start to talk of complex and wondrous things like democracy and the like.* For these are issues anchored in an existential core of personality.[19]

Today I am even more confused about the presence or absence of conditions which could lead to more democratic functioning. Somedays I wake up feeling "nasty, brutish, and short," and, other times, feeling benign, generous, and short. This may be true of the general population, for the national mood is erratic, labile, depending on repression or anarchy for the "short" solution to long problems.

Let us consider Lane's[20] "democraticness scale," consisting of five items: (*a*) willingness or reluctance to deny the franchise to the "ignorant or careless"; (*b*) patience or impatience with the delays and confusions of democratic processes; (*c*) willingness or reluctance to give absolute authority to a single leader in times of threat; (*d*) where democratic forms are followed, degree of emphasis (and often disguised approval) of underlying oligarchical methods; (*e*) belief that the future of democracy in the United States is reasonably secure.

Unfortunately, there has been relatively little research on the "democratic personality," which makes it risky to forecast whether conditions today will facilitate or detract from its effective functioning. On the one hand, there is interesting evidence that would lead one to forecast an increased commitment to democratic ideals. Earlier I mentioned Flacks' work on the "transformation of the American middle-class family," which would involve increased equality between husband and wife, declining

---

*See Sartori.[21] "No wonder, therefore, that the more 'democracy' has become to be a universally accepted honorific term, the more it has undergone verbal stretching and has become the loosest label of its kind [p. 112]."

distinctiveness of sex roles in the family, increased opportunity for self-expression on the part of the children, fewer parental demands for self-discipline, and more parental support for autonomous behavior on the part of the children. In addition, the increase in educated persons, whose status is less dependent on property, will likely increase the investment of individuals in having autonomy and a voice in decision making.

On the other hand, it is not difficult to detect some formidable threats to the democratic process which make me extremely apprehensive about an optimistic prediction. Two are basically psychological, one derived from some previous assumptions about the environment, the other derived from some recent personal experience. The third is a venerable structural weakness which at this time takes on a new urgency.

1. Given the turbulent and dynamic texture of the environment, we can observe a growing uncertainty about the deepest human concerns: jobs, neighborhoods, regulation of social norms, life styles, child rearing, law and order; in short, the only basic questions, according to Tolstoi, that interest human beings are How to live? and What to live for? The ambiguities and changes in American life that occupy discussion in university seminars and annual meetings and policy debates in Washington, and that form the backbone of contemporary popular psychology and sociology, become increasingly the conditions of trauma and frustration in the lower middle class. Suddenly the rules are changing—all the rules.

A clashy dissensus of values is already clearly foreshadowed that will tax to the utmost two of the previously mentioned democraticness scale items: "impatience or patience with the delays and confusions of democratic processes" and the "belief that the future of democracy in the United States is reasonably secure."

The inability to tolerate ambiguity and the consequent frustration plus the mood of dissensus may lead to the emergence of a proliferation of "minisocieties" and relatively impermeable subcultures, from George Wallace's blue-collar strongholds to rigidly circumscribed communal ventures. Because of their rejection of incremental reform and the establishment, and their impatience with bureaucratic-pragmatic leadership, their movements and leadership will likely resemble a "revolutionary-charismatic" style.[22]

2. The personal observation has to do with experience over the past two years as an academic administrator, experience obtained during a particularly spastic period for all of us in the academy.* I can report that we, at Buffalo, have been trying to express our governance through a thorough and complete democratic process, with as much participation as anyone can bear. There are many difficulties in building this process, as all of you are undoubtedly aware: the tensions between collegiality and the bureaucratic-pragmatic style of administrators, the difficulty in arousing faculty and

---

*I am reminded here of Edward Holyoke's remark, written over 200 years ago on the basis of his personal experience: "If any man wishes to be humbled or mortified, let him become President of Harvard College."

students to participate, etc. I might add, parenthetically, that Buffalo, as is true of many state universities, had long cherished a tradition of strong faculty autonomy and academic control. Our intention was to facilitate this direction, as well as encourage more student participation.

When trouble erupted last spring, I was disturbed to discover—to the surprise of many of my colleagues, particularly historians and political scientists—that the democratic process we were building seemed so fragile and certainly weakened in comparison to the aphrodisia of direct action, mass meetings, and frankly autocratic maneuverings. The quiet workings of the bureaucratic-democratic style seemed bland, too complex and prismatic for easy comprehension, and even banal, contrasted to the headiness of the disruptions. Even those of us who were attempting to infuse and reinforce democratic functioning found ourselves caught up in the excitement and chilling risks involved.

Erich Fromm[23] said it all, I reflected later on, in his *Escape from Freedom,* but what was missing for me in his formulation was the psychic equivalent for democratic participants.

During this same period, I came across a paper by Argyris[24] which reinforced my doubts about the psychological attractiveness of democracy. Using a 36-category group observational system on nearly 30 groups, in 400 separate meetings, amounting to almost 46,000 behavioral units, he found that only 6 of the 36 categories were used over 75% of the time, and these 6 were "task" items such as "gives information, asks for information," etc. Almost 60% of the groups showed no affect or interpersonal feelings at all, and 24% expressed only 1% affect or feelings. These groups represented a wide cross-section of bureaucratic organizations, research and development labs, universities, and service and business industries.

Argyris' data, along with my own personal experience, have made me wonder if democratic functioning can ever develop the deep emotional commitments and satisfactions that other forms of governance evoke, as for example, revolutionary-charismatic or ideological movements? The question which I leave with you at this time is not the one from the original paper ("Is democracy inevitable?"), but, "Is democracy sexy?"

3. The structural weakness in present-day democracy, using that term in the broadest possible political sense, is the 200-year-old idea first popularized by Adam Smith (1776) in *The Wealth of the Nations.* This was "the idea that an individual who intends only his own gain is led by an invisible hand to promote the public interest." The American Revolution brought about a deep concern for the constitutional guarantees of personal rights and a passionate interest in individuals' emotions and growth, but without a concomitant concern for the community.

In a recent issue of *Science,* Hardin,[25] the biologist, discusses this in an important article, "The Tragedy of the Commons." Herdsmen who keep their cattle on the common ask themselves: "What is the utility to me of adding one more animal to my herd [p. 1244]?" Being rational, each herdsman seeks to maximize his gain. It becomes clear that by adding even one animal, as he receives all the proceeds from the sale of the additional increment, the positive utility is nearly +1, whereas the negative utility is only a fraction of –1 because the effects of overgrazing are shared by all herdsmen. Thus, "the rational herdsman concludes that the only sensible course for him to pursue is to add another animal to his herd. And another, and another . . . [p. 1244] ," until

Each man is locked into a system that compels him to increase his herd without limit . . . Ruin is the destination toward which all men rush . . . Freedom in a commons brings ruin to all [p. 1244] .

A recent, less elegant example along these lines occurred at my own campus where there is a rather strong commitment against institutional racism. A recent form this commitment has taken is the admission of at least double the number of black students ever before admitted. However, more disadvantaged students could have been accepted if the students had chosen to vote for "tripling" in the dormitories. It was voted down overwhelmingly, and it was interesting to observe the editor of the student newspaper supporting increased admission for black students and at the same time opposing tripling.

The democratic process as we know it, expressed through majority vote, contains many built-in guarantees for individual freedom without equivalent mechanisms for the "public interest," as Gans'[26] recent article in the Sunday Magazine section of *The New York Times* argues.

A character in Balchin's[27] *A Sort of Traitors* expresses this structural problem with some force:

You think that people want democracy and justice and peace. You're right. They do. But what you forget is that they want them on their own terms. And their own terms don't add up. They want decency and justice without interference with their liberty to do as they like.

These are the dilemmas as I see them now: the threat to legitimacy of authority, the tensions between populist and elitist functions and interdependence and complicity in the environment, the need for fresh metaphors, the discontinuities between microsystems and macrosystems, and the baffling competition between forces that support and those that suppress the adoption of democratic ideology. All together, they curb my optimism and blur the vision, but most certainly force a new perspective upon us.

## A NEW PERSPECTIVE

These profound changes lead me to suggest that any forecast one makes about trends in human institutions must take into account the following:

- The need for fundamental reform in the purpose and organization of our institutions to enable them to adapt responsively in an exponentially changing social, cultural, political, and economic environment.

- The need to develop such institutions on a human scale which permit the individual to retain his identity and integrity in a society increasingly characterized by massive, urban, highly centralized governmental, business, educational, mass media, and other institutions.

- The significant movement of young persons who are posing basic challenges to existing values and institutions and who are attempting to create radical new life styles in an attempt to preserve individual identity or to opt out of society.

- The increasing demands placed upon all American institutions to participate more actively in social, cultural, and political programs designed to improve the quality of American life.

- The accelerating technical changes which require the development of a scientific humanism: a world view of the social and humanistic implications of such changes.

- The necessity of a world movement to bring man in better harmony with his physical environment.

- The need for change toward a sensitive and flexible planning capability on the part of the management of major institutions.

- The rising demand for social and political justice and freedom, particularly from the American black community and other deprived sectors of society.

- The compelling need for world order which gives greater attention to the maintenance of peace without violence between nations, groups, or individuals.

## A NEW FORECAST FOR PUBLIC BUREAUCRACY

The imponderables are youth, and tradition, and change. Where these predicaments, dilemmas, and second thoughts take us, I am not exactly sure. However, by way of a summary and conclusion—and at the risk of another five-year backlash, there are a number of trends and emphases worth considering.

*The Organization's Response to the Environment Will Continue*
*to Be the Crucial Determinant for Its Effectiveness*

Economists and political scientists have been telling us this for years, but only recently have sociologists and social psychologists, like Terreberry,[28] Emery and Trist,[29] Levine and White,[30] Litwak and Hylton,[31] and Evan,[32] done so. To quote Benson Snyder,[33] concerning a recent trip to California universities:

There is another consequence of this limited response to rapid change. The climate of society becomes suffused and distrait, positions ossified, and one hears expressions of helplessness increase, like dinosaurs on the plains of mud. Each in his own way frantically puts on more weight and thinks this form of strength will serve him. He doesn't know he had lost touch until the mud reaches the level of his eyes.

Three derivatives of this protean environment can be anticipated: First, we will witness new ecological strategies that are capable of anticipating crisis instead of responding to crisis, that require participation instead of consent, that confront conflict instead of dampening conflict, that include comprehensive measures instead of specific measures, and that include a long planning horizon instead of a short planning horizon.

Second, we will identify new roles for linking and correlating interorganizational transactions—"interstitial men."

Third, and most problematical, I anticipate an erratic environment where various organizations coexist at different stages of evolution. Rather than neat, linear, and uniform evolutionary developments, I expect that we will see both more centralization (in large-scale instrumental bureaucracies) and more decentralization (in delivery of health, education, and welfare services); both the increase of bureaucratic-pragmatic and of revolutionary-charismatic leadership; both the increase in size and centralization of many municipal and governmental units and the proliferation of self-contained minisocieties,* from the "status-spheres" that Tom Wolfe writes about like Ken Kesey's "electric kool-aid acid-heads" and the pump-house gang of La Jolla surfers to various citizen groups. Ethnic groups organize to "get theirs," and so do the police, firemen, small property owners, and "mothers fighting sex education and bussing," and so on.

*Large-Scale Public and Private Bureaucracies Will Become More Vulnerable Than Ever Before to the Infusion of Legislative and Juridical Organs*

These probably will become formalized, much like the Inspector General's office in the Army. In one day's issue of a recent *New York Times*, three front-page stories featured: (*a*) the "young Turks" within the State Department who are planning to ask the Department to recognize the Foreign Service Association as the exclusive agent with which the Department would bargain on a wide scale of personnel matters, (*b*) antipoverty lawyers within the Office of Equal Opportunity who have organized for a greater voice in setting policy, and (*c*) the informal caucus of civil rights lawyers in the Justice Department to draft a protest against what they consider a recent softening of enforcement of the civil rights laws.

I have always been fascinated by Harold Lasswell's famous analogy between the Freudian trinity of personality and the tripartite division of the federal government. Most bureaucracies today contain only one formal mechanism, that is, the executive or

---

*Sometimes it is difficult to distinguish the reform groups from the reaction groups, except that the affluent, particulary the young, uncommitted affluent, have already begun to invent and manage environments, cutting across class and ethnic lines, that reflect unique life styles. And these begin and end as rapidly as boutiques on Madison Avenue, which in many ways they resemble, rather than the massive, more familiar conglomerates of yesteryear.

ego functions. The legislative (id) and the judicial (superego) have long been under-represented; this will likely change.*

### *There Will Be More Legitimization for "Leave-Taking" and Shorter Tenure at the Highest Levels of Leadership*

One aspect of "temporary systems" that was underplayed in my 1964 paper was the human cost of task efficiency. Recently, James Reston observed that the reason it is difficult to find good men for the most responsible jobs in government is that the good men have burnt out, or as my old infantry company commander once said, "In this company, the good guys get killed." Perhaps this creates the appearance of the Peter Principle, that is, that people advance to the level of their greatest incompetence. What is more likely is that people get burnt out, psychologically killed. Many industries are now experimenting with variations on sabbaticals for their executives, and I think it is about time that universities woke up to the fact that a seven-year period, for a legalized moratorium, is simply out of joint with the recurring need for self- and professional renewal.†

It may also be that leaders with shorter time horizons will be more effective in the same way that interregnum Popes have proven to be the most competent.

### *New Organizational Roles Will Develop Emphasizing Different Loci and Commitments of Colleagueiality*

Aside from consultants and external advisory groups, organizations tend to arrogate the full working time and commitments of their memberships. One works for Ford, or the Department of Health, Education and Welfare, or Macy's, or Yale. Moonlighting is permitted, sometimes reluctantly, but there is usually no doubt about the primary organization or where there might be a possible "conflict of interest." This idea of the mono-organizational commitment will likely erode in the future where more and more people will create pluralistic commitments to a number of organizations.

To use my own university as an example once again, we have set up one new experimental department which includes three different kinds of professors, different

---

*The labor unions have been relatively unsuccessful in organizing either top levels of management or professionals. They have failed to do so, in my view, because they have operated at the lowest level of the Maslow hierarchy of needs, economic, physiological, safety, failing to understand the inducements of most professional development. Ironically, this has provided more "due process" and, in some cases, more legitimate participation to nonsalaried employees than to higher level personnel. It is no coincidence that the cutting edge of last year's French revolution, in addition to the students, were middle-class professional employees and technicians.

According to William Evan,[34] the lack of "due process" for the high-ranking managerial and professional personnel has led to or reinforced the "organization man."

†At Buffalo, we have tried to develop a policy whereby all administrators would hold an academic appointment as well as an administrative post. They would be expected to return to their academic calling after no longer than 5, possibly 10, years. The response to this formulation was less than positive, and I suspect that the basic reason for its unpopularity was the psychological blow to the self-concept which equates role-leaving (without manifest promotion) to failure.

in terms of their relatedness and loci to the department. There is a core group of faculty with full-time membership in the department. There is an associated faculty with part-time commitments to the department, but whose appointment is in another department. And finally, there is a "network faculty," who spend varying periods of time in the department, but whose principal affiliation is with another university or organization. Similar plans are now being drawn up for students.

Similarly, a number of people have talked about "invisible colleges" of true colleagues, located throughout the world, who convene on special occasions, but who communicate mainly by telephone, the mail, and during hasty meetings at airports. I would wager that these "floating crap-games" will increase, and that we will see at least three distinct sets of roles emerge within organizations: those that are *pivotal* and more or less permanent; those that are *relevant*, but not necessarily permanent; and those that are *peripheral*. A person who is pivotal and permanent to one organization may have a variety of relevant and peripheral roles in others.

There are many reasons for this development. First and most obvious is the fact that we live in a jet age where air travel is cheap and very accessible. (A good friend of mine living in Boston commutes daily to New York City for his analytic hour and manages to get back to his office by about 10:30 A.M.) Second, the scarcity of talent and the number of institutions "on the make" will very likely lead more of the top talent to start dividing their time among a number of institutions. Third, the genuine motivational satisfaction gained from working within a variety of comparable institutions seems to be important not for all, but among an increasingly growing fraction of the general population.

We must educate our leaders in at least two competencies: (a) to cope efficiently, imaginatively, and perceptively with information overload. Marxist power was property. Today, power is based on control of relevant information. (b) As Michael[35] says in his *The Unprepared Society:*

We must educate for empathy, compassion, trust, nonexploitiveness, nonmanipulativeness, for self-growth and self-esteem, for tolerance of ambiguity, for acknowledgement of error, for patience, for suffering.

Without affective competence, and the strength that comes with it, it is difficult to see how the leader can confront the important ethical and political decisions without succumbing to compromise or to "petite Eichmannism."

We will observe in America a society which has experienced the consequences of unpreparedness and which has become more sanguine about the effects of planning— more planning not to restrict choice or prohibit serendipity, but to structure possibilities and practical visions.

Whether or not these forecasts are desirable, assuming their validity for the moment, really depends on one's status, values, and normative biases. One man's agony is another's ecstasy. It does appear as if we will have to reckon with a number of contradictory and confusing tendencies, however, which can quickly be summarized:

1. More self- and social consciousness with respect to the governance of public bureaucracies.

2. More participation in this governance by the clients who are served, as well as those doing the service, including lower levels of the hierarchy.

3. More formal, quasi-legal processes of conflict resolution.

4. More direct confrontations when negotiation and bargaining processes fail.

5. More attention to moral-ethical issues relative to technical efficiency imperatives.

6. More rapid turnover and varying relationships within institutions.

I think it would be appropriate if I concluded this paper with a quote from the earlier 1964 paper which still seems valid and especially pertinent in light of the new perspectives gained over the past five years. I was writing about the educational requirements necessary for coping with a turbulent environment:[36]

Our educational system should (1) help us to identify with the adaptive process without fear of losing our identity, (2) increase tolerance of ambiguity without fear of losing intellectual mastery, (3) increase our ability to collaborate without fear of losing our individuality, and (4) develop a willingness to participate in social evolution while recognizing implacable forces. In short, we need an educational system that can help make a virtue out of contingency rather than one which induces hesitancy or its reckless companion, expedience.

## NOTES

1. Bennis, W.G., Future of the social sciences, *Antioch Review*, 28 (1968), 227.

2. Helmer, O., Political analysis of the future. Paper presented at the annual meeting of the American Political Science Association, New York, September 4, 1969.

3. Bennis, W. G., Organizational developments and the fate of bureaucracy. Paper presented at the annual meeting of the American Psychological Association, Los Angeles, September 4, 1964.

4. DeMott, B., *Supergrow*. New York: Dutton, 1969.

5. Bennis, 1964.

6. Bennis, 1964.

7. Bennis, 1964.

8. Trist, E., *The Relation of Welfare and Development in the Transition to Post-Industrialism*. Los Angeles: Western Management Science Institute, University of California, 1968.

9. Gamson, W.A., *Power and Discontent*. Homewood, Ill.: Dorsey Press, 1968.

10. Kelman, H.C., In search of new bases for legitimacy: Some social psychological dimensions of the black power and student movements. Paper presented at the Richard M. Elliott Lecture, University of Michigan, April 21, 1969.

11. Flacks, R., Protest or conform: Some social psychological perspectives on legitimacy, *Journal of Applied Behavioral Science*, 5 (1969), 127-150.

12. Trow, M., Urban problems and university problems. Paper presented at the 24th All-University Conference, University of California at Riverside, March .23-25, 1969.

13. Gross, E., Universities as organizations: A research approach, *American Sociological Review,* **33** (1968), 518-544.

14. Parsons, T., The academic system: A sociologist's view, *The Public Interest,* **13** (1968), 179-197.

15. Greer, S., *The Logic of Social Inquiry.* Chicago: Aldine, 1969.

16. Duhl, L., Letter to the editor, *Journal of Applied Behavioral Science,* **5** (1969), 279-280.

17. Julian, J.W., and E.P. Hollander, A study of some role dimensions of leader-follower relations (Tech. Rep. No. 3, Office of Naval Research Contract No. 4679), State University of New York at Buffalo, Department of Psychology, April, 1966.

18. Hollander, E.P., and J.W. Julian, Contemporary trends in the analysis of leadership processes, *Psychological Bulletin,* **71** (1969), 387-397.

19. Bennis, W.G., When democracy works, *Trans-action,* **3** (1966), 35.

20. Lane, R.E., *Political Ideology.* New York: Free Press, 1962.

21. Sartori, G., Democracy, in E.R.A. Seligman (Ed.), *Encyclopedia of Social Sciences.* New York: Macmillan, 1957.

22. Kissinger, H.A., Domestic structures and foreign policy, *Daedalus,* **96** (1966), 503-529.

23. Fromm, E., *Escape from Freedom.* New York: Farrar & Rinehart, 1941.

24. Argyris, C., The incompleteness of social-psychological theory: Examples from small group, cognitive consistency, and attribution research, *American Psychologist,* **24** (1969), 893-908.

25. Hardin, G., The tragedy of the commons, *Science,* **162** (1968), 1243-1248.

26. Gans, H.J., We won't end the urban crisis until we end majority rule, *New York Times Magazine,* **119** (August 3, 1969), Section 6.

27. Balchin, N., *A Sort of Traitors.* New York: Collins, 1949.

28. Terreberry, S., The evolution of organizational environments, *Administrative Science Quarterly,* **12** (1968), 590-613.

29. Emery, F.E., and E.L. Trist, The causal texture of organizational environments, *Human Relations,* **18** (1965), 1-10.

30. Levine, S., and P.E. White, Exchange as a conceptual framework for the study of interorganizational relationships, *Administrative Science Quarterly,* **6** (1961), 583-601.

31. Litwak, E., and L. Hylton, Interorganizational analysis: A hypothesis on coordinating agencies, *Administrative Science Quarterly,* **6** (1962), 395-420.

32. Evan, W.M., The organization-set: Toward a theory of interorganizational relationships, in J.D. Thompson (Ed.), *Approaches to Organizational Design.* Pittsburgh: University of Pittsburgh Press, 1966.

33. Snyder, B., Personal communication, 1969.

34. Evan, 1966.

35. Michael, D., *The Unprepared Society.* New York: Basic Books, 1968.

36. Bennis, 1964.

## TRENDS AFFECTING THE FUTURE OF TRAINING AND DEVELOPMENT

*Gordon L. Lippitt*

To project the future of the training and development profession and the American Society for Training and Development, it is necessary to examine the trends of the future that will be affecting such changes. Some of the larger trends that we will be confronting will be the greatly increased standard of living in our own country and throughout the world; an increasing gap between those who possess power and money and those that are unable to exert influence and are poor; a rapid increase in the world population; continued changes in our value systems; the increased influence of local, state and federal government; an increasing expression of desire for influence in power by minority groups by age, sex, and race; a continued increase in the influence of mass media; the extensive development of education as it applies to continued growth and development; a shift from the production to service economy; a continued increase in technology; the development of new avocations and vocations in society; increased international interdependence; continuation of the East-West conflict; an increased mobility of people with a lessening of commitment to an organization or community; an increased size of the social systems of mankind so that there will be a greater feeling of powerlessness on the part of members of such institutions.

It is appropriate to explore the implications of the key changes confronting our United States as they impact on the role of training and development. I wish to examine some issues that have risen out of our technological revolution, civil rights revolution, student revolution, moral revolution, and the anti-establishment revolution that is so much in the center of our social economic forces in today's America. The issues that arise from these causes will create for those of us in the training and development field some major changes in the way we prepare ourselves for our jobs,

From Lippitt, Gordon L., *Leadership for Learning.* American Society for Training and Development, 1970, 5-8. Reprinted by permission of the American Society for Training and Development.

the way we conduct our jobs and the criteria for determining our effectiveness.

What are the implications of these trends for the training profession? What are the implications for the American Society for Training and Development?

### 1. Organizations Will Require New Structures and New Process to Cope With Change.

Organizations of the future will become increasingly complex in terms of size, financial resources, manpower utilization and product diversification. Traditional structures will not be adequate. Organizations need to use "temporary systems." Task forces, project groups and other such operations will be required to help an organization adapt and react to its environment. To permit an organization to be proactive rather than reactive, matrix organization concepts will emerge. This will provide the flexibility to utilize resources wherever they can be found to effectively meet the needs of the organization. A greater emphasis will be placed on processes and systems within the organization that will permit self-renewing activities and innovation. The implications of this trend for education and development are:

a.   Training and development professionals will have to understand and learn to apply the principal of matrix organizations. We will need to recognize that many early organization theories and assumptions are obsolete. Training and development will proceed from the assumption that people can and should be used anywhere in the organization that their talents are required. Focus will be on getting the job done. Systematic efforts will be made to prevent emphasis on working through organizational channels which tend to choke and prevent organizational growth and effectiveness.

b.   Training professionals must learn to make organization analysis and to interpret the results for management.

c.   Trainers must place greater emphasis on being communications linkers within the organization.

d.   Training and development people must focus attention on helping people become comfortable in the presence of change and to work effectively within organizations characterized by continuous change.

### 2. Many Jobs and Skills Will Become Obsolete.

The obsolescence rate of people in the organization of the future will make it necessary for individuals to cope with change in their own lives, careers, and organizations. We will need to confront the reality that people must have second and third careers in order to keep up with the rapid change required in the job and manpower market. The continued rapid growth of a service-oriented society will change the complexity and nature of many organizations and jobs. The implications for education and training are:

a.  There must be a better balance between focus on individuals and focus on organization development, so that we may assist the organization to adapt more effectively in meeting its objectives and utilizing its human resources more creatively.

b.  New methods of training and development will place greater emphasis on creativity and innovation. It will become increasingly futile to teach for jobs already in existence.

c.  In assuming responsibility for organizational and individual diagnosis in the adaptive process, training professionals will need to use effectively both line and staff people.

d.  Training and development people will place greater emphasis on their own development and the professionalism which will be required to face the needs of organizational change.

### 3. People Will Insist on a Greater Opportunity to be a Meaningful Part of the Organization.

People will expect a chance to influence the position and role that they perform in the organization. They will want to be part of an organization that is relevant to the problems of the day and to the community. The old way of inducing people to be loyal to the organization will no longer be appropriate. Individuals will be increasingly concerned with their own self-actualization and will be loyal to themselves rather than to organizations. Organizations will need to capitalize on this motivation by structuring jobs to allow a greater sense of self-fulfillment and job enrichment. In addition, organizations will be able to secure individual commitment and loyalty only if they show relevance of the work and the company objectives to both individual aspirations and social objectives.

Many implications for training and development personnel derive from this trend:

a.  They must find ways to appeal to individual motivations and their sense of achievement.

b.  They must help people within the organization to establish targets and achieve them. This will involve helping people "to do their own thing."

c.  They should begin to see the organization as a system designed to release human energy rather than to control human energy.

d.  They must realize that organizatons, like individuals, pass through levels of maturity, and that very often they get bogged down at the level of maintaining the status quo when they should be growing toward a mastery of change.

e.  They must help the organization set targets and objectives, particularly in relation to the development of human resources.

### 4. Conflict, Confrontation, Coping and Feedback Will Continue as a Way of Life.

We must begin to recognize that confrontation is not a "bad" thing, but necessarily a way in which people "lay it on the line" and "tell it as it is." Millions of good productive ideas have been lost in organizations where the climate does not allow for honest differences in judgments and opinions. Many times pertinent points of view are "filtered out" before they get to top management. We must strive to avoid a win-lose concept in organizational and societal life and substitute wherever possible, the concept of win-win. Openness, candor, and frank feedback should not be equated with hostility or obstructionism. Quite the contrary: those who shut off the ideas and contributions of their subordinates are really the obstructionists. We will find an increasing need to use confrontation and conflict in a constructive way. People are no longer ready to blindly accept the judgment or actions of bosses, superiors or organizational leaders. The implications for education and training of this trend are:

a.  Training and development personnel must help people learn how to handle conflict and to recognize that this is not simply a technique of "how to fight."

b.  As professionals, we must avoid hang-ups in terms of expressing and implementing convictions solely because they meet our own "needs."

c.  Training directors must be willing to confront managers with the insistence that clear-cut objectives be identified before any commitment is made to a specific training program.

d.  Training professionals must learn to help others free themselves of hang-ups, as well as learning how to free themselves.

e.  Training professionals should focus attention on changing the rewards systems in organizations as a means of rewarding new kinds of behavior and affecting organization change.

f.  The training manager must help the organization determine when confrontation and conflict are appropriate and how they can be used constructively.

### 5. The Explosion of Knowledge and Technology Will Continue.

The rapid increase of knowledge and the technological revolution makes it increasingly evident that education must be viewed as a continuing life-long process. We will need to avoid preoccupation with terminal degrees and place greater emphasis on continued education. We must find the means for involving the whole man on the job so that work and life become more meaningfully related. In this context, we must recognize that money alone is an insufficient motivator. Work itself must be viewed as a basic source of satisfaction. Organizational objectives, individual performance objectives and training objectives will need to be integrated; and in training, process and content must be integrated.

The implications of this trend are:

a.   Training and development must help people learn how to learn. This will require focus on people being able to analyze the values inherent in their experiences.

b.   People must have a greater control over their own development and learning processes.

c.   Training professionals should take a searching look at their present program designs.

d.   Training personnel should view themselves more as managers of training and development resources, and less as teachers.

### 6. There Is a Need for Greater Interface Between Government, Education, and Industry.

Increased interface between these three major segments of society will create problems. A better way will be needed to sense and identify the emerging problems before they become overwhelming. Opportunities for cross collaboration between education, industry and government will be required. Interchanging personnel among these organizational systems will increase.

The implication of this trend will be that training and development personnel will move in and out of specific training positions. They will widen their perspective by working in various types of organizational systems and develop collaborative skills with organizational systems other than their own. The trainer must learn where to turn to gain the benefits from this kind of interchange.

### 7. The Emergence of Under-Utilized Groups Must Be Recognized.

Inadequate use of minority group members, such as blacks, Mexicans, Puerto Ricans, women, and older workers, will be a constant challenge in an evolving and changing society. There will be pressure to evolve manpower utilization opportunities for the use of the total manpower resources of the country. Under-utilized resources must be recognized at both individual and organizational levels. We must recognize that the middle-class puritan work ethic under which we probably were raised may be an inappropriate frame of reference for understanding the development problems of persons raised outside of this ethic.

The implications for education and training are obvious. We must learn to communicate with, and to develop ways for recognizing human potential in all persons in the various cultures of our society. The role of attitudes in the utilization of human potential must be recognized and techniques developed for minimizing prejudice in the work situation. New ways to interpret and train people for the world of work will be required. This will require an ever-continuing involvement in creating new designs for effectively developing the capabilities of human resources.

These seven trends will have direct effect on the responsibility, quality and the *nature* of training and development. It is well for us to reflect on these areas as we see the increasing need for training and development to solve the problems inherent in these trends.

As one views the rapidly expanding field of training and development, there seems to be clear trends in both the nature and quality of effort, programming, design and activity. This applies all across the board—to industry, government, volunteer agencies, labor, community groups, and professional and trade associations. I feel these trends are indicative of increasing maturity and professionalism in our field. Let me list them as I see them:

1. *Improving performance rather than merely increasing individual knowledge.*

   It is increasingly evident that the criteria used to evaluate the effectiveness of training development now anticipate change in performance rather than the lesser goal of having people "like" or "feel good" about a learning experience.

2. *Training situations as contrasted to improving the skills of individuals only.*

   Many educational experiences do not seem to bring about change within the trainee's organization. This has tended to increase the emphasis on training and development activities that focus on solving problems, with the result that situations are confronted and coped with more effectively. A word of caution, however: while this is a trend toward supplementing the skills of the individual, it does not eliminate the need for both kinds of emphasis.

3. *Training viewed as the way management gets its job done and not solely as a function of a training department.*

   Training and development, in the best sense, is a resource by which management uses organizational manpower to a maximum. This also happens to be a task and role of management. There is more and more awareness of the relationship between learning processes and organizational achievement.

4. *Building "in-house" capabilities rather than depending on outside experts or resources.*

   During the past ten years, it has become apparent to many types of organizations that development of their own training and development capabilities is essential. This does not mean that outside groups and institutions are not helpful; it does mean that today's organizations have specialized needs.

5. *Insistence on evaluation of training instead of accepting the results on faith.*

   If training and development is undertaken only because it seems to be "the thing to do," there is a tendency to overlook adequate evaluation and research values. In such cases, management also finds it difficult to justify the expense for educational activities, even though they may feel they are necessary. At long last, we are seeing more sophisticated attempts to really evaluate the practical results of learning, and to be more selective about methods and emphasis.

6. *Designing training activities that focus on "learning how to learn."*

   Because organizational functioning is so complex and because so much diverse knowledge is required, it has become important that managers recognize learning as a continuing process. Learning must be gained from all of life's activities; it can no longer be confined to formal education or occasional training programs. Learning how to learn from situations is becoming a way of life for the successful manager.

7. *Moving away from training that is unrelated to the learner's life experiences or his organization's needs.*

   It seems to me that we are seeing a trend away from some esoteric types of training, which must be considered fads, to activities that are based on real needs of people and organizations.

8. *Less didactic, non-participative approaches to learning and more action-learning.*

   The gradual fading of the one-way communication concept of training and development seems to originate in recognition that adults need to experience learning rather than be exposed only to cognitive learning.

9. *Providing reinforcement and a follow-up experience for trainees, so that learning is enhanced by application.*

   A major criticism of educational programs has been that frequently there is no lasting effect of the learning. The observation that the new learningg "drops off" quickly has been a matter of concern to many in our field. More and more we see career programs being planned, with monthly follow-up sessions, planned reading programs, and a sequence of reinforcement activities.

10. *Learning that is self-motivated by the learner rather than imposed upon him.*

    It has often been stated that a person cannot be made to learn. He will learn when he has a goal, is dissatisfied with his own performance, or wishes to achieve socio-psychological or economic rewards. In offering opportunities for individual or group growth, more and more training and development efforts are focused on the use of self-motivation principles.

11. *Instead of the vague assurance that training will be "good for you" there is greater emphasis on goal orientation.*

    Achievement and the solution of problems best motivate people and aid organizations. With this in mind, many organizations now direct more of their training and development activities toward certain goals. This is usually accomplished through programs of learning by objectives.

12. *Greater homogenity in training groups so that people learn to function together in their organizational relationships.*

    While there is some advantage to the individual being trained, as an individual, there is greater advantage to an organization in the training of individuals as members of a "real" group. We are seeing more of this.

Although the trends mentioned above may not yet characterize the majority of training and development efforts, it is encouraging to realize that in the past few years the movement in these directions has substantially increased.

# 2.

# LEARNING RESEARCH AND THEORY: ITS APPLICATION TO TRAINING AND DEVELOPMENT

Learning and development necessarily go hand in hand, since without learning there can be no development. As a prelude to our discussion of development, this chapter presents several perspectives on learning. The articles provide historical background and describe predecessors of present day learning theory; they extend observations on learning in general, as well as adult learning and learning in organizations.

Much current emphasis is placed on the learner, the learning situation, and the learning process. No longer is the teacher the primary point of interest; results are now often measured in terms of the learner. The teacher develops objectives in terms of the learner's performance and is concerned with reinforcing the learner's knowledge or behavior, building on the person's strengths. This trend is most evident to those who are involved with classroom instruction, but its influence is extending more and more to those who develop human resources in other ways.

"Learning Theories and Training," by Leslie This and Gordon Lippitt, was selected as the first article in this chapter because of the great detail with which the authors describe the historic background and various schools of learning theory. The article goes on to discuss trends in the application of learning theory to training and development, thus serving as the chapter's focal point, as well.

Although the second article, Ronald Lippitt's "The Neglected Learner," was written about elementary education, it complements the first article by developing criteria for effective learning situations that apply to a variety of situations. R. Lippitt's observations are thoughtful and perceptive, and their insight should prove useful to anyone concerned with applying learning theory, no matter what his field.

The third selection in Chapter 2, "The Leader Looks at the Learning Climate," by Malcolm Knowles, considers the adult—his uniqueness as a learner and the type of learning situation he requires. To conclude the chapter, Warren H. Schmidt takes a look at the adult learner in an organizational setting. He offers practical observations on the teacher's and learner's roles and how their experiences should be organized in different situations in his article, "Transforming Knowledge into Impact."

This practical realization that different methods are useful for different learners has been overlooked in much of the literature on learning. Future writings will probably contain increased emphasis on the useful, innovative application of learning theory in a variety of situations. Undoubtedly they will also focus on increased application of learning theory to managerial and organizational development.

---

# LEARNING THEORIES AND TRAINING: AN OVERVIEW OF LEARNING THEORY IMPLICATIONS FOR THE TRAINING DIRECTOR

*Leslie E. This and Gordon L. Lippitt*

Attempts are often made to distinguish between training and education. Some educators feel that training directors are not engaged in education. Most training directors believe they are. Educators tend to make this distinction: training is narrow in scope and involves only learning that is directly related to job performance, while education is concerned with the total human being and his insights into, and understanding of, his entire world. These attempts to distinguish between training and education seem petty inasmuch as both are concerned with the process of human learning.

Berelson and Steiner define learning as "Changes in behavior that result from previous behavior in similar situations. Mostly, but by no means always, behavior also becomes demonstrably more effective and more adaptive after the exercise than it was before. In the broadest terms, then, learning refers to the effects of experience, either director or symbolic, on subsequent behavior."[1]

For the training director, learning would seem to imply these kind of things:

a.  Knowing something intellectually or conceptually one never knew before.

b.  Being able to do something one couldn't do before—behavior or skill.

c.  Combining two knowns into a new understanding of a skill, piece of knowledge, concept, or behavior.

d.  Being able to use or apply a new combination of skills, knowledge, concept, or behavior.

e.  Being able to understand and/or apply that which one knows—either skill, knowledge, or behavior.

Since the training director is concerned with learning, it follows that he should be concerned with learning theory. Training directors often talk about the learning theory that underlies their training. However, most of us do not have a good understanding of learning theories and their application to our training efforts. It is through the eyes of

---

From *Training and Development Journal*, **20**, Nos. 4 and 5 (April and May, 1966). Reprinted by permission of the American Society for Training and Development.

the training director that the authors have ventured into an overview of learning theory.

As they design training programs, training directors are confronted by many factors about which they must make decisions:

a.  *Desired Outcomes for the Learning Experience.* This can range from complex comprehension of organizational dynamics to simple manual skills.

The *managers* who underwrite training programs normally stipulate an entirely different set of training outcomes. These usually are identified as reduction of costs; increased productivity; improved morale; and a pool of promotional replacements. Sometimes these are confused by training directors as outcomes of training that are affected by learning theory. It seems to us that these may be results of training but that learning theory does not directly relate to these as outcomes.

b.  *Site for Learning.* Training directors are concerned whether learning best occurs on the job; in a classroom; on organizational premises or off organizational premises; university or other formal site; cultural island; or at home.

c.  *Learning Methods.* These are on a continuum from casual reading to intense personal involvement in personal-relationship laboratories.

d.  *Grouping for Learning.* Our grouping of learners can involve all combinations from dyads to audiences of 1,500.

As we work with, and manipulate, the kinds of variables listed above, we tend to confuse them with learning theory. For example, a training director will say "My theory of learning is that employees learn best when placed in small discussion groups at a training site removed from the plant." What is not clear to most training directors is that the variables identified above result in a myriad of devices and techniques that stem from, and are most effectively utilized by, a given learning theory. In and of themselves they are not learning theory.

## THEORY VS. COROLLARIES

Just as we confuse learning theory with the variables discussed, the use of the terms "learning theory" and "learning theory corollaries or principles" can be confusing. Usually the learning theory can be stated very broadly—for example, "Learning occurs when a stimulus is associated with a response." From this generalization about how learning occurs, a number of specific learning laws, rules, or statements are derived—for example, "Repetition of a response strengthens its connection with a stimulus." Thus, the statement, "problems are difficult to solve when they require the use of the familiar in an unfamiliar way" is a corollary of the Behaviorist Learning Theory School. It is the learning theory corollaries that most often serve as the application guides to the trainer.

Some research findings about learning seem to be unrelated to any particular learning theory and will be found in the literature as isolated pieces of research. Two examples follow:

a. Sleep immediately following learning results in more retention than when the subject stays awake after learning (even if he gets the same amount of sleep before the retention test).

b. Simple facts do not seem to be learned during sleep, even when they are presented throughout the night by tape recording.

We have discussed corollaries in detail because a training director sometimes chances upon one or more of these and incorporates them into his training design. He then says, "Here is the learning theory that I am employing in my training activity." Sometimes the corollaries he employs have been borrowed from, or are derived from, several learning theories and so would appear to be inconsistent. However, this may be quite valid. This is so because the content and training objectives for a given training program may include both˙ skill and conceptual training. Each of these kinds of training would tend to borrow techniques from different learning theories.

Our major point here, however, is that training directors frequently confuse a learning theory corollary with a basic learning theory. A learning theory is always greater than the corollary. In using the corollary, the training director is often unaware of the major learning theory which lies behind it.

## WHAT IS MOTIVATION?

As one plows into the learning theory literature, one is confronted by the problem of motivation. Can you motivate a learner to learn? Is understanding learning motivation a prime requisite of the training director and instructor? Immediately one runs into difficulty. It becomes obvious that learning theorists do not agree what motivation is or how it is accomplished. Generally speaking, you find these premises:

a. The learner must be self-motivated.

b. The trainer must motivate the learner through an effective learning climate.

c. We do not know enough about causes of motivation to discuss its role in the learning process.

Most training directors believe there is a factor called motivation. They seem to be evenly split as to whether the learner must be self-motivated or whether the training situation or trainer motivates the learner. Those who believe that learning must be self-motivated usually believe the trainer must provide the conditions under which self-motivation can occur. In practice, there is little to distinguish the training designs of trainers who subscribe to differing philosophies. Designed conditions under which self-motivation can occur look very much like the designs of those who attempt to motivate learners.

As the training director explores learning theory, he is confronted with another discouraging task. If anything is in print discussing, in layman terms, individual or comparative learning theories we have not found it. Learning theories are to be found in courses in educational psychology and require a strong background in psychology, research, and statistics to understand them. Some of the differences seem to a training director to be very subtle. It is extremely discouraging to attempt to understand either the individual theories or the difference between the schools embracing several theories.

## ANIMAL EXPERIMENTS VALID?

The first thing that strikes the training director is that most of the research on learning theory has been accomplished using animals and fowls for subjects. Several authors comment that at least 95% of learning research has been accomplished on data received from experiments on rats, chickens, pigeons, monkeys, dogs, and cats.

It is also interesting to note that research on animals and fowls inevitably occurs under one or both of two conditions: the animal or fowl is very hungry or is sex deprived. It may very well be that training directors have been overlooking some excellent motivational factors in this area.

Two other immediate problems present themselves. First, it is often difficult to distinguish learning theories differentiated as to general schools. Second, it is even more difficult to distinguish between individual learning theories within the general schools.

This difficulty is compounded because of the technical language and equations used to express the theories or portions of the theories. Usually aspects of the theories are stated mathematically and then expressed in prose. Neither of these are done in such a way that a training director can easily comprehend them. He is then faced with the problem of trying to determine what the technical language expresses and restating them in words he can understand.

## LEARNING THEORY SCHOOLS

Generally, learning theories seem to fall into six general schools.

The first school is known as the *Behaviorist School*. Primarily, these theories hold that learning results from the rewards or punishment that follows a response to a stimulus. These are the so-called S - R Theories.

E.L. Thorndike was one of the early researchers into learning. Generally he held that learning was a trial-and-error process. When faced with the need to respond appropriately to a stimulus, the learner tries any and all of his response patterns. If by chance one works, then that one tends to be repeated and the others neglected. From his research he developed certain laws to further explain the learning process—for example, the Law of Effect: if a connection between a stimulus and response is satisfying to the organism, its strength is increased—if unsatisfying, its strength is reduced.

E.R. Guthrie basically accepted Thorndike's theory, but did not accept the Law of Effect. He came up with an "S - R Contiguity Theory" of learning. His position was that the moment a stimulus was connected to a response—the stimulus would thereafter tend to elicit that response. Repeating the connection would not strengthen the association. Thus, if I am learning a poem and learn it sitting down, I can probably recall that poem best when sitting rather than standing. Generally he did not attach much significance to reward and punishment—responses will tend to be repeated simply because they were the last ones made to a stimulus.

Clark Hull introduced a new concept—not only was a stimulus and response present in learning—but the *organism* itself could not be overlooked. The response to a stimulus must take into account the organism and what it is thinking, needing, and feeling at the moment. We now had the S-O-R concept.

B.F. Skinner is usually identified with the Behaviorist School. Rather than construct a theory of learning, he seems to believe that by observation and objective reporting we can discover how organisms learn without the need of a construct to explain the process. He depends heavily upon what is called operant conditioning. He makes a distinction between "Respondent" and "Operant" behavior. Respondent behavior is that behavior caused by a known stimulus—operant behavior is that behavior for which we cannot see or identify a stimulus, though one may, and probably does, exist. If we can anticipate an operant behavior, and introduce a stimulus when it is evidenced, we can provide the occasion for the behavior by introducing the stimulus—but the stimulus does not necessarily evoke the behavior. Thus the emphasis in learning is on correlating a response with reinforcement. This is at the heart of programmed instruction—a correct response is reinforced.

Other researchers have developed variations of the theories described above. Some assume that the organism is relatively passive but that the response is in the repertoire of the learner. Other theorists pay particular attention to instrumental conditioning. They assume that the organism acts on his environment and that the response may not be in his repertoire. Still others talk about mediating responses in which a period of time may elapse between the stimulus and the response—or the response may be a series of responses that stretch over a period of time. For example, a man may be desirous of marrying a girl but will work for ten years to save enough money to support her adequately before proposing.

## GESTALT SCHOOL

The second grouping is the *Gestalt School.* These theorists believe that learning is not a simple matter of stimulus and response. They hold that learning is cognitive and involves the whole personality. To them, learning is infinitely more complex than the S - R Theories would indicate. For example, they note that learning may occur simply by thinking about a problem. Kurt Lewin, Wolfgang Kohler, E.C. Tolman and Max Wertheimer are typical theorists in this school. They reject the theory that learning occurs by the building up, bit by bit, of established S - R connections. They look at

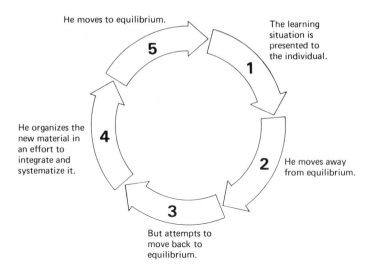

**Figure 1.**[3]    Equilibrium.

the phenomenon of insight, long-coming or instantaneous. To them, "the whole is more than the sum of the parts."

"Central in Gestalt theory is the Law of 'Pragnanz' which indicates the direction of events. According to this law, the psychological organization of the individual tends to move always in one direction, always toward the good Gestalt, an organization of the whole which is regular, simple, and stable.[2]

The Law of 'Pragnanz' is further a law of equilibrium. According to it, the learning process might be presented as follows: The individual is in a state of equilibrium, of 'good' Gestalt. He is confronted by a learning situation. Tensions develop and disequilibrium results. The individual thus moves away from equilibrium but at the same time he strives to move back to equilibrium. In order to assist this movement back to the regular, simple, stable state, the learning situation should be structured so as to possess good organization (e.g., simple parts should be presented first; these should lead in an orderly fashion to more difficult parts). The diagram in Figure 1 represents the movement toward equilibrium in the learning process."

A third school is the *Freudian School.* This is a difficult school to capsulize. "It is no simple task to extract a theory of learning from Freud's writings, for while he was interested in individual development and the kind of re-education that goes on in psychotherapy, the problems whose answers he tried to formulate were not those with which theorists in the field of learning have been chiefly concerned. Psychoanalytic theory is too complex and, at least at the present time, too little formalized for it to be presented as a set of propositions subject to experimental testing."[4]

A fourth school are the *Functionalists.* These seem to take parts of all the theories and view learning as a very complex phenomenon that is not explained by either the Gestalt or the Behavioral Theories. Some of the leaders in this school are John Dewey, J. R. Angell, and R. S. Woodworth. These men borrow from all the other schools and are sometimes referred to as "middle of the roaders."

A fifth so-called school are those who subscribe to *Mathematical Models*. To these researchers, learning theories must be stated in mathematical form. Some of these proponents come from different learning theory schools but tend to focus on mathematical models such as the Feedback Model, Information—Theory Model, Gaming Model, Differential Calculus Model, Stochastic Model, and the Statistical Association Model. As one tries to understand this school, it occurs to one that they seem to have no theory of their own but are expressing research findings of other theorists in mathematical terms.

A sixth school is more general in nature and can best be characterized by calling it *Current Learning Theory Schools*. These are quite difficult to classify and seem to run the range of modifying Gestalt Theories, modifying Behavioral Theories, accommodating two pieces of both theories, assuming that training involves the whole man—psychological, physiological, biological, and neurophysiological. Some of these are the Postulate System of MacCorquodale and Meehl and the Social Learning Theory of Rotter.

## CURRENT RESEARCH

Some of the more exciting kinds of current research seem to be in the neurophysiological interpretations of learning. One example of this was shown on a national television program, "Way Out Men," February 13, 1965. In this research, flatworms are trained to stay within a white path. If they deviate from the white path, they receive an electrical shock. After the flatworms learn to stay within the prescribed path, they are then chopped up and fed to a control group of worms. This control group learns to stay within the white path in about half the learning time. This has led some theorists to talk about the possibility of eventually feeding students "professorburgers."

Additional research is going on in this area and we have recently seen two or three other related pieces of research. It seems to indicate a key as to where memory and instincts are stored so that they can be transmitted to offspring. One is intrigued by this research when one remembers popular beliefs such as "Eating of the Tree of Knowledge," eating fish is a good brain food, and the practice of cannibals eating the brain of an educated man to become smart or to eat the heart of a brave man to become courageous.

## TRANSFER OF LEARNING

One of the problems that often confront a training director is the transfer of learning. Some of the major ways in which learning theories attempt to provide for the transfer of that which is learned to the work situation are the following:

*1. Actually doing the "that" which is being learned.* In this instance, we believe transfer is best when learning occurs on or in live situations. This is so because little or no transfer is needed—what is learned is directly applied. Instances employing this technique are on-the-job training, coaching, apprenticeship, and job experience.

*2. Doing something that is similar to that which is to be learned.* This transfer principle is applied when we use simulated experiences—the training experience and techniques are as similar to the job as possible. Sometimes we let the trainee discover the principles and apply them to his job. In other instances, particularly in skill training, he works on mock-ups which closely resemble the actual equipment on which he will work. Other techniques employed would include role playing, sensitivity training, and case studies.

*3. Reading or hearing about that which is to be learned.* In this instance, the trainer or a book gives the trainee the principles and then discusses and illustrates them. The trainee must now figure out the ways in which what he has heard or read applies to his job and how he can use it. Illustrative training techniques would be lectures, reading, and most management and supervisory training programs featuring the "telling" method.

*4. Doing or reading about anything on the assumption it will help anything to be learned.* In this instance there is an assumption that a liberalized education makes the trainee more effective in whatever job he occupies or task he is to learn. This might be termed the liberal arts approach. It assumes that a well-rounded, educated person is more effective, and more easily trained in specifics, if he understands himself, his society, his world, and other disciplines. Obviously, this would be a somewhat costly way of training. It would involve perceptual living and generalized education.

Much research has gone into the transfer of learning. Most of this occurs in the S - R Theories. It seems to be less of a problem in the other major theories. This is quite understandable as one compares the theories of learning. For example, the S - R Theories become quite concerned with questions like "Will the study of mathematics help a person learn a foreign language easier and more quickly?" This has led to much research regarding the conditions under which the transfer of learning best occurs. It is also applicable to conceptual learning. For example, will learning how to delegate responsibilities to children be useful in the delegation process in the work organization?

## ADULT LEARNING

Recent research at the University of Nebraska indicated:

1. The average older adult in an adult education program is at least as intellectually able, and performs as well, as the average younger participant.

2. Adults who continue to participate in educative activity learn more effectively than similar adults who do not. This would simply seem to indicate that learning skills require practice to be maintained.

3.  Adults learn far more effectively when they are permitted to learn at their own pace.[5]

## CONDITIONS FOR LEARNING

The concerns about motivating individuals to learn, and the recognition that there is such a thing as a learning process, have led training directors and training psychologists to explore the condition under which learning seems best to occur. Numerous lists of conditions for learning exist. They vary depending on the learning theory school to which the author subscribes. However, there is a remarkable acceptance of some general conditions that should exist for effective learning regardless of the learning theory employed. One of these composite lists follows:[6]

*1.  Acceptance that all human beings can learn.* The assumption, for example, that you "can't teach an old dog new tricks" is wrong. Few normal people at any age are probably incapable of learning. The tremendous surge in adult education and second careers after retirement attest to people's ability to learn at all ages.

*2.  The individual must be motivated to learn.* This motivation should be related to the individual's drives.

  a. The individual must be aware of the inadequacy of unsatisfactoriness of his present behavior, skill, or knowledge.

  b. The individual must have a clear picture of the behavior which he is required to adopt.

*3.  Learning is an active process, not passive.* It takes action and involvement by and of the individual with resource persons and the training group.

*4.  Normally, the learner must have guidance.* Trial and error are too time-consuming. This is the process of feedback. The learner must have data on "how am I doing" if he is to correct improper performance before it becomes patternized.

*5.  Appropriate materials for sequential learning must be provided:* cases; problems; discussion; reading. The trainer must possess a vast repertoire of training tools and materials and recognize the limitations and capacities of each. It is in this area that so many training directors get trapped by utilizing the latest training fads or gimmicks for inappropriate learning.

*6.  Time must be provided to practice the learning;* to internalize; to give confidence. Too often trainers are under pressure to "pack the program"—to utilize every moment available to "tell them something." This is inefficient use of learning time. Part of the learning process requires sizable pieces of time for assimilation, testing, and acceptance.

*7.  Learning methods, if possible, should be varied to avoid boredom.* It is assumed that the trainer will be sufficiently sophisticated to vary the methods according to their usefulness to the material being learned. Where several methods are about equally useful, variety should be introduced to offset factors of fatigue and boredom.

*8. The learner must secure satisfaction from the learning.* This is the old story of "you can lead a horse to water . . ." Learners are capable of excellent learning under the most trying of conditions if the learning is satisfying to one or more of their needs. Conversely, the best appointed of learning facilities and trainee comfort can fail if the program is not seen as useful by the learner.

*9. The learner must get reinforcement of the correct behavior.* B.F. Skinner and the Behaviorists have much to say on this score. Usually learners need fairly immediate reinforcement. Few learners can wait for months for correct behavior to be rewarded. However, there may well be long-range rewards and lesser intermediate rewards. We would also emphasize that rewarded job performance when the learner returns from the training program must be consistent with the learning program rewards.

*10. Standards of performance should be set for the learner.* Set goals for achievement. While learning is quite individual, and it is recognized that learners will advance at differing paces, most learners like to have bench marks by which to judge their progress.

*11. A recognition that there are different levels of learning and that these take different times and methods.* Learning to memorize a simple poem is entirely different from learning long-range planning. There are, at least, four identifiable levels of learning; each requiring different timing, methods, involvement, techniques, and learning theory.

At the simplest level we have the skills of motor responses, memorization, and simple conditioning. Next, we have the adaption level where we are gaining knowledge or adapting to a simple environment. Learning to operate an electric typewriter after using a manual typewriter is an example. Third, is the complex level, utilized when we train in interpersonal understandings and skill, look for principles in complex practices and actions, or try to find integrated meaning in the operation of seemingly isolated parts.

At the most complex level we deal with the values of individuals and groups. This is a most subtle, time-consuming, and sophisticated training endeavor. Few work organizations have training programs with value change of long-standing, cultural or ethnic values as their specific goal. Many work organizations, however, do have training programs aimed at changing less entrenched values.

The reader will recognize that this listing of conditions under which people learn contains concepts and principles from most of the learning theory schools. Most training directors are generalists, and seldom do their training programs focus on a constant single-objective outcome. It is perhaps inevitable that his own guiding training concepts and principles will be a meld from many theories. It is important however, that he understand the theories of learning so that he is using those concepts and principles which can best assure he will accomplish his organizations' training objectives in specific training programs.

As the training director explores learning theory, he finds the following points of view:

a.   There are individual exponents of a given theory who insist that their theory alone accounts for the way people learn.

b.   There are those who insist that we do not know what learning theory is and that learning theorists do not contribute to the real problems of training.

c.   There are those who will be frank in saying to a training director, "You are heavily on your own. Learning theory in its present state will not materially help you. Experiment. If it works and gets you the results you want—don't worry about what learning theory lies behind your success."

It is encouraging to note that some social scientists are aware of this breach between research and practice:

". . . Knowledge is not practice and practice is not knowledge. The improvement of one does not lead automatically to the improvement of the other. Each can work fruitfully for the advancement of the other but also, unfortunately, each can develop separately from the other and hence stuntedly in relation to the other."[7]

"It should be clear that the linking of social theory to social practice, as well as the development of a practice-linked theory of the application of social science knowledge to practice, is an intellectual challenge of the first magnitude. But it is one that many social scientists—particularly those who rarely leave the university system—have neglected."[8]

"Lewin is credited with remarking that one can bridge the gap between reality only if one can tolerate 'constant intense tension.' Roethlisberger and his colleagues described these tensions all too well for the person trying to improve the practice of administration when they wrote on 'Training for a Multidimensional World'[9] which I have already recommended to anyone seriously planning to enter this field."[10]

In relating learning theory to learning goals, learning theory corollaries, and the designed learning experience or training program, Figure 2 is a model that is useful in visualizing their interrelationship and their time sequence.

Two points are critical regarding the model in Figure 2:

a.   The model describes either a single training program or a series of training programs separated by a span of months or even years.

b.   The dashed lines indicate that the process is not a single revolution—but a continuous process. In the life of a single training program, the learning goals may be modified—or the design, learning corollaries, or even the learning theory employed may undergo on-the-scene modification if they are not producing the desired learning goals.

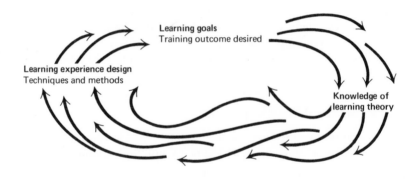

**Figure 2**

The model does not exist in a vacuum, nor is the choice of its component parts a matter of whim, preference, or intellectual selection. It is always related to the forces within the organization, the trainees, the trainers, and the situation, as is indicated in Figure 3.

A simplified mathematical statement of this model is:

$$\text{Learning Goal(s)} = \frac{\text{Present state of the organization + present state of trainees + recognized need for change}}{\text{Appropriate learning theory + appropriate training design + supportive climate for changed trainee behavior}}$$

If we accept (1) that effective training always takes into account the major forces impinging upon it and (2) that trainees have insights into factors that facilitate their learning, then it follows that we should listen attentively to trainee observations. Some of the more frequently mentioned are:

a. Participants almost always rate very high, as a training benefit, their interactions with each other. This seems particularly true in heterogeneous groups. They comment that they have become aware that their problems are not peculiar; it has been helpful to learn about other programs; they have learned from each other; and they have become more perceptive and broadened in the understanding of their role. We have, in the past, looked upon this as a minor side benefit of heterogeneous training. We are now inclined to believe this may be one of the major benefits of such training.

b. Participants always complain that they need time to internalize, digest, reflect, and to be left alone. We usually answer by scheduling more night meetings. Perhaps we need to experiment with two hours of training and six hours of internalization.

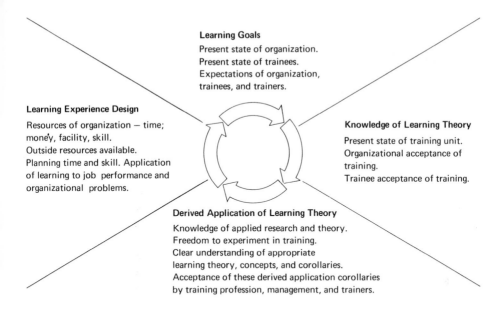

**Learning Goals**
Present state of organization.
Present state of trainees.
Expectations of organization,
trainees, and trainers.

**Learning Experience Design**
Resources of organization — time;
money, facility, skill.
Outside resources available.
Planning time and skill. Application
of learning to job performance and
organizational problems.

**Knowledge of Learning Theory**
Present state of training unit.
Organizational acceptance of
training.
Trainee acceptance of training.

**Derived Application of Learning Theory**
Knowledge of applied research and theory.
Freedom to experiment in training.
Clear understanding of appropriate
learning theory, concepts, and corollaries.
Acceptance of these derived application corollaries
by training profession, management, and trainers.

**Figure 3**

c. Participants like "bull sessions."

d. Participants say they need more recreation to release some of their emotional and physical energy.

e. The use of dyad conversations seem useful—even if these are forced. They seem to serve a helpful purpose of reaction, clarification, and feedback.

f. Time for reading pertinent articles and books seems to have excellent payoff. Training directors generally feel that managers would not accept training time being used for reading purposes.

g. Some limited experimentation seems to indicate that it is desirable to attempt to bring all participants up to a minimum level of knowledge before placing them in a training program. This can be accomplished by preliminary reading or programmed instruction.

**NO SINGLE THEORY**

We are inclined to think that by listening to the comments of participants as to what *they* believe enhances their learning, and designing training programs to meet these expressed needs, might have very excellent payoff in training programs even if the training director could not find support for the technique within existing learning theories. What we suspect is that there is no *single* learning theory that should be embraced by a training director or a training program.

This feeling seems to be supported as one surveys the current trends in training programs. These trends would seem to borrow from most of the Schools of Learning Theory. To illustrate, the authors believe that the following trends can be identified:

1. A trend toward a focus on *improved performances* rather than on increased individual knowledge.

2. A trend to *train situations* rather than individuals.

3. A trend to see training as the way *management gets its job done* rather than a function of the training department.

4. A trend toward building up *in-house* capabilities rather than dependence on outside experts.

5. A trend toward insistence on *evaluation* of training rather than accepting it on faith.

6. A trend toward designing learning that will focus on *learning-how-to learn.*

7. A trend toward training that is *reality-based* as against training that is highly unrelated to the learners' life experience.

8. A trend toward training that has an *action-learning* base rather than based on one-way communication.

9. A trend toward training that provides *reinforcement* and followup experience for trainees rather than "graduating" them from a training program.

10. A trend to depend more on the learning to be *self-motivated by the learner* rather than imposed on the learner by the trainers.

11. A trend for training to be *goal-oriented* rather than vague assurance that it will be "good for you."

12. A trend toward greater *homogeneity* in the persons being trained. [11]

**FITTING SPECIFIC NEEDS**

There would appear to be different learning techniques and conditions that are applicable to different kinds of training and learning. The training programs within a work organization are not all aimed at the same kind of learning. Perhaps different learning theories apply according to the nature of the subject to be taught and learned, the nature of the organization, the nature of the trainees, and the available teaching resources. This would indicate that no single learning theory can be applied across-the-board to all learning activities.

We suggest the following format as one that would be useful to a training director:

**Step 1.**   What is the learning outcome desired? This will indicate what is to be taught—orientation, problem solving, decision making, knowledge, memorization, changed attitude, changed behavior, manual skill, creativity, self-insight, lessened resistance to change, person-to-person relationships, group-to-group relationships, technical knowledge, communication, self-development, executive development, or understanding principles and theory.

**Step 2.**    Based on what is to be taught, select the learning theory most applicable to that content; i.e., Behavioral Theory, Cognitive Theory, Functionalism, Mathematical Model, Psychiatric, Neurophysiological, or total man and environment.

**Step 3.**    The basic learning theory should be utilized by examining the derived Corollary Theories and principles useful in effectively training toward the desired end. For example; knowing others better, knowing related programs better, reflection time, informal interaction, exercise, recreation, advance preparation, immediate reward, delayed reward, learning plateau, practice-rest-practice, reading with recitation, meaningful material, "A-na" phenomena, immediate use, material known previously, important material, pleasant material, concept formation, concrete concept, part-whole versus whole-part, positive instances versus negative instances, general to specific, maturation task relatedness, fatigue factor, and motivation.

**Step 4.**    These considerations would then suggest specific decisions on the following factors:

a.    The learning site—on-the-job; classroom-organizational premises; classroom-off organizational premises; university or other formal site, cultural island, or home.

b.    The grouping. (1) Related to size—one, dyad, trio, groups 5-8, groups 9-15, groups 16-30, and audience style—any number. (2) Related to relationships of participants—all male, all female, mixed sex; little experience, much experience, mixed experience; old, young, mixed age groups; known to each other, not known to each other; same organization—vertical, horizontal, diagonal; other organization—homogeneous, mixed; same educational level, mixed educational level; and same task or mixed tasks.

c.    The learning methods to be employed—lecture, panel, symposium, debate, laboratory, programmed instruction, experience, coaching, job progression, job rotation, job enlargement, apprenticeship, situational training, personal reading, correspondence, liberal arts, formal school, formal outside program, workshop, conference, institute, seminar, visitation, or discussion groups.

d.    The training aids to be used—movies, instantaneous replay movies, telephone—loudspeaker, TV, role play, exercises, in-basket, gaming, film strips, slides—transparent, tape recorder, blackboard, newsprint easel, flannel board, magnetic board, self-administered instruments, tests and quizzes, case studies—no printed discussion, case studies—printed discussion, case studies—incident process, experiments, models—mockups, and group—generated data.

e.    The type of resource persons or instructors—written material, experience, instrumentation, self, organizational technical expert, outside technical expert, organizational resource people, professors, industrial resource people, training department, supervisor, or peers.

f.    How much attention needs to be paid to transfer of learning: direct transfer; live, simulated reality; principle to be applied; no direct application; known stimuli—opposite response; familiar to be used in unfamiliar way; or principle to be learned and applied.


## CHANGE ON THE JOB

As training directors, we strive very hard to establish response patterns that hopefully will be carried over and continued in the work situation. This is at the heart of one of the criticisms managers level at training programs—the behavior of participants back in the work situation too often seems relatively unchanged.

As one examines this phenomena, one is struck that most training programs in the conceptual areas of supervision and management lean very heavily upon Theory "Y" assumptions. We do not know of any programs that pointedly train toward Theory "X" assumptions. Conversely, organizations still have a goodly amount of Theory "X" assumptions underlying both their operations and supervisory and management practices.[12]

This raises two questions:

1.  In our zeal to get away from the mechanistic approach to organizational dynamics, we have underplayed the role of these factors in the total organization as they affect training outcomes. We have tended to train as if such realities did not exist and that the only dynamics that were operable were the human factors in the training. This has created a breach between the training office, the operating people, and management.

2.  The S-R phenomenon not only operates within the training situation but is very much operable within the work situation. People react in the direction of the rewards they receive. The S-R patterns initiated in a training session have very little chance of survival when they come up against different S-R patterns of rewards in the work situation. For example, among the work situation S-R patterns rewarded are the following:

"Research paper production gets you promoted—not supervisory ability or a skill."

"Promotions depend on who you know—not what you know."

"I don't give a damn how your people feel—we've got a job to do."

"OK, you've been to a training program. Say something new."

"Seniority is what really counts around this place."

## REWARD PATTERNS

If a S-R pattern, initiated in a training program, is to be maintained in the work situation, then it must be rewarded by the organization. If the pattern is in conflict with rewarded patterns, the newly-learned patterns do not have much chance to survive. We believe that this accounts for a great deal of supposedly poor results of training. The training is not in harmony with the reward patterns of the organization. As training directors, we would have much better success if we would train according to the pattern rewarded, and apparently desired by the organization.

The research into learning theory has indicated a need that has not been recognized fully by the training profession. We are amazed that a critically needed overview of the field of learning theory has not been written to assist the training director. We need an identification of the existing learning theories that appear to be best researched and validated, the statement and comparison of these theories in language that the training director can comprehend and understand, and suggested guidelines for ways in which the training director can utilize these learning theories to the enhancement of his training activities. We believe such a publication is long overdue and would be highly welcomed by almost all training directors. We believe it would add much to the professionalization of the training job. More importantly it would very well make our training programs more effective in meeting the needs of our organizations.

## HELPFUL GUIDELINES

Beyond the implications for training directors that this exploration into learning theory has suggested, there seems to be some guidelines from such an exploration that are useful to a manager:

1. The sophistication needed to understand and utilize the implications of learning theory have much to say about the kinds of qualifications and skills a training director should bring to the job. The naive assumption that the bestowal of title and salary makes one a training director is tragic. Similarly, the managerial assumption that an employee who has the knack of making cute speeches or who once taught elementary school is training director material is inadequate. We would even go further and suggest there are some questionable implications of taking an employee who never managed even a small subunit and entrusting him with the training of other managers.

2. We have already commented on why we believe much of our training is not effective. Operational and organizational climate must support the training received. In addition, managers need to be much more realistic and expect that very few entrenched S-R responses can be changed in a week's training program.

3. We need to relook at the anxiety about evaluation of training. We are not even sure how people learn and this creates real problems in trying to evaluate the effectiveness of our learning process efforts. We know people do learn but we are not

sure why. When one looks at the tremendous number of complicated, tenuous, and conceptual ideas that are discussed within the span of one week in the average supervisory or management training program, it seems naive in the least to expect that very much by way of established new patterns of behavior could possibly emerge. The expectations of management are too high, and we as training directors have promised too much.

## ENCHANTMENT OF THEORY

We see no other trap. As we become concerned with learning theory, we must expect to find conflicting theories and conflicting practices within the profession. We must keep our focus on our objectives and not become seduced by enchantment with the theories.

Theories . . . attempt to organize existing knowledge, they attempt to provide guiding threads or hypotheses toward new knowledge, and they may also furnish principles by which what is known can be used. This practical outcome is seldom central in the thinking of the constructor of theory, and it is not surprising, therefore, that the person seeking advice from the learning theorist often comes away disappointed . . .

It turns out, however, that many of the quarrels of the theorists are internal ones, not very important in relation to immediate practical problems; there are, in fact, a great many practically important experimental relationships upon which the theorists are in substantial agreement . . . If the theoretical differences are irreconcilable, and one position eventually wins out over the other, there will ultimately be an effect upon practice. But advice for practical people today need not wait for the resolution of these theoretical controversies.[13]

This, then, is the challenge to those of us desiring to meet the critical problem of developing effective training programs to meet the changing manpower needs of today's organizations.

## NOTES

1. Berelson, Bernard, and Gary A. Steiner, *Human Behavior—An Inventory of Scientific Findings*. Harcourt, Brace, and World, 1964.

2. Koffka, Kurt, *Principles of Gestalt Psychology*. Harcourt, Brace, 1935, 110.

3. Marsh, Pierre J., Selected learning theories: their implications for job training. Master's thesis, George Washington University, School of Business and Public Administration, Washington, D.C., August 6, 1965, 56-57.

4. Hilgard, Ernest R., *Theories of Learning*. Appleton-Century-Crofts, 1956, 290.

5. Knox, Alan B., and Douglas Sjogren, Research on adult learning, *Adult Education* Spring, 1965, 133-137.

6. Composite drawn from: (a) Lippitt, Gordon L., Conditions of learning affecting training, unpublished notes; and (b) Miller, Harry L., *Teaching and Learning in Adult Education*. MacMillan, 1964.

7. Roethlisberger, Fritz J., in introduction to Clark, James V., *Education for the Use of Behavioral Science*. Institute of Industrial Relations, University of California, Los Angeles, 1962, 4.

8. Clark, *op. cit.*, 89.

9. Roethlisberger, Fritz J., and others, *Training for Human Relations: An Interim Report*. Division of Research, Harvard Business School, Boston, Mass., 1954, Chapter 9.

10. Clark, *op. cit.*, 91.

11. Lippitt, Gordon L., Changing trends in organized development. Talk before the Public Administration Society, University of Michigan.

12. McGregor, Douglas, *The Human Side of Enterprise*. McGraw-Hill, 1960. See Chapters 3 and 4, 33-37, for detailed explanation.

13. Hilgard, Ernest R., *Theories of Learning*, 485.

# THE NEGLECTED LEARNER

*Ronald Lippitt*

Lawrence Senesh of the University of Colorado has used the term "orchestration" to describe his view of how social scientists from the various disciplines should work together on the construction of social studies materials. This article is concerned with another type of orchestration problem—getting teachers and children to play in the same orchestra. For the most part, teachers and children are now playing in quite different orchestras.

In this paper, I will probe into the conditions of student life and the confrontations of identity, self-esteem and sense of personal worth and potency which enter into the student's readiness to be a receiver of educational opportunities. I will try to point out some data which will help us identify with the situation of the young ones on whose collaboration we have to depend if meaningful learning transactions are to occur.

In a previous statement I proposed six phases of curriculum development and change that bridge from the intellectual activity of the producer or integrator of knowledge to the learning activities of the child.[1] The phases were identified as: 1) the process of discovery, creation, formulation, or integration of basic knowledge; 2) the conversion of this knowledge into curriculum resource units, materials, frameworks,

From Morrissett, Irving, and W.W. Stevens, Jr. (eds.), *Social Science in the Schools: A Search for Rationale*. New York: Holt, Rinehart, and Winston, 1970. Reprinted by permission of Holt, Rinehart, and Winston and the author.

etc.; 3) a double phase—distribution of new resources by linking agents (such as publishers, regional laboratories, ESEA Title III projects, and schools of education) and the search for them by teachers, curriculum directors and, in a few interesting cases, groups of parents; 4) the adoption or adaptation of the new resources; and 6) consumption and utilization of new resources by learners.

I am concerned here only with the last step in this process, the activity of consumption or learning by the students. My observations are organized under five questions:

*How do we neglect the learner?*

*What is the learner's existential learning situation as he sits in the classroom?*

*How does the learner cope with our educational efforts?*

*What are the conditions of an effective learning situation?*

*How do we train a learner to become a good learner?*

## HOW DO WE NEGLECT THE LEARNER?

There are a number of ways in which we tend to neglect the learner in our teaching efforts or our preparation of materials for teaching. First, our major focus of enthusiasm and commitment is to our own specialized area of knowledge. We are concerned that our discipline or specialty get a significant amount of the child's ear, eye, and think time.

Second, our communication is often, sometimes necessarily, focused on gate-keepers rather than learners. What adaptations of our materials will be acceptable to curriculum decision-makers and teachers who must be reached? We are not pressed to give equal attention to the needs and readiness of the children.

Third, our conceptions of the consumer-learner and of his learning needs tend to be abstract, global, and occupationally oriented. We classify the learner as an age-graded or social-background cluster or group. We generalize about "the fourth grader," "the high school senior," "the central city child," etc. We also make the error of thinking of the learner as a separate entity, an individual student interacting with a teacher. This is of course an abstraction from the reality in which the learner is a member of several social contexts with many simultaneous loyalties, many commitments, and many directions of interest at any one moment. We tend to think of him in the future in producer-occupational roles like ourselves, rather than someone who now and in the future will spend most of his time as a consumer who is an intelligent or unintelligent user of the resources and services produced by others.

Fourth, we tend to ignore the young in our curriculum thinking by assuming a lack of readiness and motivation on their part to be involved in educational planning and choosing—by assuming inadequate maturity and perspective to make significant contributions to the selection of educational goals, methods, resources, or groupings.

Anyone who has taught children, field-tested materials, or closely observed the educational scene in other ways can probably add to this list.

## WHAT IS THE EXISTENTIAL LEARNING SITUATION?

What is the actual life-space of a young learner?

We must always remember that each day for our student is a medley of interventions aimed at influencing him in some way—interventions by parents, teachers, peers, friends, neighbors, TV. He is very busy responding, reacting, initiating contacts, seeking responses.

If we focus on the classroom group, as a group, we find a number of crucial factors that interact with the teacher's efforts to provide learning opportunities and to stimulate interest in curriculum resources. In a large proportion of the classrooms in our studies, over half the children believe that the majority of other classmates disapprove of active collaboration with the teacher, of reciting and showing enthusiasm for classroom projects, of asking the teacher for help, and of being friendly with him.[2] Actually, in a significant proportion of these classrooms, the majority of the children privately feel otherwise, but they take their clues from the active, anti-learning, more hostile and impulsive members of the classroom group.

In most classrooms, the distribution of interpersonal acceptance and power among children is skewed like the curve of distribution of wealth in the nation, or more so. A few students have most of the positive acceptance of their peers and most of the influence, while most of the students have very little. This state of deprivation focuses the energy of most students on interpersonal status issues and away from academic learning challenges. Those with deprivation of interpersonal status are found to be under-utilizers of their intellectual capacities in comparison with high-accepted children. There is little incentive to excel in school work to improve one's status since other skills and resources are valued much more highly.

We find the teacher's behavior reinforcing peer interactions. Low-status children get far more negative feedback from the teacher than do high-status children, and they reciprocate with negative alienation from the teacher. The findings show, impressively, that the more negative the child feels toward the teacher, the less the teacher can influence him to accept learning opportunities.

When we study the child's self-concept, or self-worth feelings, we find that most frequently he perceives teachers and other adults as seeing him more critically than positively, and as being inaccessible to influence by him in terms of having his needs heard. Negative self-conception is highly related to low motivation to learn.

Although the child's occupational role for many years from the first grade on is that of learner, few young ones have a meaningful conception of and commitment to the role of learner or a concern about the skills of competence as a learner. There is no meaningful or active involvement in learning goals, no vision of one's self as a learner, no sense of collaboration with peers in learning. For example, in one study the most frequent meaning of "helping each other in the classroom" was "cheating."

Evidence concerning the role of parents in education indicates that there is a tremendous lack of parental collaboration; that there is little orientation toward such collaboration; that there is resentment on the part of parents toward teachers; and that parents apply pressure on their children in relation to school achievement in very unskilled ways.

Still other data show a marked lack of congruence and communication between school systems and other major socialization programs of the community.

The findings just reviewed display a sample of the confused, competing, deprived learning situation of the learner-consumer in the classroom and in the larger educational community.

## HOW DOES THE LEARNER COPE WITH OUR EDUCATIONAL EFFORTS?

How does the student cope with variety of efforts to influence him, to get him to listen, to get him to learn something? To understand our consumer's behavior at this point we need to use the social-psychological concept of overlapping situations. The child, as he sits in the classroom, exists simultaneously in several psychological and social fields, each of which exerts an influence on him. We have already identified such fields as the teacher, peer-friends, peer-group, parents, and older peer models. There are others. In a typical study not long ago, teenagers identified from ten to forty persons and groups influencing their decisions and behavior in a week. At any one moment the child probably cannot report clearly all the competing inputs, but they do exist in different degrees of potency and awareness. What does he do to manage these often competing, confusing inputs? Four of these problem-solving postures are offered as illustrations.

One posture is what might be called "the compartmentalized solution," or "situational opportunism." Whatever stimulation is dominant at the moment is heeded at that time and other influences are blocked out. The teacher's presentation of curriculum opportunities will be attended to only when situationally more salient than peer relations or other interests. There is obviously little development of personal decision-making identity and internal commitment to learning with situational opportunism as a problem-solving posture.

A second problem-solving posture is what we call "the pervasive dominant loyalty." This method simplifies the problem by making one reference group or figure the dominant loyalty and behavioral guide across all situations, blocking out, rejecting, or withdrawing from other competing voices. This reduces the discomfort of decision-making. It also inhibits the development of the student as a self-initiating inquirer, learner, or decision-maker, and often results in a conforming dependency on parents, teacher, or peer-group.

Yet another problem-solving posture is that of "striking a balance," sometimes called a "computer solution." This is a posture of trying to please everyone as much as possible—finding compromises, doing school work but also meeting the demands of friends, trying to do projects but also following the clues of the popular kids. The amount of commitment to learning depends on the balance between all the confrontations active at any one time.

Another familiar solution has been called "a plague-on-all-your-houses"—the rejection of all external authority pressures. This posture is used frequently by dropouts and delinquents, as well as by others. The irritation and confusion of competing demands for the young person's energy made by parents, teachers, and others result in behavior which seems to say, "If you can't agree, then I am free to do whatever seems attractive to me at the moment—my impulses are my best guide." This withdrawal from the influence arena receives support from the child's need for autonomy, from his negative feelings about authority, and from the attractiveness of the inner pleasure-seeking voices.

Even when the teacher does successfully attract or compel the focal energy of the child, his learning behavior usually leaves much to be desired. Most frequently, the learning effort which is made and rewarded is a lip-service response, or "cognitive closure"—something that can be intellectually categorized and fed back to the teacher in some form. There is very little sense of relation to here-and-now living, to emotional commitment, to value confrontation, or to action challenge. The child may learn to be an observer or analyst, but not an actor or volunteer. He may develop skills as a critic, but not as a creator. He may become sophisticated, but not committed. He may become a very sensitive responder to clues and cues, but not an initiator of questions for action.

While creative educators today are focusing, more than ever, on the problems which I have outlined, our total educational effort is still one in which motivation is discouragingly low and learning opportunities are squandered. It is certainly one of the most tragic resource wastages in our culture.

## WHAT ARE THE CONDITIONS OF AN EFFECTIVE LEARNING SITUATION?

What are some conditions of an effective learning situation that can be derived from the preceding findings? All of us want the young ones to consume more learning opportunities. The derivations I make from the conditions described are the following:

*1. The teacher must involve the learners in the development of learning goals and norms.* Group norms must support rather than inhibit learning; they must involve the students in the development and maintenance of learning conditions.

Let us take an example from a fifth-grade class which will illustrate how these norms can be developed. The class has been asked to respond to this confrontation: "If a visitor from Mars walked in here today who was interested in education but knew nothing about American education, what would be the things that, if he saw them, would be signs that we were having a good learning day, and what would be the signs that we were having a bad learning day?" A steering committee which changes each week has been set up. The first steering committee represents four of the sociometric power figures of the class—two pro-learning and two anti-learning leaders. They appoint the next steering committee, which appoints the next one, and so on, the rule being that everyone goes through steering committee membership before anyone is on a second time. By the time the less influential children become members of the steering committee, group norms about how the process operates have been established.

The first task of the steering committee is to provide leadership in establishing criteria for good and bad learning days. They post the criteria on two large sheets of newsprint. The teacher, of course, has helped to train the steering committee to lead a problem-solving discussion and to avoid, for example, being punitive toward others who express "queer" ideas. The teacher contributes her own criteria and is active in stimulating the search for resources and ideas in addition to those the children first put up.

Each day, during the last fifteen minutes, a member of the steering committee reports his observations with respect to the two sets of criteria concerning how the class has done that day. There may also be discussion and decisions about changing the criteria before the next day begins. At the end of the week, the whole steering committee leads a half-hour discussion on whether they want to revise the criteria before they turn the material over to the next steering committee.

This example is but one way in which learners can become involved in setting their own goals and norms.

*2.   The teacher must accept the reality of the peer power structure.* There are others in the classroom group who in many ways have more power than the teacher does about the learning process. He must involve these peer leaders in improving the learning conditions of the classroom in ways similar to that mentioned above or in planning meetings in which he frankly requests the collaboration of student leaders.

*3.   The teacher must work to change the distribution of acceptance and influence in the classroom.* Though the teacher must, of necessity, work with the existing student power structure, he should try to encourage the class to develop norms of acceptance and support for varied ability and for recognition of the differences in developmental levels of people of the same age in the same group at the same time. I am reminded, for example, of a sixth-grade classroom that I recently visited. At the back of the room was a directory of "who is good at what in our class." If anyone needed help, whether it was shooting baskets in the gym, or working on math or whatever it was, they used the directory to find out who would be a good tutor or helper for their particular need.

*4.   The teacher must open up channels of communication between himself and students and among students in order to identify and work on the problems which block learning.* Not long ago, I was in a classroom where the children were doing ratings of the way in which they perceived the teacher and her help to them in learning, and the teacher was rating them as a learning group. After making the ratings, they put the two sets of data on the board so they could see how the teacher rated them and how she was rated by them. Then they discussed who needed to change in what ways to make the class a better place in which to learn.

There would be, I think, a great upsurge in the quality of education and the motivation of students if the school staff acted as though there were a National Association of Students for the Improvement of Education with an active chapter in their building. This would make a great difference in the psychological orientation of teachers.

*5. The teacher must do everything feasible to adapt the learning opportunities and tasks to the differential needs, capacities, and interests of the individual pupils in the class.* I have mentioned the resource directory. There are many other ways of developing the norm of peers helping peers in the classroom. One of the crucial elements often left out of the helper plans is that there must be peer training in the techniques of helping.

One of the most exciting projects that we have been engaged in is that of older students acting as academic helpers of the youngers.[3] Currently in one central city school system, thirty high school volunteers act as academic aides in the junior high and elementary schools. There are also about thirty junior high school students working in the elementary school and about thirty fifth- and sixth-graders in the first and second grades. The high school helpers are in a behavioral science course for which they get regular credit. They get three periods of field work a week, being teachers and helpers, and two periods of seminar work on understanding the motivation of young ones and the techniques of helping. One of the greatest results is that the academic achievement and commitment of the olders increases immediately, as does the individualization of instruction for the youngers.

*6. Everything possible must be done to increase the congruence and continuity of the child's relations to his various teachers and to the other socialization agents and to increase his own active role in decision-making in reciprocal influence relations with them.* The learner must become an active selector among the medley of opportunities, and he must become an intelligent defender of his personal integrity and selfhood against the many demands which to him are meaningless, or which demand dependence, or which are inappropriate to his own level of readiness and maturity. He must learn to be an intelligent defender against all the encroachments on his time and energy.

*7. Finally, everything possible must be done to involve parents in the learning objectives of their children and to achieve congruence and collaboration between teachers and parents in providing support for learning.* There are many interesting ways to brief parents on what would be helpful support: for example, the telephone conference. In our work with teachers, we sometimes have eight or nine teachers at once in different locations in telephone conferences. The same procedure would be quite helpful in the briefing of parents. Another method would be to use an electronic secretary, so that parents could call a telephone number and record any information they have, to be picked up at any time during the day by the teacher. The development of room meetings as genuine work sessions rather than as show-off periods is also important.

## HOW DO WE TRAIN A CHILD TO BECOME A GOOD LEARNER?

No matter how well we provide better conditions for learning, one of the most exciting and neglected jobs is the direct consumer education of the child. He must learn to seek, use, and create better educational opportunities. It seems clear that we want and need learners who are initiators—active seekers rather than passive recipients. We want consumers who are selective, who can use criteria of relevance rather than being uncritical buyers of what is offered. We want consumers who are eager for new learning tastes, eager for new risks rather than conforming and self-satisfied with having gotten such-and-such a score on a test. We want consumers who can reward themselves for good decision-making and for significant action efforts, rather than for getting the answers right for the teacher. With these criteria in mind, let us review briefly what we know about motivation and learning by means of the following types of training for learning. I have seen all of these approaches used, and they seem to be a critical part of the educational enterprise.

*1. Training in the attitudes and skills of learning from adults, of having creative, active, cross-generational communication.* We have in our social studies curriculum for example, a unit on "learning from grownups," in which the students role-play behavioral specimens of relations between teachers and students.[4] The students in the roles soliloquize: "What is going on? Why are they not asking for help?" or "Why are they asking for help all the time and being over-dependent?" Other pupils observe, analyze in lab teams, and come up with proposals of how these situations might be changed and how communication between teachers and pupils might be improved. Then the teams put on demonstrations of improvements, giving their evidence on what would cause a difference in learning if a new outlook on learning from grownups were developed.

*2. Training in how to use resource persons other than the teacher.* In our training classes, a resource person often observes students putting on the board questions they really want to explore, which demonstrates where they are in their thinking. The bottom third of the board is left empty. The resource person is then asked to add his expert questions which help get at the kinds of information the students want to know. Then we move into a dialogue of the group with the resource person.

*3. Training in the skills and responsibilities of reciprocal influence.* Instead of using the slow-down and sit-in, which are negative resistance postures and procedures, students should learn positive, responsible methods of influencing adults. These skills are developed frequently through mutual feedback and evaluation of what is going on in the classroom. The teacher reports ways in which he feels the learner role is being played inadequately and the pupils give their thoughts about ways in which they are not getting the kind of help they would like.

In our "bridging the generations" project, we have had, for several years, lower-class and middle-class teenagers working together on the problems of communication with adults. They decided to initiate teacher- and parent-education programs to get adults involved in understanding the way teenagers look at the world. With consultation, they developed teacher and parent nights in which typically they would put on a role-playing episode of a problem of communication between teenagers and adults. Teachers, parents, and teenagers would sit in diagnostic teams, observing this episode and collecting data on what they felt were the reasons for the problem of communication and ways to change and improve the situation. They moved from these diagnostic teams into demonstrations of how communication might be facilitated.

*4. Training in linking learning intentions or commitments to learning actions and efforts.* When the citizens of one city became aware of the lack of correlation between knowledge of right and wrong and actual behavior patterns of youth, they formed a curriculum development committee made up of religious, business, and educational leaders to work on an educational program which is now called "The Deciders." They worked out a curriculum in value education and decision-making that would be acceptable to both the values experts and the school system. They came out with a very exciting program—a "hit" in training materials.

The training groups usually were led by pairs of citizens, sometimes a teacher and a layman, sometimes a husband and wife. They worked on the problem of linking what we know is the thing to do with actually doing it. Among the self-inquiry projects generated were equilibrium analyses of questions such as "What are the forces for and against putting more learning effort into a committed learning task?" and "What are the forces for and against my doing any of the things I have just planned to do?"

*5. Training in using peers as learning resources.* The lack of communication where help-seeking and help-giving is not a norm is a tragedy. I have mentioned a classroom helper directory as one method of facilitating mutual assistance in peer groups. In most situations, we need to start with methodological training in skills of giving and getting help.

*6. Practice and support for practice in identifying with good teachers, or modeling.* Learning to teach others is another one of the important learner-training techniques that I have mentioned. The great response of failing lower-class black students in becoming active learners as they study the problems of young ones like themselves is inspiring. They are really studying themselves at a safe distance—looking at their own problems of motivation and ego needs. They talk very freely in sixth-grade and junior-high seminars about ego needs, about overcoming resistance, about being a good model, and about not creating dependency.

*7. Training to function in problem-solving inquiry teams.* There are lots of notions about the need for inquiry, but very little training in how to be a good team. Students often experience serious failures; if the teacher has to step in frequently, dependency is fostered. Therefore, training in skills to make learners productive in group situations is essential, no matter what the curriculum content.

*8. Training to develop internalized bases of self-reward and the feelings of success.* Children can get great excitement from working on questions such as "What is the meaning of learning for me?" and "What are the signs that I am learning something?"


## CONCLUSION

All this may sound a bit idealistic or impractical in terms of expectations for teachers; but my observation is that such a program of learner sensitivity training is crucial. It is the basic linkage between the curriculum and the learner. It is the determiner of the educational payoff.

Our experience is that teachers can be taught to do the job, if they are given the opportunity to learn. They, too, have been neglected. An amazing number of teachers are eager learners when they have the opportunity to experience the potential for self-renewal in personal and professional improvement opportunities. This is particularly true when they see that professional improvement can release them from energy-depleting burdens of caretaking activities for half-hearted pupils and permit them to move toward the exhilirating role of designer of inquiry opportunities—a teacher of how to learn, a presenter of exciting problem confrontations, a guide to learning resources.

But teacher training is another story. I have been concerned here with the problem of the learner and what he does with opportunities presented to him. We can design a great curriculum but have very poor consumption of it.


## NOTES

1. Ronald Lippit, "Processes of Curriculum Change," in Robert R. Leeper (ed.) *Curriculum Change, Direction and Process.* Washington, D.C.: Association for Supervision and Curriculum Development, NEA, 1966, 43-59.

2. The reference is to research activities of the Center for Research on the Utilization of Scientific Knowledge at the University of Michigan.

3. This refers to the *Cross-Age Helping Program* designed by Peggy Lippitt, Jeffrey W. Eiseman, and Ronald Lippitt (copyright, University of Michigan, 1968).

4. Lippitt, Ronald, Robert Fox, and Lucille Schaible, *Social Science Laboratory Units*. Chicago: Science Research Associates, Inc., 1969, Unit 7.

---

# THE LEADER LOOKS AT THE LEARNING CLIMATE

*Malcom S. Knowles*

## A LEADER OFTEN WANTS TO KNOW . . .

1. What motivates adults (my subordinates, my organization's members, my friends, ME) to learn?
2. How do adults differ from young people in their learning processes?
3. What techniques can I use to help people learn best?
4. Can I help people learn when I am not really a teacher by training or position?
5. Can adults learn equally well at every age through their life span?
6. What difference does previous education make?
7. Do adults learn some things better than others?
8. Is there a "best time" for some things to be learned?

## SOCIAL SCIENCE AND PRACTICAL EXPERIENCE TELL US . . .

### 1. Adults can Learn Throughout Their Life Span.

In 1928 the great psychologist of Columbia University, Edward L. Thorndike, in *Adult Learning* shattered for all time the ancient myth that "you can't teach old dogs new tricks." His studies proved that adults can learn at all ages, but showed a tendency towards a gradual decline in learning ability from twenty-five years of age on. Later studies by Irving Lorge and others have discounted even this gradual decline theory on the score that it is not the capacity to learn but only the *rate* of learning that diminishes with age. And even this slow-up of speed in learning appears to occur primarily in adults who get out of the practice of learning. Those who keep in practice can learn most things as well at sixty as they could at twenty, and some things better (especially when experience makes a difference). From the point of view of the leader

---

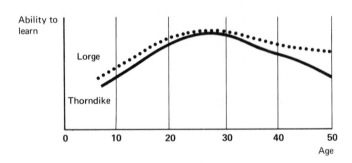

Contrast of Lorge's and Thorndike's general
curve of ability to learn in relation to age.

who wants to help other people learn, differences among a group of people that spring
from such factors as social status, educational background, occupational level, and
native intelligence, are greater than age differences in affecting their learning ability.

### 2. Certain Physiological Changes
### Take Place During the Adult Years Which Affect Learning.

All adults experience a decline in their physical abilities as they grow older, some of
which affects their learning. Fortunately most of these losses can be compensated in
various ways.

**A decline in visual acuity**, which can be offset by better illumination, larger print,
seating older people closer to the blackboard, and using sharp contrasts of color.

**A decline in hearing**, which can be compensated for by speaking more slowly and
distinctly, using amplification, using the blackboard freely, eliminating diverting
noises, seating older people in the front, and having "watchdogs" alert the speaker
when someone isn't hearing.

**A slowing up in physical tempo** and lowering tolerance for cold, heat, and fatigue,
which can be compensated for by permitting adults to choose their own work tempo,
by providing comfortable, well-ventilated and heated meeting rooms, by providing
frequent rest breaks, and by scheduling meetings at times most convenient to the
group.

It is important to realize that not all changes are necessarily in the direction of
decline. For example, although muscular strength, vigor, and speed of reaction tends
to decline, skills tend to increase with long practice. Though there may be less intense
drive or ambition, there may be an increasing loyalty and reliability, calmness and
serenity, and a greater concern for accuracy over volume.

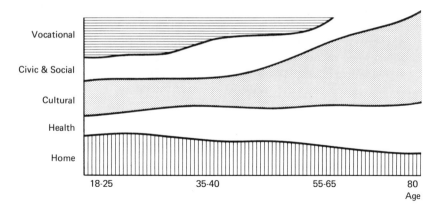

Vocational

Civic & Social

Cultural

Health

Home

18-25    35-40    55-65    80

Age

The changing pattern of adult concerns.

### 3. Patterns of Interest Change During the Adult Years.

In general, the things we like most at twenty-five years of age are liked better and better with increasing age, and the things we like least at twenty-five are liked less and less. There seems to be a slight decrease in the total volume of interests from the twenties to the fifties, but this decrease is largely in physical activities. The interests needed to support learning show no decrease. But the pattern of these interests tends to change somewhat with the normal shifts in focus of concern that take place during the several phases of the life cycle. These changing patterns of concern have been broadly charted by one of America's leading adult educators, Dr. Thurman White, of the University of Oklahoma, as follows:

The young adult, according to this theory, is likely to be most interested in learning those things that will contribute to his establishing himself in a vocation and in a home. Once he becomes relatively secure in these aspects of his life, his interests will tend to shift in the middle years to include more in the way of civic and social activities, especially in performing leadership roles. Then, as he nears retirement age, he becomes increasingly interested in learning things that have to do with his health and with cultural and religious aspects of life. These are the tendencies in our population as a whole, but individual differences are great. We all know young people who are overly concerned with health and older people who are still working on vocational advancement.

### 4. Learning Is a Complex Process Involving the Whole Person, Not Just His Mind.

Learning may be defined as a relatively lasting modification of behavior resulting from a "learning experience." It is an internal process that takes place wholly within the learner and involves his intellect, his feelings, his values, and his interests. The traditional notion that education consists of one person transmitting knowledge to another has been dispelled by modern research into the psychology of learning. Learning occurs when an individual experiences a problem or recognizes a gap between where he is and where he wants to be, and then institutes a self-inquiry in which he draws on whatever resources are available (teacher, literature, his own or other's experience) to acquire the learnings necessary to solve the problems or close the gap. *In the last analysis, all education is self-education*; a teacher can't really teach another person—he can only help him to learn.

### 5. The Most Effective Role of the Teacher Is NOT that of Simply Transmitting Knowledge, but Rather that of Facilitating Self-Directed or Mutual Learning.

The new insights into the nature of the internal learning process have led to a shift in the definition of the role of the teacher from the traditional one of *the transmitter of subject matter* to one of *procedural and resource person in the process of inquiry*. The art of teaching accordingly has shifted in emphasis from lecturing, lesson planning, and testing toward involving the learners in diagnosing, planning, conducting, and evaluating their own learning. The highest art of the teacher or resource person is the art of ego-involvement. Let's turn now to the practice of this fine art.

### A LOOK AT BASIC CONCEPTS—ADULT LEARNERS DIFFER FROM YOUTHFUL LEARNERS

Most teachers (and trainers) of adults know what they know about teaching from having been taught as youths or from having been trained to teach youth. Their approach to the teaching of adults tends, therefore, to be based on assumptions about learning that are derived from the traditions of youth education.

But adults have at least four characteristics as learners that are different from the characteristics of youths as learners (at least as typically assumed in tradition schooling). And a growing awareness of these differences is producing a technological ferment in the field of adult education out of which is evolving a uniquely adult approach to the learning-teaching transaction.

What are these differences? And what are their implications for helping adults to learn?

### 1. Difference in Self-Concept.

Youths tend to see themselves as essentially dependent persons. They expect that most of the important decisions affecting their lives will be made for them by adults. They enter into an educational activity, accordingly, with the concept that their role is the more or less passive one of receiving the information adults have decided they should have. They may gripe about particular impositions of the adult world's will on them, but they accept them as being congruent with their self-concept of dependency.

Adults, on the other hand, tend to see themselves as responsible, self-directing, independent personalities. In fact, the psychological definition of adulthood is that point at which an individual becomes self-responsible and self-directing. For this reason, adults have a deep psychological need to be treated with respect, to be perceived as having the ability to run their own lives. They tend to avoid, resist, and resent being placed in situations in which they feel they are treated like children—told what to do and what not to do, talked down to, embarrassed, punished, judged. Adults tend to resist learning under conditions that are incongruent with their self-concept as autonomous individuals.

*Implications . . .*

- More attention should be given to the quality of the learning environment. It is important to create a climate of mutual respect between leader and learners. An "adult atmosphere" is established by arranging the physical setting to provide comfort and easy interaction (chairs at tables or in circles, not in rows). The teacher is supportive rather than judgmental. An adult learning situation is friendly and informal—not aloof and formal.

- Adults can be helped to diagnose their own needs for learning. Good developers of adults are skillful in creating non-threatening situations (case discussions, role playing episodes, laboratory projects) in which individuals can discover for themselves what they need most to learn. Naturally, there are other needs that must be taken into account—those derived from the teacher's experience with the subject matter and those of the sponsoring institution. These needs, however, are negotiated with the learners in the spirit of "Let's create learning experiences that will meet both your needs and our needs"; they are never imposed on learners to the exclusion of their own concerns.

- Adults can be involved in planning and conducting their own learning. In the new technology of adult education, great emphasis is placed on the resource person and the learners working together on translating diagnosed needs into specific educational objects and then designing learning experiences to achieve these objectives. A modern adult learning situation is alive with meetings of small groups—planning committees, project teams, task forces—sharing responsibility for helping one another learn.

- Adult learners can evaluate their own progress toward their learning goals. In modern adult education the trainer does not set himself up as the judge of how well the students are doing. Instead, he devotes his energy to helping the adults create devices and procedures for getting evidence about the progress they are making. In fact, many of the same procedures that are used to diagnose needs for learning (case problems, skill performance exercises, etc.), can be used as before-and-after measures of progress in learning.

## 2. Difference in Accumulated Experience:

A given adult enters into any educational activity with a different background of experience from that of his youth. Having lived longer, he has accumulated a greater volume of experience. He also has had different *kinds* of experience: few youths have had experience in making their own living, marrying, having children, taking real community responsibilities, or being responsible for the welfare of others.

For this reason, adults are themselves a richer resource for one another's learning than youths usually are. They are less dependent on the vicarious experiences of teachers, experts, and textbooks.

Another advantage grows out of the psychological principle that new learnings can usually be grasped more easily when they can be related to past experiences. Adults have a broader foundation of past experience on which to *base* new learnings.

Because of their past experience, adults may have more fixed habits of thought, and sometimes this gets in the way of their learning better habits. This unconscious or spontaneous dependence on habit can make creative thinking and innovation difficult without some external encouragement toward change.

*Implications . . .*

- Greater emphasis can be placed on techniques that tap the experience of the adult learners, such as group discussion, the case method, the critical incident process, simulation exercises, role playing, skill practice exercises, field projects, action projects, laboratory training, demonstrations, group interviews, seminars, and audience participation patterns. A great ferment of inventiveness since World War II has produced a large reservoir of such experimental techniques. These have largely displaced the traditional transmittal procedures, such as lectures, assigned readings, quizzes, and canned audio-visual presentations, as the backbone of adult educational methodology.

- Greater care must be taken to illustrate new concepts or broad generalizations with life experiences drawn from the learners.

- Special attention should be given to introductory activities that help adults to "unfreeze" their fixed habit patterns. Leaders of adults often devote as much as the first third of a total program to establishing an atmosphere in which people feel free to admit deficiencies, providing objective and nonthreatening feedback to learners on their performance, and engaging them in a process of self-diagnosis of their needs and goals for learning.

## 3. Difference in Readiness to Learn:

It is now widely accepted in our culture that children and youth learn best those things that are necessary for them to advance from one phase of development to another. Each of these "developmental tasks" produces a "readiness to learn" that at its peak presents a "teachable moment." For example, we all have to accept the fact that we can't make a child learn to walk until he has mastered the art of crawling and has become frustrated at not being able to stand up and walk over to turn the T.V. knob by himself. At that point, and only then is he ready to learn, for it has become *his* developmental task.

Recent research indicates that the same phenomenon is at work during the adult years. Adults too, have their phases of growth and resulting developmental tasks. Robert Havighurst of the University of Chicago, who pioneered in this area of research, divides the adult years into three phases: "early adulthood," "middle age" and "later maturity," **and** identifies the main developmental tasks for each phase as follows:

*Early Adulthood:*

>    Selecting a mate

>    Getting started in an occupation

>    Starting a family

>    Rearing children

>    Managing a home

>    Finding a congenial social group

>    Taking civic responsibility

*Middle Age:*

>    Relating to one's spouse as a person

>    Achieving social and civic responsibility

>    Establishing and maintaining an economic standard of living

>    Assisting teen-age children to become happy and responsible adults

>    Getting to the top of the vocational ladder

>    Adjusting to aging parents

>    Developing adult leisure-time activities

*Later Maturity:*

>    Adjusting to decreasing physical strength and health

>    Adjusting to retirement and reduced income

>    Adjusting to death of a spouse

>    Establishing satisfactory physical living arrangements

Notice that these developmental tasks are related to what Havighurst calls "the ten social roles of adulthood": worker, mate, parent, homemaker, son or daughter, citizen, friend, organization member, religious affiliate, and user of leisure time. It is possible, therefore, to trace the changes in developmental tasks, and consequently in readiness to learn, through the changes that occur in the requirements of each of our social roles.

For example, in a person's role of worker his first developmental task is to get a job. At that point he is ready to learn anything required to get a job, but he definitely isn't ready to learn to become a supervisor. Having landed a job, he is faced with the task of mastering it, and at that point he is ready to learn the special skills it requires, the standards that are expected of him, and how to get along with his fellow workers. Having mastered his basic job, his task becomes one of working up the occupational ladder. Now he becomes ready to learn to become a supervisor or executive. Finally, after reaching his ceiling, he faces the task of dissolving his role of worker—and is ready to learn about retirement or substitutes for work.

*Implications . . .*

- The sequence of learnings should be strongly influenced by the developmental tasks of the learners, not just by the logic of the subject matter or the needs of the sponsoring institution. For example, an orientation course for new workers fresh from school would not start with the history and policies of the company; it would probably start with a practice try-out in their new work.

- Learners should be grouped according to their developmental tasks. For some kinds of learning, they are grouped homogeneously. (For example in a program on child care, young parents would be dealt with separately from middle aged parents.) For other kinds of learning they might be grouped heterogeneously (e.g., a program of human relations training in which the objective is to help people learn to get along better with all kinds of people, the groups would cut across age and status levels.)

## 4. Difference in Time Perspective

Youths tend to perceive most of their learning as being for use later in life; their time perspective is one of postponed application. They regard learning as a process of accumulating a pool of subject-matter knowledge and skills that may prove to be worthwhile when they become adults. They tend to enter any educational activity in a *subject-centered* frame of mind.

Adults, on the other hand, engage in learning largely in response to pressures they feel from current life problems; their time perspective is one of immediate application. They regard learning as a process of improving their ability to deal with problems they face now. They tend, to enter any educational activity in a *problem-centered* frame of mind.

*Implications . . .*

- The starting point of all learning activities can be the problems and concerns the adult learners bring in with them. Where the opening session of a youth education program might be titled, "What this course is all about," the opening session in an adult education program would be titled, "What are you hoping to get out of this course?", and one of the early activities would be a problem census or a diagnostic exercise through which the participants would identify the specific problems they want help on. Of course, there may be other problems that the teacher or the sponsoring institution are expecting to deal with, and these can be introduced into the picture along with the participants' problems.

- The central organizing principle for sequences of learning units should be *problem* areas rather than logical *subject-matter* divisions. For example, instead of a sequence on supervision being organized into such units as "Elementary Principles of Supervision," "Supervisory Theory and Practice," and "Advanced Supervisory Techniques," it would be more likely to be organized into such units as "Getting Ready to be a Supervisor," "Dealing With the Daily Problems of a Supervisor," and "Improving Your Ability to Help Subordinates Develop."

- Leaders and teachers of adults can emphasize their function of helping their students learn to cope better with their problems, rather than telling them what would be good for them. The modern teacher of adults is person-centered (and therefore also problem-centered) rather than subject-centered.

Now that a case has been made for adults being different from youth as learners, the question might well be raised: "Wouldn't youth learn better, too, under conditions in which they felt respected, were involved in the planning and conducting of their own learning, actively contributed their experience, had their learning sequenced according to their developmental tasks, and conducted their intellectual inquiry in terms of real life problems?" The chances are probably pretty good that they *would* learn better, and some strides are being taken in this direction in some of the new high school curriculums. But we know that these conditions *must* prevail in adult education because adults are voluntary learners who have the freedom to withdraw from situations that violate their integrity, whereas youth are compulsory learners who have little choice as to whether to accept imposed instruction or not.

## TRANSFORMING KNOWLEDGE INTO IMPACT—SOME THOUGHTS ON THE TEACHING-LEARNING PROCESS

*Warren H. Schmidt*

Educators of adults are more than distributors of knowledge; they are creators of learning experiences. Their task becomes increasingly complex when the desired outcome of the learning involves changes in attitudes, assumptions and approaches to human problems.

1.  The adult educator and training specialist needs a frame of reference for making strategic decisions.

    ...  The spectrum of the specialists' activities may range from teaching simple clerical tasks to organization development.

    ...  The body of knowledge in almost every field is increasing at a phenomenal rate.

    ...  The variety of available media and methodology is multiplying.

    ...  The number of educational institutions, educational businesses and consultants is growing.

    ...  The pace of change within organizations—and hence, the need for constant re-tooling of individuals, is up sharply.

2.  The training specialist may function as:

    ...  a *distributor of knowledge* (he arranges for information and techniques to get to the man who needs them)

    ...  a *bridge-builder* (he brings the person who has power and little knowledge together with the person who has knowledge and little power)

    ...  a *designer of creative learning experiences* (which is much more than simply bringing knowledge to one who needs to know)

3.  A critical variable in any learning situation is the relevance of the learner's past experience to the educational objective:

    ...  Some learning is designed to help the individual *organize his past experiences* in new ways.

---

This is an outline that was used as a handout by the author for a presentation at the 1969 national convention of the American Society for Training and Development. It was not prepared for publication. The editors felt, however, that it gave useful practical insight into the use of learning theory in organizational settings, and it is included for that reason. It is reprinted by permission of the author.

- Counselling, sensitivity training, and some kinds of management training help the individual to get better "handles" on what he already knows—but of which he has not been fully aware.

... Some learning is designed to *give new knowledge*, new experience, new skill—to push the individual beyond his present knowledge, assumptions and skill.

- Learning to program a computer would be an example.

4. Building from these extremes, we can derive this

Continuum of learning processes.

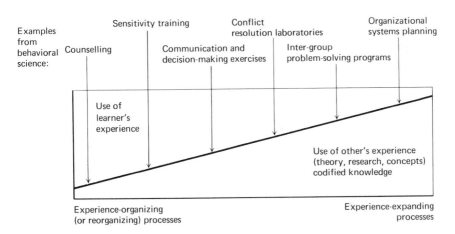

5. The position of a given learning experience on this continuum has implications for

- the preparation and orientation of the learner
- the learning climate and pace
- the role of the instructor
- the role of the learner
- conditions for success of the learning effort

6. To make clearer (and at the risk of over-simplifying) let's look at the extremes of the Learning Continuum. . .

When the Primary Emphasis is on. . .

| | Organizing the Learner's Experience | Expanding the Learner's Experience |
|---|---|---|
| The preparation and orientation should. . . | . . . make it comfortable for the learner to make explicit his past successes & failures<br><br>. . . emphasize the value of analyzing past experience to "get handles" on similar problems in the future | . . . emphasize the kinds of problems which the learner cannot now solve — and will be able to solve after mastering the new material<br><br>. . . help the learner deal with his inadequacy in confronting new material (it's "normal") |
| The climate and pace of the learning situation should be. . . | . . . thoughtful, not rushed<br><br>. . . strongly influenced by the learner's reactions and desires | . . . exciting, absorbing<br><br>. . . most strongly determined by the nature of the content |
| The Instructor's role is primarily. . . | . . . to set a climate<br><br>. . . to create conditions for making experience explicit<br><br>. . . to facilitate analysis of the experience<br><br>. . . to put the learner's experience into perspective | . . . to identify real problems and concerns of the learner<br><br>. . . to clarify learning goals and their relevance<br><br>. . . to describe the process by which the learner will achieve the near competence |

When the Primary Emphasis is on. . .

| | Organizing the Learner's Experience | Expanding the Learner's Experience |
|---|---|---|
| | . . . to give "feedback" on the possible consequences of past behavior<br><br>. . . to help the learner to generalize from his past experience | . . . to provide the new data and concepts or demonstrate the new behaviors |
| The learner's role is primarily. . . | . . . to provide data about his own experience, assumptions<br><br>. . . to analyze that experience<br><br>. . . to examine alternative ways of conceptualizing his experience | . . . to absorb the new data and concepts<br><br>. . . to test the new data, concepts, skills in dealing with problems<br><br>. . . to practice until the new material is internalized<br><br>. . . to apply the new material to real situations |
| Success is heavily dependent on. . . | . . . the extent to which the climate is free of threat<br><br>. . . the learner's feeling of need to find new approaches to old problems<br><br>. . . the learner's willingness to risk exposure of weaknesses | . . . the clarity of presentation of new material<br><br>. . . the learner's respect for the educator's competence<br><br>. . . the relevance of the new material (as perceived by the learner) |

When the Primary Emphasis is on. . .

| | Organizing the Learner's Experience | Expanding the Learner's Experience |
|---|---|---|
| Problems to anticipate: | . . . the learner may not feel that he has learned anything new<br><br>(or)<br><br>. . . the learner may reject any analysis or theory which does not agree with his own<br><br>. . . feelings of threat to learner in exposing his own experience | . . . feelings of inadequacy on the part of the learner<br><br>. . . communications problems<br><br>. . . the educator may over-estimate or under-estimate learner's knowledge |

7.  This analysis is based on the *primary* learning process to be emphasized. Within a single learning situation the emphasis may shift from time to time.

8.  The instructor should make clear to the learner where on the Learning Continuum he is focusing at any given time (i.e., what assumptions he is making about the relevance of the learner's past experience).

9.  Regardless of the process to be emphasized, the instructor of adults will find these guidelines useful:

    •   Adults learn what they feel a need to learn.

    •   Adults learn best by doing (by being actively involved).

    •   Adults learn best through problem-solving.

    •   Adults want to know how they are doing.

    •   Adults prefer an informal learning environment.

10.  Finally—what really counts is *what the learner learns (not* what the teacher teaches). To insure that this emphasis is kept in mind. . .

    •   Objectives should be stated in terms of what the learner should "take away" from the experience (not in terms of what the instructor does in the training session).

- The instructor should remember that in the final analysis all learning is really self-learning—with the instructor facilitating the process through stimulation, resources and setting. Kahlil Gibran put it this way:

> The teacher who walks in the shadow of the temple, among his followers, gives not of his wisdom but rather of his faith and his lovingness.
>
> If he is indeed wise he does not bid you enter the house of his wisdom, but rather leads you to the threshold of your own mind.
>
> The astronomer may *speak* to you of his understanding of space, but he cannot *give* you his understanding. . .
>
> For the vision of one man lends not its wings to another man.

> — from *The Prophet*

# 3.
# A SYSTEMS APPROACH TO DEVELOPING HUMAN RESOURCES

As we have noted, the use of systems to describe and develop human resources has been increasing during the past few years. The primary appeal of systems is that they provide a logical, thorough approach to the matter at hand.

In human resource development this method has been most fully utilized in the design of instructional systems to meet the needs of specific groups of people. These systems have been applied mainly to technical or skills training. This is because the systems approach to training requires very specific objectives that can be accurately measured and evaluated. In addition, the systems approach is time-consuming and costly; proper application must be both thorough and painstaking, even for simple problems.

Because management and organization development are less tangible than technical or skills training, it is more difficult to apply the systems approach to these areas. Yet the use of systems in management and organizational matters will probably increase, because systems can be helpful in describing, understanding, and evaluating as well as in controlling development—which is its primary use in training. The systems model provides a thorough description of the organization. It offers a unique method for understanding the organization *in toto* and for placing problems in a broad perspective. The use of systems models for broad developmental purposes will come with time, but initially we are likely to see them used much more for descriptive purposes.

The selections in this chapter emphasize the description and understanding of total organizations and subsystems of organizations. The first three give broad pictures of organizations as systems. Selection number one is from the already classic work on this subject, *The Social Psychology of Organizations*, by Daniel Katz and Robert Kahn, published in 1966. The second selection, from Edgar Schein's *Organizational Psychology*, discusses several important earlier systems models of organizations and presents his views on how the definition of an organization should be enlarged. The third, from Gordon Lippitt's *Organization Renewal*, discusses organizations as social systems and presents a typology of social systems that enlarges on the first two selections.

The fourth selection, from Amitai Etzioni's *Modern Organizations*, contrasts systems models with other approaches, thus evaluating the strengths and weaknesses of the systems concept. It provides a summary of the first three articles and serves as an introduction to the remaining two, which are somewhat more practically oriented. William Evan's "A Systems Model of Organizational Climate" is the fifth selection. It describes how the concept of systems can be applied to specific aspects of organizations and offers suggestions for the practical use of Evan's model of organizational climate. In the final selection, Paul Lawrence and Jay Lorsch present a system model intended for use in developing organizations, in an excerpt from *Developing Organizations: Diagnosis and Action.*

From what has been said here, it is evident that the editors believe that systems will be used increasingly to describe and develop management and organizations. Practical applications of systems will increase, but slowly. Development of the concept will require much time and effort, and the most meaningful of this development will have to take place within organizations, through intensive study and long-term application.

# ORGANIZATIONS AND THE SYSTEM CONCEPT

*Daniel Katz and Robert L. Kahn*

The aims of social science with respect to human organizations are like those of any other science with respect to the events and phenomena of its domain. The social scientist wishes to understand human organizations, to describe what is essential in their form, aspects, and functions. He wishes to explain their cycles of growth and decline, to predict their effects and effectiveness. Perhaps he wishes as well to test and apply such knowledge by introducing purposeful changes into organizations—by making them, for example, more benign, more responsive to human needs.

Such efforts are not solely the prerogative of social science, however; common sense approaches to understanding and altering organizations are ancient and perpetual. They tend, on the whole, to rely heavily on two assumptions: that the location and nature of an organization are given by its name; and that an organization is possessed of built-in goals—because such goals were implanted by its founders, decreed by its present leaders, or because they emerged mysteriously as the purpose of

From Katz, Daniel, and Robert L. Kahn, *The Social Psychology of Organizations.* New York: John Wiley and Sons, Inc., 1966, 14–19 and 26–28. Reprinted by permission of John Wiley and Sons, Inc., and the author.

the organizational system itself. These assumptions scarcely provide an adequate basis for the study of organizations and at times can be misleading and even fallacious. We propose, however, to make use of the information to which they point.

The first problem in understanding an organization or a social system is its location and identification. How do we know that we are dealing with an organization? What are its boundaries? What behavior belongs to the organization and what behavior lies outside it? Who are the individuals whose actions are to be studied and what segments of their behavior are to be included?

The fact that popular names exist to label social organizations is both a help and a hindrance. These popular labels represent the socially accepted stereotypes about organizations and do not specify their role structure, their psychological nature, or their boundaries. On the other hand, these names help in locating the area of behavior in which we are interested. Moreover, the fact that people both within and without an organization accept stereotypes about its nature and functioning is one determinant of its character.

The second key characteristic of the common sense approach to understanding an organization is to regard it simply as the epitome of the purposes of its designer, its leaders, or its key members. The teleology of this approach is again both a help and a hindrance. Since human purpose is deliberately built into organizations and is specifically recorded in the social compact, the by-laws, or other formal protocol of the undertaking, it would be inefficient not to utilize these sources of information. In the early development of a group, many processes are generated which have little to do with its rational purpose, but over time there is a cumulative recognition of the devices for ordering group life and a deliberate use of these devices.

Apart from formal protocol, the primary mission of an organization as perceived by its leaders furnishes a highly informative set of clues for the researcher seeking to study organizational functioning. Nevertheless, the stated purposes of an organization as given by its by-laws or in the reports of its leaders can be misleading. Such statements of objectives may idealize, rationalize, distort, omit, or even conceal some essential aspects of the functioning of the organization. Nor is there always agreement about the mission of the organization among its leaders and members. The university president may describe the purpose of his institution as one of turning out national leaders; the academic dean sees it as imparting the cultural heritage of the past, the academic vice-president as enabling students to move toward self-actualization and development, the graduate dean as creating new knowledge, the dean of men as training youngsters in technical and professional skills which will enable them to earn their living, and the editor of the student newspaper as inculcating the conservative values which will preserve the status quo of an outmoded capitalistic society.

The fallacy here is one of equating the purposes or goals of organizations with the purposes and goals of individual members. The organization as a system has an output, a product or an outcome, but this is not necessarily identical with the individual purposes of group members. Though the founders of the organization and its key members do think in teleological terms about organizational objectives, we should not accept such practical thinking, useful as it may be, in place of a theoretical set of constructs for purposes of scientific analysis. Social science, too frequently in the past, has been misled by such short-cuts and has equated popular phenomenology with scientific explanation.

In fact, the classic body of theory and thinking about organizations has assumed a teleology of this sort as the easiest way of identifying organizational structures and their functions. From this point of view an organization is a social device for efficiently accomplishing through group means some stated purpose; it is the equivalent of the blueprint for the design of the machine which is to be created for some practical objective. The essential difficulty with this purposive or design approach is that an organization characteristically includes more and less than is indicated by the design of its founder or the purpose of its leader. Some of the factors assumed in the design may be lacking or so distorted in operational practice as to be meaningless, while unforeseen embellishments dominate the organizational structure. Moreover, it is not always possible to ferret out the designer of the organization or to discover the intricacies of the design which he carried in his head. The attempt by Merton[1] to deal with the latent function of the organization in contrast with its manifest function is one way of dealing with this problem. The study of unanticipated consequences as well as anticipated consequences of organizational functioning is a similar way of handling the matter. Again, however, we are back to the purposes of the creator or leader, dealing with unanticipated consequences on the assumption that we can discover the consequences anticipated by him and can lump all other outcomes together as a kind of error variance.

*It would be much better theoretically*, however, to start with concepts which do not call for identifying the purposes of the designers and then correcting for them when they do not seem to be fulfilled. The theoretical concepts should begin with the input, output, and functioning of the organization as a system and not with the rational purposes of its leaders. We may want to utilize such purposive notions to lead us to sources of data or as subjects of special study, but not as our basic theoretical constructs for understanding organizations.

Our theoretical model for the understanding of organizations is that of an energic input-output system in which the energic return from the output reactivates the system. Social organizations are flagrantly open systems in that the input of energies and the conversion of output into further energic input consist of transactions between the organization and its environment.

All social systems, including organizations, consist of the patterned activities of a number of individuals. Moreover, these patterned activities are complementary or interdependent with respect to some common output or outcome; they are repeated, relatively enduring, and bounded in space and time. If the activity pattern occurs only once or at unpredictable intervals, we could not speak of an organization. The stability or recurrence of activities can be examined in relation to the *energic input* into the system, the *transformation of energies within the system*, and the *resulting product or energic output*. In a factory the raw materials and the human labor are the energic input, the patterned activities of production the transformation of energy, and the finished product the output. To maintain this patterned activity requires a continued renewal of the inflow of energy. This is guaranteed in social systems by the energic return from the product or outcome. Thus the outcome of the cycle of activities furnishes new energy for the initiation of a renewed cycle. The company which produces automobiles sells them and by doing so obtains the means of securing new raw materials, compensating its labor force, and continuing the activity pattern.

In many organizations outcomes are converted into money and new energy is furnished through this mechanism. Money is a convenient way of handling energy units both on the output and input sides, and buying and selling represent one set of social rules for regulating the exchange of money. Indeed, these rules are so effective and so widespread that there is some danger of mistaking the business of buying and selling for the defining cycles of organization. It is a commonplace executive observation that businesses exist to make money, and the observation is usually allowed to go unchallenged. It is, however, a very limited statement about the purposes of business.

Some human organizations do not depend on the cycle of selling and buying to maintain themselves. Universities and public agencies depend rather on bequests and legislative appropriations, and in so-called voluntary organizations the output reenergizes the activity of organization members in a more direct fashion. Member activities and accomplishments are rewarding in themselves and tend therefore to be continued, without the mediation of the outside environment. A society of bird watchers can wander into the hills and engage in the rewarding activities of identifying birds for their mutual edification and enjoyment. Organizations thus differ on this important dimension of the source of energy renewal, with the great majority utilizing both intrinsic and extrinsic sources in varying degree. Most large-scale organizations are not as self-contained as small voluntary groups and are very dependent upon the social effects of their output for energy renewal.

Our two basic criteria for identifying social systems and determining their functions are (1) tracing the pattern of energy exchange or activity of people as it results in some output and (2) ascertaining how the output is translated into energy which reactivates the pattern. We shall refer to organizational functions or objectives not as the conscious purposes of group leaders or group members but as the outcomes which are the energic source for a maintenance of the same type of output.

This model of an energic input-output system is taken from the open system theory as promulgated by von Bertalanffy.[2] Theorists have pointed out the applicability of the system concepts of the natural sciences to the problems of social science. It is important, therefore, to examine in more detail the constructs of system theory and the characteristics of open systems.

System theory is basically concerned with problems of relationships, of structure, and of interdependence rather than with the constant attributes of objects. In general approach it resembles field theory except that its dynamics deal with temporal as well as spatial patterns. Older formulations of system constructs dealt with the closed systems of the physical sciences, in which relatively self-contained structures could be treated successfully as if they were independent of external forces. But living systems, whether biological organisms or social organizations, are acutely dependent upon their external environment and so must be conceived of as open systems.

Before the advent of open-system thinking, social scientists tended to take one of two approaches in dealing with social structures; they tended either (1) to regard them as closed systems to which the laws of physics applied or (2) to endow them with some vitalistic concept like entelechy. In the former case they ignored the environmental forces affecting the organization and in the latter case they fell back upon some magical purposiveness to account for organizational functioning. Biological theorists, however, have rescued us from this trap by pointing out that the concept of the open system means that we neither have to follow the laws of traditional physics, nor in deserting them do we have to abandon science. The laws of Newtonian physics are correct generalizations but they are limited to closed systems. They do not apply in the same fashion to open systems which maintain themselves through constant commerce with their environment, i.e., a continuous inflow and outflow of energy through permeable boundaries.

At this point we should call attention to some of the misconceptions which arise both in theory and practice when social organizations are regarded as closed rather than open systems.

The major misconception is the failure to recognize fully that the organization is continually dependent upon inputs from the environment and that the inflow of materials and human energy is not a constant. The fact that organizations have built-in protective devices to maintain stability and that they are notoriously difficult to change in the direction of some reformer's desires should not obscure the realities of the dynamic interrelationships of any social structure with its social and natural environment. The very efforts of the organization to maintain a constant external environment produce changes in organizational structure. The reaction to changed inputs to mute their possible revolutionary implications also results in changes.

The typical models in organizational theorizing concentrate upon principles of internal functioning as if these problems were independent of changes in the environment and as if they did not affect the maintenance inputs of motivation and morale. Moves toward tighter integration and coordination are made to insure stability, when flexibility may be the more important requirement. Moreover, coordination and control become ends in themselves rather than means to an end. They are not seen in full perspective as adjusting the system to its environment but as desirable goals within a closed system. In fact, however, every attempt at coordination which is not functionally required may produce a host of new organizational problems.

One error which stems from this kind of misconception is the failure to recognize the equifinality of the open system, namely that there are more ways than one of producing a given outcome. In a closed physical system the same initial conditions must lead to the same final result. In open systems this is not true even at the biological level. It is much less true at the social level. Yet in practice we insist that there is one best way of assembling a gun for all recruits, one best way for the baseball player to hurl the ball in from the outfield, and that we standardize and teach these best methods. Now it is true under certain conditions that there is one best way, but these conditions must first be established. The general principle, which characterizes all open systems, is that there does not have to be a single method for achieving an objective.

A second error lies in the notion that irregularities in the functioning of a system due to environmental influences are error variances and should be treated accordingly. According to this conception, they should be controlled out of studies of organizations. From the organization's own operations they should be excluded as irrelevant and should be guarded against. The decisions of officers to omit a consideration of external factors or to guard against such influences in a defensive fashion, as if they would go away if ignored, is an instance of this type of thinking. So is the now outmoded "public be damned" attitude of businessmen toward the clientele upon whose support they depend. Open system theory, on the other hand, would maintain that environmental influences are not sources of error variance but are integrally related to the functioning of a social system, and that we cannot understand a system without a constant study of the forces that impinge upon it.

Thinking of the organization as a closed system, moreover, results in a failure to develop the intelligence or feedback function of obtaining adequate information about the changes in environmental forces. It is remarkable how weak many industrial companies are in their market research departments when they are so dependent upon the market. The prediction can be hazarded that organizations in our society will increasingly move toward the improvement of the facilities for research in assessing environmental forces. The reason is that we are in the process of correcting our misconception of the organization as a closed system.

Emery and Trist have pointed out how current theorizing on organizations still reflects the older closed system conceptions. They write:

In the realm of social theory, however, there has been something of a tendency to continue thinking in terms of a "closed" system, that is, to regard the enterprise as sufficiently independent to allow most of its problems to be analyzed with reference to its internal structure and without reference to its external environment .... In practice the system theorists in social science ... did "tend to focus on the statics of social structure and to neglect the study of structural change." In an attempt to overcome this bias, Merton suggested that the "concept of dysfunction, which implied the concept of strain, stress and tension on the structural level, provides an analytical approach to the study of dynamics and change." This concept has been widely accepted by system theorists but while it draws attention to sources of imbalance within an organization it does not conceptually reflect the mutual permeation of an organization and its environment that is the cause of such imbalance. It still retains the limiting perspectives of "closed system" theorizing. In the administrative field the same limitations may be seen in the otherwise invaluable contributions of Barnard and related writers.[3]

**NOTES**

1.  Merton, R.K., *Social Theory and Social Structure*, Revised Edition. New York: Free Press, 1957.

2.  von Bertalanffy, L., General system theory, *General Systems*, Yearbook for the Society for the Advancement of General System Theory, 1, p. 1-10.

3.  Emery, F.E., and E.L. Trist, Socio-technical systems, *Management Sciences Models and Techniques*, Vol. 2. London: Pergamon Press, 1960, 84.

---

# THE ORGANIZATION AS A COMPLEX SYSTEM

*Edgar H. Schein*

The complex interactions between how an individual is inducted into the organization, trained, assigned, and managed; the interaction between the formal organization and the various informal groups which arise inevitably within it; the disintegrative forces which formal organizational mechanisms stimulate among subgroups; and the inconsistencies which arise out of assumptions about man which fit formal organizational logic but not the realities of how he functions—all of these points argue for a redefinition of organizations along more dynamic lines. As I have stressed throughout, the complexity and high degree of interaction of the parts of an organization, whether these parts be functions, groups, or individuals, indicate a redefinition in terms of complex systems criteria.

Perhaps the most important argument for a systems conception of organization is that the environment within which organizations exist is becoming increasingly unstable. With the rapid growth of technology, the expansion of economic markets, and rapid social and political change, come constant pressures for organizations to change, adapt, and grow to meet the challenges of the environment. And, as one examines this process, one is struck that it is the total organization, not merely some key individuals, who must be studied if this process is to be properly understood.

## THE ORGANIZATION IN RELATION TO ITS ENVIRONMENT

The relationships between organizations and their environments are complex and as

---

From Schein, Edgar H., *Organizational Psychology*. Englewood Cliffs, New Jersey: Prentice-Hall, Inc., 1965, 88–95. Reprinted by permission of Prentice-Hall, Inc.

yet not well conceptualized. First of all, it is difficult to define the appropriate boundaries of any given organization under analysis and to determine what size its environment is. Where does a business concern—with its research departments, suppliers, transportation facilities, sales offices, and public relations offices—leave off and the community begin? Is the relevant environment society as a whole, the economic and political system, other companies in the same market, the immediate community, the union, or all of these?

Secondly, organizations generally have several basic purposes or fulfill multiple functions, some primary, some secondary. The business concern whose ultimate survival depends on making a useful product for a profit may have as a secondary function the provision of secure, adequately paid, meaningful jobs for its community. The cultural and social norms which dictate this secondary function are just as much a part of the relevant environment as are the economic forces which demand a good product at minimum cost. Yet these sets of forces may impose conflicting demands on the organization. When the organization has several primary functions, as does, say, a university-connected hospital, the differential pressures from different parts of the environment may be even more acute and difficult to conceptualize.

Thirdly, the organization carries within itself representatives of the external environment. Employees are not only members of the organization which employs them, but they are also members of society, other organizations, unions, consumer groups, and so on. From these various other roles they bring with them demands, expectations, and cultural norms. How should an organization theorist describe a system which carries representatives of its external environment within itself?

My point in mentioning these difficulties is to warn you that theory in this area is imperfect and incomplete. Systems conceptions take us much farther in clarifying organizations than did the simple mechanical models of early organization theory, but they still leave much to be desired. Having said this, let us examine some proposed conceptual scheme to illustrate the type of theory toward which, I believe, we must move.

### The Tavistock Model[1]

Some of the most vigorous proponents of the systems approach to organizational phenomena have been the group of social scientists associated with the Tavistock Institute in London. Out of their studies of changing technology in the coal mining industry and the redesign of work in Indian textile mills, they developed, first, the important concept of the socio-technical system and then the more general open-system definition of organizations.

The idea of a socio-technical system as put forth by Trist implies that any productive organization or part thereof is a combination of technology (task requirements, physical layout, equipment available) and a social system (a system of relationships among those who must perform the job). The technology and the social system are in mutual interaction with each other and each determines the other. In keeping with this concept, it would make just as little sense to say that the nature of the work will *determine* the nature of the organization which develops among workers as it would to say that the socio-psychological characteristics of the workers will *determine* the manner in which a given job will be performed. As the Hawthorne studies and Trist's coal-mining studies have shown, each determines the other to some degree.

The open-system model of organizations as discussed by Rice argues that any given organization "imports" various things from its environment, utilizes these imports in some kind of "conversion" process, and then "exports" products, services, and "waste materials" which result from the conversion process. One important import is the information obtained from the environment pertaining to the primary task—that is, what the organization *must* do in order to survive. Other imports are the raw materials, money, equipment, and people involved in the conversion to something which is exportable and meets some environmental demands.

If we now combine these two ideas, we can see the importance of multiple channels of interaction between the environment and the organization. Not only must the organization deal with the demands and constraints imposed by the environment on raw materials, money, and consumer preferences, but it must also deal with the expectations, values, and norms of the people who must operate the work organization. The capacities, preferences, and expectations of the employee are, from this point of view, not merely something he brings with him; they are also something which is influenced by the nature of the job and the organizational structure during his working career. Consequently, one cannot solve the problem merely by better selection or training techniques. Rather, the initial design of the organization must take into account both the nature of the job (the technical system) and the nature of the people (the social system).

For example, in the coal mining studies previously cited, if it is true that mining induces anxiety and that anxiety can best be managed in small cohesive work groups, then a technology which prevents such work group formation is likely to be ineffective. On the other hand, if one starts with the concept of open socio-technical systems, one would ask, "What *combination* of technology, initial worker characteristics, and organizational structures would most likely result in an effective work organization?"

An answer to this question might require the reassessment of the relative importance of different environmental inputs relative to the basic task. Economic demands and technological developments might both argue for a work method and structure which undermines the social system. The organization planner might then have to reassess whether the gains of an effective social organization in terms of long-run economic gains outweigh the gains of short-run maximum efficiency. In order to make this reassessment, he would have to consider a variety of other environmental characteristics—for example, changing aspects of the labor force, particularly on key variables like anxiety proneness; technology in related fields, such as methods of improving mine safety; trends in labor-management relations and union policies; and so on.

### The Homans Model[2]

One especially useful model of social systems, whether at the level of the small group or large organization, has been proposed by the sociologist George Homans. This model, as we will see, is not fundamentally at odds with the Tavistock model, but is somewhat more differentiated and complex. Any social system exists within a three-part environment: a *physical* environment (the terrain, climate, layout, and so on), a *cultural* environment (the norms, values, and goals of society), and a *technological* environment (the state of knowledge and instrumentation available to the system for the performance of its task). The environment imposes or specifies certain activities and interactions for the people involved in the system. These activities and interactions in turn arouse certain feelings and sentiments among the people toward each other and the environment. The combination of activities, interactions, and sentiments which are primarily determined by the environment are called the *external system.*

Homans postulates that activities, interactions, and sentiments are mutually dependent on one another. Thus, any change in any of the three variables will produce some change in the other two; in some cases, the direction of the change can be specified. Of particular interest, here, is the relationship postulated between interaction and sentiments, which is that *the higher the rate of interaction of two or more people, the more positive will be their sentiments toward each other.* Or vice versa: the more positive the sentiment, the higher the rate of interaction. The seemingly obvious exception of two people who come to hate each other as a result of interacting is explained if we realize that over the long run these people will reduce their interaction as much as possible. If they are forced into continued interaction, they often find good sides to each other so that positive sentiment in the end grows with increased interaction.

Whether propositions such as the one cited are true or false is, for the moment, not as important as the dynamic conceptualization which Homans provides, because from it can be derived several other important concepts. Homans notes that with increasing interaction come not only new sentiments which were not necessarily specified by the external environment, but also new norms and shared frames of reference which generate new activities, also not specified by the external environment. In the Hawthorne studies, it was found that the workers developed games, interaction patterns, and sentiments which were not suggested and not even sanctioned by the environment. Homans has called this new pattern which arises out of the external system, the *internal system.* The internal system corresponds to what most theorists have labelled the informal organization.

Homans further postulates that the internal and external systems are mutually dependent. This means that any change in either system will produce some change in the other. A change in the work technology will produce a change in patterns of interaction, which in turn will change (or sometimes temporarily destroy) the internal system. (The longwall coal mining method destroyed some of the primary work groups.) On the other hand, if the internal system develops certain norms about how life should be organized, it will often change the way the work is actually performed, how much of it will be done, and what quality will result. (The members of the bank-wiring room developed patterns of job trading, a concept of a fair day's output, and their own leadership.)

Finally, the two systems and the environment are mutually dependent. Just as changes in the environment will produce changes in the formal and informal work organization, so the norms and activities developed in the internal system will eventually alter the physical, technical, and cultural environment. For example, out of workers' informal problem-solving may come ideas for technological innovations (change in technical environment), redesigned work layouts (change in physical environment), and new norms about the nature of the psychological contract between workers and management (change in cultural environment).

The most important aspect of this conceptual scheme is its explicit recognition of the various mutual dependencies. Empirical research studies have shown again and again how events in one part of the organization turn out to be linked to events in other parts or in the environment. Similarly, consultants have found how changes in one part of an organization produce unanticipated and often undesired changes in other parts. Conceptualizations such as those of Homans, Trist, and Rice make it possible to analyze and anticipate such events.

## The Likert Overlapping-Group Model[3]

Likert's model of organizations adds two important ideas to the models already presented. First, organizations can be usefully conceptualized as systems of interlocking groups; and second, the interlocking groups are connected by individuals who occupy key positions of dual membership, serving as linking pins between groups.

This conception does not conflict with either of the above, but it draws our attention to two important points. First, the relevant environment for any given group or system is likely to be, not something impersonal, but rather a set of other systems or groups. This set is composed of three parts: (1) larger-scale systems, such as the whole complex of organizations performing a similar job or society as a whole; (2) systems on the same level, such as other organizations like itself, consumer and supplier organizations, community groups, and so on; and (3) subsystems within the given system, such as the formal and informal work groups.

Second, the organization is linked to its environment through key people who occupy positions in both the organization and some environmental system, and the parts of the environment may well be linked to each other through similar key people. To the extent that this model is correct, it suggests not only a relevant point of entry in analyzing system-environment relations (the location of linking pins), but also implies that the parts of the environment are not independent of each other. Consequently, if an organization is to understand and deal with its environment, it must seek out and understand these interdependencies.

Katz and Lazarsfeld's analysis of the "two-step" flow of communication provides a good example of the point I am trying to make here.[4] These investigators discovered that influence on consumer beliefs and preferences does not result from direct exposure of the individual to relevant information and advertising, but rather from exposure to "opinion leaders" in the community. Thus, if an opinion leader in the realm of fashions or political beliefs changed his outlook, a great many individual consumers would follow suit. The effect of advertising on the opinion leader is therefore the critical variable.

If this phenomenon is indeed general, it argues that a business must sell to the opinion leaders in its environment, not to its individual consumers. These leaders then can act as linking pins between the organization and its clients or consumers. Similarly, if several consumer groups are involved and their opinion leaders influence each other, it is important for the selling organization to know that the two groups are not independent portions of the environment. If it influences one, it may influence the other as well.

### The Kahn Overlapping-Role-Set Model[5]

Robert Kahn and his colleagues have pointed out that while the overlapping-group model is closer to organizational reality, it still misses the important point that psychological groups and formal groups may be different. In Likert's model, no clear provision is made for distinguishing between types of groups, and thereby accurately identifying the linking pins. Kahn has proposed that instead of groups, one should consider what sociologists have termed "role sets." If one considers the formal positions in an organization as "offices," and the behavior expected of any person occupying an office as his "role," one can then ask, "What other offices are linked to the particular one under consideration in the operating organization?" Or, to put it in terms of the role concept, one can ask, "Given a focal person fulfilling an organizational role, with whom else is he connected or associated in performing his role?" The set of people—supervisors, subordinates, peers, and outsiders—with whom he has role-related relationships then constitutes his "role set." The organization as a whole can then be thought of as a set of overlapping and interlocking role sets, some of which transcend the boundaries of the organization.

The behavior of members of an organization can then be studied in terms of the concept of either role *conflict*—where different members of the role set expect different things of the focal person—or role *ambiguity*—where members of the role set fail to communicate to the focal person information he feels he needs to have in order to perform his role, either because they do not have the information or because they withhold it. The kinds of expectations which members of the role set hold, the manner in which they attempt to influence the focal person, his perceptions of their expectations and influence attempts, his feelings and reactions to these, and his attempts to cope with the feelings and tensions which may be generated—these can then be related to organizational factors (rank, type of job, reward system, and so on), to personality factors in the focal person or the role senders, and to interpersonal factors which characterize the nature of the relationship between role senders and the focal person (degree of trust, relative power, dependence, and so forth).

For example, in their study, Kahn and his colleagues show that role conflict will be greater if the role set includes some members who are inside and some who are outside the organizational boundaries; role conflict and ambiguity also tend to be greater the higher the rank of the focal person in the organization structure; coping responses of the person who experiences tension as a result of role conflict or ambiguity often reduce tension but at the expense of organizational effectiveness. For example, the person who perceives conflict may deal with it by ignoring or denying some of the legitimate expectations which some members of his role set have communicated, resulting in a portion of the job remaining undone. People do not attempt to resolve the conflict by bringing together the role senders whose demands are conflicting, thus making it impossible to achieve an integrative solution.

The point which Kahn's study underlines is again the great degree of interdependence of organizational variables like rank, location of position in the structure, role expectations, perceptions of such expectations, coping patterns in response to perceived conflict, and effectiveness of role performance. Kahn's focus on the concept of role also highlights the possibility that more abstract concepts of organization (for instance, overlapping role-sets) are amenable to empirical research.

To summarize, I have attempted to show in the above several examples of theorizing about organizations the trend toward systems-level concepts which take into account the interactions and mutual dependencies of internal organizational and environmental variables. If one attempts to build a definition of organization in terms of such concepts, one must go beyond the traditional one with which we started.

## TOWARD A REDEFINITION OF ORGANIZATION

I will not attempt to give a tight definition of organization in systems terms because this cannot as yet be done. Instead, I will attempt to highlight where a new definition has to enlarge upon or change the traditional one.

First, the organization must be conceived of as an open system, which means that it is in constant interaction with its environment, taking in raw materials, people, energy, and information, and transforming or converting these into products and services which are exported into the environment.

Second, the organization must be conceived of as a system with multiple purposes or functions which involve multiple interactions between the organization and its environment. Many of the activities of subsystems within the organization cannot be understood without considering these multiple interactions and functions.

Third, the organization consists of many subsystems which are in dynamic interaction with one another. Instead of analyzing organizational phenomena in terms of individual behavior, it is becoming increasingly important to analyze the behavior of such subsystems, whether they be conceived in terms of groups, roles, or some other concept.

Fourth, because the subsystems are mutually dependent, changes in one subsystem are likely to affect the behavior of other subsystems.

Fifth, the organization exists in a dynamic environment which consists of other systems, some larger, some smaller than the organization. The environment places demands upon and constrains the organization in various ways. The total functioning of the organization cannot be understood, therefore, without explicit consideration of these environmental demands and constraints.

Finally, the multiple links between the organization and its environment make it difficult to specify clearly the boundaries of any given organization. Ultimately, a concept of organization is perhaps better given in terms of the stable *processes* of import, conversion, and export, rather than characteristics such as size, shape, function, or structure.

## NOTES

1. I have labelled this section the Tavistock model because of the many people involved in formulating this model. Most of the material discussed is drawn from two primary sources: (1) Trist, E.L., and others, *Organizational Choice*. London: Tavistock Publications, 1963. (2) Rice, A.K., *The Enterprise and its Environment*. London: Tavistock Publications, 1963.

2. Homans, G.C., *The Human Group*. New York: Harcourt, Brace & World, 1950.

3. Likert's theory is most clearly presented in Likert, R., *New Patterns of Management*. New York: McGraw-Hill, 1961. The concept as expounded there deals primarily with the internal relationships among parts of the organization. However, the conceptualization is also useful in thinking about organization-environment relationships, hence I am extending it to this other focus.

4. Katz, E., and P.F. Lazarsfeld. *Personal Influence*. Glencoe, Ill.: The Free Press, 1955.

5. Kahn, R.L., D.M. Wolfe, R.P. Quinn, J.D. Snoek, and R.A. Rosenthal, *Organizational Stress: Studies in Role Conflict and Ambiguity*. New York: Wiley, 1964.

# SOCIAL SYSTEM ELEMENTS OF ORGANIZATIONS

*Gordon L. Lippitt*

A *social system* may be defined as a "stable pattern of interaction between interdependent social units." It is a set of parts which stand in definite relationship to one another. This concept can be applied to *individuals*, in which case there is an interaction between the different roles that the individual person performs. It can be applied to *organizations*, in which case there is an interaction between social institutions (e.g., economic system, political system). An organization, in common with individuals, groups, and communities, may be regarded as an open, organismic system. We see the organization as a set of dynamic elements that are in some way interconnected and interrelated and that continue to operate together according to certain laws and in such a way as to produce some characteristic total effect. This serves equally well in referring to individuals, groups, organizations, or communities. All four levels of systems have their boundaries which separate them from their environment; each is constantly exchanging material and energy with this environment; each has a number of sub-systems within it which have to be functioning together to form a dynamic unity.

Such a social system performs certain necessary functions:

1. To keep the random actions of its members within limits so that they behave in accordance with *role* definitions. Supervisors are expected to supervise, workers to work, managers to administer, custodians to maintain the building, and so forth.

2. To reduce randomness and uncertainty in the relationships among the individuals or groups that make up the system, i.e., to meet man's need for structure and predictability.

3. To satisfy the shared needs and fulfill the shared goals of its members, both the implicit (usually not talked about) and the explicit (talked about), as defined by the system.

4. To survive as a system by meeting new concerns of its members and new demands directed toward it from the outside.

The nature of such a social system, however, is not all that obscure. It can be simplified for the purpose of examination. Figure 1 illustrates the progression from the individual human being to a complex organization of many human beings. The basic, micro-organismic unit—the sub-system we know as the *individual*—is indisputably as complex as other parts of the system, a fact which explains one of the reasons why

From Lippitt, Gordon L., *Organization Renewal*. New York: Appleton-Century-Crofts, Educational Division, Meredith Corporation, 1969, 46–52. Reprinted by permission of Appleton-Century-Crofts, Educational Division, Meredith Corporation.

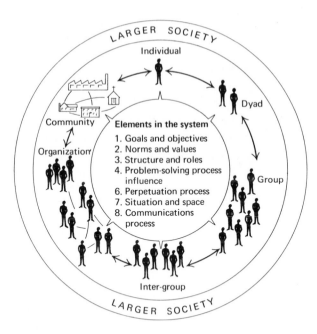

**Figure 1.**    Behavioral factors in social systems.

organizations have problems. Two individuals constitute a *dyad*, more than two individuals form a *group*. Both the dyad and the group are sub-systems. The *intergroup* is created when two or more groups establish a relationship. An *organization* usually is comprised of two or more groups having a more or less common reason for working together, although an organization can at any time consist of only a single group. A *community*, which in this scale is macro-organistic, is made up of individuals, groups and organizations in various intermixtures and associations. Schematically, as well as practically, all this forms a never-ended circle, and the whole of a society is made up of countless such circles interlocked like chainmail.

If we consider an organization to be a socio-technical system comprised of subsystems—i.e., individuals, dyads, and groups—we find that the subsystems are influenced by certain behavioral elements regardless of their size or complexity. Prior to examining these elements, however, it will be helpful to realize that they are manifested in both *formal* and *informal* contexts, or as *closed* or *open* states of the organization. Subsystems and the total organization manifest both open and closed aspects of their nature. One of the social scientists who has contributed a great deal to our understanding of this field is Milton Rokeach.[1] He took as a point of departure the writings of Eric Fromm on authoritarian character structure (in *Escape From Freedom*), Abraham Maslow (on the structure of authoritarian personality), and, of course, the massive work, *Authoritarian Personality*, by T.W. Adorno, E. Frenkel-

Brunswik, D.J. Levinson, and R.N. Sanford. Rokeach proposes that every person and organization has a belief system which represents the total beliefs, opinions, sets, and expectancies—conscious or unconscious—that are accepted as being true; at the same time, he has a system of disbeliefs, which are defined as a *series of sub-systems* related to and not in agreement with the belief system.[2] Thus, for example, a person may accept a system of thought concerning a social organizational structure as being "true for a particular situation." If this is taken as a belief system, he simultaneously rejects, to a greater or lesser degree, all other organizational value systems.

If we applied Rokeach's characteristics of open-closed systems to organizations we could observe the following:

An organization system is open to the extent that the *specific content* of beliefs by people in the organization is to the effect that the organizational work life *environment is primarily friendly*; it is closed when the work world is seen as a threat.

Open organization systems hold to a scheme of values founded on the belief that *authority is rational and tentative*, and that persons are not to be judged according to their agreement or disagreement with authority. In closed systems the value is that authority is considered absolute, and that persons are to be accepted or rejected in accordance with their relation to such authority.

Open organization systems will value and practice a relative *open communication* pattern among persons, and in a closed system the converse will apply.

The closed organization tends toward formal and inflexible structure, communications, and relations. An open organization is more flexible in its structure, informal in its human relationships, and leveling in communication. The formal aspect puts the individual at the summons of external demands—forces which originate outside his personality and are only indirectly fashioned out of his needs. The necessary submission brings its cost to the human personality; it causes fatigue, drains nervous energy, and produces anxiety. Formal relations need not, however, impair or destroy personality because the individual usually is revitalized and refreshed through the informal. It is a mixing of the formal with the informal that makes social systems bearable. Both are necessary; they are in dynamic relationship to each other. For each of the following elements, therefore, it is necessary to recognize the potential for reciprocal modification of the informal by the formal, and vice versa.[3]

## Goals and Objectives

Each sub-system has certain goals toward which its behavior is directed. The conscious or unconscious perception of these goals may range from clear to vague. They may be short range or long range, fixed or flexible, explicit or implicit. Although not necessarily with absolute certainty or unanimously, goals reflect what the sub-system "wants to do." In small, informal, face-to-face groups the relevant goals are those which involve the interaction of the members of the group. In formal organizations, goals are the rationally contrived purposes of the organizational entity.[4] The goals set up by organizational subsystems may be sought in different degrees as a result of the clarity with which they are conceived, their consistency with other goals, and the extent to which such goals are integrated with the next larger unit in the social system.

The functioning of an organization is often strongly affected by the nature of both its formal and informal goals and the extent to which those goals are understood and accepted by all members of the system. Vague or mixed goals tend to produce apathy and internal competitiveness; clear, accepted goals tend to produce greater commitment and interdependence.

## Norms and Values

As it interacts with the environment, an organizational system will develop expected and prescribed ways of acting in relationship to its goals and objectives. These standards of behavior will be influenced by what has happened in the past as well as new experiences and requirements. These norms will include how people dress, whether personal relations are stiff or relaxed, how much "enthusiasm" about one's work is appropriate—and dozens of similar unspoken but powerful dictums. To act contrary to the norms may bring severe censorship or even total rejection by the group. Some norms are functional in getting the organization's task done; others may be incidental and nonproductive. Standards may rest on tradition as well as on changes produced by new experiences and requirements. Because norms and values sometime persist beyond the point where they are functional, some groups and organizations find it useful in the renewal process to periodically make their operative norms explicit. They ask, "Is this the way we really want to behave? What purpose is served by this norm?"

Norms and values form the culture in which people work.

. . . a social system is a function of the common culture, which not only forms the basis of the intercommunication of its members, but which defines, and so in one sense determines, the relative statuses of its members. There is, within surprisingly broad limits, no intrinsic significance of persons to each other independent of their actual interaction. Insofar as these relative statuses are defined and regulated in terms of a common culture, the following apparently paradoxical statement holds true: what persons *are* can only be understood in terms of a set of beliefs and sentiments which define what they *ought to be*. This proposition is true only in a very broad way, but is none the less crucial to the understanding of social systems.[5]

## Structure and Roles

A social system develops a pattern of expected behavior that determines the interrelationships of individuals and groups and, thereby, the structure of the organization. In the small group, organization for work is flexible, and can meet both group goals and member needs. The positions in the group are interchangeable and usually there is no stable, sharp role differentiation. Occupants of a position (e.g., group member, chairman) can move in and out of it with relative ease. The behavior of members is highly visible to all. Finally, the sequence of work operations can be relatively casual and circuitous without serious difficulty.

In the formal organization, on the other hand, we have closely defined positions in a network. These positions have *continuity*—they are maintained by the expectations of occupants of other positions. All this makes for more stability, but less flexibility. The positions usually are *not* easily interchangeable (e.g., the sales manager may not understand and therefore could not perform the chief engineer's job). Positions are clearly differentiated for an effective division of labor. Position occupants accordingly cannot easily move in and out of positions other than their own. Job behavior is not highly visible (e.g., most members do not know very much about what other members *do*) and sequence becomes very important (e.g., order slips have to be routed *this* way or we'll have confusion).

This behavioral element will both raise and answer many questions. How much social distance should exist between a boss and his subordinates? What sphere of influence does the controller have—and what data can he ask for without being accused of invading the privacy of some person or department? These role expectations, like norms, become powerful determinants of behavior within the organization.

## Problem-Solving Process

Each sub-system adopts a way to resolve its internal and external conflicts, and to eliminate threat or ambiguity. These processes may result in such behavior as flight, fight, or dependency; or they may involve behavior which copes with the situation *as it is* through analysis, progression, and evaluation. Members of the organization develop a general feeling that "We're pretty realistic here" or "We really don't know how to come to grips with problems." In some systems, problem-solving is viewed as primarily an individual responsibility; in others it is viewed as group effort.

Again, basically, organization renewal is the process of realistically confronting situations so that problems are resolved in such a manner as to produce growth of individuals, groups, and the organization, as well as mature the process of problem-solving itself.

## Power, Authority, and Influence

This element reflects the ability of a sub-system to exert change on other sub-systems within the same organization, and the ability of that organization to effect change within its sub-systems or to influence change in other organizations. Some of the factors affecting the results of power and authority are the sub-system's place in the hierarchy of the organization, the sanctions imposed upon it, the expertise it possesses, the capacity of one sub-system to reward or punish another, and the interpersonal skills which are brought into play. Power, in the sense of capacity to influence behavior, becomes more and more central as positions become more differentiated. Authority is here used to mean "legitimized" power (who has the right to make this particular decision), but it is clear that much "illegitimate" power is exerted in keeping any organization going.

Influence by participation in small, work group decision-making can be full and complete. Non-face-to-faceness, however, unavoidable in the large formal organization, means that participation in *all* decisions by *all* persons is an impossibility and would be highly disruptive and ineffective. Trust or mistrust of those with greater power and efficiency becomes a pattern in organizations. As members of an organization gain sophistication, skill, and self-confidence, they increasingly resist direct commands and respond to the more sophisticated and sometimes informal influence of involvement and recognition.

### Perpetuation Process

Every sub-system in an organization wishes to maintain its existence. The need felt by each sub-system to continue functioning is a dynamic factor in the development and growth of an organization, either positively or negatively. This need is a dynamic factor behind attempts to reorganize a personality or an organization. To demonstrate the power of this behavioral element, one needs only to note the number of committees, agencies, and organizations that continue to exist long after their stated mission has been accomplished.

### Situation and Space

Every system and sub-system exists within the sphere of influence of an even larger system, and the limits constraining each system or sub-system are determined by its particular circumstances with respect to situation and space. Studies in the field of socio-technical systems underscore the impact of physical arrangements on the operation of an organization. The location of one's office inevitably affects who he talks to most frequently and what persons enter his sphere of influence. The recognition of this fact—that physical arrangements can strongly influence inter-personal relations—has led some to complain that too often architects and engineers determine the climate of the organization without fully realizing the nature of their impact.

### Communication

A social system must communicate to survive and grow. Communication is the means for providing information which permits the system or subsystem to change, grow, and achieve its goals. In the small group, the communication net usually is fully interconnected—all persons can talk to all other persons, either singly or as a group. Under these circumstances, few rules are necessary to channel communications, and members follow these rules because they are clearly functional (e.g., one person should talk at a time). Since people are face-to-face, information is transmitted with less distortion. Small group information-handling is as good as possible because errors can be checked and corrected immediately ("Joe, do I hear you saying that . . . ?").

In a formal organization, on the other hand, the communication net limits and channels communication. Much information must travel through a number of persons in sequence; distortion increases sharply as data are abstracted and simplified, as some information is blocked, or some is added deliberately or via projection. Rules for communication become important (X reports to Y and sends carbons to Z, *only*). As work and authority problems mount, occupants of positions almost inevitably find that the formal communications channels are providing data of poor quality or insufficient quantity. Therefore, the rules are circumvented, persons are "gone around," coffee-break chats become essential, and an informal communication network appears. Finally, correcting information in an organization is a difficult and lengthy process (phone calls, memos, special meetings). Many problems can be attributed to "break-downs in communication." This process has been studied extensively and much is now known about the conditions which facilitate effective communications.[6]

## NOTES

1. Rokeach, Milton, *The Open and Closed Mind*. New York: Basic Books, 1960.

2. *Ibid.*, 33.

3. The list of elements of a social system is a revised version of pp. 14—17 in the author's monograph written with Warren Schmidt, *Managing the Changing Organization* (Washington, D.C.: Leadership Resources, Inc., 1968). Used by permission.

4. Tannenbaum, Robert, Irving R. Weschler, and Fred Massarik, *Leadership and Organization* (New York: McGraw-Hill Book Co., Inc., 1961), 28-29.

5. Parsons, Talcott, *Social Structure and Personality*. New York: The Free Press, 1964, 22.

6. Haney, William V., *Communication and Organizational Behavior*. Homewood, Ill. Richard D. Irwin, Inc., 1967.

## GOAL MODELS AND SYSTEM MODELS

*Amitai Etzioni*

Thus far we have implicitly followed the widely held approach to organizational analysis that focuses on the study of goals and of organizations as their servants, obedient or otherwise. This approach has some distinct disadvantages both for studying and evaluating organizations. Those disadvantages are best brought into focus by comparing this more traditional approach with a newer one, which I advocate, and which will prevail, in much of the rest of this volume.

It is common for an outsider, if he is a researcher or evaluator (let us say a journalist or politician), to measure an organization against its goal or goals; the question most commonly asked about organizations is: How close did it come to achieving its assignment?

This approach has two potential pitfalls. First it tends, though not invariably, to give organizational studies a tone of social criticism rather than scientific analysis. Since most organizations most of the time do not attain their goals in any final sense, organizational monographs are frequently detoured into lengthy discussions about this lack of success to the exclusion of more penetrating types of analysis.[1] Low effectiveness is a general characteristic of organizations. Since goals, as symbolic units, are ideals which are more attractive than the reality which the organization attains, the organization can almost always be reported to be a failure. While this approach is valid, it is only valid from the particular viewpoint chosen by the researcher. This *goal-model* [2] approach defines success as a complete or at least a substantial realization of the organizational goal. Here the researcher is analogous to an electrical engineer who would rate all light bulbs "ineffective" since they convert only about 5 per cent of their electrical energy into light, the rest being "wasted" on heat. In practice, we find it more meaningful to compare light bulbs to one another rather than to some ideal "super bulb" that would turn all energy into light. It then becomes significant that brand "A" converts only 4.5 per cent of the energy into light while brand "B" converts 5.5 per cent. From the Olympian height of the goal—light without heat—both results are hopelessly inadequate. From the realistic level of comparative analysis, one bulb is 22 per cent more effective than the other (and may even be the most effective light bulb known).

Thus the goal-model approach is not the only means of evaluating organizational success. Rather than comparing existing organizations to ideals of what they might be, we may assess their performances relative to one another. We would not simply say that practically all organizations are oligarchic; we would rather try to determine which ones are more (or which are less) oligarchic than others. The comparative

From Etzioni, Amitai, *Modern Organizations*. Englewood Cliffs, N.J.: Prentice-Hall, Inc., 1964, 16-19. Reprinted by permission of Prentice-Hall, Inc.

analysis of organizations suggests an alternative approach which we refer to as the *system model*. It constitutes a statement about relationships which must exist for an organization to operate.

Using a system model we are able to see a basic distortion in the analysis of organizations that is not visible or explicable from the perspective of goal-model evaluation. The latter approach expects organizational effectiveness to increase with the assignment of more means to the organization's goals. In the perspective of the goal model, to suggest that an organization can become more effective by assigning fewer means to goal activities is a contradiction. The system model, however, leads one to conclude that just as there may be too little allocation of resources to meet the goals of the organization, so there may also be an over-allocation of these resources. The system model explicitly recognizes that the organization solves certain problems other than those directly involved in the achievement of the goal, and that excessive concern with the latter may result in insufficient attention to other necessary organizational activities, and to a lack of coordination between the inflated goal activities and the de-emphasized non-goal activities. Thus a bank may pay all its attention to making money and completely ignore the morale of its employees. This lack of attention to non-goal activities may result in staff dissatisfaction which may express itself in poor work by the clerks which in turn results in decreased efficiency, or even in a wave of embezzlements which ultimately reduces the bank's effectiveness.

The system model is not free from drawbacks; it is more exacting and expensive when used for research. The goal model requires that the researcher determine the goals the organization is pursuing—and no more. If stated goals are chosen, this becomes comparatively easy. Real goals, those the organization actually pursues, are more difficult to establish. To find out the organization's real orientation, it is sometimes necessary not only to gain the confidence of its elite but also to analyze much of the organizational structure.

Research conducted on the basis of the system model requires more effort than a study following the goal model, even when the goal model focuses on real goals. The system model requires that the analyst determine what he considers a highly effective allocation of means. This often requires considerable knowledge of the way an organization of the type studied functions. Acquiring such knowledge is often quite demanding, but (1) the efforts invested in obtaining the information required for the system model are not wasted, since the information collected in the process of developing the system model will be of much value for the study of most organizational problems; and (2) theoretical considerations may often serve as the bases for constructing a system model. This point requires some elaboration.

A well-developed organizational theory will include statements on the functional requirements[3] various organizational types must meet. Just as human beings have different needs, so organizations require different things to operate successfully. An awareness of these needs will guide the researcher who is constructing a system model for the study of a specific organization. In research where the pressure to economize is great, the theoretical system model of the particular organizational type may be used directly as a standard and guide for the analysis of a specific organization. But it should be pointed out that in the present state of organizational theory, such a model is often not available. At present, organizational theory is generally constructed on a high level of abstraction, dealing mainly with general propositions which apply equally well—but also equally badly—to all organizations. The differences among various organizational types are considerable; therefore any theory of organizations in general must be highly abstract. It can serve as an important frame for specification—that is, for the development of special theoretical models for the various organizational types—but it cannot substitute for such theories by serving in itself as a system model, to be applied directly to the analysis of actual organizations.[4]

Maybe the best support for the thesis that a system model can be formulated and fruitfully applied is found in a study of organizational effectiveness by B.S. Georgopoulos and A.S. Tannenbaum,[5] one of the few studies that distinguish explicitly between the goal and system approaches to the study of effectiveness. Instead of focusing on the goals of the delivery service organizations under study, the researchers constructed three indexes, each measuring one basic element of the system. These were: (1) station productivity, (2) intraorganizational strain as indicated by the incidence of tension and conflict among organizational subgroups, and (3) organizational flexibility, defined as the ability to adjust to external or internal change. The total score of effectiveness thus produced was significantly correlated with the ratings on effectiveness which various experts and "insiders" gave the 32 stations. The stations were compared to one another on these dimensions rather than to an idealized picture of what a delivery station should be.

Further development of such system-effectiveness indexes will require elaboration of organizational theory along the lines discussed above, because it is necessary to supply a rationale for measuring certain aspects of the system and not others.

### Survival and Effectiveness Models

A system model constitutes a statement about relationships which, if actually existing, would allow an organization to maintain itself and to operate. There are two major sub-types of system models. One may be called a survival model—i.e., a set of requirements which, if fulfilled, allows the system to exist. In such a model, each relationship specified is a prerequisite for the functioning of the system; remove any one of them and the system ceases to operate, like an engine whose sparkplugs have been removed. The second sub-type is an effectiveness model. It defines a pattern of interrelations among the elements of the system which would make it most effective in the service of a given goal, as compared to other combinations of the same or similar elements. The question here is: Which type of sparkplug makes the engine run smoothest?

There is considerable difference between the two sub-models. Alternatives which are equally satisfactory from the viewpoint of the survival model have a different value from the viewpoint of the effectiveness model. The survival model gives a "yes" or "no" score when answering the question: Is a specific relationship necessary? The effectiveness model tells us the relative effectiveness of several alternatives; there are first, second, third, and n'th choices. Only rarely are two patterns full-fledged alternatives in this sense—i.e., only rarely do they have the same effectiveness value. The survival model would not record significant changes in organizational operations; the model only asks whether the basic requirements of the organization are being met. The use of the effectiveness model evaluates changes that have occurred in the organization, and how they affect the ability of the organization to serve its goals, as compared to its earlier state or other organizations of its kind.

## NOTES

1. For a discussion of this viewpoint and references to it in the literature, see Etzioni, Amitai, Two approaches to organizational analysis: a critique and a suggestion, *Administrative Science Quarterly* (1960), 5:257-278.

2. For a discussion of the concept model, see Inkeles, Alex, *What is Sociology? An Introduction to the Discipline and Profession*. Englewood Cliffs, N.J.: Prentice-Hall. It is used here to refer to conceptual constructs, or meta-theories.

3. Functional requirements here simply refer to the requirements that have to be met for the specific unit under discussion to function—that is, to operate. For a more extensive discussion of this important concept, see Inkeles' *What is Sociology?*

4. For an effort to provide models for the analysis of various types of organizations, see Etzioni, Amitai, *A Comparative Analysis of Complex Organizations*. New York: The Free Press of Glencoe, 1961.

5. Georgopoulos, B.S., and A.S. Tannenbaum, A study of organizational effectiveness, *American Sociological Review*, 22, (1957), 534-540.

## A SYSTEMS MODEL OF ORGANIZATIONAL CLIMATE

*William M. Evan*

In the interdisciplinary field variously known as organization theory, organizational behavior, complex organizations and formal organizations, the distinction between individual unit data and aggregate unit data is often blurred. It is not surprising that psychologists gather data on an individual unit level and that sociologists, economists, operations researchers, and others gather data on an aggregate unit level.[1] The growing interest in the phenomenon of organizational climate is an example of the intersection of these two levels of analysis.

The utility of a concept such as "organizational climate" may be judged with the aid of at least two standards: (1) Does it help us perceive phenomena hitherto not perceived or identify problems hitherto not identified? (2) Does it link up with other concepts in organizational analysis, thereby generating empirically testable propositions and contributing to the development of theory? Whether the concept of organizational climate is scientifically useful in terms of these two standards may be considered an open question. What is manifestly not an open question is whether the concept is phenomenologically real. People do sense and react to the climate of an organization whether they belong to it or not.

The use of this concept involves us in an interesting dilemma: from a scientific point of view, it appears to be so gross and ambiguous as to be of doubtful utility; however, from a common-sense point of view, it appears to be useful. Although common sense is scarcely a reliable source of ideas for conceptualization in science, in the case of organizational climate it may prove instructive. The social-psychological reality of this concept is not unrelated to what Merton calls the "Thomas theorem": "If men define situations as real, they are real in their consequences."[2]

The purpose of this paper is threefold: (a) to propose a tentative definition of organizational climate, (b) to integrate this concept with that of an organization-set[3] in the context of a systems model of organizations, and (c) to develop several potentially testable propositions about the climate of an organization.

### A PROVISIONAL DEFINITION OF "ORGANIZATIONAL CLIMATE"

Among the multitude of concepts used in organizational research, organizational

From Tagiuri, Renato, and George H. Litwin (eds.), *Organizational Climate: Explorations of a Concept*. Boston: Division of Research, Graduate School of Business Administration, Harvard University, 1968, 107-124. Reprinted by permission of the Division of Research, Graduate School of Business Administration, Harvard University, and the author.

*Author's Note*: I am indebted to Professors Renato Tagiuri and George Litwin for invaluable comments on an earlier version of this paper. I also wish to express my gratitude to Choon Chen, Conrad Grundlehner, and Mrs. Judith Milestone for many helpful suggestions.

climate is not yet firmly established. Nevertheless, increasingly it is the subject of inquiry as witness the studies of Michael,[4] Halpin and Croft,[5] Carlin,[6] and Pelz and Andrews.[7] The concept suggests, as noted above, a union between an individual and an aggregate level of analysis.

Among the various kindred concepts that may suggest a definition of organizational climate, several are noteworthy. Argyris,[8] in effect, equates organizational climate with "organizational culture." This has the advantage of linking the concept with components of culture and with such a related concept as "subculture." However, if we take culture to mean the set of beliefs, values, and norms that constitute blueprints for behavior, then the concept of culture as the basis for a definition of organizational climate seems too broad.

Another cognate concept is "organizational prestige," as used, for example, by Perrow.[9] This concept relates to the public image of the products or services of an organization.

If an organization . . . [is] well regarded, it may more easily attract personnel, influence relevant legislation, wield informal power in the community, and insure adequate numbers of clients, customers, donors, or investors. Organizations may be placed along a continuum from unfavorable to favorable public images. A predominantly favorable image we shall call 'prestige,' and it may range from low to high.[10]

While this concept is suggestive in directing attention to the image that nonmembers have of an organization, it is needlessly restrictive in not including the image members themselves have of the organization; nor does it include the public image of organizational attributes other than products or services.

Yet another conception relevant to organizational climate is Margulies' idea[11] of organizational culture which he defines as the degree to which the organization is capable of adapting to its dynamic environment. This conception is not distinguishable from the concept of "organizational flexibility" advanced a decade ago by Georgopolous and Tannenbaum,[12] nor does it capture the subjective or perceptual dimension conveyed by the term.

To exploit the phenomenological reality of the concept, Halpin and Croft use the metaphor of personality in their study of the organizational climate of schools. Their metaphorical definition guided their construction of the Organizational Climate Description Questionnaire.[13] The impetus for their study was the observation that schools differ in their "feel." Halpin's explanation of his metaphorical definition of organizational climate is as follows:

Anyone who visits more than a few schools notes quickly how schools differ from each other in their "feel." In one school the teachers and the principal are zestful and exude confidence in what they are doing. They find pleasure in working with each other; this pleasure is transmitted to the students, who thus are given at least a fighting chance to discover that school can be a happy experience. In a second school the brooding discontent of the teachers is palpable; the principal tries to hide his incompetence and his lack of a sense of direction behind a cloak of authority, and yet he wears this cloak poorly because the attitude he displays to others vacillates randomly between the obsequious and the officious. And the psychological sickness of such a faculty spills over on the students, who in their own frustration, feed back to the teachers a mood of despair. A third school is marked by neither joy nor despair, but by hollow ritual. Here one gets the feeling of watching an elaborate charade in which teachers, principal, and students alike are acting out parts. The acting is smooth, even glib, but it appears to have little meaning for the participants; in a strange way the show just doesn't seem to be "for real." And so, too, as one moves to other schools, one finds that each appears to have a "personality" of its own. It is this "personality" that we describe here as the "Organizational Climate" of the school. Analogously, personality is to the individual what Organizational Climate is to the organization.[14]

For present purposes, I would like to venture the following definition:

*Organizational climate is a multidimensional perception of the essential attributes or character of an organizational system.*

In this provisional definition I deliberately limit the concept to "multidimensional perceptions" rather than posit some inherent properties such as might be implied in the concept of "organizational culture" or organizational structure. The term "multidimensional" is necessary because the "essential attributes" are not likely to be perceived along one dimension only.

This definition differs from that developed by Tagiuri in his introductory essay in this volume in two respects: (1) it does not limit the concept to perceptions of members since nonmembers may also perceive the climate of an organization; and (2) it does not incorporate the effect of organizational climate on behavior, which can be conceived as the dependent variable in any empirical research on organizational climate.

## A SYSTEMS MODEL OF ORGANIZATIONS

On the assumption that complex systemic relations give rise to "multidimensional perceptions of the essential attributes" of an organization, a systems model of organizations will now be explored. Such a model may also have the advantage of integrating the concept of organizational climate with other concepts in organization theory. A systems approach to organizational phenomena minimally involves identifying input elements, process elements, output elements, and feedback effects. It also focuses attention on the interrelation of at least three levels of analysis: the subsystems of an organization, the organizational system in its entirety, and the suprasystem. Analyzing the subsystems of an organization entails a study of the interaction patterns of the various subunits; analyzing the organizational system includes an examination of the cultural, structural, and technological components; and analyzing the suprasystem requires, at the very least, an inquiry into the network of interactions of the given organization with the various organizations in its environment. In short, to ascertain the determinants and consequences of organizational

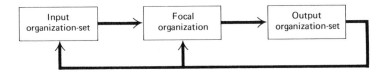

**Figure 2.** Some elements of an organization-set model of inter-organizational relations.

climate, as here defined, a model is required of the internal and external relations of an organization.

The model to be explored posits a particular organization or a class of organizations whose behavior is of interest to the investigator, and which is processing various inputs from its environment and generating various outputs. Following Gross, Mason, and McEachern's use[15] of the term "focal position" in their outstanding study of role analysis, I have referred to the organization or class of organizations that is the point of origin of inquiry as the "focal organization."[16] In the study of roles, the "focal role" is viewed in terms of its relation to a set of roles with which it interacts, namely, the "role set."[17] Similarly, the focal organization interacts with a complement of organizations in its environment, which I refer to as an "organization-set." A systems analysis perspective suggests that we divide the organization-set into an "input organization-set" and an "output organization-set." By an input organization-set, as the term suggests, I mean a complement of organizations that provides some type of resources to the focal organization. Similarly, by an output organization-set I mean all organizations that receive the goods and services, including organizational decisions, generated by the focal organization. Furthermore, a systems analysis requires that we trace feedback effects—positive and negative, anticipated and unanticipated—from the output organization-set to the focal organization and thence to the input organization-set, or directly from the output to the input organization-set. Figure 2 summarizes the rudimentary elements of an organization-set model of interorganizational relations.

Thus, if we take as our focal organization the Ford Motor Company, the input organization-set may include a variety of suppliers of raw materials, trade unions, government agencies, courts, universities, research and development organizations, etc. The input resources are very heterogeneous indeed, including human, material, financial, legal, etc. These inputs are transformed by the focal organization's social structure and technology into products and services that are exported to the members of the output organization-set, which principally includes automobile dealers. The output organization-set may also include advertising agencies concerned with increasing the sale of its products; community chest organizations to which financial contributions are made; trade associations to which information is provided and which may undertake to influence the course of future legislation, etc. The success with which the focal organization—in this case, the Ford Motor Company—manages its multifaceted relations with the members of its output organization-set in turn feeds back into the input organization-set which again triggers the cycle of systemic relations.

## A MODEL OF ORGANIZATIONAL CLIMATE

To relate the systems model of organizations to organizational climate, consider the following assumptions about the latter:

1. Members as well as nonmembers have perceptions of the climate of the "focal organization," i.e., the organization or class or organizations which is the object of analysis.

2. Organizational members tend to perceive the climate differently from nonmembers because of the prevalence of different frames of reference and different criteria for evaluating an organization.

3. Perceptions of organizational climate, whether real or unreal, have behavioral consequences for the focal organization as well as for elements of the organization-set, i.e., the complement of organizations with which the focal organization interacts.

4. Organizational members performing different roles tend to have different perceptions of the climate, if only because of (a) a lack of role consensus, (b) a lack of uniformity in role socialization, and (c) a diversity in patterns of role-set interactions.

5. Members of different organizational sub-units tend to have different perceptions of the climate because of different role-set configurations, different sub-goals, and a differential commitment to the goals of sub-units compared to the goals of the organization as a whole.

With the aid of these concepts and assumptions, a systems model of organizational climate will now be developed for analyzing organizational climate. In other words, a systems approach by itself does not dictate the constituents of the model used in analyzing a particular phenomenon. It merely identifies the basic elements of analysis, viz., input, process, output, and feedback. Nor does it define which input, process, and output elements to select and which feedback effects to study.

In Figures 3 and 4 a systems model of organizational climate is presented. Although the cycle of systemic relations can be analyzed from any starting point in the flow chart in Figure 3, we shall begin with the focal organization's interface with the input elements in its environment, proceed to the process elements, viz., the internal processes of the focal organization, then turn to the output elements and finally consider the feedback effects.

As an "open system" the focal organization (Figure 3A) depends upon various

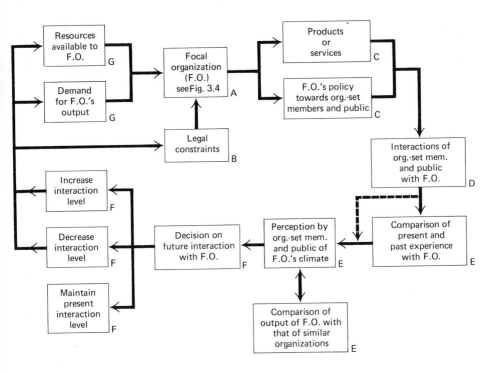

**Figure 3.** Flow chart of a systems model of organization climate.

resources—human, material, financial, etc. (Figure 3G). Whatever its goals, unless the focal organization performs a function vis-à-vis some external organization, client system, or constituency, the demand for its product or service will diminish or disappear (Figure 3G).

Yet another input are the legal constraints (Figure 3B) in the form of laws concerning incorporation, taxes, employment, etc. Implementing these laws are the various courts and administrative agencies of the local, state, and federal government.

The level and quality of the inputs at any particular time activate the complex of intra-organizational processes within the focal organization (Figure 4).

The goals of an organization (Figure 4A), whether explicitly or implicitly defined, condition the decision-making process of top executives (Figure 4B). The decision making of top executives is functionally equivalent to the action of legislators in a governmental context in that it may have system-wide structural ramifications. In this respect, executive decision making is to be distinguished from administrative decision making of lower echelons which officially involves implementing policies or "laws"[18] formulated by top executives.

If the organization is enjoying a steady level of inputs and there are no administrative or technical problems of any significant size looming on the horizon,

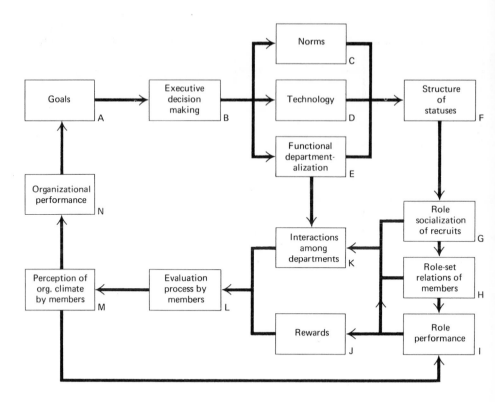

**Figure 4.** Processes within the focal organization generating an organizational climate.

the "law making" activities of executives will be minimal. When, however, changes either internal or external to the organization threaten inputs and/or outputs, the policy-making activities of top management are activated, setting off the chain reaction of effects the system model describes. In other words, some internal organizational processes are primarily responsive to the level and quality of inputs while others are primarily responsive to *changes* in the level and quality of those inputs. Management's policy-making activities are an example of the latter while role socialization, for example, is an instance of the former.

The decisions of top executives result in (a) the choice of technology with which to produce the organization's goods or services, (b) the formation of functional sub-units, and (c) the development of norms designed to regulate the behavior of members (Figure 4C, D, E).[19] As a consequence of these three processes, a structure of statuses emerges, typically of an hierarchical nature[20] (Figure 4F), which affects the socialization of new members (Figure 4G). As new members are recruited they are socialized, by formal and/or informal means, into a particular role which involves the recruit in a network of interactions with various role partners—peers, superiors, and possibly also subordinates (Figure 4H). These role-set relations, directly or indirectly, influence the member's role performance (Figure 4I). In turn, role performance tends to affect the distribution of rewards (Figure 4J), particularly in organizations governed by norms of rationality and universalism.

The processes of role socialization, role-set interactions, and role performance collectively influence the type of interdepartmental relations that develop (Figure 4K). In addition, functional specialization among sub-units generates not only varying degrees of cooperation but also varying degrees of competition and conflict over the allocation of scarce resources. The rewards received by members for their role performance and their intradepartmental and interdepartmental experiences lead them to evaluate the character of the organization (Figure 4L). This evaluation process, influenced in part by the commitment of members to their role, their sub-units, and the total organization, results in the formation of a perceived organizational climate (Figure 4M). The collective perceptions by members of the organizational climate, possibly because of their feedback effects on role performance (Figure 4M-I), influence the organizational performance (Figure 4N). And the level and quality of organizational performance in turn influence the degree of goal attainment and future goal-setting behavior (Figure 3A), which again triggers the cycle of intra-organizational processes.

The various intra-organizational processes, which give rise to an *internal* organizational climate, are subject to modifications as a result of external relations of the focal organization with various members of its organization-set and the public at large. Initiating these external relations are the outputs of the focal organization and the accompanying policies regarding its outputs (Figure 3C). For example, the modes of interaction between the focal organization and members of its organization-set may run the gamut of conflict, competition, coalition formation, and amalgamation (Figure 3D).[21] Organizations that are willing to forego formal contractual relations in interactions with members of their organization-set create a different impression from those that uniformly adhere to commercial practices,[22] similarly, organizations that are scrupulously fair and reasonable in their transactions create a quite different impression from organizations that are prone to terminate arbitrarily contracts with members of their organization-set.[23] The impressions created in the course of interactions between the focal organization and organization-set members are evaluated in the light of past experiences (Figure 3E). If an organization-set member has had no previous interactions with the focal organization, it bypasses this phase and proceeds directly to evaluating the focal organization's outputs—products or services and policies toward organization-set members—in comparison with those of similar organizations. The outcome of this evaluation process is a perception by organization-set members and the public at large of the focal organization's essential attributes of character, viz., its climate. These collective perceptions constitute the *external* organizational climate.[24]

The focal organization might be disposed to ignore perceptions of its climate by organization-set members and the public at large if the perceptions were not translated into behavior. However, as in the case of other types of perceptions, we would expect that organization-set members' perceptions of the focal organization's climate would in fact influence their decisions regarding future interactions—whether to increase, decrease, or maintain the present level of interactions (Figure 3F).

Whatever the decisions of the organization-set members regarding future interactions, the feedback effects on the input resources of the focal organization are decisive. They partly determine the flow of revenue from products or services, the flow of new personnel, the flow of information, and the flow of other resources (Figure 3G). When the changed inputs are fed back to the focal organization, a new cycle of intraorganizational processes is generated which may tend to maintain or alter the internal organizational climate and thereafter affect the state of the external organizational climate.

### SOME TESTABLE PROPOSITIONS

The systems model of organizational climate sketched above may prove to be heuristic. As in the case of any theory, the test of a systems model is whether it generates verifiable and significant propositions. Several illustrative propositions, suggested by our systems model, concerning the problem of changing an organizational climate are as follows:

1. The climate of an organization tends to be perpetuated from one generation of members to another unless the structure of inputs and outputs and intra-organizational processes are changed along with the feedback effects. This hypothesis, if true, in effect cautions against the inclination to solve an organizational climate problem by recruiting a new executive. He is not likely to succeed unless he is sufficiently knowledgeable, powerful, and charismatic as to alter the inputs, the intra-organizational processes, the outputs, and the feedback effects.

2. Inertial forces maintaining organizational climate tend to increase with the size of an organization. As the size of an organization increases, differentiation increases both as regards number and type of statuses and number and type of sub-units. Accompanying an increase in status and functional differentiation is an increase in the scope of problems of role socialization, role performance, and inter-sub-unit coordination. In the face of mounting problems associated with an increase in size, the difficulties of deliberately modifying the internal organizational climate are correspondingly greater.

3. If the organizational climate as perceived by members of the focal organization is more favorable than the climate as perceived by members of organizations comprising the organization-set, there will be a lower rate of innovation because of a reduced motivation to change. Conversely, if the climate as perceived by members of the focal organization is less favorable than the climate as perceived

by members of organizations comprising the organization-set, there will be a higher rate of innovation.

4. Organizational climate is more susceptible to deliberate efforts to modify it when there is a low degree of consensus regarding it. As between *internal* and *external* organizational climate, it is probably easier to alter the former than the latter because of the greater control that the focal organization can exercise over its members than over the members of organizations comprising its organization-set.

5. As differences in sub-unit climates of an organization increase, there is a tendency for a greater conflict to arise concerning proposals for innovation and for a discrepancy to occur in the rate of technical and administrative innovations, viz., for the degree of "organizational lag" to increase.[25]

6. Technical innovations, because they are manifested in the products or services of an organization, are more likely to generate faster changes in the external organizational climate than administrative innovations.[25]

If we are to close the gap between the common-sense meanings of organizational climate and the scientific utility of the concept, systematic research is necessary on the theoretical as well as on the methodological front. Theoretically, it is necessary to experiment with more refined concepts of organizational climate, especially with various dimensions of climate, e.g., value climate, interpersonal climate, and task climate. The value climate of an advertising agency, for example, with its emphasis on profit is obviously quite different from that of a social work agency with its emphasis on service.[26] This contrast is probably translated into different interpersonal and task climates. Together, these three dimensions of organizational climate probably have traceable consequences for the internal and external relations of an organization.

Methodologically, it is necessary to explore the utility of various research strategies in studying organizational climate: observational studies, surveys, field experiments, computer simulations, etc.[27] Whichever strategy is employed, past researches on organizations suggest that a comparative approach would probably maximize the chances of identifying the antecedents and consequences of contrasting organizational climates.[28]

On a quite different methodological plane is the critical problem of developing and testing alternative procedures for assessing climate: adjective check lists, sets of descriptive statements, the semantic differential, etc.[29] The labor involved in developing research instruments that would prove both reliable and valid is indeed formidable, but unless progress is made in operationalizing the concept of organizational climate it will remain a common-sense rather than a social science concept.

**NOTES**

1. Cf. Lazarsfeld, P.F., and H. Menzel, On the relation between individual and collective properties, in Etzioni, Amitai (ed.), *Complex Organizations: A*

*Sociological Reader*. New York: Holt, Rinehart and Winston, 1966.

2.  Merton, R.K., *Social Theory and Social Structure* (revised edition). Glencoe: Free Press, 1957, 421.

3.  Cf. Evan, W.M., The organization-set: toward a theory of inter-organizational relations, in Thompson, J.D. (ed.), *Approaches to Organizational Design*. Pittsburgh: University of Pittsburgh Press, 1966.

4.  Michael, J.A., High school climates and plans for entering college, *Public Opinion Quarterly*, 25 (1961), 585-595.

5.  Halpin, A.W., and D.B. Croft, *The Organizational Climate of Schools*. Chicago: University of Chicago, Midwest Administrative Center, 1963.

6.  Carlin, J.E., *Lawyers' Ethics*. New York: Russell Sage Foundation, 1966.

7.  Pelz, D.C., and F.M. Andrews, *Scientists in Organizations: Productive Climates for Research and Development*. New York: Wiley, 1966.

8.  Argyris, C., Some problems in conceptualizing organizational climate: a case study of a bank, *Administrative Science Quarterly*, 2 (1958), 501-520.

9.  Perrow, C., Organizational prestige: some functions and dysfunctions, *American Journal of Sociology*, 66 (1961), 335-341.

10.  Perrow, 1961.

11.  Margulies, N., *A study of organizational culture and the self-actualizing process*. Unpublished doctoral dissertation, University of California, Los Angeles, 1965.

12.  Georgopoulos, B.S., and A.S. Tannenbaum, A study of organizational effectiveness, *American Sociological Review*, 22 (1957), 534-540.

13.  Halpin and Croft, 1963.

14.  Halpin, A.W., *Theory and Research in Administration*. New York: Macmillan, 1966.

15.  Gross, N., W.S. Mason, and N.W. McEachern, *Explorations in Role Analysis: Studies in the School Superintendency Role*. New York: Wiley, 1958.

16.  Evan, 1966 (The organization-set. . .).

17.  See Merton, 368-380, and Gross, Mason, and McEachern, 48-74.

18.  For an analysis of legal processes in private organizations compared with those of government, see Evan, W.M., Public and private legal systems, in Evan, W.M., (ed.), *Law and Sociology*. New York: Free Press, 1962.

19.  The underlying assumption of this assertion is that the strength and time span of these activities depicted in the flow chart are of the same order of magnitude. This assumption becomes evident when parallel paths (branches) are drawn, for example, from C-D-E to F to G-H-I to J-K to L and from E to K to L in Figure 3. If they are not of the same order of magnitude, the effects of one branch would predominate.

20.  Cf. Evan, W.M., Indices of the hierarchical structure of industrial organizations, *Management Science*, 9 (1963), 468-477.

21. Cf. Evan, 1966 (Organization-set. . .), 183-184.

22. Cf. Macaulay, S., Non-contractual relations in business: a preliminary study, *American Sociological Review,* **29** (1963), 55-67.

23. Cf. Ridgeway, V.F., Administration of manufacturer-dealer system, *Administrative Science Quarterly,* **2** (1957), and Macaulay, S., Changing a continuing relationship between a large corporation and those who deal with it: automobile manufacturers, their dealers, and the legal system, *Wisconsin Law Review* (1965) Summer, 483-575 and Fall, 740-858.

24. For a relevant analysis of problems of external organizational climate, see Riley, J.W., Jr. (ed.), *The Corporation and its Publics.* New York: Wiley, 1963.

25. For a discussion of the distinction between administrative and technical innovations and an analysis of the concept of "organizational lag," see Evan, W.M., Organizational lag, *Human Organizations,* **25** (1966), 51-53 and Evan, W.M., and G. Black, Innovation in business organizations: some factors associated with success or failure of staff proposals, *Journal of Business,* **40** (1967), 519-530.

26. Cf. Bensman, J., *Dollars and Sense.* New York: Macmillan, 1967.

27. See Vroom, V.H. (ed.), *Methods of Organizational Research.* Pittsburgh: University of Pittsburgh Press, 1967.

28. Cf. Blau, P.M., The comparative study of organizations, *Industrial and Labor Relations Reviews,* **18** (1965), 323-338; Udy, S.H., Jr., The comparative analysis of organizations, in March, J.G., (ed.), *Handbook of Organizations.* Chicago: Rand McNally, 1965; Burns, T., The comparative study of organizations, in Vroom, V. (ed.), *Methods of Organizational Research.* Pittsburgh: University of Pittsburgh Press, 1967.

29. Cf. Halpin and Croft, 1963, and Halpin, 1966.

---

# CONCEPTS FOR DEVELOPING ORGANIZATIONS

*Paul R. Lawrence and Jay W. Lorsch*

The creation of a framework for thinking about any topic such as organization development is an essential step toward understanding and action. We shall present below an interrelated set of ideas that have proved useful to us in ordering many diverse observations about organization life. They can help us make sense out of the examples that will follow and provide guidelines for application in new situations.

From Lawrence, Paul R., and Jay W. Lorsch, *Developing Organizations: Diagnosis and Action.* Reading, Mass.: Addison-Wesley, 1969, 9-14. Reprinted by permission of Addison-Wesley and the authors.

After some brief comments on systemic analysis, we will present the concepts of differentiation and integration and relate them to our question about determining the directions for organization-development work and also to the stages of the process of organizational development.

## SYSTEMS ANALYSIS

Without attempting to spell out all the implications of a systems view of organization, we would emphasize now two crucial ideas. The first of these is the idea of an essential interdependence between the elements of the organization. In our treatment in Chapter 1 of developmental problems, we have, for purposes of simplicity, presented them as independent issues. But an organization is not a mechanical system in which one part can be changed without a concomitant effect on the other parts. Rather, an organizational system shares with biological systems the property of an intense interdependence of parts such that a change in one part has an impact on the others.[1]

For example, the activities required by a given transactional strategy, such as making shoes, can be spelled out in mechanical terms and broken into a very fine division of labor. When machines are available that can do the complete job, things might go well. But when human contributors must be engaged in the process, the situation is different. An optimal division of labor from a mechanical standpoint could generate serious costs if it is discovered that the simple repetitive work is distasteful to the available people and the inducements required to obtain their contributions become excessive.

Such examples can be cited in regard to any element of an organization. The point has been made many times, but it is especially relevant to the chapters ahead where we will be exploring these interfaces on a one-at-a-time basis, as any writer must. As human beings, the readers and the writers share a bounded rationality—we can deal in our minds with only about seven variables at a time, while the organizational world we would master is obviously much more complex. We must proceed with caution, recognizing that in treating topics one at a time, we are not recognizing all the interdependencies in organizational systems.

The second relevant critical idea deriving from systems analysis is the idea that social systems such as organizations, unlike mechanical and even biological systems, have the ability to modify themselves in basic structural ways. Buckley terms this the *morphogenic property* of organizations, and cites it as the prime identifying feature of organizations.[2] A machine cannot alter its gear train, an animal cannot develop an extra leg, but an organization can and does do analogous things. A business, a church, a bank can add or subtract new departments and modify its communication and authority structure. A social agency can change its constitution. This happens by a cybernetic process through which an organization's members compare the *desired* results of strategy with the *actual* results. Important discrepancies are defined as a problem and a search is undertaken for causes and remedies. Most frequently in this process some error is detected or a procedural routine is modified, but repeated discrepancies between plans and results start people exploring alternative modifications in the existing strategy and/or in the organization structure. By this feedback process, organizations literally hitch themselves along into the future.

An outsider, watching, over a period of time, the external manifestations of this process, might wrongly conclude that the organization had a long-term purpose of its own. But we now see that this is an illusion created by the viewer's point of observation. Such changes are a result, instead, of a group of individual problem-solvers identifying their welfare to a greater or lesser extent with the organizational welfare, and bringing their different purposes to a problem-solving situation on behalf of the organization. From the outside, large organizations often appear to be monolithic entities run as if by a single mastermind and moving inexorably along a predetermined path. From the inside, they frequently appear to be in a chaotic situation, trying to move in all directions at once. The truth is somewhere in between. But it is this semichaotic, semi-planned process of self-correcting and self-modifying which gives organizations the morphogenic properties that make them potentially such a flexible and powerful tool for the extension of man's control over his environment.

With this general view of organizations as highly interdependent and morphogenic systems, we want to look in detail at the concepts of differentiation and integration and how they help us understand the organization-and-environment and the group-to-group interfaces.

## THE DIFFERENTIATION-AND-INTEGRATION MODEL

The notions of differentiation and integration and associated concepts dealing with the management of intergroup conflict have been presented as a comprehensive conceptual model elsewhere.[3] We want only briefly to summarize them here. In doing so, we need to emphasize two points.

1. The model is based on empirical study of ten organizations in three different environments. Further, these findings have been corroborated by our consulting activities in several additional settings.

2. The model is fully consistent with the view of organizations as systems. That is, instead of providing a universal prescription of the one best way to organize, it provides a framework, based on the demands of the organization's environment, by which we can understand what organizational characteristics are required if an organization is to perform effectively in its particular environment.[4]

### Differentiation

To understand the environmental demands on an organization, we start first by looking at how much differentiation should exist among the various groups. As already suggested, this depends upon what internal characteristics each group must develop to carry out planned transactions with its assigned part of the environment. More specifically, it depends primarily upon the extent to which the certainty of information within the various parts of the environment is similar or different. If these parts of the environment (e.g., the market, scientific knowledge, techno-economic or manufacturing factors) are fairly homogeneous in their degree of certainty, the units will need to be fairly similar in formal organizational practices and members' orientations. If these parts of the environment have quite different degrees of certainty, the units will need to be more differentiated. Our evidence indicates that these needed differences are not minor variations in outlook but, at times, involve fundamental ways of thinking and behaving.

**Integration**

This model focuses attention not only upon the degree of differentiation necessary but also upon the integration required among organizational units. We need to be concerned with two aspects of the integration issue: which units are required to work together and how tight the requirement is for interdependence among them. But there is a strong inverse relationship between differentiation and integration. As we have suggested, when units (because of their particular tasks) are highly differentiated, it is more difficult to achieve integration among them than when the individuals in the units have similar ways of thinking and behaving. As a result, when groups in an organization need to be highly differentiated, but also require tight integration, it is necessary for the organization to develop more complicated integrating mechanisms. The *basic* organizational mechanism for achieving integration is, of course, the management hierarchy. In organizations with low differentiation, we have found that this is often sufficient to achieve the required intergroup collaboration. However, organizations faced with the requirement for both a high degree of differentiation and tight integration must develop *supplemental* integrating devices, such as individual coordinators, cross-unit teams, and even whole departments of individuals whose basic contribution is achieving integration among other groups. By using this model, then, we are able to understand not only the pattern of differentiation and integration required to deal effectively with a particular environment, but also the formal structural devices needed to achieve this pattern.

**Conflict Management Variables**

This model also points to another set of variables which are important—the behavior patterns used to manage intergroup conflict. As individuals with different points of view attempt to attain unity of effort, conflicts inevitably arise. How well the organization will succeed in achieving integration, therefore, depends to a great extent upon how the individuals resolve their conflicts. Our work indicates that the pattern of behavior which leads to effective conflict resolution varies in certain respects depending upon environmental demands, and in other respects is the same *regardless* of variations in environmental demands.

Those conflict management factors which vary with environmental demands include the pattern of influence or power within and among groups. The influence within groups means the organizational level *at which influence or power resides* to make decisions leading to the resolution of conflict. If conflict is to be managed effectively, this influence must be concentrated at the point in the various group hierarchies where the *knowledge* to reach such decisions also exists. Obviously, this will vary depending upon the certainty of information in various parts of a particular environment. The required pattern of influence among groups also varies with environmental demands. The groups which have more critical knowledge about environmental conditions are the ones which need to have high influence in resolving intergroup conflict if the organization is to be effective in resolving such conflict.

The factors which lead to effective conflict-resolution under all environmental conditions are the mode of conflict resolution and the basis from which influence is derived. In organizations existing in quite different environments, we have found that effective conflict management occurs when the individuals deal openly with conflict and work the problem until they reach a resolution which is best in terms of total organizational goals. In essence, effective organizations confront internal conflicts, rather than smoothing them over or exercising raw power or influence to force one party to accept a solution.[5]

In organizations dealing effectively with conflict, we have also found that the individuals primarily involved in achieving integration, whether they be common superiors or persons in coordinating roles, need to have influence based largely upon their perceived *knowledge and competence.* They are followed not just because they have formal positional influence, but because they are seen as knowledgeable about the issues which have to be resolved.

To summarize, the differentiation and integration model provides a set of concepts which enable us to understand what characteristics an organization must have to be effective in a particular set of environmental circumstances. It directs our attention to environmental demands on the organization in terms of the degree of differentiation, the pattern and degree of integration, integrative mechanisms, and conflict-resolving behaviors. In sum, it provides a way of understanding much of what needs to happen at both the organization-and-environment and group-to-group interfaces.

**NOTES**

1. We are not suggesting that a biological system is a complete analogy for an organization. As will become apparent in a later paragraph, for example, we see organizations, unlike biological systems, as having the capacity to change their own form and structure (be morphogenic). In this regard, we share Buckley's concern that the biological view of organizations has led to inaccurate and overly pessimistic conclusions about the capacity of organization members to change the shape of their organizations. (Buckley, W., *Sociology and Modern Systems Theory*. Englewood Cliffs, N.J.: Prentice Hall, 1967.) Nevertheless, the biological

analogy is useful to describe the interdependence of the parts of organizational systems.

2. Buckley, *op. cit.*

3. Lawrence, P. R., and J. W. Lorsch, *Organization and Environment: Managing Differentiation and Integration.* Boston: Division of Research, Harvard Business School, 1967.

4. As we shall explain in more detail below, the relationship between organizational performance and internal organizational characteristics can lead to effective performance, but feedback of results also affects the way organizational states and processes develop. For example, in a high-performing organization, knowledge of success may create an atmosphere where differences in viewpoint are more acceptable and where conflict involves less tension. However, in this discussion, we will deal with the relationship as unidirectional—certain organizational characteristics leading to effective performance. We feel justified in doing this because from the viewpoint of managers or consultants concerned with corrective action, changing these internal organizational characteristics provides the best opportunity for ultimately improving performance. The reader should realize that awareness of the need to make changes is a result of feedback in the other direction (about past organizational performance).

5. This finding is consistent with the theory and findings of others. See especially (Blake, Shepard, and Mouton, *Managing Intergroup Conflict in Industry.* Houston: Gulf Publishing Co., 1964).

# 4.
# ORGANIZATION GROWTH — THE NEED
# FOR ORGANIZATION DEVELOPMENT

*Organization development* or *organization renewal* gradually emerged during the 1960's as a concept of concern to training directors and organizations. A number of organizations have set up departments with OD in the title; the demand for OD practitioners has expanded significantly, and literature has burgeoned with articles about the subject.

Despite the dramatically heightened interest, until recently there was little agreement upon how OD should be defined, what an OD program looked like, or what kind of qualifications or skills were needed by the change agent. Gradually consensus is beginning to emerge along these fronts.

Several years ago most definitions of OD centered upon self-growth, self-insight, and intragroup effectiveness. Today the focus is upon improved problem solving, decision making, and planning. Organizations are concerned less with the training of individuals than with the training of work groups—mostly aimed at improved decision making and planning. As would be expected, the current emphasis is upon on-site rather than off-site training, but this can be expected to change within the next few years. The term that most appropriately describes the learning thrust is "learn as you earn."

There is also an awareness that OD embraces the total organization and its total processes: organization systems, for example, are now acknowledged to be a concern of and a part of OD. Currently the field is just beginning to identify and define the knowledge and skills required of the practitioner. These include the ability to work effectively within a macrosystem, and in this area we are discovering that we know very little. Most of the research in the past 15 years has been on the individual in groups and microsystems.

Organizations initiating OD programs are not sure about what kind of person they are looking for, and they find very few resources to help them train their OD personnel. Most of the resources purporting capability to train such personnel still place a heavy emphasis on individual awareness and sensitivity. This situation appears due for dramatic change. The emerging skills seem to be those that the field has tended to view as unworthy of a professional—directive approach, assuming the role of an advocate, knowledge and use of organizational power structures, mass communication and consensus techniques, etc. The next five years will probably see a completely new focus upon macrosystems and macrosystem dynamics.

In this chapter's first selection, "Organization Development: Fantasy or Reality," Leslie This discusses the many early and current interpretations of what OD is all about, how it can be defined, and the basic elements involved in the concept and process. From the several differing concepts he abstracts the issues that have emerged and are currently being resolved.

Next, "Crucial Issues in Organization Development" by Paul Buchanan looks at ten case studies of OD in various settings. One of the interesting things about this article is that it deals with seven successful experiences and three failures. Most of the literature, quite understandably, deals with successes only. There is a strong possibility that we could learn as much if not more from reported failures as from successes. OD practitioners should be encouraged to contribute more of these examples to the literature. Buchanan's article isolates 33 issues from these 10 case studies and discusses the three issues found to have been most crucial in determining the success of the OD venture.

Our third article turns to some of the more commonly used organizational interventions in introducing OD. Gordon Lippitt, in "Team Building for Matrix Organizations," recognizes the work team as a critical element of matrix organizations. He discusses ten characteristics of teamwork and describes the two- to three-day team-building confrontation conference as an initiating intervention in OD. For the fourth selection Wendell French, in "Organization Development Objectives, Assumptions and Strategies," lists seven objectives normally found in an OD program. He looks at assumptions most programs hold, and discusses action research, team-building sessions, and laboratory training.

"An Organic Problem-Solving Method of Organizational Change" is our fifth selection. Author Sheldon Davis describes in detail the use by TRW Systems of the intervention of sensitivity training as the vehicle to carry forward the OD objectives. This article offers a good example of an organization using this intervention—one which seems to have lost some favor in the past two to three years but is still staunchly defended by some change agents.

The chapter closes with a look at broader issues in the field. Most of the OD efforts throughout the fifties and sixties involved small groups, units, or organizations. This was probably a natural outgrowth of the laboratory method and its limited application. The field is indebted to these early pioneers and to the dynamics, awareness, and strategies they developed in the micro-setting. Increasingly, however, practitioners are finding that the problems demanding their attention are macrosystems—total organizations and external social systems. Little exists to help the practitioner here, but a body of knowledge is beginning to emerge. Peter Vaill, in "Organization Development: Ten New Dimensions of Practice," is one of the first writers to explore this area. His focus is on OD in a macrosystem. He lists and discusses ten skills and abilities that seem to be critical in a change agent if he is to make meaningful organizational interventions.

# ORGANIZATIONAL DEVELOPMENT: FANTASY OR REALITY

*Leslie E. This*

"When I use a word, it means exactly what I want it to mean," said the Mad Hatter to Alice.

"And when I use a word," says the personnel director, training director, or social scientist, "it means exactly what I want it to mean—even if I'm not sure what I mean."

This is the semantic jungle through which a well-intentioned and operations-buffeted manager is supposed to find his way and commit agency (or company money) and employee time to activities that every "enlightened" management is sponsoring and supporting.

Currently this verbal barrage is centering around activities that somehow are related to "productivity maximation" or "profit maximation," development of employees as "full individuals," flexibility and innovativeness to stay abreast of a kaleidoscoping world, and effective decision-making.

The words and phrases used to encompass these activities are called systems development, organization development, manpower development, employee development, management development, organizational renewal, confrontation training, laboratory training, organization planning, team training, planned change, organizational change, organizational growth, and a host of similar word combinations.

What makes analysis and understanding even more difficult is that there is no consistency in the definition of the words or phrases. For example, laboratory training can mean a three week experience designed for sensual development akin to the hippies' goals, a two week experience examining group forces and one's impact on the effect of these forces, a five year developmental in-house experience, a role play, a case study, or a two hour training experience. All of these definitions can be found in the literature.

It is our general goal to sort out these terms so the manager can better know what he is dealing with. It is our express goal to clarify the term "organization development."

Any management concept, piece of organizational research, or organizational experience that seems insightful appears to go through five phases:

*Phase 1.* The piece of research, the concept, or the organizational experience is reported in a paper read at a scientific or professional meeting—or is reported in a technical journal. The wording is precise, complex, replete with equations and tables, and heavily foot-noted. It is politely applauded, published, and creates little attention. In the meantime, operating people are doing a job—using experience and common

This selection was originally published by the Society for Personnel Administration as *Supervisor Booklet No. 7* (1969). Reprinted by permission of the Society for Personnel Administration, 485-87 National Press Building, 14th and F Streets, N.W., Washington, D.C. 20004.

sense. Asked to comment on the concept, they look blankly and comment, "Look, I'm working or making steel–or profits–or selling. Don't mix me up unless you can show me it will produce more or make more money."

*Phase 2.* The researcher or author is himself a management consultant or speaker. Private management firms and consultants scour the research frontiers for something new. Over a period of 1–4 years the key findings are high-lighted, over-simplified, over-generalized, footnotes dropped, technical language reduced to man-in-the street terms, gimmicky displays dreamed up, and jokes added. Now it is peddled in the workshop and conference circles and in brochures for management as "the greatest break-through since scientific management and atom-smashing. Send your managers to this two-day course and increase productivity (or company profits) by 736%". The market is ready since the operating people read and hear of the new "break-through" and evidence interest in a gimmick that will guarantee instant success. They don't want to study or think–"Give me your panacea in a presentation from 9:11 to 9:23 and let's get on with the show."

*Phase 3.* The market is fairly well saturated and the terminology accepted–if not understood. Now the peddlers (and we include training directors, personnel men, and managers) begin to hunt for variations and "dress-up" techniques. Some hitherto neglected small piece of the research is highlighted. The same article or workshop gets a new, jazzy title. The consultant/author asks, "What would industry/business/government like to hear?" and directs his material in this direction. "Down with human relations–fire the SOB's." The operators begin to lose interest and increasingly ask "But how do you apply the concept?"

*Phase 4.* At this stage other researchers/consultants/authors begin to attack the validity of the original work. Reports are published re "Where the original study was faulty and went astray." The battle of semantics emerges–original meanings are lost. Other researchers whose own pet theories are threatened bellow their anguish and pain. Off-beat applications or forced-relationships with other concepts are made. The initial study or concept can no longer be identified–a discussion of the concept is a Babel of tongues.

*Phase 5.* A lone prominent voice is raised in a critical speech or journal saying, "Look, we've lost our way. We got along without the concept before it was identified. There's such a thing as living and production or profits–let's forget the whole thing." Everyone is weary of the concept–some of the terminology is now within the professional circles–and, besides, another concept or research report is now out and is the fashionable thing to talk about. But–don't discard your notes–this old one will reappear again in 10-14 years. The words may be different–but the concept will be there.

The author recently traced several major concepts emerging in the past ten years, through 65 journals. The pattern we have sketched above is remarkably constant.

The concept of "organization development" is currently enmeshed in this process. It is in Phase 3 and rapidly emerging into Phase 4. It is a fashionable phrase. Few self-respecting managers and organizations would dare admit they don't understand the term or subscribe to the concept. Beautifully art-decorated brochures proclaim our interest. But asked to define the concept, images range from "a case study used in a training course" to "man's relating himself to all the micro-and macro-systems in our society."

A report on the initial American Society for Training and Development's "Program For Specialists in Organization Training and Development," compiled in December 1967, states that "Douglas McGregor is credited with being the first person to talk about OD, and that was no longer than ten years ago."

Warren Bennis notes that OD is very new.[1] The earliest academic attempt he references is "the Organization Studies Group at MIT started about 1959."

These kinds of date-fixing are misleading. OD is not a new concept—just as social scientists did not discover human relations or interpersonal relationships.

What is new is the term—or the way the term is used—not the concept. All that is currently embosomed by OD—has long been identified by some organizations and managers—they simply did not have the labels or some of the more sophisticated techniques now available.

For example, as far back as 1956 the American National Red Cross recognized the need not only to train individuals, but entire macro-systems. The effort was called "situational training." It also recognized the inter-relationship of the organization and its sub-parts to the forces and factors outside the organization. The National Training Laboratories, in its early years and at about this same time, also recognized this need and approach, though later its efforts were to take a more limited focus.

At that time, the Red Cross saw the role of the training function for management related to organization problems and objectives in this way:

### Preserving the Human Organzation

| Improved technical skills | Improved performance, attitudes, and behavior | Improved procedures and processes |
|---|---|---|

### Planning the Future Organization

| Introducing new technical skills | Helping people to grow for new responsibility | Planning the organization to meet new demands |
|---|---|---|

As an early program paper stated, "New requirements necessitate focusing on situations and organization development. The focus on situational training is on what training can do to reach operational goals rather than on increasing the competence of the individuals."

The preoccupation with organizational development reminds one of the preoccupation some years ago with the "liberal arts" approach to managerial/organizational development. There was an assumption that managers were too in-bred and insufficiently aware of the world around them—the world in all its facets. It was presumed a manager could function more effectively if he was "well-rounded"—liberal arts educated. A great deal of activity ensued. A management development program could include anything—on the assumption that anything he could study was related to the world, and therefore, the job of the manager. This approach really had much in common with the present diffused thrusts in OD.

Let us now examine the various definitions of OD. It should be remembered that seldom does an author or consultant consciously define the term. The Author has tried to illustrate the definitions by quoting from the literature—but acknowledges that he may sometimes seem to be extrapolating more than the quotation warrants. However, he believes from other writings and the context of articles quoted, that his assessment is valid.

1.  Those who use OD in the context of organizations developing from simple to complex forms—or a given organization "developing" from birth to maturity. Blau and Scott use the term in this manner.

Large and complex formal organizations do not spring into existence full-blown but develop out of simpler ones. We shall examine such developmental processes in this first part of the chapter.[2]

A variation of this use of the words "development" and "organization" is to be found in an article by Gordon L. Lippitt and Warren H. Schmidt, "Crises in a Developing Organization."[3] Here the authors are thinking of a specific organization and the six stages it goes through as it develops: the need to be born—to survive—to gain stability—to gain reputation and develop pride—to achieve uniqueness and adaptability—and to contribute to society. Organization development in this sense is quite different from other uses of the term.

2.  Those who see the process as one of training. This major division has a number of sub-schools:

    a.  Those who believe that OD primarily is concerned with training of individuals—for self insight, self awareness, personal growth, and understanding. They depend heavily on the laboratory method—but laboratories slanted in the directions indicated. The labs may be instrumented or trainer-led.

    b.  Those who believe OD primarily is concerned with the training of groups and effective working and problem-solving within groups. The targets of training can be in heterogeneous labs, but there is a pronounced movement to train within the organization in family groups: vertical—horizontal—or diagonal. Again, the laboratory method of training is preferred—both instrumented and trainer-led.

c. A tighter definition would favor the group/team approach—but confine the training to "managers." Many organizations subscribe to this view. Generally it is equated with "management development."

d. A fourth sub-school would equate the term with the "development" of all the employees in the organization—particularly in the areas of social science research.

The differentiation among the three sub-schools listed above are not always discrete and clear. Several quotations will indicate the line of thinking—and the overlapping.

OD has joined the long list of 'initialisms' and acronyms with which we try to tag the complex functions of the modern world. It stands for Organization Development, itself a short title for a way of looking at the whole human side of organizational life.[4]

Warren Bennis clarifies the two schools (individual and team training) that equate organizational development with the human relationships aspects of organizations. The effort is headed by a change agent who is a professional holding a doctorate in the behavioral sciences. Tracing the use of the T-groups as a main instrument in organizational change, he notes that since 1947 "The main objective at first was personal change of self-insight. Since the fifties the emphasis has shifted to organizational development, a more precise date being 1958, when the Esso Company inaugurated a series of laboratories at refineries over the country————."

He references the Managerial Grid system developed by Robert Blake and the Esso Refinery model as examples of this approach. Generally such models involve the use of training, consulting, and applied research. The thrust of this definition of OD is clear when he notes that he sees the normative goals of change agents as

improving interpersonal competence of managers; effecting a change in values so that human factors and feelings come to be considered legitimate; developing increased understanding among and within working groups to release tensions; developing 'team management'; developing better methods of 'conflict resolution' than suppression, denial, and the use of unprincipled power; viewing the organization as an organic system of relationships marked by mutual trust, interdependence, multigroup membership, shared responsibility, and conflict resolution through training or problem solving.[5]

Silxon, Mullen, and Morton note that organization training emphasizes team training rather than individual growth and training:

Sensitivity training hopes to produce improvement in the way people understand themselves, get along with others, communicate with and trust others.

On the other hand, organization training emphasizes team decision making and problem solving. It is concerned with how effectively a team uses its material and human resources.[6]

To some, OD is equated with management development. This is referenced by Schein and Bennis[7] when they comment that many laboratories "select their delegates in terms of fairly rigid requirements." They observe "Two examples would be: (1) the Organization Development Program, an alumni program, developed by an NTL committee, for directors of management development activities who were presumed to be already in influential change agent roles in their organizations————." Here the OD program was seen as designed for directors of management development activities.

3.   A third school has a definition similar to those described above, but interestingly, and understandably, equate OD with laboratory training. The two terms are identical to this group; We have observed that England seems to subscribe to this definition—but many U.S. organizations also hold to this definition.

4.   The fourth school would equate the term OD with systems development, systems research, or training/developing/improving a sub-system. Sometimes this appears to be in the sense of laboratory training—others equate it with any sub-system improvement including procedures, hardware, technological, time-motion studies, etc.

James S. Winston[8] defines "system" from Paul M. Fitts[9] as "An assemblage of man/machine information processors. These processors, while they have their own distinct characteristics, interact with each other, are interrelated and interdependent. The processor, tied together by a common information flow network produces outputs."

In this instance, organizational development would seem to be concerned with the improvement of an organization sub-system. This could include the total configuration of all relevant parts—employees, equipment, space, communications, etc. The focus can vary: some emphasize the training of employees; others emphasize efficient system functioning and may be more intrigued with equipment, flow, and the mechanical side of the operation.

That this approach is often equated with organization development can be seen in the author's observation, "In industrial training the use of the systems analysis approach will improve the quality of training, reveal deficiencies in training and can stimulate the entire organization to make effective use of education and simulation to develop the organization and the personnel within the company framework."

5.   A fifth school, and this seems to be growing, equates OD with being concerned not only with the organization's human resources—but the non-human resources and factors as well. Many of this school, despairing of getting the term OD to be understood in this sense, have coined another phrase to encompass their concept—"organizational renewal."

Increasingly in recent months, there has been a heightened awareness that OD connotes more than improving the human resources of the organization—that non-human aspects must also be considered. This is increasingly seen in comments of men who have predominantly, in the past, seen OD as primarily concerned with the human side of organizations.

Warren Bennis, discussing "The Managerial Revolution" in "What's Wrong With Work?"[10] comments:

The challenge for organization development and the challenge for education, it seems to me, are these:

1. How do we produce in our organizational development programs 'learning men, men who have poise, men who can adapt, men to have the right balance between commitment and inquiry, and men who will be able to tolerate future shock?

2. How do we develop problem-centered organizations, organizations that react to problems as they emerge and don't get overcommitted to techniques that worked yesterday but can't work tomorrow?

3. How can we develop within our organizations 'centers for revitalization,' centers for development, if you will, that have as their main mission organizational adaptation and helping to shape the future of society?

4. Finally, how do we develop a system of organization which is oriented to the future, to possibilities and potentials, rather than basing most of its learning on a past that will no longer be adequate to handle very new kinds of problems, problems which we can't even contemplate today?

In the past, then, OD has been equated with such unlike things as an enlightened wage and salary program—on-going training programs—role plays—case studies—T-groups—laboratory training—operations research—systems research—etc., etc.

Part of this is attributable to researchers and consultants making speeches and writing popular articles in assigned topics and loosely using the term OD or applying it in a misleading context. It is not unusual to find a basic speech or article of an author/speaker/researcher appearing in several journals with only changes in the title: the title is slanted to the occasion or journal and is completely misleading when correlated to the content.

Part of the dilemma, as one reviews the literature, is that, like many concepts, OD changes with the passing months. Accordingly, and understandably, a leader in the field refines, elaborates, or limits his understanding of the term as the months go by.

Lastly, terms like "OD" become popular and no self-respecting professional is going to be caught with it missing from his vocabulary and printed materials—even if he hasn't the foggiest notion of what it means.

As organizations use the term, a lot depends on their philosophy. If the criteria of success is growth and better-than-industry return to shareholders—you get one view of what OD is. If the organization has a philosophy that also to be considered are the employees, their goals and aspirations, and the meaning of work to man—you get still another view. If the organization has a philosophy that both of the above are important, and add concerns of the nation, our way of life, our partnership with government, an awareness of community and social "good"—still another meaning of OD evolves.

A better understanding into the confused concepts of OD can be had when we consider the meaning of work. Very little research and study has gone into the real meaning of work in the lives of men. Until fairly recently, most men thought of work as something undesirable a man did to earn a living to enable him to do the things he really wanted to do. Few thought of their jobs in terms of "self-fulfillment."

This is changing rapidly. There is now a wide acceptance that "work" is something one would want to do even if an adequate livelihood was assured. The social scientist is moving along these lines—and thus his overpowering concern with the human side of OD. Many organizations, however, are still very heavily committed to concerns about profits, production, bigness, share of the market, etc. There is some concern about people—but this is something they concede rather than seek. Their concept of OD is obviously more non-people oriented.

There is, it would follow, a group of organizations and managers who earnestly are striving to meet the needs both of their human resources and their non-human resources and factors. OD has still another meaning to them.

With these broad and sharp variations, it is quite understandable why OD is so very differently defined and programs constructed that look so different.

Several issues are emerging. The key thread in OD seems to be the increased ability of the organization to solve problems and to make decisions. Whether this is done by individuals, intra-group, or inter-group dictates the methodology employed.

Another key issue revolves around whether the key change agent should be external—or can be internal. Those who lean towards the personal insight and inter-personal relationships focus favor the use of an outside social scientist consultant.

A third issue revolves around whether a change effort in a sub-system of the organization constitutes an OD program—or whether the entire organization must be simultaneously, or consciously planned progressively involved.

A fourth issue relates to whether OD can be called OD unless the need for development is seen by, initiated, and supported by top management.

The cardinal issue seems to be whether a program can be called OD if it focuses solely, or primarily, on individual or group training to improve personal insight and group effectiveness—particularly in open communication, problem solving, and decision making. Some feel yes—others feel an OD program must concern itself with all the internal and external forces, factors, and systems that affect the organization—human and non-human.

John W. Gardner, if he did not coin, brought the term "organization renewal" into the vocabulary of OD practitioners. As initially used by Gardner the term had a fairly restricted meaning.

"———John W. Gardner terms a 'self-renewing agency' one in which the total organization (and the consumer of the services) participates in redefining its own problems. Successful self-renewal depends upon employing the model of complex causality and remaining alert to ever changing goals."[11]

A number of men concerned with OD began uncomfortably to suspect that the "development" of an organization had something to do with more than training and teamwork. There was a suspicion that the following kinds of things might just possibly be related to the organization's effectiveness and future:

| | |
|---|---|
| Budgeting | Leisure |
| Machinery | Meaning of work |
| Equipment | Privacy |
| Work methods | Crime |
| Plant facility | Value analysis |
| Procedures | Specialization |
| Supply and procurement | Automation |
| Corporation gifts | Time-motion studies |
| Ethics | Financial controls |
| Changing societal values | Division of labor |
| World hunger | Hierarchical authority/power structure |
| Population trends | Rules and regulations |

Because of the difficulty in gaining common acceptance of an expansive definition of "organization development," these practitioners began to use the term "Organization Renewal."

For example, Dr. Gordon Lippitt, in his new book "Organization Renewal,"[12] makes this differentiation:

Organization Development is the strengthening of those human processes in organizations which improve the functioning of the organic system so as to achieve its objectives. Organization Renewal is the process of initiating, creating, and confronting needed changes so as to make it possible for organizations to become or remain viable, to adapt to new conditions, to solve problems, to learn from experiences, and to move toward greater organizational maturity.

It is apparent that Dr. Lippitt, with others, has acknowledged that "organization development" is so variously defined as to defy understanding, and so has employed the phrase "organization renewal" to convey the concept "organization development" was initially meant to convey. This may be inevitable. Other social scientists are also using this term, such as Matthew B. Miles, Paul C. Buchanan, and Dale G. Lake.

Some reject the term, feeling that "renewal" connotes that something has gotten old and is being "renewed"—as "urban renewal," while "development" connotes an attempt to keep the organization in cue with internal and external factors and is more consonant with the concept.

One confusing aspect in discussing organization development is the way the term is frequently "hooked up" with "planned change." Many use the two terms synonymously. Planned change generally seems to assume resistance to the change—organizational development does not necessarily seem to imply this inevitable resistance. Planned change generally implies the use of an outside change agent—OD most often is considered an internal operation. The focus in planned change seems to be on human relationships—OD is not so limited. The change efforts in planned change usually involve a limited goal: stop smoking, introduction of a new billing system installation of a new machine—OD implies broader, more significant change goals over a longer period of time. OD must, of course, concern itself with planned change, and limited change goals introduced sequentially to reach a broader change goal. It would seem to be helpful if this differentiation was clearly made. It is the same as confusing a skirmish with a war.

Paul C. Buchanan illustrates the general definition block when he uses OD, planned change, and self-renewal in the same title: "The Concept of Organization Development, or Self-Renewal, as a Form of Planned Change."[13] He says:

Organization development is directed toward developing the capabilities of an organization in such a manner that the organization can attain and sustain an optimum level of performance; it is a problem-solving process; it is undertaken on a collaborative basis by the members of an organization and behavioral science practitioners; and it reflects the belief that even in organizations which are operating satisfactorily or adequately there is room for further improvement.

[It] Has these characteristics:

— Goal is to become sufficiently viable to continuously adapt to its changing environment and its own internal forces.

— Focus of development efforts is on an organization.

— Aspects of the organization's operation to be changed are determined by the unit members.

— Way organization should operate is determined by unit members.

— Unit members determine rate and amount of change effort.

— Unit members are assisted by consultants or change agents.

The parameters of OD in this broad perspective, and the reasons for organizational concern, were sketched by Norman J. Ream in a panel discussion on "The State of Information Retrieval and Date Processing in the Year 2000 and its Implications for Management."[14] He was not discussing OD per se, but the world of pronounced change and complexity in the years ahead. He said:

— No product will be safe in an innovating world.

— No enterprise, however big, is safe in an era of radical change; all organizations must live dangerously and try to hear the potentialities in the market place.

— No management technique can survive as a conditioned response to a given situation, for the situations will not remain static.

— No business or marketing plan can avoid becoming obsolete when there are vast swings into mass habits, when there is intense and imaginative competition.

— No member of management is secure in his position unless he can cope with extreme changes. Past successes will not secure his future.

One of the best concepts of the force-field with which this concept of organization development is trying to cope is found in a recent issue of *Kaiser Aluminum News.* [15]

A more recent way of looking at corporations is to consider them as energy exchange systems in which there is an input of energy from the environment, and a patterned internal activity that transforms the energy into output, which in turn provokes a new energy input. The corporation is thus seen as an open system engaged in constant transactions with its environment, which can be visualized as a system of systems. These systems include the sub-systems within the corporations (divisions, departments) which are constantly engaged in energy exchanges, and the systems operating outside the corporation, but affecting it—other members of the same industry, members of competing industries, suppliers, government institutions, etc. The energy exchanges—transactions—that place both internally and externally occur in a field of force operating in space/time and made up of all the patterned but individual desires and aspirations of all the people who make up both internal and external environmental systems. This way of looking at a corporation offers a picture that is fairly close to modern physical theory and one which should be capable of expression and measurement in scientific, quantitative terms.

In summary, this article has sketched the various ways in which organization development is defined and treated by researchers, teachers, and organizational practitioners.

There is an accelerating awareness that while an organization does nothing without people, conversely, people do little without organization and tools and non-human resources. Somehow the two inter-face and are interrelated and the squabble over theory X or theory Y does not materially help.

The concept "OD" seems to be moving toward encompassing both human and non-human factors. It may well be that the term "organization renewal" may be used to describe this concept—while "OD" will be left to those who wish to focus on the "human" side. One last issue needs to be surfaced and confronted—an issue that is not dealt with in the current literature. Organizations are said to be either reactive or proactive. Few organizations would admit to being reactive—responding to emergencies and forces only when they present themselves and demand a response.

The critical issue for organization development or organization renewal would seem to be this: Is it possible for either an individual or an organization to sustain high interest, awareness, and constantly make the changes, decisions, and planning that is called for in such a viable concept?

Those who would answer affirmatively would point to such efforts as training programs, safety programs, planning groups within the organization, and specific programs such as "Zero Defects." They would also point to all kinds of regulatory and control bodies.

It is our position that such sustained interest and viability is not possible. Man's nature and past experience would seem to offer abundant evidence he is not capable of sustaining even, continuous adaptation.

We know the attention span of children is limited. We have learned that in teaching adults we must count on a limited learning/attention span. We have learned that punishment is best when not sustained. Man listens by spurts. His whole orientation seems to be focus–let up–focus–let up. He does not seem capable of sustained attention.

This would also seem to operate in his organizational life. We have air safety regulatory bodies of all kinds. Most are manned by conscientious men who make an effort to stay viable and maintain pressure on air safety. Yet every time there is a major air crash, or a series of crashes, we have a host of evidence to indicate laxity in enforcement, individual neglect, and non-adaptation to emerging forces and factors. There is a general outcry and a rash of legislation to plug the gaps.

The same phenomena occurs whether we are looking at nursing home safety, health problems and health regulatory bodies, rail safety, or national security. One of the more recent examples came from the death of 78 coal miners in Mannington, West Virginia. After such an event you inevitably find expressions such as this one quoted from the Washington Evening Star of Tuesday, November 26, 1968.

Rep. Ken Hechler, D-W. Va. called for a nation-wide clamor for enactment and strict enforcement of tough mine safety laws. He said he will introduce legislation to strengthen existing laws.

"Hopefully," Hechler told a press conference, "disasters such as a Mannington could be avoided in the future." Hechler blamed everyone–Congress, the coal companies, state and federal inspectors, union officials and the miners themselves, who he said "have come to accept disasters as inevitable."

This author remembers when unions became active within the federal service a few years ago. This issue was highlighted in one of the United States Department of Agriculture divisions that had responsibility for inspecting meats at the packing houses. The particular negotiation item had to do with standards of performance. The organization officials were holding out for 100% accuracy–no diseased carcass would be missed. To admit otherwise would be to bring down a flood of public criticism–each individual would be sure he had gotten meat from the missed carcass. The union negotiators held that no man could be 100% perfect or accurate–volume, the way the men felt, lighting, boredom, speed-ups–a thousand factors would argue against 100% standards.

To say that the concept of organization development or organizational renewal is capable of attainment seems naive. Particularly is this true when you look at the realities of organizational life that militate against such an approach.

- The organization's needs for reliability, standardization and predictability
- The "Don't rock the boat" syndrome

- The temptation to "freeze" success or profitable undertakings
- Emergencies such as death of the company president
- Market breakdowns
- Government regulations
- Merger
- Recession
- Technological changes
- War—hot or cold
- Territorial imperative as practiced by employees, including executives
- Man's inertia

It is a recognition of factors such as these that led a minister to reflect, as the congregation had a lively meeting to celebrate the burning of a mortgage incurred to replace a roof burned off three years previously—"I'd like to see it burn every three years. That roof burning gave us cohesion and activity we will not be able to sustain now that the mortgage is paid off."

This is partly why, we suspect, Warren Bennis[16] recently cynically observed, as he noted the relatively ineffective results of individual change efforts, "The change agents in our own society are the lawyers, the architects, the engineers, the politicians, and the assassins."

We would not be as pessimistic as Bennis, but we think some real cautions and reality should be injected into the concept of organization renewal as it emerges from a concept into organizational programs. The human frailties of complacency, fixation, security, tenure and inertia are potent ones. Man does not seem capable of sustained attention—even to viable decision-making.

The organization would probably be much better advised to attempt such an approach, but to recognize it will have to adapt to its changing environment and internal changes by periodic concentrated attention and effort. To do otherwise runs a heavy risk of being lulled into "program hypnosis." Certainly such an approach would be more sympatico with human nature.

But—this concept is probably 5-10 years ahead of its time. The present concept must be allowed to wend its course and later the field will begin to ask, "Is it possible to do what we are attempting?"

## NOTES

1. *"What's Wrong with Work?"* National Association of Manufacturers, New York, 1967, 38.

2. Blau, Peter M., and W. Richard Scott, *Formal Organizations*. San Francisco: Chandler Publishing Co., 1962, 224.

3.  Lippitt, Gordon L. and Warren H. Schmidt, Crises in a developing organization, *Harvard Business Review*, **45**, No. 6 (Nov.-Dec. 1967), 102-112.

4.  *News and Reports*, NTL Institute, **2**, No. 3 (June, 1968), 1.

5.  Bennis, Warren G., Theory and method in applying behavioral science to planned organizational change, *The Journal of Applied Behavioral Science*, **2**, No. 4 (Oct.-Dec. 1965), 337-360.

6.  Silxon, John E., Donald P. Mullen, and Robert B. Morton, Sensitivity training for individual growth-team training for organization development? *Training and Development Journal*, **22**, No. 1. (January, 1968), 47-53.

7.  Schein, Edgar H., and Warren G. Bennis, *Personal and Organizational Change Through Group Methods.* New York: John Wiley and Sons, 1966.

8.  Winston, James S., A system approach to training and development, *Training and Development Journal*, **22**, No. 6 (June, 1968), 13-20.

9.  Paul M. Fitts. *Notes and Selected Reading on Human Engineering Concepts and Theory* University of Michigan, College of Engineering, August, 1959.

10.  *Op. cit.*, 43.

11.  Duhl, Leonard J., Planning and predicting: or what to do when you don't know the names of the variables. *Daedalus,* **96**, No. 3 (Summer, 1967), 786.

12.  Lippitt, Gordon L., *Organization Renewal.* New York: Appleton-Century-Crofts, 1969.

13.  Buchanan, Paul C., The concept of organization development, or self-renewal, as a form of planned change, in Watson, Goodwin (ed.), *Concepts for Social Change.* Published for Cooperative Project for Educational Development by National Training Laboratories, NEA, 1967, 1-9.

14.  *Management 2000.* New York: American Foundation for Management Research, Inc., 1968, 80-81.

15.  The corporation as a creative environment, *Kaiser Aluminum News.* No. Two/67, 12.

16.  Bennis, Warren, The case study. *The Journal of Applied Behavioral Science,* **4**, No. 2 (1968), 228.

# CRUCIAL ISSUES IN ORGANIZATIONAL DEVELOPMENT

*Paul C. Buchanan*

## INTRODUCTION

Organization development has become an important area of concern to behavioral scientists as well as to executives in educational, industrial, and other kinds of organizations, and several strategies of development have been formulated and applied. In the present paper I examine several cases of organization development in order to determine if there are any common and critical issues discernible among the different strategies applied in a selected group of cases.

The relevance of this analysis of organization development to self-renewal in school systems is a further question. Presumably the answer hinges upon the similarities and differences between industries and schools as social systems, a topic discussed in the chapter in this book by Miles.

## METHOD OF STUDY

As a basis for attempting to identify crucial issues in organization development (OD), I first located as many studies[1] as I could which (a) met the concept of OD as outlined in my paper "The Concept of Organization Development, or Self-Renewal, as a Form of Planned Change"(Buchanan, 1967), and (b) provided sufficient information to indicate the outcome of the undertaking. These two criteria are interrelated, in that to be a program of OD rather than organization improvement there needs to be indication that planned improvement continued after the OD project itself was terminated. There must be indication that a "take off" point has been passed and the organization continues to improve under its own initiative and with its own resources. On this basis it is necessary to "track" a program over an extended period of time. Thus, in this study several cases have been excluded which, on the basis of short-range data, were imaginative and promising,[2] Other studies similar to OD in objective but focusing on communities[3] have been excluded since I believe it would unduly complicate the task of identifying differences between successful and unsuccessful cases to introduce too great a variety in the kind of system which was the focus of development effort. However, there will be occasion to refer to some of these cases in analyzing crucial issues later on in this paper. The same is true regarding the growing body of information on the development of nations—it seems to me there is much to be gained from analysis of case studies of organization, community, and national development.

Cases of OD to which I had access at the time I undertook this study and which I considered to be "successful" were Guest (1962), Blake and Mouton as described by Greiner (1965), Jaques (1951), Beckhard (1966), Shepard and Buchanan's work with a refinery (Buchanan, 1964a), Dennis (1964), and Zand, Miles, and Lytle (1964). Cases which I considered to be "unsuccessful" were Argyris (1962), Buchanan and Brunstetter (1959), and Buchanan (1964b).

An explanation is in order regarding the classification of cases. In one—that reported by Argyris—the change effort in many ways attained the objectives toward which it was directed, since changes occurring in the interrelations among the top management group were identifiable several months after the major "interventions." I list it as a failure, however, since the changes in the relationships among the top group did not spread to their relations with other members of the organization and apparently did not resuit in further improvements. Two cases (Buchanan and Brunstetter, 1959, and Buchanan, 1964b) achieved initial success, one for a period of about two years and the other for about six months, in that the changes spread throughout the unit which was the focus of the effort and involved more and more dimensions of the operations of the units; however, both became failures later, for reasons which are examined below.

Having selected the cases, I tried to identify the strategy, or main action steps, in each. This is not easy and is bound to be only roughly accurate since some of the cases are not reported in much detail. These strategies are presented in the following section of this paper.

Next, on the basis of a study of these cases, and after examining analyses which have been made of the process of planned change (Argyris, 1960; Bennis and others, 1961; Schein and Bennis, 1965; Sofer, 1962), I attempted to identify issues or elements of strategy which the process involves. Most relevant in this regard is the work by Lippitt, Watson & Westley, *The Dynamics of Planned Change*, trom which I have borrowed heavily. A summary of issues from these sources, augmented by my own experiences, is given in the second section below.

Finally, from comparison of the successful and the unsuccessful cases, and by looking at similarities and differences among the successful cases, I attempted to identify which of these issues were "crucial"—*which made a difference*—in the process of organization development. Again, this is a difficult process, since many of the questions one would like to ask are not answerable from the case descriptions.

## STRATEGIES OF ORGANIZATION DEVELOPMENT

In this section an attempt is made to outline the major steps in the different strategies reported in the cases selected for study.

1. **"Socio-analytic consultation" (Jaques).**    In describing his approach, Jaques (1964) says it ". . . requires that an individual or individuals in an organization with a problem concerning the working of the organization should seek the help of an analyst in sorting out the nature of the problem." Once this help is sought the steps appear to be as follows:

a)  The relationship between the consultant and the client system is worked out, written down, and made known to all members of the organization.

b)  At the request of the individuals, the consultant discusses with them, individually or in small groups, problems raised by the members. He "listens for the principles and concepts behind the words."

c)  The consultant formulates a report consisting of information obtained from members of a work group ("command team") and of his analysis of this information.

d)  The consultant presents his report at meetings of the work group.

e)  He regularly attends the periodic meetings of the work group during which his role again is to listen for principles and concepts behind the words, and to help members identify and work through issues they are avoiding, anxieties which influence their problem-solving abilities, and so on.

f)  This leads to the formulation of projects undertaken by special task forces or command groups, in which, if the members request it, the consultant participates in the role indicated previously: listening for principles, identifying and helping the group work through issues being avoided, and so forth.

In Glacier Metals, where Jaques did this work, he was available on a full-time basis for four years, during which major changes were made in the functioning of the company. Projects included change in the appeals procedures of the company, modification of the executive system, working out a new method for measuring performance, modification of the pay system, changes in company policy, and others. One of the consequences was the development within the company of ability to "continue socio-analytic consultation under its own steam," and subsequently Jaques has been used only on a part-time basis.

2.  **Survey-feedback-training-problem solving**:    Two of the cases (Dennis, 1964, and Buchanan, 1964a) involved strategies which were basically similar yet included some variations will be identified:

a)  Survey of all members of management to determine what the members considered to be problems in working effectively. This was done by interviews.

b)  Formulation of the survey data into a conceptual scheme considered appropriate by the consultants.

c)  Report-back and analysis of the findings in a series of meetings of the top management group and the consultants.

d)  Laboratory training for all members of management. In one case this was a conventional one-week laboratory (Dennis, 1964); in the other it was a modified laboratory, with the training groups assigned responsibility for studying the survey report, formulating issues requiring further work, and exploring means of increasing teamwork in the plant (Buchanan, 1964a).

e)  Systematic problem solving. In one case (Dennis, 1964) this was done by utilizing a modified form of the Scanlon Plan (Lesieur, 1958). In the other, task groups were formed around issues formulated at the laboratory sessions, the project being coordinated by a committee representing each of the training groups. At the end of a year, groups composed of members of management who worked on the same product met for two days off the job to again identify problems and develop action plans. These plans were systematically discussed with the top management group and then carried through with assistance as needed from top management.

3.  **Cyclical survey-feedback-problem-solving-team training.** Beckhard used an approach similar to that outlined above, but sufficiently different to be described separately:

a)  Interviews with the top management team.

b)  Formulation of the data into a conceptual scheme considered appropriate by the consultant.

c)  Series of 3-day meetings of top management, with the task being carefully controlled so the group first understood the data, then set priorities for action, then determined the group or person responsible for action, and then worked on those which were within the action responsibility of the managers who participated in the meeting.

d)  Steps (a) through (c) followed by successively lower levels of managers, with the top manager joining each group toward the end of each group's meeting to hear and consider issues requiring attention at his level.

e)  Introduction of theory and some skill-practice in the problem-solving meetings.

f)  Laboratory training conducted for middle levels of management, and technical training for those entering jobs for which they needed additional skills.

g)  Intergroup problem-solving sessions held by groups where the need was indicated.

h)  Teams formed to open new plants (hotels) received team training.

A variation of Beckhard's approach was used by Zand, Miles, and Lytle: Instead of gathering information in advance, consultants and members of management met for three days away from the job, the middle and upper level managers meeting one week and the first-line supervisors meeting the following. With both groups some time was spent in training regarding the problem-solving process, but the major activity was to identify and plan action regarding on-the-job problems. A unique aspect of the design was that the consultants carefully separated the group's work in the various stages of problem solving: diagnosis of difficulties was completed before effort was made to formulate problems; agreement among the participants regarding the statement of problems was reached before attempts were made to formulate possible solutions; and so on. A second unique aspect was that several of the higher level managers participated in the last day of the meeting of the first-line supervisors and thus provided a means of integrating the plans of the two groups. The third phase of the program involved task groups carrying out, on the job, plans made in the previous phases, with guidance and support from a steering committee formed from both groups. The effectiveness of this approach as OD, or self-renewal, is indicated by the fact that the task groups completed their work; then the total group of managers met again (without a consultant), they formulated additional action plans, and they were continuing their developmental efforts at the time the case report was prepared (two years after the first off-the-job meeting was held).

4. **Survey-feedback-team training.**   Argyris proceeded as follows:

   a)   He interviewed and observed members of the top management group to determine the extent to which their values as reflected in their job behavior conformed to a predicted set of values.

   b)   He fed the results back to the group in a meeting away from the job. On the basis of their interpretation of these findings, the group decided improvement was called for.

   c)   The managers as a team participated in a T-group.

   d)   The group analyzed its own manner of working by having part of the team conduct problem-solving meetings while being observed by the other members and by consultants, the analysis being used to determine the extent to which they were applying what they had decided from their T-group experience to be desirable.

5. **"Managerial Grid Organization Development."**   Although Blake and Mouton (1964) described their program as consisting of six phases, the case description (Greiner, 1965) that I am using in this paper involved some important additional steps. To keep the record straight, I will star the steps mentioned by Blake and Mouton.

   a)   The consultant spent approximately two weeks in the target system, getting a "feel" for it and its problems.

   b)   The top management group in the plant and a group in headquarters to whom they reported met for three days to explore and improve each group's perceptions of the other and to improve their ability to work effectively with one another.

   c)   The top manager and a few members of the plant participated in a public managerial grid laboratory.

d)  A pilot managerial grid laboratory was conducted within the plant for managers from all levels and departments of the plant.

e)  *All members of management in the plant participated in a managerial grid laboratory.

f)  *Family groups, beginning with the top, met to improve their working relations and their effectiveness as teams. (This was done in only a few of the teams in the case reported by Greiner.)

g)  *Meetings were held of members of groups which had working interrelationships, the purpose and procedure being similar to Step (b) above. (In the case described by Greiner such meetings were held only by top plant and headquarters management.)

h)  *Organizational improvement goals were worked out. Beginning in the grid laboratories and in the team development meetings, conditions requiring change were formulated in systematic terms. In this phase, action goals were formulated on a personal, team and organization-wide basis, and "unresolved problems preventing attainment of organization competence" were identified and plans for solving them were worked out.

i)  *Plans for attaining established goals were carried out. This was done in part by use of "task paragraph discussions" which followed a procedure designed to facilitate effective problem solving (Blake and Mouton, 1964, p. 277ff.).

j)  *Stabilization. This step involved "establishing a sound relationship between goals and actions previously set in motion and current activities." Greiner presents little information regarding what, if anything, was done in this phase of the program.

6.  **Change conducted by a new manager (Guest).**   Unlike all the other cases in this study, Guest (1962) describes one in which there was no consultant, the change being planned and effected by the new plant manager. The steps taken were as follows:

a)  Higher management changed its actions in relation to the plant manager. How this came about is not made clear in the case description, although Guest speculates that a new corporate officer urged the division manager to allow the plant manager latitude in "running his own show."

b)  The new plant manager communicated (by action and words) his philosophy and approach to all members of plant management.

c)  The plant manager held informal meetings to find out the problems of the plant as seen by all levels of the management group.

d)  The manager initiated regular problem-solving meetings with his high-level subordinates. Steps (b), (c), and (d) resulted in a new pattern of interaction

○

between superiors and subordinates, and among peers, which spread to all levels of the management group.

e)  Many managers were transferred laterally within the plant.

f)  Plans were put into effect as changes were agreed upon in staff meetings. These consisted of changes both in the plant's technical system and in procedures. In this phase the manager "played an increasingly important role in gaining divisional support of such changes."

g)  Long-range plans, based upon consensus of the management group, were formulated and carried out.

As can be noted from even these brief summaries of strategies, the cases utilized a variety of types and mixtures of "inputs" (interventions) while still having the similarities mentioned in my earlier paper (Buchanan, 1967). The next section lists some dimensions on which these comparisons can be made.

## ISSUES IN ORGANIZATION DEVELOPMENT

The following are issues which appear to be potentially important as a consultant attempts to help an organization develop its effectiveness:[4]

1.  Clarify or develop the client's motivation to change.

2.  Assess the change agent's potential helpfulness:

    a.  Relevance of his resources, interests, and competence to the client's need.

    b.  His job security in relation to the client system.

    c.  Relations among members of the change-agent team.

    d.  Compatibility of his different objectives (to help the client, to conduct research, to get promoted within the company, and so on).

    e.  Time he has available.

3.  Establish effective relations between the change agent and the client system.

    a.  Role of each in planning and conducting the program.

    b.  Expectations of each regarding the amount and kind of effort required of each in the change program.

    c.  Restrictions (if any) upon the kinds of changes which are allowable.

    d.  Who the client is—whom the change agent's relations are with.

    e.  Expectations regarding the role(s), or kind(s) of help, the change agent is to provide.

4. Clarify or diagnose the client system's problems.

    a.    Concepts in terms of which diagnosis is to be made.

    b.    How information is to be obtained, and from whom.

    c.    Use of data in diagnosis.

    d.    Develop diagnostic skills of members of the system.

    e.    Determine the boundaries of the client system.

5. Establish instrumental objectives for change. (How should we operate?)

6. Formulate plans for change.

    a.    Link to other persons, issues, and/or parts within the internal system.

    b.    Link to other persons, parts, and/or issues in the external system.

    c.    Develop time schedule and build time expectations.

    d.    Develop procedures and/or structures for carrying out plans.

    e.    Provide for anticipatory testing of plans.

    f.    Develop competence of those involved in taking actions.

    g.    Develop motivation for carrying out plans.

7. Carry out plans for change.

    a.    Maintain support and understanding from the larger system.

    b.    Obtain feedback on consequences of early action steps.

    c.    Coordinate efforts of different people and groups involved.

8. Generalize and stabilize changes.

    a.    Assess the effects of the change upon the total system.

    b.    Look for "regression."

    c.    Facilitate spread to other parts of target system and to adjacent inter-dependent systems.

9. Institutionalize planned development or self-renewal.

    a.    Develop problem-sensing and problem-solving skills and mechanisms in all components of the system.

    b.    Develop reward systems which facilitate innovation.

    c.    Establish a change-agent role in the system.

We are now in a position to determine which, if any, of these issues are "crucial" by returning to an examination of the ten actual cases outlined in the previous section.

## CRUCIAL ISSUES IN ORGANIZATION DEVELOPMENT

*Comparing the successful and the unsuccessful cases,* the issue which appears to be most conspicuous is that of *linkage between the target system and the larger system* (Issue 6b). In two of three unsuccessful cases, changes were initiated and progress was being made, only to come to a halt because of action by management above the top man in the target system. While the change agents in these cases recognized the importance of linkage with higher management, steps taken to accomplish such linkage were not effective. The difficulty[5] in one case was partly due to disagreement among members of the change-agent team regarding the approach to be followed (Issue 2c), and in part to the way the change agents related to the company president (Issue 3a). The program in question was initiated by the head of a department in a large company, and he requested help from both an inside and an outside consultant. The consultants were in agreement that the program plan of the department should be fully understood by corporate managers, and a two-day conference to accomplish this was worked out by the outside consultant and the president. The consultants jointly planned the two-day conference, but under the tensions which arose regarding the corporate officers' reactions to the meeting, the consultant who had the central role in the conference changed the plan, creating tension and role ambiguity between the consultants. This reduced the quality of the meeting, and at the end of the first day the president postponed the second day of the conference—which was never held. The department decided to go ahead with its program, with the support of a vice president, and it proved to be highly effective. Then the vice president left the company, leaving the change program in the target department going full swing but with no effective links between it and an uninterested and rather hostile corporate management. Shortly after the vice president left, a higher official called the top managers of the focal department into his office and said, in effect, "You do the technical work and leave the management to me."

In the other case, work was being done to effect the linkage, but the meeting where this was intended to be accomplished was not effective, apparently due to Issue 3b, expectations by the top man regarding what was required of him, and to the lack of competence (Issue 2a) and/or job security (Issue 2b) of the change agent. Thus, when the changes being made in the norms, reward system, and methods of decision making in the department required accommodating changes in the practices and values of higher management, such changes were not possible. Furthermore, higher management replaced the three key people in the target department with managers who were unfamiliar and unsympathetic with the change program, and the development effort was discontinued.

In the third unsuccessful case (Argyris, 1962), there is no indication that the issue of linkage upward arose. Perhaps this was due in part to the fact that a high-level manager (division president) initiated and was a participant in the program, and in part because the kinds of changes which resulted did not require accommodating changes in other parts of the company.

In contrast to two of the unsuccessful cases, there is indication of effective linkage with the external system in two of the successful ones. Both Greiner (1965) and Guest (1962), in describing the cases, emphasize the importance of this issue. In three other cases the top manager of the organization was included in the target system (Jaques, 1951; Dennis, 1964; and Beckhard, 1966). In another case (Zand, Miles, and Lytle, 1964) linkage was not given much attention, and this almost led to termination of the program: A higher level manager heard of the meetings the first-line supervisors were holding, and he called the head of the target unit, wanting to know about the "unionization of foremen." The head of the focal unit was able to explain the program to the higher manager's satisfaction. In the seventh case (Buchanan, 1964a) the plant which was the target system was sufficiently autonomous so that relations with higher levels didn't become a problem during the four years of the program. There was a change of manager during this time, but the new one had participated in a training laboratory and was enthusiastic about the program which was going on when he took over. Yet the top managers in the plant took "linking" steps which are worth noting. At the third of a series of off-the-job meetings during which they were formulating long-range plans, the plant managers asked two key managers from headquarters to meet with them. They were thus enabled to integrate plant plans with headquarters' plans.

A case described by Schein and Bennis (1965, p. 255ff) adds further support of the importance of linkage to the larger systems (Issue 6b). Laboratory training was undertaken with lower levels of management, only to be abruptly terminated when the top manager learned about what was going on.[6] Linkage has also been highlighted as a factor in effective community development (see Lasswell, 1962, p. 122). Additional support of the importance of this issue, and an interesting way of trying to attain it, are reported by Whyte and Hamilton (1965): One consultant worked with lower managers and employees, the other with the general manager.[7] As the one working with lower levels encountered difficulties resulting from the behavior of the general manager, he talked with the other consultant, who brought up the issues in his next meeting with the general manager. But the method seemed to be only partially successful; while the general manager approved of changes requested at lower levels, and he encouraged the development effort, he seemed not to become involved. In sharp contrast is the method of linking used by Blake (see Greiner, 1965). Sensing that the plant managers and their superiors in headquarters disagreed over important issues, he proposed a three-day meeting of the two groups to explore their perceptions of each other. The openness, mutual understanding, and role clarification which resulted from the meeting seemed to be an important factor in the magnitude and depth of change which was subsequently accomplished in the plant. In contrast to the Whyte-Hamilton case, the linkage was made not via the consultant as intermediary but through direct changes in the relations between the plant and headquarters managers.

Another issues suggested by comparison of the successful and unsuccessful cases is *linkage with other persons, issues, and/or parts within the target system* (Issue 6a). The case described by Argyris indicates success in effecting the change which that program attempted: members of the top management group who were involved in the program seemed to have become more authentic and open in their dealings with each other. However, the evidence seems rather clear that this change did not lead to changes in their dealings with their subordinates, nor was there a spread of the program to other units of the organization or to other dimensions of the unit's operation.

In all the successful cases linkage with several levels of people within the target system was established either as part of the change-induction plan (Blake, 1964; Buchanan, 1964a; Dennis, 1964; Zand, Miles, and Lytle, 1964), or by steps taken early in the program which led to such action (Beckhard, 1966; Jaques, 1951; Guest, 1962). It seems that such linkage was either in the form of *working on operating problems* which involved units or groups beyond the original focal unit (for example, in one case work on the issue of cost reduction led to involving the union in the development program), or linkage was in the form of involving large numbers and levels of organizational members at the problem-identification phase of the program.

Support for the centrality of Issue 6a also comes from the field of community development. In describing their work in Peru, Holmberg and Dobyns state that "the project has selected values and institutions to change which would then foster more change by the [members of the community] themselves" (Holmberg and Dobyns, 1962, p. 107).

Now what can be learned from *differences among the successful cases*?

One thing which stands out is the variety of ways in which the different programs coped with many issues listed in the previous section:

1. One difference among the successful cases was the *kind* of model introduced by the change agents, both as a basis for diagnosis (Issue 4a) and for determining how the members thought they should try to operate their organization (Issue 5). There appear to be three types of models used in the seven cases: *cognitive, process,* and *procedural.* While most of the cases involve more than one, it appears that Blake and Mouton make primary use of the cognitive one, in the form of the managerial grid: through assigned readings, tests on the readings, and demonstration exercises, managers are taught the distinctions among five managerial styles and some consequences of the use of each. Jaques used primarily a process model: he focused on how members related to each other and on the fact, for example, that the way they felt about exercising authority influenced their effectiveness. Zand, Miles, and Lytle used primarily a procedural model: they guided the managers through a carefully controlled series of steps in identifying, diagnosing, and planning action regarding problems in the operation of the target system. (Guest's manager used a procedural model, while Beckhard, Buchanan, and Dennis used mixtures of process and procedural models.)

2. The cases also varied greatly in the *manner* in which models for formulating goals were introduced into the organization. In the case of Blake and Mouton it was done primarily by an extensive training program. At the other extreme, Guest introduced

the model by the example set by the change agent—the top manager: in his first meeting with his management group he described how he intended to operate; then he set about illustrating it, with the result that the procedure spread to all levels of the organization. It appears that Jaques introduced a model partly by demonstrating it (see Bennis, 1963, for an analysis of Jaques' method) and partly by helping members identify "spontaneously emerging solutions to problems" by "listening for the principles and concepts behind the words" (Jaques, 1964) and holding them up for examination and comparison with current practices. Beckhard, and Zand, Miles, and Lytle (although in somewhat different ways) also demonstrated use of a problem-solving procedure.

What strikes me as of special significance is that each of these different approaches resulted in the introduction of a model which was incorporated into the practices of the organization—it became institutionalized. It is my impression, although I cannot prove it from these cases, that successful introduction of a new and viable model, relating to a fundamental aspect of the organization's operation, was one of the single most important contributions of the change agent in the successful cases.

In light of the differences in (1) the kind of model used and (2) the way it was introduced, it appears that a change agent should be wary of believing that he alone holds the key to utopian organizations.

3. In one case the change agent was the top manager in the target system (Guest), in two they were "internal" consultants from headquarters working with a plant (Buchanan, Dennis), while in the rest they were "outside" consultants. Apparently the location of the change agent was not, in itself, a crucial factor. This is consistent with the fact that the "catalysts" in General Electric's Program of Business Effectiveness, which appears to be successful in accomplishing organization development, also are "internal" consultants. However, it seems likely that the location of the change agent is closely related to several other issues: role of the change agent in planning (Issue 3a), the change agent's motivation (Issue 2d), who his "client" is (Issue 3d), and his job security (Issue 2b).

4. While all of the successful cases involved all levels of management in the target system, they differed in the time at which additional levels were involved. In Beckhard's case the main program began with the top management group; then as issues were identified and progress made, the same or similar activities were undertaken at successively lower levels (activity at the higher levels being continued). In three cases (Jaques; Blake; and Zand, Miles, and Lytle) all levels of management—and in Jaques' case some non-managers—were involved during the early stages of the program. In the case described by Guest there was some activity involving all levels of management. At an early meeting of all management personnel the change agent announced his intention, and he immediately began obtaining information and ideas from a sample at all levels; yet the major work was done at the top of the target unit. While it is difficult to draw generalizations from Guest's case, since the change agent was the manager, this case suggests that we hold open the issue of whether the change

agent is needed at all levels, or whether if significant changes on a central issue are made at the top, they will spread throughout the subordinate organization.

Finally, we need to look at what can be learned from the *similarities in the successful cases*.

1. As has been indicated, in all seven cases the top manager of the target system was actively involved in the project. It appears that this is important, although this was not an issue which differentiated the successes from the failures. Determining the boundaries of the target system (Issue 4e) is probably of more importance, since this helps define who is the "top person in the system."

2. In all cases the change agent introduced a model for collecting data and for diagnosing the system's needs (Issue 4a), which could be considered by the members of the system in establishing goals for improvements (Issue 5).

3. Although the models differed, and were introduced into the system in different ways, all concerned the problem-solving processes of the organization.

4. All of the models resulted in changes in the power structure of the target system such changes being in the *kind* of power or influence used (away from authority and toward increased use of information), in the *distribution* of influence among the members of management (proportionately greater influence by people at lower levels), and in the total *amount* of influence exerted, or in the "size of the influence pie" (after the development program, the target systems appeared to have more self-control, and their operation appeared to be less determined by chance or by forces outside the system).

5. The models used also emphasized the development of norms and of skills which facilitated a shift from relationships based on negotiation or bargaining toward relationships based on problem solving or collaboration.

Obviously the cases varied in the extent of change in the above respects; yet because of the crude measurements used in assessing the cases, it is difficult to determine which resulted in the most change and, therefore, which strategy of development was most effective.

6. In all cases the change agent came from outside the target organization and was new to the target system. Since this was also the situation in the three unsuccessful cases, it is difficult to assess the implications.

## CONCLUSIONS AND IMPLICATIONS

Of approximately 33 issues which there was some reason to believe are important in organization development, three have been identified as being of particular centrality in this study of ten cases. These issues are:

1.  Introducing a new model of operation which the members of an organization can consider as a basis for formulating improvement goals regarding a dimension or operation which is central to the performance of the organization (Issue 5).

2.  Sequencing objectives and action steps in such a way that linkage is established between the initial point of change and other persons, parts, and dimensions of operation *internal* to the target system (Issue 6a).

3.  Sequencing objectives and action steps in such a way that linkage is established between the initial point of change and other persons, parts, and dimensions of the *external* system with which the target system has important interdependency (Issue 6b).

Why did so few issues emerge as crucial?

One possibility is that the cases studied all represent a similar approach to organization development—what Leavitt calls the "people approaches" and what Bennis refers to as "change agents working on organizational dynamics" (Bennis, 1963, p. 140). It is to be expected that the more the similarity of approach, the less any differences are highlighted, and thus the greater the difficulty in discerning crucial or significant differences.

Perhaps of greater importance is the fact that the differences in the outcomes of what I have called the successful and unsuccessful cases were not as pronounced as my discussion of them has implied. Probably cases that are "really" failures do not get reported, and so we do not have access to cases required for a thorough study of the effectiveness of change strategies and of issues which are crucial to the process.

A third, and in my judgment the most important, possible explanation for the emergence of so few crucial issues is that information required to determine the importance of each of the 33 issues listed earlier in this paper was not included in the case reports. The reports vary considerably in what is reported, and the reasons for the inclusions and omissions are not clear. It may be that the reporter is including what he considers most important either in the particular case or in cases in general; he may be reporting either what he is willing to reveal about his own work or what the organization concerned will permit him to print. At any rate, it appears to me that if organization development is to advance as an application of behavioral science, and if we are to practice our own beliefs, it is important to engage in systematic self-study. This can be done only if we document our work in such a form that it can be studied by ourselves and our associates. And this, it seems to me, requires that we agree upon a format, or at least upon some key issues to be covered in reports. I hope that the list of issues presented in the middle section of this paper is a fruitful beginning of such a format.

**NOTES**

1. One will note that all of these cases involve what Leavitt (1964) refers to as the "People Approaches" to change. One reason for this is that the "People Approaches," more than others, emphasize *development* or *self-renewal.*

2. Examples: Sofer's work with a small company, the research unit in a hospital, and a department of a technical college (Sofer, 1962); Morton and Weight's work at Aerojet (Morton & Weight), the work of General Electric's Business Effectiveness Staff, and Whyte and Hamilton's work with a hotel (Whyte and Hamilton, 1965).

3. Examples: Klein's work with a community in New England (in Schein and Bennis, 1965); Holmberg's work with a community in Peru (Holmberg, 1965).

4. In addition to the sources mentioned earlier, I have also benefited from comparing issues in my preliminary list with observations made about the change process by people familiar with the Vicos Project of Community Development in Peru. (See Holmberg, 1965; Holmberg and Dobyns, 1962; and Lasswell, 1962.)

5. The information upon which these observations are made is not in the case reports, but was available to me from direct sources.

6. Schein and Bennis interpret this failure as due to introducing a set of values in a component of an organization where the prevailing value system is too greatly different from that being introduced. I believe the linkage issue is a better way of formulating the difficulty, since the cases described by Guest and by Greiner indicate that a change program can be effective even when the new values are distinctly different from those currently prevalent in the system. However, the analysis by Schein and Bennis regarding "crucial issues" in the use of laboratory training is very relevant to our subject. (See Schein and Bennis, 1965, chapter 10.)

7. Fantini and Weinstein (1966) report a similar approach to linkage in their work with a school system.

# TEAM BUILDING FOR MATRIX ORGANIZATIONS[1]

*Gordon L. Lippitt*

Organizations of the future will need to develop new structures and processes to meet the rapidly changing demands placed upon them. These new structures and processes will increase the need for the creative and flexible use of the human resources of the organization. More and more we will see the emergence of *matrix organization* concepts wherein people will be seen as resources to be utilized at any time their capabilities are needed to solve organizational problems. The old concepts of "going through channels," autonomous departments, and line-staff delineation is no longer completely valid in modern organizational management. The use of project teams, task forces, and other types of "temporary systems" will be the appropriate way for organizations to optimize the different capabilities of its human resources. As predicted by Bennis: [2]

I suspect that we will see an increase in the number of planned-change programs . . . toward less bureaucratic and more participative, 'open system' and adaptative structures. Given the present pronounced rate of change, the growing reliance on science for the success of the industrial enterprises, and the 'turbulent contextual environment' facing the firm, we can expect increasing demand for social inventions to revise traditional notions of organized effort.

It is frequently found that organizational problems are no longer the province of just one group, but that they cut across the multiple human, structural and technological resources of an organization. The need for a *matrix organization* concept in practice is a trend in making modern organizational systems viable.

The development and utilization of special groups and sub-systems in organizations to solve problems is an example of the temporary societies concept of Bennis. [3] He points out that the characteristics of temporary systems are as follows:

Time Boundary (either chronologically or in terms of a task completion).
Insulation between the system and "outside" influences.
Intensive Involvement (in most cases).

To cope with these characteristics, people in the organization will need to be able to be many things and to take various roles, to identify with the adaptive and change process, and to develop an ability to modify their commitments as needs arise. People in organizations will need to move in and out of various kinds of work group relations which may have a short or long range time dimension. It will be necessary to foster and encourage teamwork in these different group situations. Helping a group of people

---

This selection was originally published by the Society for Personnel Administration as *Supervisor Booklet No. 6* (August, 1969). Reprinted by permission of the Society for Personnel Administration, 485-87 National Press Building, 14th and F Streets, N.W., Washington, D.C. 20004.

to work together is a difficult and complex undertaking. A leader or a member of a group needs to be aware that teamwork is manifested in the way a group is able to solve problems. Let's examine some of the characteristics of teamwork and ways to achieve it.

**1. Teamwork requires an understanding and commitment to the group goals.** Whether a regular work group, a project team, or a special task force, the need for the group to determine and understand its goals will be a prerequisite for effective teambuilding. It is not just an understanding of the immediate task, but an understanding of the role of the group in the total organization, its responsibilities, and the morale objectives to which they are related. As indicated earlier, those goals operate at the level of the organization, task group, and individual. They will be both long and short-range in nature. The members of the group, to achieve teamwork, will need not only to understand these goals but have a degree of commitment to them so as to work effectively toward their achievement.

Obviously, it is not a task-oriented group unless it has a goal or combination of goals—to solve a specific problem, to plan a specific action, to produce a specific report, to make specific recommendations, and so forth.

Obviously, too, such goals do not exist in a vacuum, but are a part of the larger goals of the organization within and for which the group exists. The first requirement of team effectiveness is that these goals must be clearly defined. The time spent in arriving at a goal definition here, by a member or by the group itself, helps make the time used by the group meaningful. Writing down goals is not the same as preparing an action plan, but a better plan can be prepared from a well thought out statement of goals. The second requirement is that all members of the group must know and understand with equal conciseness what these group goals are. This is often not the case, and where even a few members have only a general idea of the group's goals, they tend to have quite different ideas about group achievement.

**2. Teamwork requires the maximum utilization of the different resources of individuals in the group.** The group may be used effectively for problem-solving when the type of problem to be solved is one in which there is a quantitative and qualitative need for various points of view and opinions. This might be especially true where there is a complex problem that has no easy solution within the resources of a single individual. Similarly, inasmuch as people tend to better carry out decisions in which they share, a decision might be best made in a group when the people comprising it will be the ones who will carry out what is decided. Thus, a leader or administrator will find it extremely worthwhile to involve in the process of making the decision those who will ultimately implement it. Different people in an organization will have had different experiences, background, and technical knowledge which frequently will be helpful in arriving at a decision.

Frequently, in modern organizations, the complexity of a problem requires the specialized knowledge and experience of all the individuals in the group to find a realistic solution. A team knows the different resources of the individuals in their group. A supervisor and leader is the coordinator of these resources in getting group action. A good question [for the manager] to ask is: "Have I heard the ideas of everyone who can make a significant contribution to the solution of this problem?"[4]

Teamwork will maximize the utilization of individual resources to achieve group goals.

**3. Teamwork is achieved when flexibility, sensitivity to needs of others, and creativity are encouraged.** A group of persons does not spring into mature group action just because its members happen to be assigned to the same section of the building or to a similar function. A group of persons may need to deal with some of the emotional problems of its members' inter-personal relationships before it can reach decisions effectively. Team action is a complex thing. Group decision-making, at its best, depends on the kind of working relationships in which disagreement, creativity, and shared responsibility can flourish. When such an atmosphere is established, the group normally is ready to reach decisions effectively.

The old cliche that "two heads are better than one" is not always true. In some cases a manager can implement, develop, or think through various plans without getting the advice and suggestions of others. Conversely, when working on a new or complex problem, or a situation that affects a large segment of the organization, more effective resolution might be achieved if a number of people participate in a group problem-solving situation.

The interstimulation of a number of persons can frequently emerge with an idea which is the outgrowth of the group process and not that of any single individual. Many people have their best thoughts stimulated by the thoughts of others. This kind of creative thinking is the goal of good group teamwork, and it is one of the crying needs of management today. Too many conferences, groups, and task groups are sterile because they stick to a rigid agenda and right procedures, and because they have poor interpersonal relationships.

**4. Teamwork is most effective where participative leadership is manifested.** A group of persons brought together in a problem-solving situation will not function at maximum efficiency if its members are "rubber-stamp" or "yes" men for a manager or leader. In such a situation a group leader is merely communicating his own ideas. If a supervisor is interested both in assuming his own responsibility for leadership, and in developing the membership of a group so that the functions of leadership are shared, his attitude will go a long way toward achieving effective decision-making.

This criterion might be embarrassing to many who are reluctant to exert a team type of leadership. If a manager's motivation in calling together a group is to get his own way, he should not pretend to be seeking a group decision. If he has already made up his mind, he should not imply consultation; he should announce his decision and communicate it to those who need to know. It is another matter if he is asking a group of people to think and act together as a means of helping him to reach a decision.

**5. Teamwork requires a group to develop procedures to meet the particular problem or situation.** We are all familiar with the use of a voting procedure in group decision-making situations. There have been a number of research studies showing that in many cases it is not the most appropriate tool for group action. In fact, in many settings it is only a way by which the leader can keep control of the group—or, at its worst, an ideal procedure for "railroading" ideas. In most situations in which group action is taken, there is little need for a voting procedure.

This is not to say that parliamentary procedures are not appropriate in certain situations, for instance, for a working legislative body or a policy body such as a board of directors where there is a need for a historical or legal record. There are also some situations in which a group will not be using strictly parliamentary procedure but will decide on an issue by a vote, or it might develop some procedure such as a majority or two-thirds rule. The creation of a minority group in such a situation, however, frequently poses problems later on, unless the group members show an unusual degree of maturity, or the decision to be made is so inconsequential that no one really cares who wins. To get away from the vote-taking situation, there has been a great deal of talk about trying to get "unanimous" group decision. As laudable as this might be in group decision-making, it is extremely difficult and may be impractical. People being as complex as they are, it is unlikely that one can get unanimous decisions very often; in many cases, it would take a great deal of time and an extraordinary amount of patience for a group to reach perfect unanimity. There is a difference between unanimous decision-making and a "consensus" decision. In a consensus-type decision, the members of the group agree on the next steps, with those who are not in agreement reserving the right to have the tentative decision tested and evaluated for later assessment. In other words, certain members of the group will agree that on a "provisional try" or a "first-time" basis the organization might try out a particular alternative; but they want to ensure certain evaluative means for testing whether or not the feelings of the majority indicate the most appropriate action. In a very real sense, this is different from compromise, where the decision is taken from two opposing points of view and becomes something quite different from either of them. In the consensus decision, individuals in the group might be saying they are "not sure" of the best decision, but, realizing the need for action, they will accept agreement to one of the alternatives for action after thorough discussion and minority points of view are heard, and with the understanding that the temporary decision will be reviewed and evaluated at a later date.

**6. Teamwork is characterized by the group's ability to examine its process so as to constantly improve itself as a team.** When two or more people work together for a purpose, there tends to be interaction, interpersonal relationships, group goals, and communication, all with varying degrees of success. Someone has made the observation that a collection of normal individuals can make a neurotic group. In this sense, the word "neurotic" is used to describe a group which is unable to focus on the problem, is erratic in group discussion and unable to reach a decision, and which constantly bickers and fights. Such ineffective behavior is only one example of the pattern of forces and group dynamics which every task group inevitably exhibits. The leader and each group member might well ask himself some pertinent questions so as to learn from interaction:

- What are the motivations of the various members of the group?
- What are the real reasons for these people wanting to be members of the group?
- What are the various relationships among them?
- Are there underlying animosities which will reduce the group's productivity?
- What effect will conditions of status have on the group?
- Will any members of the group have difficulty in communicating with other members?
- Can the group maintain a clear purpose?
- How cohesive is the group?

By setting up a process of analyzing its own actions a group can learn from its experiences how to improve its teamwork. A manager should always devote some time to developing group effectiveness -- by helping the group confront its own process and initiating appropriate team building opportunities.

**7. For a group to function effectively as a team, the climate of the organization should encourage the manager to utilize the practices of team leadership.** Most managers behave in accordance with the example set by their superiors, and with the implicit and explicit reward systems existing throughout the organization. If the top management of an organization tends to feel that the only good decisions are individual decisions, a subordinate manager probably will feel uncomfortable in using groups very frequently to aid in the problem-solving process. On the other hand, if top management puts value on those leaders who utilize and develop others through team experiences, he will feed encouraged to use group action whenever it seems to him to be appropriate. Even for top management, however, this is not always a clear-cut issue:

An organization built on the assumptions and values of self-actualizing man is more likely to create a climate conducive to the emergence of psychologically meaningful groups because of the organization's concern with the meaningfulness of work .... The effective integration of organizational and personal needs probably requires a climate based on the assumptions of complex man because groups are not the right answer to all problems at all times. Those organizations which are able to use groups effectively tend to be very careful in deciding when to make use of a work team or a committee and when to set up conditions which promote or discourage group formation. There are no easy generalizations in this area, hence a diagnostic approach may be the most likely to pay off. [5]

**8. Teamwork utilizes the appropriate steps and guidelines for decision-making in the solution of problems.** As work groups, task forces, management teams, project groups, or other types of groups initiate and decide an action in the renewal process, they should use the appropriate steps and guides in decision-making that can be identified as follows:[6]

*A clear definition of the problem.* If the problem is ambiguous and the group is unable to understand it, the decision-making process will be greatly impeded. In many cases, a problem is so general that the group is unable to come to grips with it. A problem should be defined clearly, the limits of group responsibility should be set, and any clarification relative to the problem should be encouraged.

*A clear understanding as to who has the responsibility for the decision.* When a group is asked to assume responsibility for a decision, it should have an understanding as to its freedom to act and the degree of its responsibility.

*Effective communication for idea production.* It is important to get the ideas of the group out in the open. Too often the group will seize on the first solution or suggestion to solve a problem, but too early evaluation of an idea can block effective decision-making. Such methods as brainstorming and encouraging the group not to associate ideas with people are often valuable.

*Appropriate size of group for decision-making.* If a group is too large for decision-making, it should use sub-groups in trying to reach a decision. A group often gets "bogged down" because of its size.

*A means of effective testing of different alternatives relative to the problem.* If a group is to effectively make a decision, it should have some means of getting data about the effects of the different alternatives it is considering. It is unfair to ask a group to make a decision without adequate data. It might be that a group needs to postpone making a decision until it can get additional data.

*A need for building commitment into the decision.* A group needs to realize that the reaching of a decision is only one step in a process which also involves implementation. There is a need to build into its planning some responsibility, and the delegation of it, for carrying out the indicated action. Frequently, failure to pin down responsibility renders a decision pointless and necessitates further meetings, with resultant frustration and apathy on the part of group members.

*Honest commitment of the manager or leader to the group decision-making process.* A leader should be essentially interested in the process and not in a predetermined idea or opinion of his own. This does not mean, however, that the leader, or any other status person, does not have the right to make a contribution, although for him to do so too early is a mistake. If the group members feel he has a particular solution, they will tend to react to it and not creatively introduce new ideas.

*A need for agreement on procedures and methods for decision-making prior to deliberation of the issues.* Issues which are particularly controversial, or likely to cause a "split" in the group, make decision-making a real problem. It is helpful to have the group spend some time at the beginning of the meeting to reach agreement on the methods and procedures it will use in reaching its decision. If it can agree on the criteria and standards it will use, it will have established the basis of agreement for later decision-making. It is advantageous for a group to take time to prepare itself so that it does not make a hasty decision before there is true readiness for group action.

**9. Teamwork requires trust and openness in communication and relationships.** An important dimension of effective team leadership is the ability to develop a trusting relationship among one's associates. Such a trust relationship will encourage open and frank communications. It will manifest a high tolerance for difference of opinions and personalities. Teamwork is manifested best when such behavior is common to all members of the group, including the leader.

**10. Teamwork is achieved when the group members have a strong sense of belonging to the group.** A degree of cohesiveness is needed for teamwork to be manifested. Such cohesiveness will be built upon commitment to the goals, commitment to the group, and respect for the members of the group. This sense of belonging is not just a matter of blind loyalty, but a sense of wanting to work with other members of the group in accomplishing goals which are meaningful to the individual member. It is not predicated on everyone's liking each other, a highly unlikely occurrence, but is a more mature level of respect and openness which emerges out of common commitment to the task and to working together to accomplish the goals.

It should be apparent from all that has been discussed so far that teamwork depends as much upon the behavior and contribution of each member as it does on the skill of the leader, but this is not to say that the leader is unimportant. The group supervisor or leader is an essential factor in effective group functioning and growth.

The question that now emerges is the ways in which such teamwork can be developed. One approach that this author has found valuable is to hold a team-building two or three day conference which focuses on both the task confronting the group and developing the interpersonal effectiveness of members of the team.

The problem-oriented conference discussed in this paper is an attempt to stimulate an organization climate which fosters both individual growth and team-building. In these extended weekend conferences the executives of a single organization participate throughout the learning experience. The principal method of these conferences has been the mutual identification and exploration of key group concerns and problems in the organization. The main goal has been organizational development by improved understanding of the process of problem-solving in teamwork situations.

The general goals are developed before the conference with the group-planning committee. Normally these purposes include the following:

... to develop further the management team;

... to identify and diagnose common concerns affecting the team;

... to explore some research-based principles on leadership and management applicable to the work of the team;

... to share ideas concerning improvement of the management team;

... to develop plans to follow-up the conference back on the job.

Advance preparations for the team-building conference is extensive. It will probably involve an internal or external organization development type of conduct. In this connection the many functions of the members of the planning committee are signally important. They assist the group and the consultants in general planning; they act as a special communication channel for the other participants and help interpret the conference and its purposes to them; and they work on evaluation procedures and follow-up plans.

Problem identification is a key pursuit, and this begins well before the conference. Interviews with individuals are conducted prior to the conference to secure perceptions and facts about the present functioning of the organization. An early task of the planning committee and the consultants is to examine major problem areas in the organization and to discuss methods most likely to stimulate a productive interchange at the conference. This process is continued on the first day of the conference when all the conferees, in small groups, develop a "problem census."

The value of developing this census is *not* in the list of topics. The value is in the probing process which produces many consequences other than the list itself, including a climate for the entire conference and a foundation which influences the ensuing process. Following the initial problem census, the resource consultants reappraise with the Planning Committee the tentative agenda.

As the foregoing indicates, a considerable emphasis in this team-building conference is placed on experience-centered and action-centered learning. Several assumptions underlie this emphasis. First, of course, is a recognition that the individual and collective resources of the conferees are very considerable. The process of the conference is designed to bring out these resources in a variety of ways. A second principle is the importance of peer learning. We can learn many things more readily from appropriate interactions with our associates than we can from the best of instruction by our superiors or by the experts. A third assumption is that organizational change and team-building is most likely to occur when managers, as a group, work at becoming more sensitive to the essential conditions and climate for organizational growth. This involves a mutual examination of the underlying nature of many team management problems, including the motivation of available human resources and the release of creativity within the organizational team. Most of the conference time is devoted to small group or total group sessions.

The group sessions are used for many purposes: for problem identification; for analysis of experience, for observation and other skill practice; for planning and problem-solving; and for experimentation with a range of methods which can be employed back in teamwork action in the organization. A continuing objective is to evoke a substantial number of "live incidents" which have appeared as "helps" or "hindrances" in accomplishing the team-building mission of the organization. These incidents take on personal meaning to the participants because of their part in identifying them. The consultants, by reference to similar or analogous situations, frequently bring in outside data. But the group "listens" within their organizational frame of reference.

With few exceptions, the small group activity received favorable mention in the open-ended evaluations I have collected at the end of prior conferences. In speaking of what he likes best, one participant wrote of the "use of small group sessions to initiate and discuss problems. Also the use of such group sessions to suggest solutions considered. Use of true-life situations in the organization."

It is important to note that some of the interactions in the small group were not all sweetness and light. Differences in experiences and perceptions will frequently lead to disagreement and occasionally to open conflict. The pace of the "digging" at times causes impatience and some yearning for a more structured process. Concerning the small group work, one participant wrote in his evaluation:

The small group discussions were the most difficult sessions of this conference. These discussions were not the least valuable, but certainly were the least pleasant of the conference . . . . At least a knowledge and awareness of our interaction in small groups is recognized.

A part of every manager's job, of course, is listening perceptively and patiently to observations he may think are *not* as well or as succinctly phrased as he would like or which are not in agreement with his own. One of the functions of the resource person is to help the conferees cope with the differences and frustrations which are part and parcel of this kind of learning experience. Thus, such "difficult" experiences offer great learning potential in these conferences.

Team-building can take place with the operating group examining its process in the work environment. These conferences I am now describing were held "off the job" to help the group initiate their team-building process.

The conference has certain characteristics common to all "off the job" meetings of managers. They spring from a conviction that occasionally there is real value in a common exodus from the usual work setting. This gets busy people away from the demands of daily operations, thus providing an atmosphere permitting concentration without interruption and deliberation without routine pressures.

Many of these kinds of conferences are held in a rural area at a facility which offers the necessary conference rooms and equipment, and which also provides opportunities for individual recreation and reflection.

The conferences discussed here have usually spanned a weekend beginning on a Thursday evening or Friday morning and continuing until Sunday afternoon. The conferees have usually included a top management team from the organization.

There are two other reasons why these executive team-building conferences have included a Saturday and Sunday. First, the cost to the organization has been reduced. Second, this has enabled the participants to contribute two days of their own time to a program that has important dimensions for individual growth as well as for organizational improvement.

The question of the amount of time and its best use is always a complex matter, but the almost unavoidable demands upon the top echelons of an organization are inescapable. If it is agreed that more time is required, then it might be well to conduct the conference in two stages, the first separated from the second by several weeks or more.

### Number of Participants for Team-Building Conferencing

How many participants should there be? What is the proper cut-off point? The answers to these questions depend upon the number of executives of the organization with direct and substantial influence in policy-making and decision-making work groups. The main object is to have a group which can function as peers concerned with major management problem-solving. Whether you wish to focus on building one group team or developing a number of teams will be a key factor in the number in attendance.

Final selection is usually made by the key leaders of the company, after consultation with a planning committee. A great deal does depend upon the organization's peculiarities.

### Participant Reaction to the Achievement of Conference Goals

Assuming proper goals, the ultimate criterion in evaluating a team-building program is the extent to which it achieved them. Although depth research would be preferable in measuring results, the fact is that the immediate post-program responses of the executives in such programs is usually relied upon in judging the success or failure of such an effort. The reliability of these reactions can be increased greatly if they include written questionnaires which are carefully phrased, open-ended, and anonymous.

### Improving Work Group Relations

The number of evaluations from previous conferences which specifically mentions work group relations makes it clear that this is a key important concern of top management people. One participant concluded:

I believe the greatest value to the organization to be the breaking down of barriers between individuals compartmentalized on a functional basis by reason of the informal and uninhibited manner in which the seminar was conducted and by removal of the conference to the pleasant and remote environment in which this course has been conducted.

Another wrote that the experience would help him "in securing greater cooperation from my staff and workers — in furnishing clear-cut goals and objectives for my organization." Others said, "I believe a more flexible approach to my everyday problems will result in benefit to the organization." The experience "brought people closely together in an atmosphere of thought expressions that cannot exist in every day-to-day work. Enabling a better understanding of people with whom one seldom comes in contact."

### Developing the Management Team

A common criticism of many management development programs is that management functions are treated as entities rather than as integral parts of the total management picture. In situational training of the kind discussed here, more emphasis is placed upon improved organizational performance than upon increasing individual competence. Several of the declared goals of the conferences speak to this point, and many of the participants direct a considerable part of their evaluations to the development of teamwork.

One previous participant said, "As a whole, these sessions have welded the primary staff into a better team. This will assist us in effecting our mission." Another felt one result would be "to secure a closer, more intimate knowledge of the areas where conflict and duplicating effort are now existing." One felt that the experience "should be of definite value in establishing an improved teamwork concept."

Several mentioned closer understanding of other team members as a valuable consequence of the joint learning endeavor: "A better understanding between each of us. Those who can learn together can work together." "We are now more of a unit. We have more knowledge of ourselves and our colleagues and of our roles."

Nothing in the evaluations suggests that the stresses of some of the interactions had a deleterious effect on teamwork. On the contrary, the respect of the participants for one another appears to have increased. In this vein one participant said: "I better understand the other members of our organization. Some bore out to a greater extent my past opinions of them while some completely surprised me (pleasantly, that is) when I got to know them better."

### Self-Insight

Each of the conference goals is keyed to organizational improvement. Still, the organization works only through its human resources, and these are individual persons. In the final analysis, the insightfulness of individual managers concerning themselves and the organization is what counts. It is striking, therefore, that so many of the assertions in the evaluations deal with different aspects of self-insight and self-improvement. Each of the following quotes is from the evaluation of a different participant in one of the team-building conferences:

"It (the seminar) has caused me to reflect on my own role and to take a look at my own shortcomings."

"It has served to cause me to know myself and others better. It has especially caused me to take a self-analysis of my own weakness and shortcomings."

"By opening your mind to self-analysis, you see yourself, faults in your personality that undoubtedly keep you from becoming as good a leader as you might become if you are willing to be flexible enough to change your tactics and approaches to cope with various problems and situations.

"It has awakened a determination for occasional self-evaluation."

## Planning Follow-up To the Team-Building

Developing plans to implement learning from the conference back on the job is discussed at any early meeting of the planning committee — and, of course, it is the principal topic for the wind-up session. The individual notebooks of each participant contain some pertinent literature and a bibliography as helpful resources for individual development after the conference. However, the evaluations show considerable concern for what is likely to happen in the organizational setting after the conference is over.

One participant wrote: "At follow-up sessions, which have already been planned, these team-building conferences, have indicated various weak areas where it is possible to help individuals to improve and develop themselves." Another stated that the conference "will cause some reassessment of past handling of problems. Probably result in broader views of problems, particularly in relationship to other divisions of the organization." Some wrote more generally: "The final results of this conference will be demonstrated in the months to come."

Others were less sanguine about the long-term result. In speaking of the value of the conference one wrote: "For awhile an attempt (will be made) to develop both individually and as a team. But without nurturing this may gradually die out." Still another showed a similar concern:

"This cannot be a 'one shot' affair as this type of conference is like a 'shot in the arm,' a rededication, an awakening, a realization that we begin to slip after some time. Having refresher opportunities would maintain the degree of enthusiasm and keep everyone stimulated."

Post conference slippage is a continuing concern of good managers, training directors, and organizational consultants, and no simple answers are available. Hopefully, these conferences are pointed in the right direction by focusing on organic organizational functioning. They are designed as a sequence of the on-going processes of the management group itself; their focus is on meanings which relate to everyday management and they endeavor to make follow-up an integral part of the goals of the learning experience.

The most valuable follow-up will be for the various temporary and permanent groups in the organization to build process analysis into their problem-solving activities.

## Prerequisites for a Successful Conference

It may be wasteful to attempt team-training of this kind unless there is genuine readiness for the learning experience within the organization itself. In this connection, I suggest that there are six basic requirements for a successful conference:

1. Recognition of a need for improvement in the processes of management teamwork.

2. Support for the program by the top executives in the company.

3. Sustained attention to advance planning and developing readiness.

4. Close collaboration with competent professional resource persons with experience in organization development either inside or outside the organization.

5. Willingness to give time and care to plan evaluation.

6. Commitment to "follow-up" as an integral part of the plan and program.

There are a variety of ways to begin the team-building process to enable people to function effectively in a matrix type of organization. Such skills could be required for the organization that is able to solve problems quickly, be adaptable, and optimize the human resources of the organization.

The approach reported in this paper is calculated to be a significant element in the total organizational development plan for an organization. It requires for success the real commitment of the key executives. No one activity or approach is adequate, but conferences such as these seem to be a helpful step in initiating action toward organizational improvement through executive team development.

### NOTES

1. Portions of this article are adapted from the author's book, *Organizational Renewal* (New York: Appleton-Century-Crofts, 1969, 107-113), and, by special permission from the American Society for Training and Development, from an article co-authored by Dr. G.L. Lippitt with Drexel Sprecher, Management development in the Federal Government, ASTD *Journal* (April 1964), 8-16.

2. Bennis, Warren G., and Philip E. Slater, *The Temporary Society*. New York: organizational change, *Journal of Applied Behavioral Science*, 1, No. 4 (1965), 357.

3. Bennis, Warren G., and Philip E. Slater, *The Temporary Society*. New York: Harper & Row, 1968, 127.

4. Schmidt, Warren H., The leader looks at the leadership dilemma, *Looking into Leadership Monographs*, Washington, D.C., Leadership Resources, Inc., 1961, 9.

5. Schein, Edgar H., *Organizational Psychology*. Englewood Cliffs, N.J.: Prentice-Hall, 1965, 72-73.

6. Lippitt, Gordon L., Improving decision-making with groups, *Y-Work With Youth* (a publication of the Program Services Dept., National Council of YMCA's), April 1958.

# ORGANIZATION DEVELOPMENT OBJECTIVES, ASSUMPTIONS AND STRATEGIES

*Wendell French*

Organization development refers to a long-range effort to improve an organization's problem solving capabilities and its ability to cope with changes in its external environment with the help of external or internal behavioral-scientist consultants, or change agents, as they are sometimes called. Such efforts are relatively new but are becoming increasingly visible within the United States, England, Japan, Holland, Norway, Sweden, and perhaps in other countries. A few of the growing number of organizations which have embarked on organization development (OD) efforts to some degree are Union Carbide, Esso, TRW Systems, Humble Oil, Weyerhaeuser, and Imperial Chemical Industries Limited. Other kinds of institutions, including public school systems, churches, and hospitals, have also become involved.

Organization development activities appear to have originated about 1957 as an attempt to apply some of the values and insights of laboratory training to total organizations. The late Douglas McGregor, working with Union Carbide, is considered to have been one of the first behavioral scientists to talk systematically about and to implement an organization development program.[1] Other names associated with such early efforts are Herbert Shepard and Robert Blake who, in collaboration with the Employee Relations Department of the Esso Company, launched a program of laboratory training (sensitivity training) in the company's various refineries. This program emerged in 1957 after a headquarters human relations research division began to view itself as an internal consulting group offering services to field managers rather than as a research group developing reports for top management.[2]

## OBJECTIVES OF TYPICAL OD PROGRAMS.

Although the specific interpersonal and task objectives of organization development programs will vary according to each diagnosis of organizational problems, a number of objectives typically emerge. These objectives reflect problems which are very common in organizations:

1. To increase the level of trust and support among organizational members.

2. To increase the incidence of confrontation of organizational problems, both within groups and among groups, in contrast to "sweeping problems under the rug."

3. To create an environment in which authority of assigned role is augmented by authority based on knowledge and skill.

4. To increase the openness of communications laterally, vertically, and diagonally.

5. To increase the level of personal enthusiasm and satisfaction in the organization.

6. To find synergistic solutions[3] to problems with greater frequency. (Synergistic solutions are creative solutions in which 2 + 2 equals more than 4, and through which all parties gain more through cooperation than through conflict.)

7. To increase the level of self and group responsibility in planning and implementation.[4]

### DIFFICULTIES IN CATEGORIZING.

Before describing some of the basic assumptions and strategies of organization development, it would be well to point out that one of the difficulties in writing about such a "movement" is that a wide variety of activities can be and are subsumed under this label. These activities have varied all the way from inappropriate application of some "canned" management development program to highly responsive and skillful joint efforts between behavioral scientists and client systems.

Thus, while labels are useful, they may gloss over a wide range of phenomena. The "human relations movement," for example, has been widely written about as though it were all bad or all good. To illustrate, some of the critics of the movement have accused it of being "soft" and a "hand-maiden of the Establishment," of ignoring the technical and power systems of organizations, and of being too naively participative. Such criticisms were no doubt warranted in some circumstances, but in other situations may not have been at all appropriate. Paradoxically, some of the major insights of the human relations movement, e.g., that the organization can be viewed as a social system and that subordinates have substantial control over productivity have been assimilated by its critics.

In short, the problem is to distinguish between appropriate and inappropriate programs, between effectiveness and ineffectiveness, and between relevancy and irrelevancy. The discussion which follows will attempt to describe the "ideal" circumstances for organization development programs, as well as to point out some pitfalls and common mistakes in organization change efforts.

### RELEVANCY TO DIFFERENT TECHNOLOGIES AND ORGANIZATION SUBUNITS

Research by Joan Woodward[5] suggests that organization development efforts *might be more relevant to certain kinds of technologies and organizational levels, and perhaps to certain workforce characteristics, than to others.* For example, OD efforts may be more appropriate for an organization devoted to prototype manufacturing than for an automobile assembly plant. However, experiments in an organization like Texas

Instruments suggest that some manufacturing efforts which appear to be inherently mechanistic may lend themselves to a more participative, open management style than is often assumed possible.[6]

However, assuming the constraints of a fairly narrow job structure at the rank-and-file level, organization development efforts may inherently be more productive and relevant at the managerial levels of the organization. Certainly OD efforts are most effective when they start at the top. Research and development units—particularly those involving a high degree of interdependency and joint creativity among group members—also appear to be appropriate for organization development activities, if group members are currently experiencing problems in communicating or interpersonal relationships.

## BASIC ASSUMPTIONS

Some of the basic assumptions about people which underlie organization development programs are similar to "Theory Y" assumptions[7] and will be repeated only briefly here. However, some of the assumptions about groups and total systems will be treated more extensively. The following assumptions appear to underlie organization development efforts.[8]

### About People

Most individuals have drives toward personal growth and development, and these are most likely to be actualized in an environment which is both supportive and challenging.

Most people desire to make, and are capable of making, a much higher level of contribution to the attainment of organization goals than most organizational environments will permit.

### About People in Groups

Most people wish to be accepted and to interact cooperatively with at least one small reference group, and usually with more than one group, e.g., the work group, the family group.

One of the most psychologically relevant reference groups for most people is the work group, including peers and the superior.

Most people are capable of greatly increasing their effectiveness in helping their reference groups solve problems and in working effectively together.

For a group to optimize its effectiveness, the formal leader cannot perform all of the leadership functions in all circumstances at all times, and all group members must assist each other with effective leadership and member behavior.

**About People in Organizational Systems**

Organizations tend to be characterized by overlapping, interdependent work groups, and the "linking pin" function of supervisors and others needs to be understood and facilitated.[9]

What happens in the broader organization affects the small work group and vice versa.

What happens to one subsystem (social, technological, or administrative) will affect and be influenced by other parts of the system.

The culture in most organizations tends to suppress the expression of feelings which people have about each other and about where they and their organizations are heading.

Suppressed feelings adversely affect problem solving, personal growth, and job satisfaction.

The level of interpersonal trust, support, and cooperation is much lower in most organizations than is either necessary or desirable.

"Win-lose" strategies between people and groups, while realistic and appropriate in some situations, are not optimal in the long run to the solution of most organizational problems.

Synergistic solutions can be achieved with a much higher frequency than is actually the case in most organizations.

Viewing feelings as data important to the organization tends to open up many avenues for improved goal setting, leadership, communications, problem solving, intergroup collaboration, and morale.

Improved performance stemming from organization development efforts needs to be sustained by appropriate changes in the appraisal, compensation, training, staffing, and task-specialization subsystem—in short, in the total personnel system.

## VALUE AND BELIEF SYSTEMS OF BEHAVIORAL SCIENTIST-CHANGE AGENTS

While scientific inquiry, ideally, is value-free, the applications of science are not value-free. Applied behavioral scientist-organization development consultants tend to subscribe to a comparable set of values, although we should avoid the trap of assuming that they constitute a completely homogeneous group. They do not.

One value, to which many behavioral scientist-change agents tend to give high priority, is that the needs and aspirations of human beings are the reasons for organized effort in society. They tend, therefore, to be developmental in their outlook and concerned with the long-range opportunities for the personal growth of people in organizations.

A second value is that work and life can become richer and more meaningful, and organized effort more effective and enjoyable, if feelings and sentiments are permitted to be a more legitimate part of the culture. A third value is a commitment to an action role, along with a commitment to research, in an effort to improve the effectiveness of organizations.[10] A fourth value—or perhaps a belief—is that improved competency in interpersonal and intergroup relationship will result in more effective organizations.[11] A fifth value is that behavioral science research and an examination of behavioral science assumptions and values are relevant and important in considering organizational effectiveness. While many change agents are perhaps overly action-oriented in terms of the utilization of their time, nevertheless, as a group they are paying more and more attention to research and to the examination of ideas.[12]

The value placed on research and inquiry raises the question as to whether the assumptions stated earlier are values, theory, or "facts." In my judgment, a substantial body of knowledge, including research on leadership, suggests that there is considerable evidence for these assumptions. However, to conclude that these assumptions are facts, laws, or principles would be to contradict the value placed by behavioral scientists on continuous research and inquiry. Thus, I feel that they should be considered theoretical statements which are based on provisional data.

This also raises the paradox that the belief that people are important tends to result in their being important. The belief that people can grow and develop in terms of personal and organizational competency tends to produce this result. Thus, values and beliefs tend to be self-fulfilling, and the question becomes "What do you choose to want to believe?" While this position can become Pollyannaish in the sense of not seeing the real world, nevertheless, behavioral scientist-change agents, at least this one, tend to place a value on optimism. It is a kind of optimism that says people can do a better job of goal setting and facing up to and solving problems, not an optimism that says the number of problems is diminishing.

It should be added that it is important that the values and beliefs of each behavioral science-change agent to be made visible both to himself and to the client. In the first place, neither can learn to adequately trust the other without such exposure—a hidden agenda handicaps both trust building and mutual learning. Second, and perhaps more pragmatically, organizational change efforts tend to fail if a prescription is applied unilaterally and without proper diagnosis.

## STRATEGY IN ORGANIZATION DEVELOPMENT: AN ACTION RESEARCH MODEL

A frequent strategy in organization development programs is based on what behavioral scientists refer to as an "action research model." This model involves extensive collaboration between the consultant (whether an external or an internal change agent) and the client group, data gathering, data discussion, and planning. While descriptions of this model vary in detail and terminology from author to author, the dynamics are essentially the same.[13]

Figure 1 summarizes some of the essential phases of the action research model, using an emerging organization development program as an example. The key aspects of the model are *diagnosis, data gathering, feedback to the client group, data*

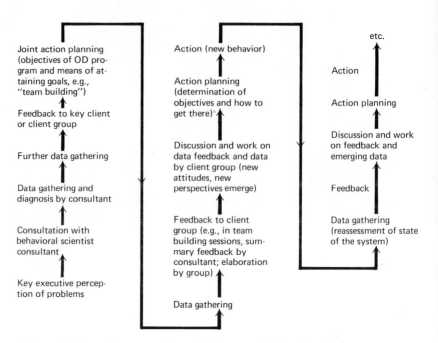

**Figure 1.**  An action research model for organization development

*discussion and work by the client group, action planning, and action.* The sequence tends to be cyclical, with the focus on new or advanced problems as the client group learns to work more effectively together. Action research should also be considered a process, since, as William Foote Whyte says, it involves "... a continuous gathering and analysis of human relations research data and the feeding of the findings into the organization in such a manner as to change behavior."[14] (Feedback we will define as nonjudgmental observations of behavior.)

Ideally, initial objectives and strategies of organization development efforts stem from a careful *diagnosis* of such matters as interpersonal and intergroup problems, decision-making processes, and communication flow which are currently being experienced by the client organization. As a preliminary step, the behavioral scientist and the key client (the president of a company, the vice president in charge of a division, the works manager or superintendent of a plant, a superintendent of schools, etc.), will make a joint initial assessment of the critical problems which need working on. Subordinates may also be interviewed in order to provide supplemental data. The diagnosis may very well indicate that the central problem is technological or that the key client is not at all willing or ready to examine the organization's problem-solving ability or his own managerial behavior.[15] Either could be a reason for postponing or moving slowly in the direction of organization development activities, although the technological problem may easily be related to deficiencies in interpersonal relation-

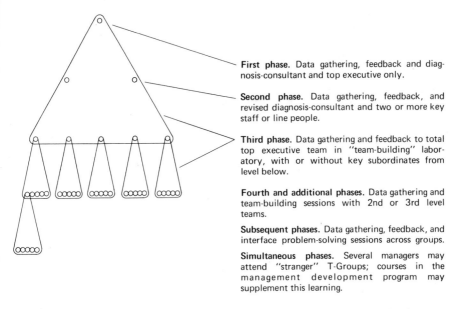

**First phase.** Data gathering, feedback and diagnosis-consultant and top executive only.

**Second phase.** Data gathering, feedback, and revised diagnosis-consultant and two or more key staff or line people.

**Third phase.** Data gathering and feedback to total top executive team in "team-building" laboratory, with or without key subordinates from level below.

**Fourth and additional phases.** Data gathering and team-building sessions with 2nd or 3rd level teams.

**Subsequent phases.** Data gathering, feedback, and interface problem-solving sessions across groups.

**Simultaneous phases.** Several managers may attend "stranger" T-Groups; courses in the management development program may supplement this learning.

**Figure 2.**   Organization development phases in a hypothetical organization

ships or decision making. The diagnosis might also indicate the desirability of one or more additional specialists (in engineering, finance, or electronic data processing, for example) to simultaneously work with the organization.

This initial diagnosis, which focuses on the expressed needs of the client, is extremely critical. As discussed earlier, in the absence of a skilled diagnosis, the behavioral scientist/change agent would be imposing a set of assumptions and a set of objectives which may be hopelessly out of joint with either the current problems of the people in the organization or their willingness to learn new modes of behavior. In this regard, it is extremely important that the consultant *hear and understand* what the client is trying to tell him. This requires a high order of skill.[16]

Interviews are frequently used for *data gathering* in OD work for both initial diagnosis and subsequent planning sessions, since personal contact is important for building a cooperative relationship between the consultant and the client group. The interview is also important since the behavioral scientist-consultant is interested in spontaneity and in feelings that are expressed as well as cognitive matters. However, questionnaires are sometimes successfully used in the context of what is sometimes referred to as survey feedback, to supplement interview data.[17]

Data gathering typically goes through several phases. The first phase is related to diagnosing the state of the system and to making plans for organizational change. This phase may utilize a series of interviews between the consultant and the key client, or between a few key executives and the consultant. Subsequent phases focus on problems specific to the top executive team and to subordinate teams. (See Fig. 2.)

Typical questions in data gathering or "problem sensing" would include: What problems do you see in your group, including problems between people, that are interfering with getting the job done the way you would like to see it done?; and what problems do you see in the broader organization? Such open-ended questions provide wide latitude on the part of the respondents and encourage a reporting of problems *as the individual sees them*. Such interviewing is usually conducted privately, with a commitment on the part of the consultant that the information will be used in such a way as to avoid unduly embarrassing anyone. The intent is to find out what common problems or themes emerge, with the data to be used constructively for both diagnostic and feedback purposes.

Two- or three-day offsite *team-building or group problem-solving sessions* typically become a major focal point in organization development programs. During these meetings the behavioral scientist frequently provides *feedback* to the group in terms of the themes which emerged in the problem-sensing interviews.[18] He may also encourage the group to determine which items or themes should have priority in terms of maximum utilization of time. These themes usually provide substantial and meaningful data for the group to begin work on. One-to-one interpersonal matters, both positive and negative, tend to emerge spontaneously as the participants gain confidence from the level of support sensed in the group.

Different consultants will vary in their mode of behavior in such sessions, but will typically serve as *"process" observers and as interpreters of the dynamics of the group interaction* to the degree that the group expresses a readiness for such intervention. They also typically encourage people to take risks, a step at a time, and to experiment with new behavior in the context of the level of support in the group. Thus, the trainer-consultant(s) serves as a stimulant to new behavior but also as a protector. The climate which I try to build, for example, is: "Let's not tear down any more than we can build back together."[19] Further, the trainer-consultant typically works with the group to assist team members in improving their skills in diagnosing and facilitating group progress.[20]

It should be noted, however, that different groups will have different needs along a task-process continuum. For example, some groups have a need for intensive work on clarifying objectives; others may have the greatest need in the area of personal relationships. Further, the consultant or the chief consultant in a team of consultants involved in an organization development program will play a much broader role than serving as a T-group or team-building trainer. He will also play an important role in periodic data gathering and diagnosis and in joint long-range planning of the change efforts.[21]

## LABORATORY TRAINING AND ORGANIZATION DEVELOPMENT

Since organization development programs have largely emerged from T-group experience, theory, and research, and since laboratory training in one form or another tends to be an integral part of most such programs, it is important to focus on laboratory training per se. As stated earlier, OD programs grew out of a perceived need to relate laboratory training to the problems of ongoing organizations and a recognition that optimum results could only occur if major parts of the total social system of an organization were involved.

Laboratory training essentially emerged around 1946, largely through a growing recognition by Leland Bradford, Ronald Lippitt, Kenneth Benne, and others, that human relations training which focused on the feelings and concerns of the participants was frequently a much more powerful and viable form of education than the lecture method. Some of the theoretical constructs and insights from which these laboratory training pioneers drew stemmed from earlier research by Lippitt, Kurt Lewin, and Ralph White. The term "T-Group" emerged by 1949 as a shortened label for "Basic Skill Training Group"; these terms were used to identify the programs which began to emerge in the newly formed National Training Laboratory in Group Development (now NTL Institute for Applied Behavioral Science).[22] "Sensitivity Training" is also a term frequently applied to such training.

Ordinarily, laboratory training sessions have certain objectives in common. The following list, by two internationally known behavioral scientists,[23] is probably highly consistent with the objectives of most programs:

## Self Objectives

Increased *awareness* of own feelings and reactions, and own impact on others.

Increased *awareness* of feelings and reactions of others, and their impact on self.

Increased *awareness* of dynamics of group action.

*Changed attitudes* toward self, others, and groups, i.e., more respect for, tolerance for, and faith in self, others, and groups.

Increased *interpersonal competence*, i.e., skill in handling interpersonal and group relationships toward more productive and satisfying relationships.

## Role Objectives

Increased *awarness* of own organizational role, organizational dynamics, dynamics of larger social systems, and dynamics of the change process in self, small groups, and organizations.

*Changed attitudes* toward own role, role of others, and organizational relationships, i.e., more respect for and willingness to deal with others with whom one is interdependent, greater willingness to achieve collaborative relationships with others based on mutual trust.

Increased *interpersonal competence* in handling organizational role relationships with superiors, peers, and subordinates.

## Organizational Objectives

Increased *awareness* of, *changed attitudes* toward, and increased *interpersonal competence* about specific organizational problems existing in groups or units which are interdependent.

*Organizational improvement* through the training of relationships or groups rather than isolated individuals.

Over the years, experimentation with different laboratory designs has led to diverse criteria for the selection of laboratory participants. Probably a majority of NTL-IABS human relations laboratories are "stranger groups," i.e., involving participants who come from different organizations and who are not likely to have met earlier. However, as indicated by the organizational objectives above, the incidence of special labs designed to increase the effectiveness of persons already working together appears to be growing. Thus terms like "cousin labs," i.e., labs involving people from the same organization but not the same subunit, and "family labs" or "team-building" sessions, i.e., involving a manager and all of his subordinates, are becoming familiar. Participants in labs designed for organizational members not of the same unit may be selected from the same rank level ("horizontal slice") or selected so as to constitute a heterogeneous grouping by rank ("diagonal slice"). Further, NTL-IABS is now encouraging at least two members from the same organization to attend NTL Management Work Conferences and Key Executive Conferences in order to maximize the impact of the learning in the back-home situation.[24]

In general, experienced trainers recommend that persons with severe emotional illness should not participate in laboratory training, with the exception of programs designed specifically for group therapy. Designers of programs make the assumptions, as Argyris states them,[25] that T-Group participants should have:

1. A relatively strong ego that is not overwhelmed by internal conflicts.

2. Defenses which are sufficiently low to allow the individual to hear what others say to him.

3. The ability to communicate thought and feelings with minimal distortion.

As a result of such screening, the incidence of breakdown during laboratory training is substantially less than that reported for organizations in general.[26] However, since the borderline between "normalcy" and illness is very indistinct, most professionally trained staff members are equipped to diagnose severe problems and to make referrals to psychiatrists and clinical psychologists when appropriate. Further, most are equipped to give adequate support and protection to participants whose ability to assimilate and learn from feedback is low. In addition, group members in T-Group situations tend to be sensitive to the emotional needs of the members and to be supportive when they sense a person experiencing pain. Such support is explicitly fostered in laboratory training.

The duration of laboratory training programs varies widely. "Micro-Labs," designed to give people a brief experience with sensitivity training, may last only one hour. Some labs are designed for a long weekend. Typically, however, basic human relations labs are of two weeks duration, with participants expected to meet mornings, afternoons, and evenings, with some time off for recreation. While NTL Management Work Conferences for middle managers and Key Executive Conferences run for one week, team-building labs, from my experience, typically are about three days in length. However, the latter are usually only a part of a broader organization development program involving problem sensing and diagnosis, and the planning of action steps and subsequent sessions. In addition, attendance at stranger labs for key managers is frequently a part of the total organization development effort.

Sensitivity training sessions typically start with the trainer making a few comments about his role—that he is there to be of help, that the group will have control of the agenda, that he will deliberately avoid a leadership role, but that he might become involved as both a leader and a member from time to time, etc. The following is an example of what the trainer might say:

This group will meet for many hours and will serve as a kind of laboratory where each individual can increase his understanding of the forces which influence individual behavior and the performance of groups and organizations. The data for learning will be our own behavior, feelings, and reactions. We begin with no definite structure or organization, no agreed-upon procedures, and no specific agenda. It will be up to us to fill the vacuum created by the lack of these familiar elements and to study our group as we evolve. My role will be to help the group to learn from its own experience, but not to act as a traditional chairman nor to suggest how we should organize, what our procedure should be, or exactly what our agenda will include. With these few comments, I think we are ready to begin in whatever way you feel will be most helpful.[27]

The trainer then lapses into silence. Group discomfort then precipitates a dialogue which, with skilled trainer assistance, is typically an intense but generally highly rewarding experience for group members. What goes on in the group becomes the data for the learning experience.

Interventions by the trainer will vary greatly depending upon the purpose of the lab and the state of learning on the part of the participants. A common intervention, however, is to encourage people to focus on and own up to their own feelings about what is going on in the group, rather than to make judgments about others. In this way, the participants begin to have more insight into their own feelings and to understand how their behavior affects the feelings of others.

While T-Group work tends to be the focal point in human relations laboratories, laboratory training typically includes theory sessions and frequently includes exercises such as role playing or management games.[28] Further, family labs of subunits of organizations will ordinarily devote more time to planning action steps for back on the job than will stranger labs.

Robert J. House has carefully reviewed the research literature on the impact of T-Group training and has concluded that the research shows mixed results. In particular, research on changes as reflected in personality inventories is seen as inconclusive. However, studies which examine the behavior of participants upon returning to the job are generally more positive.[29] House cites six studies, all of which utilized control groups, and concludes:

All six studies revealed what appear to be important positive effects of T-Group training. Two of the studies report negative effects as well ... all of the evidence is based on observations of the behavior of the participants in the actual job situations. No reliance is placed on participant response; rather, evidence is collected from those having frequent contact with the participant in his normal work activities.[30]

John P. Campbell and Marvin D. Dunnette,[31] on the other hand, while conceding that the research shows that T-Group training produces *changes in behavior*, point out that the usefulness of such training in terms of *job performance* has yet to be demonstrated. They urge research toward "forging the link between training-induced behavior changes and changes in job-performance effectiveness."[32] As a summary comment, they state:

... the assumption that T-Group training has positive utility for organizations must necessarily rest on shaky ground. It has been neither confirmed nor disconfirmed. The authors wish to emphasize ... that utility for the organization is not necessarily the same as utility for the individual.[33]

At least two major reasons may account for the inconclusiveness of research on the impact of T-Group training on job performance. One reason is simply that little research has been done. The other reason may center around a factor of cultural isolation. To oversimplify, a major part of what one learns in laboratory training, in my opinion, is how to work more effectively with others in group situations, *particularly with others who have developed comparable skills.* Unfortunately, most participants return from T-Group experiences to environments including colleagues and superiors who have not had the same affective (emotional, feeling) experiences, who are not familiar with the terminology and underlying theory, and who may have anxieties (usually unwarranted) about what might happen to them in a T-Group situation.

This cultural distance which laboratory training can produce is one of the reasons why many behavioral scientists are currently encouraging more than one person from the same organization to undergo T-Group training and, ideally, *all* of the members of a team and their superior to participate in some kind of laboratory training together. The latter assumes that a diagnosis of the organization indicates that the group is ready for such training and assumes such training is reasonably compatible with the broader culture of the total system.

## CONDITIONS AND TECHNIQUES FOR SUCCESSFUL ORGANIZATION DEVELOPMENT PROGRAMS

Theory, research, and experience to date suggest to me that *successful* OD programs tend to evolve in the following way and that they have some of these characteristics (these statements should be considered highly tentative, however):

• There is strong pressure for improvement from both outside the organization and from within.[34]

• An outside behavioral scientist-consultant is brought in for consultation with the top executives and to diagnose organization problems.

• A preliminary diagnosis suggests that organization development efforts, designed in response to the expressed needs of the key executives, are warranted.

• A collaborative decision is made between the key client group and the consultant to try to change the culture of the organization, at least at the top initially. The specific goals may be to improve communications, to secure more effective participation from subordinates in problem solving, and to move in the direction of more openness, more feedback, and more support. In short, a decision is made to change the culture to help the company meet its organizational goals and to provide better avenues for initiative, creativity, and self-actualization on the part of organization members.

• Two or more top executives, including the chief executive, go to laboratory training sessions. (Frequently, attendance at labs is one of the facts which precipitates interest in bringing in the outside consultant.)

• Attendance in T-Group program is voluntary. While it is difficult to draw a line between persuasion and coercion, OD consultants and top management should be aware of the dysfunctional consequences of coercion (see the comments on authentic behavior below). While a major emphasis is on team-building laboratories, stranger labs are utilized both to supplement the training going on in the organization and to train managers new to the organization or those who are newly promoted.

• Team-building sessions are held with the top executive group (or at the highest point where the program is started). Ideally, the program is started at the top of the organization, but it can start at levels below the president as long as there is significant support from the chief executive, and preferably from other members of the top power structure as well.

• In a firm large enough to have a personnel executive, the personnel-industrial relations vice president becomes heavily involved at the outset.

• One of two organizational forms emerges to coordinate organization development efforts, either (a) a coordinator reporting to the personnel executive (the personnel executive himself may fill this role), or (b) a coordinator reporting to the chief executive. The management development director is frequently in an ideal position to coordinate OD activities with other management development activities.

• Ultimately, it is essential that the personnel-industrial relations group, including people in salary administration, be an integral part of the organization development program. Since OD groups have such potential for acting as catalysts in rapid organizational change, the temptation is great to see themselves as "good guys" and the other personnel people as "bad guys" or simply ineffective. Any conflicts between a separate organization development group and the personnel and industrial relations groups should be faced and resolved. Such tensions can be the "Achilles heel" for either program. In particular, however, the change agents in the organization development program need the support of the other people who are heavily involved in human resources administration and vice versa; what is done in the OD program needs to be compatible with what is done in selection, promotion, salary administration, appraisal, and vice versa. In terms of systems theory, it would seem imperative that one aspect of the human resources function such as any organization development program must be highly interdependent with the other human resources activities including selection, salary administration, etc. (TRW Systems is an example of an organization which involves top executives plus making the total personnel and industrial relations group an integral part of the OD program.[35])

• Team-building labs, at the request of the various respective executives, with laboratory designs based on careful data gathering and problem diagnosis, are conducted at successively lower levels of the organization with the help of outside consultants, plus the help of internal consultants whose expertise is gradually developed.

• Ideally, as the program matures, both members of the personnel staff and a few line executives are trained to do some organization development work in conjunction with the external and internal professionally trained behavioral scientists. In a sense, then, the external change agent tries to work himself out of a job by developing internal resources.

• The outside consultant(s) and the internal coordinator work very carefully together and periodically check on fears, threats, and anxieties which may be developing as the effort progresses. Issues need to be confronted as they emerge. Not only is the outside change agent needed for his skills, but the organization will need someone to act as a "governor"—to keep the program focused on real problems and to urge authenticity in contrast to gamesmanship. The danger always exists that the organization will begin to punish or reward involvement in T-Group kinds of activities per se, rather than focus on performance.

• The OD consultants constantly work on their own effectiveness in interpersonal relationships and their diagnostic skills so they are not in a position of "do as I say, but not as I do." Further, both consultant and client work together to optimize the consultant's knowledge of the organization's unique and evolving culture structure, and web of interpersonal relationships.

• There needs to be continuous audit of the results, both in terms of checking on the evolution of attitudes about what is going on and in terms of the extent to which problems which were identified at the outset by the key clients are being solved through the program.

• As implied above, the reward system and other personnel systems need to be readjusted to accommodate emerging changes in performance in the organization. Substantially improved performance on the part of individuals and groups is not likely to be sustained if financial and promotional rewards are not forthcoming. In short, management needs to have a "systems" point of view and to think through the interrelationships of the OD effort with the reward and staffing systems and the other aspects of the total human resources subsystem.

In the last analysis, the president and the "line" executives of the organization will evaluate the success of the OD effort in terms of the extent to which it assists the organization in meeting its human and economic objectives. For example, marked improvements on various indices from one plant, one division, one department, etc., will be important indicators of program success. While human resources administration indices are not yet perfected, some of the measuring devices being developed by Likert, Mann, and others show some promise.[36]

## SUMMARY COMMENTS

Organization development efforts have emerged through attempts to apply laboratory training values and assumptions to total systems. Such efforts are organic in the sense that they emerge from and are guided by the problems being experienced by the people in the organization. The key to their viability (in contrast to becoming a passing fad) lies in an authentic focus on problems and concerns of the members of the organization and in their confrontation of issues and problems.

Organization development is based on assumptions and values similar to "Theory Y" assumptions and values but includes additional assumptions about total systems and the nature of the client-consultant relationship. Intervention strategies of the behavioral scientist/change agent tend to be based on an action-research model and tend to be focused more on helping the people in an organization learn to solve problems rather than on prescriptions of how things should be done differently.

Laboratory training (or "sensitivity training") or modifications of T-group seminars typically are a part of the organizational change efforts, but the extent and format of such training will depend upon the evolving needs of the organization.

Team-building seminars involving a superior and subordinates are being utilized more and more as a way of changing social systems rapidly and avoiding the cultural-distance problems which frequently emerge when individuals return from stranger labs. However, stranger labs can play a key role in change efforts when they are used as part of a broader organization development effort.

Research has indicated that sensitivity training generally produces positive results in terms of changed behavior on the job, but has not demonstrated the link between behavior changes and improved performance. Maximum benefits are probably derived from laboratory training when the organizational culture supports and reinforces the use of new skills in ongoing team situations.

Successful organization development efforts require skillful behavioral scientist interventions, a systems view, and top management support and involvement. In addition, changes stemming from organization development must be linked to changes in the total personnel subsystem. The viability of organization development efforts lies in the degree to which they accurately reflect the aspirations and concerns of the participating members.

In conclusion, *successful organization development tends to be a total system effort; a process of planned change–not a program with a temporary quality; and aimed at developing the organization's internal resources for effective change in the future.*

### NOTES

1. Beckhard, Richard, W. Warner Burke, and Fred I. Steele, The program for specialists in organization training and development (mimeographed), NTL Institute for Applied Behavioral Science, Dec. 1967, ii; and Jones, John Paul, What's wrong with work? in *What's Wrong with Work?* New York: National Association of Manufacturers, 1967, 8. For a history of NTL Institute for Applied Behavioral Science, with which Douglas McGregor was long associated in addition to his professorial appointment at M.I.T. and which has been a major factor in the history of organization development, see Bradford, Leland P., Biography of an institution, *Journal of Applied Behavioral Science,* III:2 (1967), 127-143. While we will use the word "program" from time to time, ideally organization development is a "process," not just another new program of temporary quality.

2. Kolb, Harry D., Introduction to *An Action Research Program for Organization Improvement.* Ann Arbor: Foundation for Research in Human Behavior, 1960, i.

3. Cattell defines synergy as "the sum total of the energy which a group can command." Katz, Daniel, and Robert L. Kahn, *The Social Psychology of Organizations.* New York: Wiley, 1966, 33.

4. For a similar statement of objectives, see What is OD? NTL Institute: *News and Reports from NTL Institute for Applied Behavioral Science,* 2 (June 1968), 1-2.

Whether OD programs increase the overall level of authority in contrast to redistributing authority is a debatable point. My hypothesis is that both a redistribution and an overall increase occur.

5. Woodward, Joan, *Industrial Organization: Theory and Practice.* London: Oxford University Press, 1965.

6. See Myers, M. Scott, Every employee a manager, *California Management Review,* **10** (Spring 1968), 9-20.

7. See McGregor, Douglas, *The Human Side of Enterprise.* New York: McGraw-Hill, 1960, 47-48.

8. In addition to influence from the writings of McGregor, Likert, Argyris, and others, this discussion has been influenced by "Some assumptions about change in organizations," in notebook *Program for Specialists in Organization Training and Development,* NTL Institute for Applied Behavioral Science, 1967, and by staff members who participated in that program.

9. For a discussion of the "linking pin" concept, see Likert, Rensis, *New Patterns of Management.* New York: McGraw-Hill, 1961.

10. Warren G. Bennis sees three major approaches to planned organization change, with the behavioral scientists associated with each all having "a deep concern with applying social science knowledge to create more viable social systems; a commitment to action, as well as to research . . . and a belief that improved interpersonal and group relationships will ultimately lead to better organizational performance." Bennis, Warren G., A new role for the behavioral sciences: effecting organizational change, *Administrative Science Quarterly,* **8** (Sept. 1963), 157-158; and Herbert A. Shepard, An action research model, in *An Action Research Program for Organization Improvement,* 31-35.

11. Bennis, A new role for the behavioral sciences, 158.

12. For a discussion of some of the problems and dilemmas in behavioral science research, see Argyris, Chris, Creating effective relationships in organizations, in Adams, Richard N., and Jack J. Preiss (eds.), *Human Organization Research.* Homewood, Ill.: The Dorsey Press, 1960, 109-123; and Benedict, Barbara A., *et al.,* The clinical experimental approach to assessing organizational change efforts, *Journal of Applied Behavioral Science* (Nov. 1967), 347-380.

13. For further discussion of action research, see Schein, Edgar H., and Warren G. Bennis, *Personal and Organizational Change Through Group Methods.* New York: Wiley, 1966, 272-274.

14. Whyte, William Foote, and Edith Lentz Hamilton, *Action Research for Management.* Homewood, Ill.: Richard D. Irwin, 1964, 2.

15. Jeremiah J. O'Connell appropriately challenges the notion that there is "one best way" of organizational change and stresses that the consultant should choose his role and intervention strategies on the basis of "the conditions existing when he enters the client system" in *Managing Organizational Innovation.* Homewood, Ill.: Richard D. Irwin, 1968, 10-11.

16. For further discussion of organization diagnosis, see Beckhard, Richard, An organization improvement program in a decentralized organization, *Journal of Applied Behavioral Science*, 2 (Jan.-March 1966), 3-4; OD as a process in *What's Wrong with Work?*, 12-13.

17. For example, see Mann, Floyd C., Studying and creating change, in Costello, Timothy W., and Sheldon S. Zalkind (eds.), *Psychology in Administration—A Research Orientation*. Englewood Cliffs, N.J.: Prentice-Hall, 1963, 321-324. See also Miller, Delbert C., Using behavioral science to solve organization problems, *Personnel Administration*, 31 (Jan.-Feb. 1968), 21-29.

18. For a description of feedback procedures used by the Survey Research Center, Univ. of Michigan, see Mann and Likert, The need for research on the communication of research results, in *Human Organization Research*, 57-66.

19. This phrase probably came from a management workshop sponsored by NTL Institute for Applied Behavioral Science.

20. For a description of what goes on in team-building sessions, see Beckhard, An organizational improvement program, 9-13; and Margulies, Newton, and Anthony P. Raia, People in organizations—a case for team training, *Training and Development Journal*, 22 (August 1968), 2-11. For a description of problem-solving sessions involving the total management group (about 70) of a company, see Beckhard, The confrontation meeting, *Harvard Business Review*, 45 (March-April 1967), 149-155.

21. For a description of actual organization development programs, see Buchanan, Paul C., Innovative organizations—a study in organization development, in *Applying Behavioral Science Research in Industry*. New York: Industrial Relations Counselors, 1964, 87-107; Davis, Sheldon A., An organic problem-solving method of organizational change, *Journal of Applied Behavioral Science*, III:1 (1967), 3-21; Sofer, Cyril, *The Organization from Within*. Chicago: Quadrangle Books, 1961; Marrow, Alfred J., David G. Bowers, and Stanley E. Seashore, *Management by Participation*. New York: Harper and Row, 1967; Blake, Robert R., Jane S. Mouton, Louis B. Barnes, and Larry E. Greiner, Breakthrough in organization development, *Harvard Business Review*, 42 (Nov.-Dec. 1964), 133-155; Bartlett, Alton C., Changing behavior as a means to increased efficiency, *Journal of Applied Behavioral Science*, III:3 (1967), 381-403; Greiner, Larry E., Antecedents of planned organization change, *ibid.*, III:1 (1967), 51-85; and Blake, Robert R., and Jane Mouton, *Corporate Excellence Through Grid Organization Development*. Houston, Texas: Gulf Publishing Company, 1968.

22. From Bradford, Biography of an institution. See also Benne, Kenneth D., History of the T-group in the laboratory setting, in Bradford, Jack R. Gibb, and Benne (eds.), *T/Group Theory and Laboratory Method*. New York: Wiley, 1964, 80-135.

23. Schein and Bennis, 37.

24. For further discussion of group composition in laboratory training, see Schein and Bennis, 63-69. NTL-LABS now include the Center for Organization Studies,

the Center for the Development of Educational Leadership, the Center for Community Affairs, and the Center for International Training to serve a wide range of client populations and groups.

25. Argyris, Chris, T-Groups for organizational effectiveness, *Harvard Business Review*, **42** (March-April 1964), 60-74.

26. Based on discussions with NTL staff members. One estimate is that the incidence of "serious stress and mental disturbance" during laboratory training is less than one percent of participants and in almost all cases occurs in persons with a history of prior disturbance. See Seashore, Charles, What is sensitivity training, *NTL Institute News and Reports*, **2** (April 1968), 2.

27. *Ibid.*, 1.

28. For a description of what goes on in T-groups, see Schein and Bennis, 10-27; Bradford, Gibb, and Benne, 57-67; Whitaker, Dorothy S., A case study of a t-group, in Whitaker, Galvin (ed.), *T-Group Training: Group Dynamics in Management Education*. (A.T.M. Occasional Papers) Oxford: Basil Blackwell, 1965, 14-22; Weschler, Irving R., and Jerome Reisel, *Inside a Sensitivity Training Group*. Berkeley: University of California, Institute of Industrial Relations, 1959; and Glueck, William F., Reflections on a t-group experience, *Personnel Journal*, **47** (July 1968), 501-504. For use of cases or exercises based on research results ("instrumented training") see Blake, Robert R., and Jane S. Mouton, The instrumented training laboratory, in Weschler, Irving R., and Edgar H. Schein (eds.), *Five Issues in Training*. Washington: National Training Laboratories, 1962, 61-76; and Burke, W. Warner, and Harvey A. Hornstein, Conceptual vs. experimental management training, *Training and Development Journal*, **21** (Dec. 1967), 12-17.

29. House, Robert J., T-Group education and leadership effectiveness: a review of the empiric literature and a critical evaluation, *Personnel Psychology*, **20** (Spring 1967), 1-32. See also Stock, Dorothy, A survey of research on t-groups, in Bradford, Gibb, and Benne, 395-441.

30. House, *ibid*, 18-19.

31. Campbell, John P., and Marvin D. Dunnette, Effectiveness of t-group experiences in managerial training and development, *Psychological Bulletin*, **70** (August 1968), 73-104.

32. *Ibid.*, 100.

33. *Ibid.*, 101. See also the essays by Dunnette and Campbell and Chris Argyris in *Industrial Relations*, **8** (Oct. 1968), 1-45.

34. On this point, see Greiner, Larry E., Patterns of organization change, *Harvard Business Review*, **45** (May-June 1967), 119-130.

35. See Davis, Sheldon A., An organic problem-solving method.

36. See Likert, Rensis, *The Human Organization: Its Management and Value*. New York: McGraw-Hill, 1967.

## AN ORGANIC PROBLEM-SOLVING METHOD
## OF ORGANIZATIONAL CHANGE

*Sheldon A. Davis*

A few months ago, I learned from a vice-president of a large national corporation that two of the three top executives in his company had recently participated in a Presidents' Conference on Human Behavior conducted by the National Training Laboratories. I learned further that, both before and after attending the conference, these two persons were highly committed to Theory Y notions, as described by Douglas McGregor in *The Human Side of Enterprise.* My acquaintance expressed concern, however, with the form this commitment was taking. He mentioned that one of these two men had chaired a meeting during which he expressed his commitment to those assumptions stated by McGregor. As a concrete example of this commitment, he said that a few days earlier a key subordinate presented some work for approval. The "boss" did not like the quality of the work and said so. The subordinate pointed out that his people had worked very hard in producing the work and were highly committed to it. The top executive said, "OK. In that case, let's go ahead."

To me, this is *not* an example of what McGregor meant. It is an example of very soft human relationships that are not task-oriented and therefore, in my opinion, are irrational. It does represent, however, a problem presented in laboratory training. How can we eliminate some of the soft, mushy, "sweetness and light" impressions that some people feel are implicit in sensitivity training?

An example of a different approach recently took place within TRW Systems.

A section head, the lowest managerial level in the organization, discovered that a certain Quality Control procedure for Manufacturing hampered his effectiveness. He sought to get the procedure modified, only to be told that this was impossible because it covered all of the divisions and therefore could not be modified. He was further told that a change would raise the ire of at least one general manager of another division. The section head refused to accept the explanation and personally called a meeting of the general manager identified, the manager of Manufacturing—both vice-presidents of the company, and four levels above the section head—and the director of Product Assurance. Within an hour the procedure was modified in the direction desired by the section head.

The foregoing vignettes dramatize the differences which can occur because of markedly different applications of behavioral science theories within an organization. In both instances, the individuals involved were convinced that they were using the best of behavioral science techniques. The consequence of their interpretation and application had decidedly different payoffs.

## CONFRONTATION: THE MISSING ELEMENT IN BEHAVIORAL SCIENCE LITERATURE

The values that Douglas McGregor stood for and articulated regarding organizational development have within them a very real toughness: In dealing with one another, we will be open, direct, explicit. Our feelings will be available to one another, and we will try to problem-solve rather than be defensive. These values have within them a very tough way of living—not a soft way. But, unfortunately, in much of the behavioral science literature, the messages come out sounding soft and easy, as if what we are trying to do is to build happy teams of employees who feel "good" about things, rather than saying we are trying to build effective organizations with groups who function well and can zero in quickly on their problems and deal with them rationally, in the very real sense of the word. As an example of this kind of softness, I do not remember reading in any book in the field that one of the alternatives in dealing with a problem person is the possibility of discharging him.

There is no real growth—there is no real development—in the organization or in the individuals within it if they do not confront and deal directly with their problems. They can get together and share feelings, but if that is all they do, it is merely a catharsis. While this is useful, it has relatively minimal usefulness compared with what can happen if they start to relate differently within the organizational setting around task issues.

## LABORATORIES ARE NOT ENOUGH

I think one important theme of the nearly four-year organizational change effort at TRW Systems is that of using laboratory training (sensitivity training, T-Grouping) clearly as a means to an end—that of putting most of our energy into on-the-job situations, real-life intergroup problems, real-life job-family situations, and dealing with them in the here-and-now. This effort has reached a point where sensitivity training, per se, represents only 10 to 15 per cent of the effort in our own program. The rest of the effort, 85 to 90 per cent, is in on-the-job situations, working real problems with the people who are really involved in them. This has led to some very important, profound, and positive changes in the organization and the way it does many things, including decision making, problem solving, and supervisory coaching of subordinates.

One generalization I would draw from this and other similar experiences is that laboratory training in and of itself is not enough to really make the kind of difference that might be made in an organization forcefully trying to become more rational in its processes of freeing up the untapped potential of its people and of dealing more sensibly with its own realities. Attending a strangers' laboratory or, in our case, a cousins' laboratory (that is, being in a T Group with people who are not necessarily from the same job family but are from the same company) is a very useful, important experience. Most people learn much in laboratory training, as has been well documented and discussed. However, this is not enough.

We have felt that the laboratory experience (the sensitivity training experience itself) should not be just three days or a week or whatever is spent in the off-site laboratory. As a result, we have undertaken important laboratory prework as well as postwork. The prework typically consists of an orientation session where the staff very briefly presents some of the theoretical aspects of the program and an explanation of why we do laboratories. During this time, participants in the coming laboratory can ask any kind of question, such as: Is this therapy? Is the company going to evaluate my performance? and so on.

Also, we typically hand out a questionnaire to the participants for their own use (they are not asked to turn it in). It presents questions such as: "What are the three most pressing problems you feel you pose for those who have to work with you?" It is an attempt to get the person to become introspective about his own particular work situation, to begin his articulation process within himself.

Then there is the laboratory itself. This is followed up by on-site sessions several weeks apart, perhaps one evening every other week for three or four sessions. At this time a variety of actions are taken in an attempt to help people phase into their work situation. There is continued working in the small training groups; there can be exercises such as intergroup competition.

The laboratory is a highly intensive experience. Attitudes toward it can be extremely euphoric, and people can experience tremendous letdowns when they return to the ongoing culture—even a highly supportive one. Therefore, there is major emphasis on working in the ongoing situation in real-life job families as well as in intergroup situations and mergers, for example.

Recently, we have added to the follow-on work an opportunity for the wives of the participants to experience a micro-laboratory. This might be a 1:00 to 5:00 p.m. session on a Saturday for the wives, with a staff available to give some feel for the laboratory experience.

One of the problems many people have as a result of laboratory training is returning to their continuing organizational culture and finding it quite hostile to the values learned and to the approaches they would like to try. The notion very early in the TRW Systems effort was to focus on changes in the ongoing culture itself: the norms, values, rewards, systems, and processes. If all we did was to have a lot of people attend sensitivity training, this might indeed be useful to them as individuals, but its usefulness would be quite limited with respect to the total organization.

We have had other kinds of concerns with laboratory training. We have tried hard not to *send* people to a laboratory but to make it as voluntary as possible. People who are *sent* usually spend much of their time wondering why they were sent instead of working on relevant issues.

If we look at the processes of change itself, it is quite clear that it is not enough for an individual to gain enormous insight into his own situation, his own dynamics, and his own functioning. Granted, this will help him develop a better understanding of how groups work and of the complexity of communication processes. However, if he cannot take this understanding and turn it into action in the on-the-job situation, if he cannot find other people who are interested in trying some of the same ideas, if he cannot bring about a difference in his real life, the value of the laboratory is very severely minimized. In real life, what do we find? We find organizations, typically, with highly traditional methods of management and with very unrealistic assumptions about people (the kind of Theory X assumptions that Douglas McGregor stated). There has to be an emphasis on changing the ongoing organization. The direction has to be toward working in the organization on a day-to-day basis.

## ORGANIZATIONAL SETTING AND DEVELOPMENT OF PROGRAM

I should like to describe the program under way at TRW Systems as an example of this kind of effort—of a nonmechanical, organic approach to career development—the development of the careers of the individuals in the organization and the career of the organization itself, both inextricably tied.

TRW Systems currently employs about 13,300 persons. About one third are professional engineers, and half of these have advanced degrees. It is an organization with products of tremendous innovation and change. It is an organization that is highly interdependent. We have a matrix organization: there are project offices and functional areas of technical capabilities such as structures, dynamics, guidance, and control. A project office, to perform its task, must call upon capabilities and people throughout the organization. This is a highly complicated matrix of interdependencies. No one can really get his job done in this kind of system without working with others. As a result, problems of relationships, of communication, of people being effectively able to problem-solve with one another are extremely critical.

The program started at a time when the company was going through a significant change in its role—from an organization with essentially one Air Force contract for systems engineering on ballistic missile programs (Thor, Atlas, Titan, and Minuteman) to a company that would be fully competitive in the aerospace market. This has indeed happened over the past six years. We now have many contracts, many customers. Most of our work is done under fixed-price and incentive contracts; we produce hardware such as unmanned scientific satellites, propulsion engines for the Apollo mission, as well as other types of hardware. The company has become exceedingly more complex in its product lines and its mix of business.

All through this growth and diversification there has been a concern about the careers of the people in the organization, about trying to maintain certain qualities within the organization. Appendix A is a list of these qualities which was prepared in

September of 1965 and is an attempt to list qualities which seem to have a direct bearing on the kind of success we have been having over the past six years. That success has been quite striking: a tremendous increase in sales, in the number of contracts, a good record in competitions for programs in our industry, and a large increase in the number of employees.

In the middle of 1961, TRW Systems, then called Space Technology Laboratories, began to think about organizational development. At that time, Herbert Shepard, then on the faculty at Case Institute of Technology, spent a portion of the summer at TRW, including some time with key executives. The following summer he spent a month with the organization. Just prior to this visit, the director of Industrial Relations and his associate attended a laboratory conducted by the University of California at Los Angeles.

Shepard's visit and discussions centering around it led to a growing articulation of what we might want to do with respect to career development. A number of things happened in the next several months.

One was the preparation of a white paper on career development—a statement of how we might approach the subject. The paper discussed why a program was needed, assumptions to be made about employees (a paraphrase of McGregor's Theory Y), the type of organizational climate and training needed, as well as some general indications of how we might proceed.

An assumption we made was that most of the people in the organization were highly competent, very intelligent, and certainly experimental. If they could be freed up enough to look at some of their behavior, to question some of their assumptions, to look at assumptions other people were making, to try new approaches, this group could, within limits, develop their own specific management theory.

The white paper was circulated to a number of key persons. Interviews were then conducted to determine possible next steps. A series of events led from this point.

One event was the first of many team development laboratories. (By team development laboratory, I mean an activity which might, for example, be a three-day off-site meeting involving a supervisor and the people who immediately report to him. The agenda for the meeting would be "How can we improve our own effectiveness?") The first team meeting involved one of the program offices in the company. It turned out to be quite successful. With this experience under our belts, we had further discussions to formulate what we wanted to do as an organization with respect to the careers of the people comprising it.

Employees within the Personnel organization began attending sensitivity training laboratories such as the Arden House Management Work Conferences, conducted by National Training Laboratories.

A very significant event in the total development of this change effort occurred in May of 1963 when a group of 12 key executives attended a laboratory. Their co-trainers were Herbert Shepard (an outside consultant) and myself (a member of the TRW Systems organization).[1]

The participants in this first laboratory were quite positive in their feedback to the director of Industrial Relations and to the president of the company, who himself was very much interested in how people were reacting to the training. The president had given support for us to be experimental: "Let's try things. If they work, continue them. If they don't, modify them, improve them, or drop them."

A consulting team evolved over time. The consultants were not used in any one-shot way but were asked to make a significant commitment of time over a long-term period. They have become involved with us. They have learned our culture and our problems. While our consultants are all qualified T-Group trainers, most of their time is spent in on-the-job situations. There is a need to function as a team, since we are all dealing with one organization, one culture, one social system. The kind of cohesiveness that takes place during consulting team meetings has been a critical part of the program here at TRW Systems.

In one sense we started at the top of the organization, and in another we did not. In the beginning, there was a shared general understanding between the president and the key people in Industrial Relations about the type of program we wanted. There were some shared values about the organization we had and wanted to maintain, build, and develop. So, in McGregor's term, this was not Theory X management and Theory Y training effort. Both had a Theory Y quality.

In another sense we did not start at the top: the president and others of the top management team were relatively late in becoming involved in laboratory training and in applying this training to their own job families. The president of the company attended an NTL Presidents' Conference on Human Behavior early in 1965. Directly after that experience, his top team had an off-site team development meeting in March of 1965. In April 1966, they had a follow-up meeting.

Prior to this top team activity many other things had happened with a number of other people in other job families. In fact, this other activity helped us get to the point where the top management team became interested in trying to apply some of these techniques.

Since the program started, more than 500 key persons in the organization have attended sensitivity training laboratories, primarily laboratories conducted by the company. The staff of these laboratories is drawn from our consultants, the Personnel organization, and, more recently, from skilled and interested employees in line management positions.

We have also conducted more than 85 team development efforts. These vary in format, but a typical one involves interviews with each of the members of the team (a job family consisting of a supervisor and his immediate subordinates) and then perhaps a three-day off-site meeting where the interview data are fed back for the groups to work with. The team ends the meeting with explicit action items. Follow-on to the off-site meeting involves implementing the many action items.

We have been devoting much effort to intergroup problems: relationships between Manufacturing and Engineering, between Product Assurance and other parts of the organization, between various interfacing elements in the engineering organizations. We have found that these efforts have a great deal of leverage. We have done some work on facilitating mergers and with key people on approaching satellite launches. The latter become very tense, tight operations where people can become extremely competitive and behave in ways which clearly get in the way of having an effective launch.

## CHARACTERISTICS OF THE PROCESS

We "wound up" with a number of notions. We did not want to have a program that was canned but one that was experimental. We wanted participation to be voluntary rather than something that the company forced upon employees. We did not want it to be a crash program (in our industry there are many crash programs). We wanted the training to be highly task oriented. (If it were not relevant to making a difference on today's problems, it would not be a successful program.) We wanted to have the emphasis on experience-based learning, which implies, in a very general sense, the use of laboratory methods, of people really looking at how they are doing, examining the assumptions behind their management style, identifying alternate ways of problem solving, and making choices based on a wider range of possibilities. We wanted to be concerned with the careers of all employees, not those of key people only. We wanted to be concerned about company goals and the actual, on-the-job work environment, since this has a profound effect on the careers of people. We wanted to place the emphasis on measuring ourselves against our potential, on being quite introspective on how we were doing. So, for example, if there were an either/or situation (and there usually is not), we would rather not have someone come in and lecture on how to conduct staff meetings, but would have ourselves look introspectively at the conduct of our own staff meetings. And we wanted to do continuous research on how we were faring so that it could be fed back into the program for further development.

I should like to describe what I think we have come to mean by an organic approach to organizational change within TRW Systems. There are a number of points which, at least for me, tend to describe what is meant by organic methods.

1. There is the notion that if you are interested in improving a particular culture—a particular social system—you must be able to step out of it in the sense of being very analytical about it, of understanding what is going on, by not being trapped within the culture and its own particular values. If you look at a culture from the viewpoint of its own values, you are not going to come up with anything very startling and different for it to do. You have got to be able to step out of it and say, "What really would make sense here?" This ability to step out of the culture and yet not leave it, not become alienated from it, is a very important one.

2. A bias toward optimism regarding the chances for meaningful organizational development to take place increases the psychological freedom for those trying to

introduce the change. There is certainly a tremendous amount of evidence at this point that significant, even profound, changes can occur in the behavior of individuals and organizations.

3.  Taking a systems engineering approach to the effort (i.e., looking at the totality of the system, dealing with fundamentals within it, considering how a change in one part affects parts elsewhere) provides an analytical approach which increases the conceptual freedom.

4.  The extensive use of third-party facilitation is made with respect to interpersonal and organizational problems. A consultant who is not directly involved in an emotional sense in a situation can be useful just by that fact.

5.  Direct confrontation of relevant situations in an organization is essential. If we do not confront one another, we keep the trouble within ourselves and we stay in trouble. With respect to confrontation, the whole notion of feedback is crucial. Giving persons feedback on how they are doing gives them a choice to do better. Caring plays an important part. Confronting without caring can be a rather destructive process. (See Albee's *Who's Afraid of Virginia Woolf?*) It does turn out that people in general can be very caring of one another.

6.  Becoming the "other" is an important part of the organic method. This is the empathic notion that Carl Rogers and others have developed. To have a really meaningful exchange, one somehow has to look at the situation as the other sees it. For a consultant to work effectively with an organization, he has to be perceptive and understanding about the organization and its people from *their* point of view.

7.  Dealing with the here-and-now and increasing the ability of people within the organization to do the same have a great deal of leverage. It is important in an organizational development effort to start with what is going on now within the organization and to deal with those things effectively. One of our objectives is to help the organization build its own capability, to deal with its problems as they emerge. Problems are constantly emerging in any live organization, and so our objective is *not* to end up with an organization that has no problems: that would be a very fat, dumb, and happy kind of place.

8.  Multiplier planning is rather crucial in the early stages of introducing organizational change. What can we next do that will have the largest effect? There is always a wide range of alternatives and possibilities; there is never enough time, money, or energy to do all the things we might do, so we are constantly picking and choosing.

9.  Fanning out is coupled with the multiplier planning aspect. It is important in an effort of this kind—if it is not to be subversive, sub rosa, hidden, squashed out—to be something that does fan out: someone does something that leads to others doing something that leads to still others doing something.

10.  A person can act, then act again and then act again; or he can act, critique what

he just did, then act, then critique, then act. And that is the whole notion of going back and forth between content and process, between doing the job and then looking at how we are doing it. Building that into the day-to-day culture is a major objective.

11. Finally, there is the notion of testing of choices. One always has choices within any particular situation. However, it is typically true that we do not test the choices we have. So someone might say, "Well, I really can't do that because these fellows won't let me," or "Yes, I would very much like to do the following, but I can't because of so and so." Given these limits, some choices do not get tested. One of the efforts is to get people to be aware of the various possibilities they have and to test them—not to accept the stereotypes in the situation, the sacred cows, that exist in any kind of organization, but to say, "OK, this is what makes sense to me in working that problem. This is what I want to try to do."

## UNDERPINNINGS TO THE EFFORT

The principles of confrontation—that laboratory training must be seen as a means to an end, that most of the effort has to be done after people have attended the laboratory, and not in the laboratory itself—have been central to this effort. This has affected the way we budget time, the way we spend money, the assumptions we make about what we are doing.

Another significant development in this large-scale effort has been a deliberate, successful attempt to build up the internal resources to carry out the program. Two years ago, in a sensitivity training laboratory put on by the company, there would have been a staff of six, four of five of whom were outside consultants. This situation has completely reversed itself. Today, when a T-Group cousins' laboratory is conducted, four or five of the persons are from inside the organization, and only one or two are external consultants.

Furthermore, in the on-the-job aspects of the program, the effort is carried on by people within the organization, primarily individuals in Personnel and, increasingly, managers from the line organization.

A very interesting aspect of the program has focused on the question of risk taking. In my opinion, those of us engaged in this kind of work are quite often too cautious, too constrained, and not experimental enough in trying out things within the organization. We do not behave as though we fully believe the implications of McGregor's Theory Y formulation: that people are creative, that they are strong, that they are motivated, that they want to make a difference. We tend sometimes to approach them gingerly and tentatively. These are constraints more within ourselves than within others or within the situation.

Many times our consultants have reported that their experience at TRW Systems has been a very "stretching" one: they have been fully challenged; people at TRW Systems are experimental, want to try things, are saying, "OK, that was useful, what should we do next?" Much of the effort in the consulting team meetings has been to push ourselves to be more developmental, more experimental in the approaches that we take within the effort.

For example, until quite recently, many people in the field felt that laboratory training was not something one could do within a job family. It seems to me that the whole objective of sensitivity training is to develop an on-the-job culture within which we can relate to one another interpersonally just the way we do in a T Group. We at TRW want to make that transfer; we do not want the T-Group to be a separate, special kind of experience. We prefer to say: "All right, let's sit down and really level with one another. Let's do this on the job, and from day to day." That is the objective. It leads to a more effective, efficient, problem-solving organization.

Working with teams in real-life situations is exactly what we are after. Otherwise, the program can be ethereal—not particularly related to the company's real-life situations. It cannot be "gutty" if it does not come to grips with some of the tougher issues, pinpoint and deal with them, and cause people to become involved and to work actively to solve problems.

In September 1963, I put together a short paper which conceptualized several plateaus that we might be moving through as an organization in this change effort.

The first one is characterized as problem awareness—that point in time during which there is general recognition and awareness on the part of some people within the organization that there are crucial interdependencies which exist in order for us to function and that there are problems due to inappropriate means of dealing with these interdependencies.

The second plateau, the identification and freeing of key people within the organization, is seen as consisting of two parts. The first part is an effort to identify key people in the organization who seem to be perceptive about the problems the company is experiencing and have a desire to work on them. They are key people in the sense that their efforts to deal with organizational problems could produce a multiplier effect that would lead others to similar action.

The second part of this particular phase of the program is characterized by an effort to provide a situation that would initiate the process of freeing up these potential multipliers from the organizational and personal constraints which, in the past, kept them from responding effectively to their awareness of the problems. Here, the strangers' laboratories, the cousins' laboratories conducted by the company, and the team development laboratories are seen as being especially relevant.

The third phase, or plateau, involves action steps to followup—experimental steps stimulated by a participation in the various kinds of laboratories that are taking place. These action steps have taken many forms: a supervisor holding a team development laboratory within his own job family; a family group diagnosing the kinds of interaction problems it has with other parts of the organization and beginning to resolve these problems in an open, direct manner in a search for a creative solution rather than an avoidance compromise; two persons at odds moving in on the problem of relating and communicating with each other; new ways of looking at functions in the organization.

The fourth plateau occurs when the effort itself gains an independent status and becomes a self-supporting system. At this plateau there are norms within the organization that support open, direct confrontation of conflict, resolution of conflict without resorting to the power structure unless there is somehow a failure in the process, and a shared commitment to objectives as a consequence of being interdependent. These organizational norms would support the giving and receiving of feedback, openness, experimentation, and day-to-day problem solving.

In this fourth phase we are trying to build procedures into the day-to-day situation which, hopefully, put into concrete terms some of the things we have learned in the earlier phases. For example, when a new project office is started it is probably useful to program some team building early in its life. When there is a new merger within the organization, particular attention can be paid to the merger process. One of the things we have learned is that specific attention should continuously be paid to the processes within the organization: how we make decisions, how we fill key spots, how we communicate with one another, how we decide to reorganize, how we make other important decisions. There is a heavy people involvement in these processes, and, typically, they do not get enough legitimate attention. If I am concerned about the quality of staff meetings I attend, I tend to talk about them in the hallways or go home and kick the dog and tell my wife about them. I do not exert effort during the staff meetings to try to change their quality and improve them, because somehow that is not legitimate. "Let's keep personalities out of it. Don't get emotional." These are the kinds of expressions that inhibit me from dealing with the problem.

Development through the four plateaus requires considerable invention because the state of the art of organizational change, in my opinion, is such that one cannot program in advance everything he is going to do within the organization. There are some people who approach organizational change this way. I believe their efforts tend to be mechanical and relatively superficial.

Another important aspect of this effort which I think is particularly consistent with Theory Y formulation is that the direction and pace that the effort takes should be meaningful to the members who are participating in it. The consultant in any particular situation has to get in touch with the needs and concerns of the people involved from *their* point of view, not from *his*.

I have tried to suggest that in many situations in which behavioral scientists are trying to apply their principles the really serious limitations are not within the people or the organizations they are working with, but within themselves—their own skills and ability and courage to act. Theory Y has deeply ingrained in it a profound belief in the abilities, strengths, and motivations of people in general and specifically. Many times we do not act as if we fully believe or understand that set of formulations.

## NEXT STEPS

In TRW Systems, we are now moving in a number of directions, some of which I should like to describe. We are moving more toward day-to-day coaching—on-the-job feedback, if you will—with or without consultants and without calling special meetings, but just as we work together. We are paying continuing attention to process as a way of doing business. We are moving more and more toward using third-party facilitation as a standard operating procedure.

So far there has not been a heavy involvement of the rank and file. The first several years in the effort were specifically biased toward working with key people. These are the ones who have a large effect upon the culture, upon the processes of the organization, upon the tone of the climate. But we are now at a point where we want to get more and more involvement of all the employees within the organization.

I think that the experience of the past several years within TRW Systems has rather clearly demonstrated the potential high leverage of applying some of the behavioral science formulations of people like McGregor, Lewin, and Likert. I think it has also demonstrated that there needs to be much more organizational theory development based upon experience, not upon someone's sitting in a room by himself and thinking about the topic. Some of the statements written about organizational development are to me naive, impractical, unrealistic, and unrelated to organizational problems as they actually exist. Through experiences gained at TRW Systems and many other places, we should be able to develop a more sophisticated understanding of organizational development.

In my opinion, there is great potential in the development of this theory and in its application within organizations. That seems to me to be one of the leading edges within the field of behavioral science.

## NOTES

1. This has been one of the important notions in the approach at TRW Systems. We use, at this point, about nine consultants who are members of the NTL Network—people like Richard Beckhard, Michael Blansfield, James Clark, Charles Ferguson, Jack Gibb, George Lehner, Herbert Shepard, Robert Tannenbaum, and others. These people are *always* coupled in their work, either in T-Group training or on-the-job consulting, with someone inside the organization, typically a personnel manager in one of the line operating units.

## ORGANIZATION DEVELOPMENT: TEN NEW DIMENSIONS OF PRACTICE

*Peter B. Vaill*

### INTRODUCTION

"Organization Development" (O.D.) is a phrase applied increasingly to the process of deliberately seeking to improve work relationships in organizations. Richard Beckhard, a prominent management consultant, has defined O.D. as follows:[1]

Organization development is an effort (1) *planned*, (2) *organization-wide*, and (3) *managed* from the *top*, to (4) increase *organization effectiveness* and *health* through (5) *planned interventions* in the organization's "processes", using (6) *behavioral-science* knowledge.

O.D. work is a growing field of professional practice. Many of America's largest and most progressive organizations have established units whose primary purpose is to perform the function defined by Beckhard.

This article is about the men who are doing O.D. work. They will be called "O.D. practitioners" to emphasize that they are *doing* O.D. work in organizations, and training others to do it. They are not "resident intellectuals," nor are they merely another variety of personnel man.

It is true that many present O.D. practitioners have backgrounds in traditional personnel work, but many have extensive line experience also. The disciplines they draw on in their work include personality and social psychology, sociology, and cultural anthropology. Today's O.D. practitioners are largely self-educated in these disciplines. However, the new programs at such business schools as Harvard, M.I.T., Case Western Reserve, and Yale, as well as elsewhere, guarantee that tomorrow's O.D. practitioner will be professionally trained. The NTL Institute for Applied Behavioral Science has taken the lead in defining the role of O.D., and in encouraging universities to establish degree programs in O.D.

The idea of a function called Organization Development and the emergence of a professional called an O.D. practitioner are results of studies of organizational behavior that stretch back forty years. Work in the 1930's and 1940's was largely devoted to establishing the feasibility of studying human behavior in live organizational contexts. In the 1950's and 1960's, this growing body of knowledge has been codified more and more into a set of technologies which men can use to change organizations.

A key fact about this historical evolution is that the knowledge which has been developed and used is primarily about individual persons and small work groups. The individual and the group have received so much study because they are obviously important in organizational operations. They are also much more researchable than are

Reprinted by permission of the author. Author's note: I am indebted to my colleagues, Robert Tannenbaum and William McKelvey, for comments on an earlier draft of this paper.

total-organization events and processes. Thus, we know more about face-to-face communication than we know about one-to-many communication in organizations; we understand individual motivation better than we understand motivational levels which exist in whole departments or divisions; we know more about work group norms than we know about cultural norms and mores.

While much has been written about the larger-scale processes, and some excellent formal theory and research exists,[2] comparatively little of it has been codified in a way that O.D. practitioners can use it. At present O.D. work is to a large extent the practical child of its theoretical parent—the social psychology of small groups.

However, on two fronts this situation is changing. Beckhard's statement, quoted above, is a lucid example of how O.D. can be defined in *organizational* terms, rather than in terms of sub-units of the system such as persons, groups, or departments. Beckhard is echoed in the writings of many other theorists of the O.D. process. Second, many O.D. practitioners are trying to *do* O.D. work on the organization in a planned way, rather than hit-or-miss on bits and pieces of it. It is widely understood among O.D. practitioners that without an organizational focus, their efforts with individuals, groups, departments, etc., can easily be "swamped" or cancelled out by the momentum of the rest of the system.

This paper assumes that O.D. practitioners either possess or can acquire the skills to work effectively among individuals and within small groups. This includes such skills as effective listening, nondirective counseling, small group leadership, facilitation as a trainer/consultant of small group processes, assessment of individual motivation, and development of programs to change motivation. This is not to say the acquisition of such skills is easy. There is relative agreement on what these skills are, however, and we know how to train men in them.

This paper is about some new skills and abilities which it appears O.D. practitioners need if they wish to create change in *organization* processes. It is difficult to describe these skills and abilities, and at the present time it is quite impossible to say how to train men to practice them. Yet the issue must be addressed if O.D. practice is to be effective at the organizational level.

## SKILLS AND ABILITIES IN ORGANIZATIONAL INTERVENTIONS

1. Most men are quite aware of the *political realities* in the organizations where they take action. In light of this rather widespread awareness of power, power differences, and changes in power relations, it is remarkable how little reference there is to power and politics in the O.D. literature. This point is eloquently made by Bennis in a recent discussion of the "unsolved problems" of O.D. work.[3]

Even though discussion of power and politics is lacking in the literature, it is not lacking in O.D. practice. It is just not "talked about." Sensitivity to power and politics probably permeates the typical O.D. practitioner's approach to his work. It would be revealed in his awareness of what he can and can't do in a given setting; it would be revealed in his awareness of the need people in the system have to protect themselves, to look good, to not act knowingly in ways that reduce their influence on events; it would be revealed in his awareness of the role of symbols of power and status, such as large offices, impressive job titles, large expense accounts, and the like.

With the O.D. literature ignoring or positively decrying "power-based," "win-lose" political situations in the organization, the O.D. practitioner is left with feelings of behaving "unprofessionally" when he consciously takes advantage of political realities to advance his interests.

The underlying political realities are sometimes the ugly side of things. They can be a depressing subject to dwell upon, especially since the more one gazes on the Byzantine infrastructure of the average organization, the less sure one may become that any meaningful change can be achieved quickly—if, indeed, ever.

However, because they are real and cannot be wished away, the question is whether these political realities can be put to use, whether the attempt to understand them is helpful for the purpose of creating change in the organization. The question is especially important, since the O.D. practitioner's relation to politics is different in one way from everyone else in the organization. Everybody, including the O.D. man, will be "playing politics" in one way or another. But he alone is also dedicated to *reshaping* the political infrastructure itself.

2(a). The previous section discusses the ability to understand the meaning of power and politics in the organization. Next are discussed four political modes of behavior. Each of these may be useful to the O.D. man as he attempts to change the organization. First is a *knowledge and use of the chains of influence which criss-cross the organization*. It is a matter of common experience that some men are "dead ends" with regard to messages that come to them from others in the organization. They don't "pick up on the idea"; they don't reinvest the communication that comes to them with any new energy and meaning. They can't be counted on to "spread the word," to "pick up the ball and run with it." Others are "communication springboards": they do keep things moving; ideas don't die on their desks.

The O.D. practitioner needs to have a way of thinking that helps him understand these processes. He needs to know which channels will spread *his* word, for by the very nature of organizational influence, as opposed to interpersonal influence, the O.D. man is not going to be able to talk to all the people who need to understand his O.D. project.

Hand in hand with knowing the channels goes knowing the kind and degree of distortion that is likely to occur in a given channel. Some distortion takes place at every point of linkage, no matter how hard the parties try to be clear. Distortion can occur in O.D. practice with such questions as whether the O.D. man needs to attend a particular meeting, whether people at remote points in the system are getting the messages he intends, or whether he needs to spend additional time on follow-up and further explanation.

This discussion of the chains of influence may seem rather academic, since so many O.D. men will report that they are lucky if anyone in the system understands even half of what they are trying to do. Yet effective O.D. probably cannot proceed unless somehow the influence chains operate to maintain and enhance the program. A large literature exists on *how* to communicate clearly, based mainly on the psychology of the sender and receiver. The skill discussed here involves not only the "how," but also the "who," the "when," and the "where" of the communication.

2(b). A second type of political behavior involves the use of *symbols and stereotyping.* The underlying value system that tends to infuse O.D. today makes it wrong to engage in stereotyping. The O.D. man, so the doctrine goes, should not stereotype others and should not permit others to stereotype him. What is often overlooked is that a great deal of influence is exerted through symbols and stereotypes. The more removed one gets from face-to-face relationships, the more one must rely on symbols and stereotypes to reveal what others want and don't want, understand and don't understand, will react to and will ignore.

The O.D. practitioner's whole style of doing things is relevant: how he walks and talks, the kind of car he drives, what his office looks like, the hours he keeps, the tone of things he says and writes, what the people around him are like, and so forth down an almost endless list of items, small and large, that we all use to make inferences about other people. Very few of us, happily, calculate everything; all of us calculate a few things.

We draw conclusions about others from symbols they may or may not have intended. The O.D. practitioner, with his objectives of influencing others, never knows just what symbols in his style others are noting and reacting to. Thus he must walk a line between trying to be all things to all men and being wholly thoughtless of how he appears to others.

The other side of the issue of symbols and stereotypes is the use the O.D. man can make of the stereotypes he forms of others, based on symbols in their styles to which he attaches meaning. He cannot know even a fraction of all the men he would like to influence. Therefore the question is, how accurate are his stereotypes of them? And to what extent is he interpreting the symbols in other men's behavior in the way that they intend? As a specific example: when a large number of people in the organization arrive noticeably late in the morning, the O.D. man will have to figure out whether this behavior symbolizes anything else, and if so, what.

So the question is not whether to engage in stereotyping and use of symbols, but rather how to go about it. A classic instance, for example, is Douglas McGregor's distinction between Theory X and Theory Y.[4] McGregor is proposing that one stereotype about human motivation, Theory Y, be substituted for another of less value, Theory X. Unfortunately, most of the debate about Theory X and Theory Y misses this point, and focuses instead on which of the two is true. This degenerates, usually, into a philosophical argument about what people are "really" like, and no one learns anything. If the two theories, X and Y, were regarded as *both* stereotypes, neither of which is true, then discussion might focus where McGregor originally intended, namely: Under what conditions and for what purposes is it more useful to stereotype people with the Theory Y set of assumptions than with the Theory X?

The stereotypes that are available to O.D. practitioners on such dimensions as good/bad, smart/dumb, loyal/disloyal, constructive/destructive, ready for change/not ready, are of great importance. Research and theory can tell him a little about useful sterotypes to get hold of people, but to a large extent at present he has to rely on his own native sensitivity and insight.

2(c). A third mode of political behavior concerns the O.D. man's *charisma*. This factor grows directly out of the two just mentioned, for the overall impression others have of the O.D. practitioner is gained through the ways he operates in the influence networks and through the collections of symbols that accompany and infuse his style.

By introducing the idea of charisma, the suggestion is that some O.D. men will discover they have a capacity to get people to go along with things in the system that not everyone has. It is not, however, an unmixed blessing to possess charisma. There are themes in the O.D. value system implying it is becoming an applied science of sorts; a broad range of types of men ought to be able to do effective O.D. work, these themes would say, once they have been trained; there is nothing fundamentally mysterious or magical about exercising influence in social systems. What then of the O.D. man who finds that he has some of this "magic," this unnameable capacity to get others to do things just by being himself? He can't deny its existence if it is pointed out to him, nor can he affirm its existence very loudly, in this culture, without risking the label of a "messiah complex." Perhaps, however, he can take heart in the generalization (admittedly untested) that most successful O.D. programs in organizations have had behind them one or more "dynamic," "electric," "exciting" personalities whom other men instinctively follow. The adjectives are in quotes not out of cynicism but out of the conviction that they are clumsy and imprecise ways of talking about such men.

And what of the O.D. man who realizes gradually that he just doesn't have whatever this thing is? Does it mean he should get out of the organizational influence business?

Organization Development involves deep and far-reaching changes in basic values, as Tannenbaum and Davis have described so well.[5] The action of charismatic personalities and changes in basic values are interdependent processes, but the meaning of this interdependence remains to be understood in O.D. work.

2(d). Finally must be mentioned the increasing importance of *O.D. teams*. Political processes occur within the team, and between the team and the rest of the organization. All of the foregoing comments about political behavior take on a somewhat different meaning, however, when they are put in a team context. The O.D. practitioner is less free to evolve and perfect a private style; he must be prepared to adjust it to the styles of others who are pursuing the same objectives.

O.D. teams, therefore, cannot leave their own process unattended. There may be internal conflicts about objectives, about O.D. strategies, about "proper professional conduct" (often an especially sensitive matter in new professions), about authority and responsibility, about "spheres of influence" in the larger organization—these are a few matters that quickly come to mind. The team has access to the whole range of techniques for working on group problems, and presumably has the capability to do it.

3. Much of what the O.D. practitioner knows, or thinks he knows, about the organization comes to him indirectly—second or third hand. He is often in the position of having to reconstruct what is really happening at some remote point in the system in order to determine what action, if any, he should take. This *ability to reconstruct remote social events*, however, does not seem to have been identified in the O.D. literature.

Events may be remote in several ways. They may occur at a physical distance; they may have occurred at some point in the past; they may occur at several levels up or down the hierarchy from the O.D. man; events among blacks may be remote from whites, and events among women may be remote from men. One could say, in response to these comments, that therefore the O.D. man needs "empathy" so that he can bridge these barriers that separate him from events. But empathy is only part of it. It does not quite cover the full richness of *events*. A college administrator may "understand students" quite well, but this is no guarantee that he will understand the meaning of a student rally that occurred the previous evening on another part of the campus for the purpose of planning the takeover of the administration building. The administrator will get reports of the rally from various sources. His problem is to sort through the pieces of information for clues as to what really happened and to what it probably means for him.

Without the ability to reconstruct, an action-taker becomes the "prisoner" of the people who surround him. O.D. practitioners cannot afford to be imprisoned in this way if they want their actions to be appropriate to organization needs.

4. In the comments above about the O.D. man's use of communication channels that multiply his effects, and in the comments about charisma, there is an ability implied that should be highlighted. This is the ability to *sense when an organization development process has been set in motion and when it has not.*

Kurt Lewin's famous model of the change process serves well to make this point. Lewin spoke of "unfreezing" a system from its present pattern of operations, "moving" a system toward some new pattern, and "refreezing" it when it had achieved this new pattern. The O.D. man's questions are: Is the system sufficiently "unfrozen" that real movement can begin? Has a sufficient kind and degree of "movement" occurred to make "refreezing" appropriate? Has "refreezing" occurred, and are the new patterns now stable?

In the way O.D. people talk about their projects, one can detect awareness of these issues. There is much discussion, for instance, of "readiness", as in, "I think those two departments are ready to begin to work on some of the issues between them." This "readiness" is very difficult to assess, yet the effectiveness of an O.D. man's intervention may well depend on his having assessed it correctly.

Another common topic among O.D. people is "follow-up." Men will say they plan to change; ambitious plans will be laid; new patterns of organizational life will be discussed enthusiastically. Someone, however, has to keep going around the system, reminding people what they have committed themselves to and helping them to deal with second thoughts they may be having. The task falls to the O.D. practitioner, the man who presumably helped things get "unfrozen" in the first place. There is no question that most O.D. men do a lot of follow-up. But how they decide how much of what kind of follow-up to do with what people is not well understood.

5.  Several of the skills and abilities already mentioned involve a fifth talent called *detecting consensus.* Most of the literature on O.D. is devoted to the problem of how to *change* the consensus in an organization. The prior act is mentioned hardly at all, that is, the ability to determine what people are thinking and feeling in the first place. The technique of "deep sensing" as developed at TRW Systems is a device for detecting various degrees of consensus. It is one of the first techniques to do this in a way that is functional for operations. Most existing devices, like questionnaires and interview surveys by a staff man, probably alter the very consensus they are trying to measure. Hopefully, many more techniques such as TRW's will develop in the future.

But there is an additional issue. How, in the course of his daily activity, without making a "research project" out of it, can the O.D. man learn about consensus as he moves about the system? One possibility would be to ask the same question at various points in the system. Another might be to pay close attention to common usages of symbols. How consensus is detected in practice, however, is not well understood; yet it is clearly a fundamental process in effective O.D. work.

6.  To be living in, studying, and trying to change a large organization means that the O.D. practitioner needs the *ability to handle large amounts of information.* The possibility of information overload, even of glut, is great. Such a state of overload can produce any of three reactions in the O.D. man: (1) he can withdraw from the system, (2) he can become quite cynical about the system, thus allowing him to lump large amounts of information within sweeping negative categories, or (3) he can persist in dogged and unimaginative attempts to wrest meaning from the mass of information.

Quantification of data has been the traditional means of reducing information to manageable proportions without too seriously destroying its richness. The physical and engineering sciences have made great use of quantification, but the behavioral sciences are in not quite so fortunate a position. Further, we are talking about O.D. practitioners who cannot usually employ even the rudimentary measures and controls employed by the professional researchers.

Still, the O.D. man can't avoid the information, nor can he avoid the stresses which too much of it, in too ill-structured a form, produce on him. Among the various abilities that can be suggested as possibly helpful, three are mentioned below. They are: (7) the development of "program sense," (8) predictive ability, and (9) the development of a "hypothetical frame of mind."[6]

7. *Program sense* is a seventh talent whose strategic value is emerging in O.D. work. It is one thing for an O.D. man to decide that a single intervention with some person or group is needed. It is quite another thing to plan and carry off a series of interventions at planned points in the system for the purpose of producing certain consequences that are spelled out beforehand. Skill in this latter kind of O.D. work, occurring on a larger scale, involving more people, more planning, and more coordination, is "program sense."

With this idea is *not* meant the notion that the O.D. practitioner must become an ultrarational planner who develops his entire program in Pert-chart fashion down to the most minute detail before he takes any action. Such a mechanistic approach is the antithesis of the model of O.D. work which underlies this paper.

By program sense is meant the realization that a variety of inputs to a system can be made, that these inputs can reinforce each other if handled properly, that throughout the process there is an awareness of goals and priorities and of unintended consequences, and that change of organization patterns may require years of time and ultimately involve thousands of people. Program sense, furthermore, recognizes the "nonlinear" and multifaceted quality of organization change efforts. The O.D. practitioner does not proceed single step by single step, but rather on several fronts at once. The fronts are related in his mind, however, as a result of the strategic choices he has made.

In terms of the comments above about information overload, program sense helps the practitioner to order and interpret the information he receives in light of his objectives and of the methods he has adopted for pursuing them.

8. *Predictive ability* is another skill that may be of central importance to changing organizations. There is not much discussion of prediction in the O.D. literature. Emphasis tends to be on ideas about where organizations *should* be going rather than on where they are going as presently structured. O.D. people are concerned with the "shoulds," of course, but an intelligent selection of "shoulds" rests on a careful set of predictions about where an organization's established patterns are taking it.

O.D. people and the behavioral scientists from whom they have learned their theories of the change process, typically do not formalize their predictions. They may talk about their hunches and intuitions about the organization's future, but then they usually move quickly on to prescribe what in the system ought to be changed. As long as he leaves his hunches unstated, though, the O.D. practitioner does not have a very strong basis for explaining and defending the changes that he thinks make sense.

Formalizing one's predictions is a messy business, though, full of frustrations and uncertainties, and the O.D. man will be tempted not to bother. If he can learn the skill of prediction and practice it habitually, however, he should be able to handle the information he has more easily. The act of attempting to predict involves evaluating the quality of information presently in hand, and it helps pinpoint new information that is needed.

9.   Closely related to predictive ability is the *hypothetical frame of mind*. One means by which information can be processed is to evaluate it against some previously formed hypothesis about the system. The information can be interpreted in terms of whether it tends to confirm or disconfirm the hypothesis. Either way, the information has a meaning and value it would not have if the hypothesis did not exist.

The idea of a hypothetical frame of mind applies to all of the skills and abilities that have been mentioned. Hypotheses can be formed about politics and influence in the system, about various kinds and degrees of consensus, about the nature of remote social events.

The classical scientific use of hypothesis formation and testing requires a degree of precision which is not possible in O.D. work. The value of the hypothesis as a kind of cutting tool, however, is still considerable. "Futurists" have developed the technique of "scenario writing" as a method of considering the potential effects of a whole set of interrelated hypotheses. It is a technique which is well-adapted to the fact that there are multiple variables and all are relatively imprecise. The novel *1984* is a particularly vivid and detailed scenario, i.e., system of hypotheses, about a future society.

Since scenarios rest on systems of hypotheses, a change in any single hypothesis changes the whole system—and produces a new scenario. Thus an O.D. practitioner could produce one or more scenarios about the future of his organization, based on the hypotheses he has about it. If he had several scenarios, he could begin to compare them in terms of cost, likelihood, desirability, and so forth. Out of such an effort could come the basic decisions about the objectives of the O.D. program.

The hypothetical frame of mind (and such an example of it as scenario writing) is clearly an acquired mood and habit of thinking. It is paradoxical that so useful a habit should remain so little understood from the point of view of how men can be trained to practice it. Yet this is largely the case today.

10.   Finally, the *ability to correlate self and system* can be important to effective O.D. work. It is a commonplace among those concerned with O.D. that more is known about organizations and how to change them than is being applied. O.D. practitioners with access to all this theory and research may well find themselves growing faster in their ambitions than in their achievements. The O.D. literature is exciting. It is no exaggeration to say it contains many revolutionary ideas. Practical, detailed attempts to change particular organizations may seem mundane by comparison. How wide can the gap grow between what the O.D. man would like to see happening in his organization, and what he does see?

Effective O.D. work involves, quite probably, the discovery of some personal optimal level of "advancedness" between oneself and what others in the system are aware of and are ready for. By the nature of the role, the O.D. man is not "just like everyone else," but he can't be absolutely unlike everyone else either. The issue is complicated for the O.D. man by the very rapid rate at which theorists and researchers are producing new ideas about O.D. On one side, he does not want to lose touch with his organization and the men in it; on the other, he doesn't want to become "obsolete" in the behavioral science knowledge he has.

A poet's advice to aspiring writers sums up both the problem and the promise of this complex balance the O.D. man must seek:[7]

What you mean is never what anyone else means, exactly. And the only thing that makes you more than a drop in the common bucket, a particle of sand in the universal hourglass, is the interplay of your specialness with your commonness.

## RESEARCHING THE NEW DIMENSIONS OF O.D. PRACTICE

This listing and discussion of new dimensions of O.D. practice for large-scale change efforts leads to a definition of O.D. practice. It may be viewed as *practical, normative, experimentation.*

The problem-centered nature of O.D. work and its focus on organizational realities is what makes it distinctly *practical*. The *normative* character of O.D. work is in its goal-directedness and its commitment to changing the organization. O.D. work is distinctly *experimental* because we cannot say exactly how to achieve the changes desired. There are no formulas and there probably never will be. O.D. is a process of continuing experiment through time where techniques that do not work are cast off, and those which do are refined for wider and more efficient application.

In its discussion of O.D. practice, this paper has been mainly speculative and inferential. The critical need now is to collect more data on what these skills and abilities look like in the practice of O.D. It is necessary to talk with O.D. practitioners in detail and, where possible, observe them at work, to see if these abilities can be documented.

In such an effort, two important things need to be kept in mind. First, O.D. men will most probably not talk about these abilities in the way they have been discussed here. Their accounts will be in terms of their own specific projects and the behaviors those projects require of them. Second, these abilities should be treated as variables which can be practiced with different degrees of success.

This paper presents these new dimensions, therefore, as a plausible set of hypotheses about the behavior of an O.D. practitioner who seeks to change his organization. It remains now to test whether these ideas help us to understand the behavior of real men in the real world.

## CONCLUSION

The thesis of this article can be summarized with four statements:

1. It is increasingly clear to theorists and practitioners alike that effective O.D. work must focus on the entire organization, rather than on sub-units of it which are assumed to be safe from the dampening influence of the larger system.

2. An increasing number of O.D. practitioners are trying to cast their change programs in organizational terms.

3. The theory and research in the present O.D. literature is primarily derived from investigations of individual and group behavior, and contains comparatively few guidelines for one who is attempting to develop organization-wide programs and produce organization-wide consequences.

4. Ten kinds of behavior are described which are applicable to the problem of producing organization-wide consequences. These skills and abilities are presented as hypotheses in the hope that further investigation of their utility will occur.

**NOTES**

1. Beckhard, Richard, *Organization Development: Strategies and Models.* Reading, Mass.: Addison-Wesley, 1969, 9.

2. Thompson, James D., *Organizations in Action.* New York: McGraw-Hill, 1967.

3. Bennis, Warren G., Unsolved problems facing organizational development, *Business Quarterly*, **34**, No. 4 (Winter, 1969).

4. McGregor, Douglas, *The Human Side of Enterprise.* New York: McGraw-Hill, 1960.

5. Tannenbaum, Robert, and Sheldon A. Davis, Values, man, and organizations, *Industrial Management Review*, **10** (1969), 67-86.

6. The general problem of formulating courses of action in highly complex and fluid situations has been brilliantly described and analyzed by Sir Geoffrey Vickers in *Value Systems and Social Process.* New York: Basic Books, 1968.

7. Cox, Sidney, *Indirections.* New York: Viking Press, 1962, 19.

# 5.
# LABORATORY TRAINING IN DEVELOPING HUMAN POTENTIAL

From approximately 1950 through 1965 the training field was highly influenced by the methodology known as *laboratory training*. The best known adaptation of the laboratory method was sensitivity training. Sensitivity training began with a sociological focus and was used primarily for interpersonal insight and an understanding of small groups. The application was toward more effective individual functioning in man's organizations.

As the method developed, and as trainers were increasingly drawn from clinical psychology and related fields, its focus showed an increasing concentration on understanding of one's self and appreciation of one's feelings and emotions. In part it responded to the changes in man's values, motivations, and turning from the hard realities of societal problems to inward contemplation and understanding. This focus has recently culminated in encounter training, nonverbal techniques, and preoccupation with appreciating oneself. The use of the laboratory method in the new techniques and focus has tended to confuse sensitivity training with these developments.

The more dramatic techniques have received much attention in the popular press, the sensational press, and on television. There is little doubt that the current trend has attracted many participants looking for an emotional or psychological thrill or experience; it has attracted a number of questionable trainers, as well. For these and related reasons, in recent years sensitivity training has been associated with these thrusts. As a result many organizational trainers experience increasing difficulty in employing laboratory training as a methodology. Organizational managers have heard or read of the more sensational adaptations and do not differentiate between sensitivity training and encounter training. It is not the purpose of this chapter to trace this development but to summarize the rapid rise of both methods—the current trends and adaptations and some of the concerns and ethical issues now recognized.

One of the most difficult questions the field has tried to answer during the past two decades has been "What *is* sensitivity training?". Usually the answer given was something like this: "It is of such a personal nature, and the insights and learning vary so much from individual to individual, that it is impossible to give a ready answer." If the core of the method could not be described, at least the methodology and mechanics could. The article by Charles Seashore, "What Is Sensitivity Training?", is typical of the definitions offered.

During the sixties, one of the issues that arose was whether the laboratory method as employed by sensitivity training needed a professional trainer to sit constantly with the training group, or whether instruments could be used so the training group could "learn on its own." Partly this was a reflection of the shortage of qualified trainers; also, it reflected a learning philosophy which suggested that participants showed more progress when forced to learn through their own discoveries. There was also a growing awareness that the trainer—his personality style and interventions—affected what was learned. This had earlier been generally denied or ignored.

A great deal of discussion during the sixties questioned whether or not sensitivity training actually changed the performance of managers back on the job. Much evaluative research was done along these lines—some of it conflicting. During this period of questioning the effectiveness of sensitivity training, many organizations were unsure about whether the method was a useful one for their managers. To assist with this question, Leslie This and Gordon Lippitt wrote "Managerial Guidelines to Sensitivity Training." They discussed in nontechnical terms the strengths and weakness of sensitivity training as related to organizational goals and functioning. They stated realistically that the methodology was not good for an individuals or for all organizations and set out criteria to help an organization determine whether sensitivity training might be useful to it.

Bernard Bass, in "The Anarchist Movement and The T-Group: Some Possible Lessons for Organizational Development," goes a step further. He questions whether the T-group, admittedly effective for individual growth, is also good for organizational growth. He questions whether organizational needs in the interpersonal area are different from those required in the small group and discusses eight different approaches to increase the transfer of learning.

In "Some Ethical Issues in Sensitivity Training," Martin Lakin is more direct. With growing awareness that norms of training are more and more set by the trainer in a T-group, and as training tends toward the cathartic rather than the experimental and intellectual, Lakin believes that more pointed and troublesome ethical questions emerge. He identifies and discusses these questions.

Present indications are that laboratory training, and more especially sensitivity training, may have seen its peak. Increasingly, it has taken its role as a legitimate training method but is no longer viewed, except by a few, as a panacea for all individual and organizational needs.

Encounter training will probably flourish and decline in accord with Americans' preoccupation with introspection. The field will probably continue to avoid a system for licensing or accrediting trainers; this will lead to increased invasion by charlatans, increasing suspicion and avoidance of sensitivity training by work organizations. There will probably be a countermove to escape this difficulty through semantics—calling the methodology, for example, "awareness training." The chances are strong that some new methodology will soon emerge and sensitivity training will join the lecture, workshop, buzz groups, films, programmed-learning, debates, and panels as one more specialized learning tool.

---

# WHAT IS SENSITIVITY TRAINING?

*Charles Seashore*

Sensitivity training is one type of experience-based learning. Participants work together in a small group over an extended period of time, learning through analysis of their own experiences, including feelings, reactions, perceptions, and behavior. The duration varies according to the specific design, but most groups meet for a total of 10-40 hours. This may be in a solid block, as in a marathon weekend program or two to six hours a day in a one- or two-week residential program or spread out over several weekends, a semester, or a year.

The sensitivity training group may stand by itself or be a part of a larger laboratory training design which might include role playing, case studies, theory presentations, and intergroup exercises. This paper focuses mainly on the T Group (The *T* stands for *training*) as the primary setting for sensitivity training. However, many of the comments here also apply to other components of laboratory training.

## A TYPICAL T-GROUP STARTER

The staff member in a typical T Group, usually referred to as the trainer, might open the group in a variety of ways. The following statement is an example:

This group will meet for many hours and will serve as a kind of laboratory where each individual can increase his understanding of the forces which influence individual behavior and the performance of groups and organizations. The data for learning will be our own behavior, feelings, and reactions. We begin with no definite structure or organization, no agreed-upon procedures, and no specific agenda. It will be up to us to fill the vacuum created by the lack of these familiar elements and to study our group as we evolve. My role will be to help the group to learn from its own experience, but not to act as a traditional chairman nor to suggest how we should organize, what our procedure should be, or exactly what our agenda will include. With these few

---

Reproduced by special permission from *NTL News and Reports,* 2, No. 2, "What Is Sensitivity Training?" by Charles Seashore (April, 1968), 1-2. Copyright 1968 by the NTL Institute for Applied Behavioral Science, associated with the National Education Association, Washington, D.C.

comments, I think we are ready to begin in whatever way you feel will be most helpful.

Into this ambiguous situation members then proceed to inject themselves. Some may try to organize the group by promoting an election of a chairman or the selection of a topic for discussion. Others may withdraw and wait in silence until they get a clearer sense of the direction the group may take. It is not unusual for an individual to try to get the trainer to play a more directive role, like that of the typical chairman.

Whatever role a person chooses to play, he also is observing and reacting to the behavior of other members and in turn is having an impact on them. It is these perceptions and reactions that are the data for learning.

## UNDERLYING ASSUMPTIONS OF T-GROUP TRAINING

Underlying T-Group training are the following assumptions about the nature of the learning process which distinguish T-Group training from other more traditional models of learning:

1. *Learning responsibility.* Each participant is responsible for his own learning. What a person learns depends upon his own style, readiness, and the relationships he develops with other members of the group.

2. *Staff role.* The staff person's role is to facilitate the examination and understanding of the experiences in the group. He helps participants to focus on the way the group is working, the style of an individual's participation, or the issues that are facing the group.

3. *Experience and conceptualization.* Most learning is a combination of experience and conceptualization. A major T-Group aim is to provide a setting in which individuals are encouraged to examine their experiences together in enough detail so that valid generalizations can be drawn.

4. *Authentic relationships and learning.* A person is most free to learn when he establishes authentic relationships with other people and thereby increases his sense of self-esteem and decreases his defensiveness. In authentic relationships persons can be open, honest, and direct with one another so that they are communicating what they are actually feeling rather than masking their feelings.

5. *Skill acquisition and values.* The development of new skills in working with people is maximized as a person examines the basic values underlying his behavior as he acquires appropriate concepts and theory and as he is able to practice new behavior and obtain feedback on the degree to which his behavior produces the intended impact.

## THE GOALS AND OUTCOMES OF SENSITIVITY TRAINING

Goals and outcomes of sensitivity training can be classified in terms of potential learning concerning individuals, groups, and organizations.

1. *The individual point of view.* Most T-Group participants gain a picture of the impact that they make on other group members. A participant can assess the degree to which that impact corresponds with or deviates from his conscious intentions. He can also get a picture of the *range of perceptions* of any given act. It is as important to understand that different people may see the same piece of behavior differently—for example, as supportive or antagonistic, relevant or irrelevant, clear or ambiguous—as it is to understand the impact on any given individual. In fact, very rarely do all members of a group have even the same general perceptions of a given individual or a specific event.

    Some people report that they try out behavior in the T Group they have never tried before. This experimentation can enlarge their view of their own potential and competence and provide the basis for continuing experimentation.

2. *The group point of view.* The T Group can focus on forces which affect the characteristics of the group such as the level of commitment and follow-through resulting from different methods of making decisions, the norms controlling the amount of conflict and disagreement that is permitted, and the kinds of data that are gathered. Concepts such as cohesion, power, group maturity, climate, and structure can be examined using the experiences in the group to better understand how these same forces operate in the back-home situation.

3. *The organization point of view.* Status, influence, division of labor, and styles of managing conflict are among organizational concepts that may be highlighted by analyzing the events in the small group. Subgroups that form can be viewed as analogous to units within an organization. It is then possible to look at the relationships between groups, examining such factors as competitiveness, communications, stereotyping, and understanding.

    One of the more important possibilities for a participant is that of examining the kinds of assumptions and values which underlie the behavior of people as they attempt to manage the work of the group. The opportunity to link up a philosophy of management with specific behaviors that are congruent with or antithetical to that philosophy makes the T Group particularly relevant to understanding the large organization.

## RESEARCH ON SENSITIVITY TRAINING

Research evidence on the effectiveness of sensitivity training is rather scarce and often subject to serious methodological problems. The annotated bibliographies referred to in the suggested readings at the end of this paper are the best source for identifying available studies. The following generalizations do seem to be supported by the available data:

1. People who attend sensitivity training programs are more likely to improve their managerial skills than those who do not (as reported by their peers, superiors, and subordinates).

2. Everyone does not benefit equally. Roughly two-thirds of the participants are seen as increasing their skills after attendance at laboratories. This figure represents an average across a number of studies.

3. Many individuals report extremely significant changes and impact on their lives as workers, family members, and citizens. This kind of anecdotal report should be viewed cautiously in terms of direct application to job settings, but it is consistent enough that it is clear that T-Group experiences can have a powerful and positive impact on individuals.

4. The incidence of serious stress and mental disturbance during training is difficult to measure, but it is estimated to be less than one per cent of participants and in almost all cases occurs in persons with a history of prior disturbances.

---

## MANAGERIAL GUIDELINES TO SENSITIVITY TRAINING

*Leslie This and Gordon L. Lippitt*

Some strong opinions have been expressed pro and con about sensitivity training by leaders in the field of management. Dr. Douglas McGregor[1] says this kind of training can ". . . bring about significant improvements in the skills of social interaction," while Dr. George S. Odiorne[2] indicates that he feels that many human relations laboratories have become ". . .perverted into psychological nudist camps which end up mainly as self flagellation societies."

While much has been written about sensitivity training, most of the literature is either technical or descriptive of personal experience. Neither approach is helpful to the training director or manager who wants to answer the pragmatic question, "Is this kind of training desirable in my organization and related to my organization's problems, needs, and objectives?"

When trying to get an answer to this kind of question, the organizational decision-maker usually consults someone who has been through a program. Almost inevitably he is told, "Oh, I couldn't begin to tell you about it—you just have to experience it." This is not helpful for effective decision-making. The manager then turns to a professional person who usually doesn't distinguish between the direct work-related benefits and the more complex areas of personality integration, social responsibility, self-fulfillment, and other person-oriented values of such training.

This article is an attempt to help the organizational leaders answer the question, "Is sensitivity training desirable for my organization?" We have divided the material

---

From *Training Directors Journal,* 17, No. 4 (April, 1963). Reprinted by permission of the American Society for Training and Development.

into major areas of consideration or questions[3] that have frequently been asked about this kind of training.

## WHAT IS "SENSITIVITY TRAINING"?

The expression "Sensitivity Training" is an inadequate phrase that is popularly used in describing a particular theory and method utilized in human relations training. This kind of training usually includes the methods of unstructured group learning, individual feedback, skill practice, and information sessions. The theory behind such methods is based on a laboratory concept of learning which believes that individuals can best learn inter-personal and group skills through actual experience which is analyzed for the benefit of the learner.

The words "sensitivity training" were first applied to this kind of learning in connection with the three-week Human Relations Laboratories, sponsored by the National Training Laboratories at Bethel, Maine. Since those early years beginning in 1947, this training has spread to many University-sponsored laboratories, in-house organization programs, and the development of consultant service to provide this kind of training to particular clients.

## HOW IS THIS TRAINING ACCOMPLISHED?

One of the assumptions underlying sensitivity training is that the man best learns these kings of insights by self-discovery.[4] It does little good to be "spoken to," or to read, many of these kinds of learnings. The training, then, must provide the kind of setting and methods that will best enable men to discover these insights and knowledges. These methods have been found most helpful:

## 1. Sensitivity Training Groups

Participants meet in groups of 12-15 with a professional trainer. They have no formal agenda or prior-determined leader. Normally the groups meet once a day for two hours, but may meet twice a day for approximately two-hour sessions.

Participants struggle with making decisions about how to spend the time profitably and how to provide structure and leadership. They have time to "thresh out" their struggles and examine their group life. As they do, they begin to get insights into the forces that are at work—things like the leadership struggle, group structure, group objectives, accommodating individual objectives to group objectives, group standards to guide their conduct, what improves and lessens the group's appeal to them, how decisions will be made, how to handle the participation of members, how one's behavior is influencing this group, and how the behavior of other members is influencing one's behavior.

As the group pauses to study parts of their group life that has interest for them, the trainer helps them to understand the forces at work at that moment. From time to time an individual member may want to test out with others the effect his behavior is having on them—how they see him—and may ask for reactions and information (feedback)—and the members try to help him see himself as they see him in the life of the group.

## 2. Information Sessions

Usually the problems with which the learning groups and individuals are concerned about, at any given time in the training, can be fairly well predicted. Presentations are made, drawing on research and experiences, to further explain the forces or factors involved with a particular area of interest. Usually the design of the program is such that it is flexible and may be modified to meet the needs and interests of the participants. Real life experiences need to be compared and generalized from the findings of other experiences and research.

## 3. Skill Practice Sessions

As a man gets knowledge about what may be, for him, a better way to perform as a manager, he wants practice trying out the new way. Skill exercise periods are provided to let the participants try out new ways of behaving, or to test out ways that have been suggested in the presentation or by the groups. Here he has little at stake since he knows he is in a training setting and encouraged to experiment with new ways of behaving. If it seems to him to be better than his old pattern, the chances are enhanced that he will try it out in his job when he returns home.

These are the main methods employed. Other action learning methods are also utilized—skill practice, case studies, informal group discussion, film, gaming and coaching teams. All of these methods are utilized as appropriate to a particular program to provide the maximum opportunity for participants to learn.

## WHY DOES THE TRAINING SEEM SO MYSTERIOUS?

It isn't so seen by those who know what the training is designed to accomplish. However, as we indicated earlier, the learnings about oneself are so highly personal that it is difficult to share them with another person in a meaningful way. How would a superior react if you told him, "I learned that people mistake my seriousness for aggressiveness, and I'm going to try to do something about it"? It is in this area that it is difficult to explain one's learning.

Perhaps it is a reflection of our culture and the need for this training that we find it difficult to share one's own feelings, emotions, and behavior. This is the nature of the sensitivity group experience.

There is no excuse whatever for there being any misunderstanding about the content of the information sessions or the skill practice sessions. These you can listen to, talk about, read and perform. These activities form an important part of the actual content. Because the learnings of a personal nature are so vivid and meaningful, in comparison to the substantive learnings, it is understandable that the total training experience tends to be seen as that component of the learning activity in which trainees gained their most meaningful insights.

## CONTRIBUTIONS TO ORGANIZATION GOALS

Sensitivity training means many things to many people. However, it seems to us that it serves three basic organizational concerns:

### 1. A Manager Works in a Complex Organization System.

Organizations are more than the physical "things" that go on its inventory lists. It is not possible to think of an organization without thinking of people—their functions and inter-relationships. If people are removed from an organization, you are left with a catalogue of items occupying space—little more than a poorly utilized warehouse.

It is people that have organizational objectives—that need a division of labor—that do the work—or give the service—that need meetings—need directives—need policies—need methods for delegating work—need controls—need to know how to get the most from other people.

Too little is really known about the human dynamics of organizations. One of the objectives of sensitivity training is to help the participant to see "organizations" not as the eye sees the buildings—but the informal, unseen, or unnoticed functions, elements, characteristics, forms, authority, tradition and interpersonal processes at work. The premise is that the more he understands the nature of the human encounter in the organization, the better equipped he will be to utilize, release, and control the organization for the attainment of organizational objectives.

### 2. Organizations accomplish their work through the motivations of people.

Most managers know their technical specialty quite well, and usually are quite well informed about the functions in their jobs such as planning, reporting, controlling, etc.

What they are less knowledgeable about is how to get the maximum efficiency and productivity from people. Down through history one of the precepts noted by successful leaders has been "Know thyself." Whether a manager recognizes it or not, his behavior, posture, gestures, tone of voice, ways of reacting to people and situations, silence—these and many other personal factors influence greatly how other people react to him and the jobs he asks them to do.

It would follow that the more a man understands himself, and how his behavior, consciously or unconsciously, will affect others—the more effective he can be in his relationships with other human beings. The objective is not to become an amateur psychiatrist, but to be more sensitive to the influence his behavior has on others, and vice versa.

Such sensitivity is not designed to make a person "thin-skinned," but more aware of his surroundings. The human organism has the "radar" of its many senses which frequently are dormant or undeveloped. It is in the sharpening of these senses that sensitivity training can assist.

### 3. A Manager Works Frequently in Groups.

The life of today's manager is spent in settings with two or more persons in an organizational work unit, conferences, institutes, planning groups, task forces and similar groupings. Many of the factors at work in individual-to-individual contexts are also at work within groups. However, as every manager knows, when a number of individuals are brought into a group setting, additional factors and forces are manifested. Many of us have commented, "How can people, who individually are such fine persons, behave so ineffectively when I call them together to work on a task?"

There is a body of knowledge about the factors at work when people work in groups, and the more a manager understands these factors, the more effectively he can work with people in work groups. Dr. Rensis Likert has recently summarized much of the research in this area, and its implications for managers and organizations, in his book "Patterns of Management."[5] The research on morale and productivity indicate that people potentially meet their needs and accomplish work effectively in the face-to-face work unit of the organization.

These three areas, then, are the major areas of learning that sensitivity training explores. Since much of what is learned is peculiar to the individual in attendance, it is difficult to list what specific learning or insights each participant will discover. To know oneself better is a different experience for each of us, and that is why a personal insight for one person is not an insight to another. This in part explains why participants find it so difficult to agree on what they learned at a human relations laboratory experience.

People develop their skill and awareness through various learning experiences. An experience which will further interpersonal competence will need to provide the following conditions for learning:[6]

1.  The recognition on the part of the trainee of a need for improving his own human relations skills.

2.  An opportunity for a trainee to interact in a learning situation so that acutal behavior may serve as the curriculum.

3.  A supportive and helpful climate for learning created by the total experience.

4.  An opportunity for the trainees to give "feedback" on the effect of their behavior in both structured and unstructured learning experiences.

5.  A basic knowledge of individual, group, and organizational behavior to give guidance to the learner.

6. A chance to practice new skills of relating in person-to-person and person-to-group situations.

7. An opportunity to relate his learning to back-on-the-job situations.

These conditions for learning are essential elements in what has been referred to as the "laboratory" approach to human relations training.

## KINDS OF ORGANIZATIONAL PROBLEMS IT CAN AFFECT

We will immediately make two assumptions: 1, that training can affect some organizational problems; and 2, that individuals and groups may be considered organizational problems.

There are some organizational problems which are not the primary province of any kind of training. If the organizational product or service is not needed, wanted, or of a deliberate inferior quality—training isn't the answer. If the market falls out from under a product because of technological or international factors, training is out of its field in attempting to solve such a problem. There are some organizational matters that are the main province of other facets of organizational problem solving. Sometimes organizations mistakenly see training as the answer to all their problems. Organizational effectiveness, in all its aspects, can never be equated with training or the lack of training.

If, however, a manager suspects that some of the organization's effectiveness is being disturbed or affected by some of the following kinds of problems, he may well consider sensitivity training:

1. An otherwise effective manager whose attitudes, skills, relationships with his work force, relationships with other persons and sub-units, effectiveness in meetings, ability to diagnose personal relationship problems in their embryonic stage, are seen as inadequate.

2. Where the basic face-to-face units of the organization do not seem to be achieving a level of morale and productivity that is in keeping with their abilities.

3. Where the organization is concerned with public relations and its managerial staff have enough contacts with outside groups that the totality of these contacts can materially affect the organization's image.

4. Where it is important for communication to flow as uninhibitedly as possible between peers, between subordinate and superior, and between work units even though they appear as separate prongs on the organizational chart.

5. Where there is good reason to believe that managers in the organization are, by organizational practice or climate, discouraged from being inventive, creative, and

exercising or receiving appropriate responsibility, delegation of authority, and exercising initiative in meeting operational problems.

6. Where the organization gets its work done in large measure through the use of group meetings, conferences, and informal group activities.

## WHAT MUST EXIST BEFORE SENSITIVITY TRAINING?

The training should be consistent with the organizational objectives, goals, and processes of decision-making.[7] There must be an understanding, beginning at top management and permeating down through the levels to be trained, of the purpose of the training and acceptance and support of the training objectives. The training program should be designed to help solve one or more identified management problems, and tailored to fit the particular organization needs. The program and design should be carefully worked out and planned. It is usually helpful if some of top management have had a personal experience with this kind of training.

The training should be seen as voluntary, and an employee should be permitted to decline to undertake the training without punishment or embarrassment. There should also exist an organizational understanding and climate that will enable a participant to "try out" and practice his learnings in the organizational setting.

A qualified staff should be utilized for such training. The staff should include social scientists with experience in this kind of training, but they should be provided ample opportunity to become familiar with the organization and to be accepted by the management of the organization. Such training should also have a well designed evaluation plan to measure the effectiveness of the training.

Lately, we think the organization must see the training as a part of the organizational life and be committed to provide follow-up and supplementary training opportunities to reinforce the process that has been begun.

## SOME OF THE ISSUES ABOUT VARIOUS APPROACHES

This kind of training has developed a number of approaches in its application.

### 1. Length of Training

Some training programs last three weeks—others for as short a period as two days. Some organizations have a series of two-day sessions at intervals over a period of several months. There is some disagreement as to what is the desired length, or whether a continuous program is better.

There can be little assurance as to how much more learning takes place in a week's program versus a three-week's program—or a three-day program vs. a one-week program. Probably common sense is the best guide. One can expect that more can be learned in one week than in three days. Rarely has this kind of training been undertaken without having at least twelve hours of group learning time plus the other aspects of the program.

In the shorter programs the organization would need to identify what kind of skills, insights, and knowledges are most important to focus on, and to design the training program for intensive concentration in these pre-determined areas. Generally, most organizations seem to find an experience of at least one week's duration most desirable. This is particularly true if one is focusing on personal insight. It takes time to create a group atmosphere, and individual readiness, that will permit constructive and direct feedback of a helpful nature to trainees.

## 2. Heterogeneous or Family Groups

Opinions differ as to whether it is better to train men in programs made up from different organizations, within one industry or business, within one department in an organization, along peer lines, or vertically from several levels. There are advantages and disadvantages to each. Generally speaking, the advantage of "family" training is that all members of a work group, or related work groups, get the same kind of training at one time and get to know each other quite well.[8] They can also use the learning process in their day by day work to solve operating problems.

One of the major disadvantages of family groupings is that participants can never completely forget the setting and work relationships and the inter-actions among participants may be less intense and direct. It has been proven valuable in heterogeneous training to send a team of persons from an organization to increase impact back in the organization. Which pattern one chooses would depend upon the length of the program, the experience of the persons to be trained, the intensity of training desired, and the objectives of the program for the organization.

The authors have conducted sensitivity training using both approaches with governmental, community, and industrial organizations, and found real impact for organizational change to be possible in either approach.

## 3. Use of Trainer or Instruments in the Unstructured Group Phase of the Learning

Some experimentation has been done recently with so-called instrumental groups.[9] The instruments consist of both individual and group administered questionnaires in which reactions can be coded, analyzed, and then "fed back" to the participants. A trainer does not sit with the basic training group, but does assist in the design of the training activity and provides materials to help the groups analyze their behavior as they work together. The trainer may also lead data summarizing sessions or presentations as well as assist the group with practice exercises.

The results of these programs do indicate that learning does take place under such circumstances. A group, through the use of well developed data collection instruments, can feed back data to itself for effective learning.

Many of the specialists in this field feel that the trainer should be present to help with inter-personal feedback and group analysis as well as to prevent attempts at ill-advised therapy by trainees of each other.

It is also felt by some that such training can best utilize a professional at all times during the training. The experience to date would indicate the value in using both the trainer and effective data collection instruments for maximizing the learning.

### 4. Use of Outside vs Inside Organization Trainers

Some managers ask the question: "Can't my training director do this kind of training?"

Perhaps he can if he has had extensive training.[10] Certainly he can probably handle some of the elements, with proper knowledge and experience, like information presentations and skill exercises. However, the sensitivity training group experience and the integration of all the elements of the training program into a meaningful experience, requires a great deal of specialized knowledge, skill, and experience.

These can be learned by many training directors, but the expenditure in time, effort, and money is considerable. There is frequently the additional problem of the training director being handicapped by operating within the organization and not being seen as a resource in this kind of developmental process. Many organizations feel it is best to go outside the organization for professional guidance in this field of training. The training director's job has so many responsibilities that frequently he can not become an expert in this or other highly specialized areas of training if he is to most importantly serve as a consultant to management on how training can help management solve its problems.

### WHAT ORGANIZATIONS SHOULD NOT USE SENSITIVITY TRAINING?

Sensitivity training may have little to offer where the *management of the organization—*

- Is highly directive and intends to remain that way.
- Is not concerned with public relations, even though publics are a major factor in its operations.
- Is not concerned about the needs of employees being met or becoming compatible and closely related to the organization's needs.
- Is predicated on the assumption that men are motivated solely, or mainly, by money, promotional opportunity, threats and rewards.
- Believes that training is only for those in positions subordinate to them and is either anti-training or luke-warm to training.
- Sees the organization as composed of tight sub-units that have their own job to do and what happens elsewhere in the organization is none of their business.
- Operates on a "hard-nosed" basis and is solely production-centered regardless of the means employed.

One of the dangers in setting down a list such as the above is that most organizations will deny they have any of the attributes or characteristics so listed. These are not set down here in a judgmental way—they may be perfectly valid for that organization. Just because these characteristics aren't popular today doesn't necessarily mean they have nothing to recommend them. We are only suggesting that given a number of these characteristics, and intending to continue to operate in this way, an organization would not find sensitivity of sufficient benefit to warrant the investment of the required time and money. Other approaches to organizational change would need to precede the adoption of sensitivity training as a part of the development programs of this organization.

## WHAT IS MANAGEMENT'S ROLE?

Management must see the training as compatible with organizational objectives, understand the training objectives, and help managers see that management "buys" the philosophy of participative way of working with staff. Management should publicly endorse the program by its own way of behaving (men supervise as they are supervised—not as they are taught to supervise), be willing to finance the program adequately, and provide conditions that will allow men to put their learnings into operational practice.

## WHAT ARE THE RISKS?

There is always the risk that here and there an individual may be upset by the experience. A not too well integrated person may be threatened by self-knowledge. It is not demonstrated that the experience will really do more than precipitate a personal situation that existed previously.

There is the further risk that some managers exposed to this training may reach wrong conclusions about principles and ways of operating and be less effective than before. This is usually the result of the wrong application of a principle, or the misunderstanding of a learning. Specialists in laboratory training do not advocate that all decisions should be group decisions or that everyone in an organization needs to like each other, but a few participants in this type of training may draw inappropriate conclusions which is a possible consequence of any form of educational endeavor.

There is always the risk of seeing the training as a panacea for too many organizational ills. It does not guarantee results. It promises only more knowledgeable personal performance. It cannot substitute for a better product or service; or for organizational imperfections in financing, advertising, production, etc.

## WHERE DO I START?

You begin by discussions with your top staff. Are the learnings that can be enhanced by sensitivity training seen as bearing on the problems of your organization? Enough to want you to do something about them? If not, you turn to some other approach.

If it all still makes sense to you and is seen as desirable, you find a reputable university or outside professional training organization that has knowledgeable resource persons to help you look specifically at your problem and the impact this kind of training can have on them.

Constantly you keep testing the applicability of this kind of training in your organization for your kind of problems, the staff you possess, and with the other priorities facing you. And then, as with all decision making, if this course of action still seems to make good sense, you initiate the first action steps to implement it.

To summarize, if an organization wants its managers to know organization structure and dynamics, to know themselves better so that they can conduct themselves more effectively as they work with other individuals, and to know the forces and factors at work when people work in groups so they can become more effective—sensitivity training is probably a desirable part of your training program. If these concerns, or objectives, are not seen as desirable, needed, or important, an organization should not consider sensitivity training.

**NOTES**

1. McGregor, Douglas, *The Human Side of Enterprise*, McGraw-Hill, 1960, 221.

2. Odiorne, George S., Managerial narcissism—the great self development binge, *Management of Personnel Quarterly*, **1**, Issue 3 (Spring 1962), Bureau of Industrial Relations, Graduate School of Business, University of Michigan.

3. The authors wish to acknowledge the contribution of Mr. Rowland Geddie of the Atlanta ASTD chapter who organized a January 1963 chapter meeting on Sensitivity Training which raised some of these questions with Dr. Lippitt.

4. Knowles, Malcolm S., The leader looks at self development, *Looking into Leadership Monographs*, Leadership Resources, Inc., 1961.

5. Likert, Rensis, *Patterns of Management*, McGraw-Hill, 1962.

6. A more complete discussion of the conditions for laboratory learning may be found in Bradford, Leland P., The teaching-learning transaction, *Adult Education* (Spring, 1958) and also in Selected Readings Series No. 3, *Forces In Learning,* National Training Laboratories, National Education Association, 1961.

7. Niven, Jarold, and Allen Zoll, *A Survey of Sensitivity Training for Industrial Managers*, Boeing Airplane Co., Seattle, Washington.

8. One example of the "family" approach to training is reported in Argyris, C., *Interpersonal Competence and Organizational Effectiveness*. Dorsey-Irwin Press, 1962.

9. Blake, R., and J. Mouton, The instrumented training laboratory, in *Issues in Human Relations Training*, National Training Laboratories, National Education Association, Washington, D.C., 1962.

10. Lippitt, Gordon L. and Leslie E. This, Is training a profession?, *The Journal of the ASTD* (April, 1960).

# THE ANARCHIST MOVEMENT AND THE T GROUP: SOME POSSIBLE LESSONS FOR ORGANIZATIONAL DEVELOPMENT

*Bernard M. Bass*

T-Group theorists often imply that what is good for an individual's mental health and maturity is good for the organization's well-being. Therefore, they maintain that if we can train people to be better diagnosticians with greater tolerance and social awareness, organizations composed of such people will be the better for it. But this position may be as wrong as assuming that what is good for the organization is good for its members. Sensitivity training may be necessary for organizational development, but it is not sufficient. By itself, T Grouping is not enough.

Consider the following experimental results: Nine quasi-T Groups (T Groups without trainers) met for 15 weeks as part of a graduate business management program. After another 15 weeks had passed, three of the nine groups were each splintered into three parts and the parts reassembled into three new teams. Three other groups were divided in half and reassembled as three new teams. Three groups were left intact. Then the teams competed for 15 weeks with one another in the Carnegie Tech Management Game. Interpersonal comfort, openness, familiarity, communication ease, and cohesiveness were greatest in the three intact groups, according to member ratings made five weeks after company operations began. Nevertheless, it was these three intact groups that lost an average of $5.37 million in the competition with the remaining splintered groups. The splintered groups broke even or made a good profit, on the average. Yet these splintered groups were less successful interpersonally, according to member descriptions. These firms were felt to be less cohesive and were seen as less open. Members were less familiar with one another and had more difficulty in communicating. But they were much more successful in operating as business firms. Why? We think the answer may lie in the tendency we observed for these financially successful groups to make better use of management controls that avoided too heavy reliance on interpersonal confidence.

In the intact groups, with better interpersonal feelings, members expected more from one another as persons than they could actually receive; and for 15 weeks, at least, they were unable to correct this error of overdependence on one another. For instance, one team member might ask another to complete a budget analysis in time for the company to use it to make an important buying decision. In the intact group, the team member who made the request was likely to expect that it had been done. In the fractured groups, the members were more likely to depend on formal controls to see that such action had been taken. And thus it was that the intact groups made many more forecasting errors, failed often to take advantage of discount opportunities, had more shortages or overstocked inventories, and so on (Deep, Bass, & Vaughan, in press). In many respects, the intact groups were reliving, in 15 weeks, a half century of the history of the Spanish anarchists.

The Spanish anarchists[1] were a primitive social movement, yet seem to have nurtured many of the values often stressed in a T Group. Although the following sounds like Bethel, 1967, it was written by the anarchist, Francisco Pi y Margall, a Catalan writer and politician of the mid-nineteenth century:

True order supposes cohesion, yet not a cohesion obtained by the presence of exterior forces, but an intimate and spontaneous cohesion which external constraints inevitably inhibit. Every man who has power over another is a tyrant . . . In place of power relationships which should be eliminated, there can develop a natural system of relationships in their stead.

As soon as the old social order was destroyed (or as T Groupers might say, as soon as unfreezing had been accomplished), "then nature would cause new and better social organisms to arise to fill their place."

The anarchist emphasis on freedom of individuals and freedom of groups of individuals produced effects that may be seen in many an assembly of T Groups. At a congress of anarchists, the delegates assembled with the wishes and capacities of the groups they represented carefully in mind. Each would get up and say what his group was prepared and able to do. No group was urged to take any action which it did not feel itself prepared to take. No group was ever overruled by another group or had pressure put on it to act against its private convictions. Similarly, no objections were raised to local groups' or individual members' cooperating with a particular proposal, if they desired to do so.

The Spanish anarchist movement was an attempt to recover the equality and dignity of the individual faced with the everincreasing complexities of modern industrialization. It was an expression of nostalgia for the past: a fight against the strain of factory life. To some degree, the T-Group experience is seen in a similar way by Schein and Bennis (1965): "Laboratory training is singularly appropriate for dealing with some of the core crises facing contemporary society" (p. 6). They add that for the individual, life has become more problematical. He is alienated, lonely, anxious, and desperately seeking purpose and identity. Presumably laboratory training can help, just as anarchism could help the individual to cope better with his industrial environment.

Nevertheless, 60 years of anarchist leadership brought to its members practically nothing. The movement was much more effective than the competing movement of socialism in creating a feeling of need for change, yet anarchism lacked the necessary programs for bringing it about (Brenan, 1943).

Here, what may be a poor analogy ends. For the anarchists were intolerant of those who did not share their views. They were uncompromising, unsophisticated, and uninterested in social reform. They were a puritanical movement. They aimed to destroy modern society and had little to recommend in its place. Nevertheless, there may be some lessons to be learned from analyzing why they failed, lessons which may have implications for efforts to develop organizational effectiveness through T Grouping. The anarchists always put individual freedom ahead of organizational necessities. This resulted in the organization's suffering one defeat after another, despite which it usually was stronger in cohesiveness after defeat than before. The anarchists insisted that their adherents remain free and unfettered, organized in local groups, and without bureaucratic ties. They emphasized the importance of the primary group and its individual members, and deemphasized the formal organization, even to the point of providing no salaries or centralized financial resources for the movement's central leadership.

The anarchists represented a movement in which enthusiasm, interpersonal acceptance, mutual support, individual freedom, and cohesiveness of membership were maximized, yet where their effects on society were the reverse of what they had intended.[2]

The anarchists failed because they refused to accept supergroup goals, goals to which all or most of the local units could subscribe. They refused to accept building a formal organization to coordinate and direct the primary groups toward any such supergoals. This emphasis on freedom of the individual and the small group made it impossible to predict what others would do, which, in turn, made coordinated effort impossible. There was a refusal to submerge individual and small-group needs to advance organizational interests.

A second reason they failed, or more often had a reverse influence on the course of events, was the destructiveness of their unfreezing efforts. These aroused counter-forces in reaction which were even stronger in support of reaction or the status quo.

It seems to me that both of these causes of failure in the anarchist movement may be present in laboratory training programs purporting to foster both individual as well as organizational development, for what may be good for individual growth may not always be good for the organization's health. If we wish to increase our understanding of how to optimize the development of the individual *and* the organization, it may be profitable to review the parallels between the ineffectiveness of the anarchist movement and what goes on in the training laboratory.

For example, the T-Group laboratory does in miniature what the anarchists attempted to do in macroscopic proportions. Unfreezing is accomplished in the laboratory by removing the familiar props and customary social mechanisms, by violating the expectations of trainees, and by creating an ambiguous, unstructured situation for them of unclear goals and minimum cues.

The staff is aware of the need to avoid patterns of dependence and counterdependence of staff with trainees. Yet this unfreezing process may foster feelings within some trainees that echo Bakunin, the founder of the anarchist movement, who declared: "All exercise of authority perverts and all submissiveness to authority humiliates." That is, given a severe, structureless experience, it may be that some laboratory participants lose their confidence to use authority which may be needed in the future for organizational reasons. This may be neither the intent of the program nor a logical outcome, but it may occur just the same.[3] At the same time, there may be a correspondingly reduced acceptance of submissive behavior that may be necessary at times for the interests of good organization. In short, the "destruction" of the customary authority structure in the T Group in order to promote exploration and change in the individual participants, coupled with an emphasis on the values of democracy and consensus, may produce, in some participants at least, sufficient antiauthoritarian leadership attitudes to reduce their contributions to the organization at times when such directive leadership is required.

Yet one can catalog many organizational circumstances in which shared, permissive leadership would be less effective and acceptable than more authoritarian approaches, such as when interaction in the organization between superior and subordinate is restricted by infrequent meetings or poor communications; in large groups, where the superior is in the center of a communication network; when higher authority or the marketplace imposes arbitrary deadlines; or where subordinates expect authoritative direction. The culture may require more directive leadership. Recently, in a classroom roleplay I conducted in Spain, the participants rejected the democratic supervisor and showed preference for one who tried to persuade them. They felt the persuasive leader was according them the dignity to which they were accustomed. The democratic supervisor, since he did not try to change their minds, appeared to them to show less interest in them as persons.

T-Group theory emphasizes learning through discovery. It tends to ignore other powerful learning processes that may be going on simultaneously in the highly ambiguous setting where motivation is strong and coping behavior is vigorous and where reinforcement and fixation are unclear and uncertain to both staff and trainees. What is being reinforced and how and when it occurs may be unclear to both. Imitation, vicarious learning, incidental learning, and persuasion all may be operating in subtle directions counter to what is being learned through discovery. Despite these offsetting possibilities, T Groups are effective training grounds. A reasonable amount of controlled research evidence by Bunker (1965), by Miles (1965), and by Boyd (Boyd & Elliss, 1962), among others, attests to the increased interpersonal competence, back on the job, of trainees that results from a laboratory experience. Just as important are the observable changes which are seen in the trainee's increased awareness of interpersonal dynamics. (Ask any trainer!)

Thus we have considerable evidence that the T-Group experience is likely to increase a trainee's willingness, back in the organization, to try to foster mutual trust, shared decisions, and openness of communication. At the same time, the experience may decrease his willingness to withhold the release of information, to maintain social distance, or to make political alliances. Indeed, he may fail completely to recognize how differently he may need to behave when he is negotiating in the interests of his department or organization from when he is problem solving with others. Minimally, greater internal conflict and guilt feelings may be aroused in him when he is forced by organizational demands to adopt Machiavellian approaches.

There seems to be a generally accepted assumption that a considerable amount of frustration must be built up during the unfreezing process in the T Group and that the greater this frustration, the greater will be the search for solutions to the dilemmas imposed on the trainees by the ambiguous situation. This is predicated on a homeostatic model. One must need or want to change before he will change; and the greater the felt need, the greater will be the change. But one wonders whether the learning process may be hindered rather than helped by this emphasis on a model of frustration-search-fixation, a model that may be more applicable to rats than to man. Counterdependent feelings may be raised that increase rather than decrease resistance to change. All too often the trainer may become a leadership model that may be inappropriate for the organization. While I do not suggest that trainers, in general, engender more hostile counterreactions by their role repertoire, it is possible that some, perhaps out of their own aggressive needs, do make a considerable effort to knock the past out of trainees and to arouse a great deal of frustration in them.

One wonders whether all or any of this preliminary frustrating experience is necessary. More learning might occur about process and interpersonal awareness by beginning the group with a task, say, an in-basket test or a review of an organization survey—this to be followed by a shared process analysis of the experience. What would be learned might have more direct relevance for organizational affairs. We would be dealing with "How am I doing?" in the context of a simulation of an organizational issue or in the context of real organizational problems rather than "How am I doing?" in my interpersonal relations as simulated by the T Group of which I am a member. Less feeling might be aroused, but more significant learning might take place.

The question of goals which transcend the primary group goals in the laboratory often are given little emphasis. The paramount authority of the T Group is stressed. Most of the reinforcement is given for agreements, compacts, and "ground rules" established within the T Group. Participant responsibilities to the collectivity of T Groups are secondary. As a consequence, the staff faces difficulties when one T Group is ready for a lecture and another is not or when one T Group feels it wants more T-Group time and another does not.

Competitive intergroup exercises have focused attention, in some degree, on this issue of superordinate problems. With good reason, intergroup exercises focus on the dynamics of competition; for much is learned here about in-group behavior and attitudes toward out-groups. Occasionally in laboratories, organizational simulations are run that require the establishment of organizational goals to which the subordinate T Groups must subscribe; but I do not think we have achieved equal success in creating for learning purposes such cooperating experiences as we have achieved in designing competing ones. Somehow, we are going to have to provide training experiences in which we develop the same socio-emotional intensity of commitment to the laboratory as to the T Group, then place these laboratory commitments in conflict with commitments to the T Group. This will require participants to deal with the common organizational experience of superordinate goals that conflict with department goals.

As it was among the anarchists, individual freedom is fostered in the T-Group laboratory, where "the delegate is free—and is encouraged—to question (and reject) all inputs from the staff or other delegates. Self-control . . . is vigorously sanctioned; delegates are viewed . . . as free agents, autonomous volunteers in the learning process" (Schein & Bennis, 1965, p. 33). This emphasis on freedom is not usually matched by an equally important emphasis on the need for individual responsibility which may constrain the individual. This need to restrict one's freedom to maintain a more responsible stance for the good of the organization is seldom seen in the laboratory situation. Most emphasis is likely to be placed on tolerance of others' needs and on individual liberty rather than on the need for individual responsibility. For instance, the laboratory will stress that an individual is free to accept or to reject ideas, that he is free to change or not to change, that he is free to take roles or not to take them. It will be less likely to stress that he also has the responsibility to communicate to others what he has accepted or rejected, his intentions to change, and his assumption of particular group tasks. That is, if we wish to promote *both* individual and organizational effectiveness, then we need to point out that if an individual member of an organization is given considerable discretion and freedom he, in turn, must make it possible for others to take account of his actions and changes of plans. He is not free to act without ensuring that others are aware of his changes of plans. Mutual predictability seems of paramount importance to the organization if coordinated effort is to be achieved, although it may be of less consequence to a given individual.

Other important organizational needs may be underplayed when they conflict with individual values. For instance, in the intergroup competition held in many laboratories, we see increased loyalty to one's own group and increased cohesiveness within one's group. The bias of members toward their own group's product is exposed. Members who might defect are prospective traitors. The need for greater objectivity under such circumstances is seen, but I doubt whether most trainers call attention to the other aspect of the situation; e.g., on occasion, such blind loyalty may have positive organizational value. Thus, if I shared a foxhole with a fellow soldier, I would prefer that he remain blindly loyal to our side in the midst of a fire fight rather than suddenly deciding that the other side had more merit and that he was going to switch sides.

Or, consider the question of tolerance for deviant opinion. Here again, from the organization's point of view, there is a need for a two-way give-and-take. The deviant has to have some sense for tolerating the majority opinion, just as the majority needs to be able to tolerate deviants if the organization is to prosper.

Where, in the laboratory experience, is much learned about when and where individual interests may need to be subordinated for reasons of organization? Where is much learned about how to cope with the need to protect individual interests without jeopardizing the interests of the organization?

Schein and Bennis (1965) see the earlier emphasis on personal development (the yogi approach) as now being supplemented, in some degree, by concern for organizational development (the commissar approach). However, they do not seem to share with Pugh (1965) the thought that the yogi approach may reduce the contribution and effectiveness of the individual to the organization. They seem to be more in agreement with Argyris (1962), for whom interpersonal competence[4] is prerequisite to effective decision making, organizational flexibility, and freedom from defensiveness. Individual maturity is seen as essential for increasing organizational effectiveness. Pugh (1965) is not so sure.

Pugh (1965) assumes, rightly, that T-Group training, as such, is oriented toward increasing personal maturity and understanding. What happens, he asks, when the ex-T Grouper returns to a mechanistic organization? Pugh is uncertain. It may be that such an organization calls for little initiative from the ex-T Grouper and only a routine, shallow use of his skills, which results in his increased frustration and job dissatisfaction. Or it may be that the rigid, mechanistic system requires sophisticated personnel to operate it so that the increased perceptual sophistication of the ex-T Grouper increases his effectiveness.

Similarly, returning to an organic structure may be easier or more difficult for the ex-T Grouper. He may be called upon to display initiative in setting goals and in diagnosing social problems which he now can do more effectively. Or, to quote Pugh, he may be ruined; for in a fluid, organic situation "only an immature, job-centered bastard can insensitively hack his way to achievement."

Bamforth (1965) abandoned a pure T-Group effort in a firm where the T Groups were composed of "diagonal slices" of the organization so that no man was in the same T Group with his boss or immediate subordinates. Among the inadequacies of this program, Bamforth cited:

1.  T-Group discussion became a ventilation area. Yet the real boss-subordinate problems were not explored or dealt with effectively.

2.  Role conflicts at work were perceived in the T-Group discussions but were left unresolved.

3.  T-Group meetings did not result in corresponding work group meetings; i.e., there was no transfer.

In sum, as with the anarchist movement, the pure T-Group experience may generate a great deal of individual development. The T Group may bring about increased commitment to social understanding, greater self-awareness, and greater acceptance of individuality. Yet collectives of such more "mature" individuals may make less effective organizations. Moreover, the process of such individual growth, paralleling the anarchistic ideology of unfreezing, may carry with it some by-products of negative import to the individuals as effective members of an organization.

It is assumed that increased diagnostic skill and increased self-awareness are transferred from the T-Group experience back to the organization. Yet learning research clearly suggests that for such transfer to occur one must teach for transfer. In the past eight years or so, we have seen a considerable increase in attention to this need to teach for transfer, either by introducing learning experiences simulating important organizational issues or by increasing the similarity to the real organization of the setting in which the training experience takes place. Direct evidence of the utility of increasing the similarity of the training group to the work group comes from an analysis by Morton (Morton & Bass, 1964). Six T Groups of men from the same aerospace company, from different departments and levels (diagonal slices of the organization), were contrasted with six T Groups where men in a given T Group came from the same department, so that bosses and their subordinates were together in the same T Groups. Six months after training, the latter groups reported significantly more critical incidents of effectiveness back on the job that were attributable to the T-Group experience.

At least eight different approaches are now being employed to increase the transfer of training.

A common laboratory practice is to gradually reduce time in T Groups, as well as in lectures and exercises concerning individual and small-group behavior, during the course of a laboratory. In their place, the program substitutes exercises generating organizational phenomena and discussions about these phenomena. The exercises are an effort to provide quasi-real organizational experiences for participants for which they can profitably critique both the content and the process. These exercises may be business games of various degrees of sophistication and complexity. They may be miniature representations of the participants' back-home, real organization. They may be replications of organizational experiments such as the Bavelas-Leavitt communication network experiment (Bavelas, 1950) or the Leavitt one-way versus two-way communications experiment (Leavitt, 1962). I have prepared a program of such exercises which can be sandwiched in between T-Group sessions. The exercises involve organizational issues such as the multiplicity of management budgeting goals, expectations and satisfaction, compensation, leadership style, planning versus operating, and collective bargaining (Bass, 1965). The important staff input in dealing with these organizational exercises is to motivate participants to examine the processes by which they were confronted rather than to remain fixed on the more seductive structural and economic contents of the problems. At any rate, these exercises give participants an opportunity to transfer the analytic approaches they have developed in T Groups to simplified replicas of organizational situations, which process analyses they all can share in the here-and-now.

A second way of promoting organizational learning, using here-and-now experiences, is to confront the whole laboratory with real problems they have, as a laboratory. They might have to deal with a T Group that never comes into theory sessions on time, which holds up all the others. Or the staff may ask each T Group to subdivide or merge for specific purposes. Or the staff may ask members to rearrange themselves. A particularly strong socio-emotional experience can be engendered by a sort of "sociometry-in-motion," in which these rearrangements are made physically in one large room. Members literally have to get up and leave their own groups or call for the formation of new groups. Again, the learning comes not from the doing so much as from the analysis of what was done and how it was done.

A third approach picks up real organizational issues on which to work, using T-Group and laboratory structures which have developed earlier in the program. This requires that the T Groups contain men who work together in the real organization and face together real problems back on the job. For example, in the Aerojet program (Morton & Bass, 1964), in each laboratory each of four T Groups was composed of men from the same department. The last three days of the 10-day program provided opportunities for the T Groups to form consulting teams (one man from each T Group) similar to ones used earlier in the laboratory to consult on T-Group problems, but now made available to consult with the T Groups on real work problems since, as all men within a T Group were from the same department, they also could consult on real interdepartmental problems between T Groups.

A fourth approach, which could begin during a laboratory or after it, organizes a continuing series of T Groups to be held back home in the organization among men who must work together. An executive and his immediate subordinates might form such a continuing T Group.

A fifth approach was pioneered by Bamforth (1965) as a consequence of the failure of the within-plant T-Group members with whom he worked to transfer their learning to on-the-job problems. He dispensed with the T-Group experience altogether. He changed from the role of a T-Group trainer to that of a consultant to functioning, formal work-group meetings, where he helped the groups to recognize their boss-subordinate difficulties, anxieties about using or not using authority, colleague relations, role classifications, communications difficulties, resistance to the disclosure of initially unrecognized dynamics, and other sociopsychological problems.

In this approach, as a group works on its own real problems, the consultant slowly and gradually introduces process analysis of what is taking place, beginning possibly with some questions on how the group feels about its progress to date. The discussions about the group's performance may eventually move the group into a general program of education about group and organizational dynamics, using the group's own current experiences as the continuing basis for discussion and analysis (Schein & Bennis, 1965).

Along lines similar to those developed by Bamforth, Friedlander (N.D.) ran laboratory sessions for four work groups lasting four or five days. The work groups identified problems they faced and examined ways of solving them and implementing solutions. Interpersonal and intergroup processes affecting each work group were explored in this context.

In comparison with eight untrained groups, four work groups who received such training were found six months after training to describe themselves as more effective in problem solving, more mutually influential, and more involved in group meetings.

A sixth way combines several of the previously mentioned methods, again dispensing with the T Group, per se. At International Mining, for instance, participants from the same real organizational group engage in a complex business game over an extended period of time. After each set of decisions has been completed, a formal session of process analysis is completed. Participants have an opportunity to examine their sociopsychological interplay when engaged in behavior simulating real behavior in an organization (Wagner, 1965). The content of interaction among the trainees, who are an intact work group, is a simulation of real organizational problems. The process discussion gradually takes on T-Group qualities.

A seventh variant, employed by Matthew Miles (1965), among others, is more directly focused on organizational improvement as the basis for work-group deliberations. The meetings of the group primarily concern the construction, development, and evaluation of an attitude survey of the organization for which the group is responsible. Such a group might consist of a department head, his four immediate assistants, and their subordinates. Again, staff personnel gradually focus attention on the processes for the organization as a whole.

Finally, Blake's Managerial Grid (Blake & Mouton, 1964) represents still another approach that focuses a supervisor's attention on his own style of leadership and its likely effects on his contribution to his organization. The quasi-T-Group training aims to move the trainee to an optimum style of leadership and to help him see the effects of different styles of leadership on organizational performance.

These eight approaches all represent efforts to promote transfer of training. The more we can move in this direction, the more we are likely to increase the utility of laboratory methods for both personal and organizational improvement.

Thus it is that most of the recent organizational improvement programs, such as those of Esso, Pacific Finance, Space Technology Laboratory, Aluminum Company of Canada, U.S. Rubber, Hotel Corporation of America, General Electric, I.B.M., Eli Lilly, Hydro-Electric Commission of Canada, Beltone, and Aerojet-General, have involved much more than just T-Group training (Schein & Bennis, 1965). And when one considers the newness of all of these programs one cannot but feel that we are at the beginning of an era of exciting innovation in organizational psychology, an excitement not based on anarchistic destructiveness but resulting from creative developments and successes in the integration of individual and organizational well-being.

From an organizational point of view, mere T Grouping is not enough. Various supplementary activities which build upon the T-Group experience or take place in conjunction with T Grouping or as substitutes for T Grouping, in one way or another, need to be employed to promote organizational as well as individual learning and development. It should be clear that I still see the T-Group experience, or related approaches, as basic to organizational development. But as I stated in the introduction, T Grouping is necessary but not sufficient.

**NOTES**

1.  I have relied heavily on Brenan (1943) for the description and evaluation of Spanish anarchism presented here.

2.  This is not an unusual circumstance. There are many situations where a group's success at its tasks may be negatively related to its success in its interpersonal relations. For instance, the highly cohesive group may lack resources to cope with its tasks. Conversely, the group that is low in cohesion may be highly productive if the tasks are simple and the members are constrained from withdrawing by threat of punishment or promise of reward (Bass, 1965). Again, satisfactory interpersonal relations may be necessary in many circumstances for organizational productivity, but they are no guarantee of it.

3.  In one industrial laboratory, I recall overhearing some executives who were wandering around and muttering to themselves, "I must not be a leader, I must not be a leader!" Similarly, at the conclusion of another laboratory, many executives commented that they had removed their protective outer shells and were more open to experience than before but wondered whether, as a consequence, their confidence in themselves to play the authority figure "back home," as demanded, had been undermined.

4.  Giving and receiving nonevaluative feedback, owning up to one's feelings and attitudes, openness, experimenting, and helping others to experience their own attitudes.

# SOME ETHICAL ISSUES IN SENSITIVITY TRAINING[1]

*Martin Lakin*[2]

Sensitivity training, in its various forms, has evolved over the past two decades. It is a powerful form of experiential learning that includes self, interactional, and organizational understanding. It has its origins in the study of change and conflict resolution through attention to underlying as well as overt interactional processes. It has been widely used to reexamine managerial, pedagogic, and "helping relationships" from the factory to the classroom, from the community to the home. Typically, small groups of participants under the guidance of a "trainer" use the data of their own spontaneous interactions, and reactions to one another. The trainer functions to facilitate communication, to indicate underlying problems of relating, and to model construc-

From *American Psychologist*, **24**, No. 10 (October, 1969), 923-928. Reprinted by permission of the American Psychological Association, Inc., and the author.

tive feedback. He keeps the group moving and productively learning about processes and persons and helps to avoid counterproductive conflict or unnecessary damage to participants. With the evolution of mutant forms of training, particularly over the past few years, and their growing popularity, examination of latent ethical questions has become urgent. This article is presented not to censure an obviously significant and often helpful growth in American psychology, but rather to open for discussion and scrutiny elements of it that affect public welfare and reflect on professional standards.

The number of persons who have experienced some form of training is rapidly growing. However named (training, encounter, human relations), the experience invariably involves emotional confrontations and even an implicit injunction to reconsider if not actually to change personal behavior patterns. Since participants are not self-avowed psychotherapy patients but "normal" persons, and because the trainers are presumably not concerned with reparative but with learning or personal enhancement, it is difficult to draw a firm line between it and other psychotherapeutic forms. Indeed, comparison inevitably forces itself upon us and suggests strongly what many of us realize so well, that a distinction between "normal" and "pathological" behavior is hazy at best. However, the comparison also compels one to consider ethical implications of the differences between the contractual relationships between participant and trainer, on the one hand, and those between patient and therapist, on the other. Concerns about the contractual implications have been only partially met by statements of differences in the goals of training from those of therapy and by the difference in self-definition of a participant from that of a patient, as well as by the avowed educational objectives of trainers. Also, formerly it could be argued that the trainer had little therapeutic responsibility because he initiated little; that interactions of the group were the resultant of collective interchange and give-and-take, and did not occur at his instance; that is, a participant "discloses" intimate details of his life or "changes" behavior patterns as a result of a personal commitment or a collective experience rather than because a trainer directs him to do so. Training groups evolved from a tradition of concern with *democratic* processes and *democratic* change. The generally accepted hypothesis was that the best psychological protection against unwarranted influence was individual and collective awareness that could forestall insidious manipulation by dominant leaders or conformist tyranny by a group.

Many people currently involved in the various forms of training are not as psychologically sophisticated or able to evaluate its processes as were the mainly professional participants of some years ago. The motivation of many present participants is cathartic rather than intellectual (e.g., seeking an emotional experience rather than an understanding). Particularly because training is increasingly used as a vehicle for achieving social change, it is necessary to explore its ethical implications—notwithstanding our as yet incomplete understanding of its special processes. There are ethically relevant problems in setting up a group experience, in conducting the group, and following its termination.

## PREGROUP CONCERNS

A psychotherapeutic intention is clear by contrast with the training intention. Sophisticated therapists know that this clarity is not absolute; complex issues of values and commitment to specific procedures cannot really by shared with patients, despite the best intentions of a therapist to be candid. Nevertheless, the therapist's mandate is relatively clear—to provide a corrective experience for someone who presents himself as psychologically impaired. By contrast, participant expectancies and fantasies about training vary much more widely. By comparison with the therapist, the trainer's mandate is relatively ambiguous. For example, some trainers view the group experience primarily as a vehicle to produce increased awareness of interactional processes to be employed in social or organizational settings. However, currently, some others dismiss this goal as trivial in favor of an expressive or "existential" experience. Both approaches are similar in that they require a participant-observer role for the trainee. Yet, the emphasis upon rational and emotional elements differs in these approaches, and this difference makes for divergent experiences. The problem is that there is no way for a participant to know in advance, much less to appraise, intentions of trainers, processes of groups, or their consequences for him. It is not feasible to explain these because training, like psychotherapy, depends upon events that counter the participant's accustomed expectations in order to have maximum impacts. Since it is inimical to training to preprogram participant or process, the nature of the training experience depends more than anything upon the particular translations, intentions, and interventions the trainer makes. This makes it imperative for the trainer to be first of all clear about his own intentions and goals.

Training has begun to attract the participation of more psychologically disturbed persons in recent years—a higher proportion of more frustrated individuals seeking personal release or solutions. Correspondingly, there is a larger supply of inadequately prepared persons who do training. To my knowledge, only the National Training Laboratories—Institute of Applied Behavioral Science has given systematic consideration to the training of leaders, but even its accredited trainers are not all prepared to deal with the range of expectations and pathologies currently exhibited by some participants. Some people who are inadequately prepared are suggesting to other people what they feel, how to express their feelings, and interpreting how others respond to them. Some, equally poorly prepared persons, are engaged in applying training to social action and to institutions. Recently, it has come to my attention that there are inadequately prepared trainers who lead student groups on college campuses without supervision. Several eye-witness accounts of these groups suggest that highest value is placed upon intensity of emotionality and on dramatic confrontations. Screening of participants is virtually unknown and follow-up investigation of the effects of these groups is unheard of. Their leaders are usually individuals who have participated in only one or two experiences themselves. Most disturbing of all, there is no sign that these leaders are aware of or concerned about their professional limitations. I think it must be recognized that it will be difficult to restrain poorly prepared individuals from practicing training in the absence of a clear statement of standards of training, trainer preparation, and the publication of a code of training ethics. (An antiprofessional bias is very popular just now, as we all know, and training fits nicely the image of "participative decision making.") Unfortunately, accredited and competent trainers have done little to deter the belief that training requires little preparation and is universally applicable. I do not exempt the National Training Laboratories from responsibility in this regard.

"Adequate preparation" should be spelled out. One would wish to avoid jurisdictional protectionism, although a degree in a recognized educative or therapeutic discipline is certainly one index of responsible preparation. For work with the public, trainers should have had, in addition to a recognized advanced degree in one of the "helping professions," background preparation in personality dynamics, a knowledge of psychopathology as well as preparation in group dynamics, social psychology, and sociology. They should also have had an internship and extensive supervised experience.

It should be recognized that it is difficult, if not impossible, to do effective screening in order to prevent the participation of persons for whom training is inappropriate. One reason is that it is almost impossible to prevent false assertions about one's mental status on application forms. It is also true that it is difficult to assess the precise effects of training upon a particular individual. It could be argued that short-range discomfort might be followed by long-range benefits. Probably the most important step that could be taken immediately would be the elimination of promotional literature that suggests by implication that training is, indeed, "psychotherapy," and that it can promise immediate results. Why has such a step not been taken until now? I suggest that one reason is that currently many trainers do indeed view training as a form of therapy even though they do not explicitly invite psychologically troubled applicants. They do not wish to screen out those who do seek psychotherapy. But this reluctance to exclude such persons makes it almost certain that psychologically impaired individuals will be attracted in large numbers to training as a therapy.

More serious is the fact that there is little evidence on which to base a therapeutic effectiveness claim. To me it seems indefensible that advertising for training should be as seductive as it is in offering hope for in-depth changes of personality or solutions to marital problems in the light of present inadequate evidence that such changes or solutions do occur. Greater candor is necessary about the needs that are being addressed by the newer training forms. A legitimate case could perhaps be made for the temporary alleviation of loneliness that is unfortunately so widespread in contemporary urban and industrial life, but the training experience as a palliative is neither learning about group processes nor is it profound personal change. Such candor is obviously a first requisite in face of the fact that some training brochures used in promotion literally trumpet claims of various enduring benefits. I suggest that immediate steps need to be taken to investigate these claims, to reconsider the implementation of screening procedures, set up and publicize accreditation standards, and monitor promotional methods in order to safeguard the public's interest and professional integrity.

## ETHICAL QUESTIONS RELATED TO THE PROCESSES OF TRAINING GROUPS

Being a trainer is an exciting role and function. Being looked to for leadership of one kind or another and being depended upon for guidance is a very "heady" thing as every psychotherapist knows. On the other hand, training, in its beginnings, was based on the idea that participation and involvement on the part of all the members of the group would lead to the development of a democratic society in which personal autonomy and group responsibility were important goals. The trainer had only to facilitate this evolution. Personal exertion of power and influence, overt or covert, was naturally a significant issue for study and learning in group after group. Evaluation of the trainer's influence attempts was crucial for learning about one's responses to authority. The trainer was indeed an influence, but the generally accepted commitment to objectification of his function made his behavior accessible to inquiry and even to modification. Correspondingly, experienced trainers have almost always been aware that the degree of influence they wield is disproportionately large; therefore they, themselves, tried to help the group understand the need for continual assessment of this factor. Awareness of this "transference" element has stimulated trainers in the past to emphasize group processes that would reveal its operations and effects.

However, with the advent of a more active and directing training function that includes trainer-based pressures upon participants to behave in specific ways, but without provision for monitoring of trainer practices, the "democratic" nature of the group interaction is subverted. More important is the fact that there is less possibility for participants to overtly evaluate the influences exerted upon them by the trainer. In some groups that emphasize emotional expressiveness, some trainers purposefully elicit aggressive and/or affectionate behaviors by modeling them and then by inviting imitation. Some even insist that members engage one another in physically aggressive or affectionate acts. Still others provide music to create an emotional experience. Such leadership intends to create certain emotional effects. It does so, however, without sufficient opportunity to work them through. Moreover, analytic or critical evaluation of such experiences would almost certainly be viewed as subversive of their aims.

It will be argued that participants willingly agree to these practices. The fact that the consumer seeks or agrees to these experiences does not justify them as ethically defensible or psychologically sound. It should be remembered that "the contract" is not between persons who have an equal understanding of the processes involved. It cannot be assumed that the participant really knows what he is letting himself in for. At the request of the trainer, and under pressure of group approval, some aggressive displays (e.g., slappings) or affectional displays (e.g., hugging) have occurred that some participants later came to view as indignities.

The question of group acquiescence involves a related point. A crucial element in the history of training was its stress upon genuine consensus. This emphasis was a deterrent to the domination of any single power figure or to the establishment of arbitrary group norms. Action and "decision" were painstakingly arrived at out of group interaction, consisting of increasingly candid exchanges. Influence could be exerted only under continuing group scrutiny and evaluation. Some trainers who are impelled to elicit expressiveness as a primary goal are also committed to democratic values; however, owing to their primary commitment to the significance of emotional expressiveness, they may employ their sensitivities and skills to achieving it in ways that are relatively subtle or even covert. When the participant is encouraged to experience and express strong emotions, the trainer's function in promoting these is often obscured. What is often *his* decision or initiative is presented as *group* initiative. In his recent book, Kelman (1968) has suggested that a group leader has the responsibility of making group members aware of his own operations and values. I find no fault with that suggestion; however, it is very difficult to accomplish this. It is made even more difficult, if I am correct, because some trainers may even have an interest in the group remaining *unaware* of their particular manipulations because they wish to sustain the illusion that it is the group's rather than their own personal decision that results in a particular emotional process. The intention may not be to deceive consciously. It is difficult for trainers to practice complete candor with their participants and yet to facilitate the processes of training for reasons I suggested above. Nevertheless, in the light of these questions, trainers should reexamine their own activities. It might be that aroused concern will lead established trainers to take the necessary steps to educate aspirants for professional status to a new sensitivity to these issues.

### LEARNING AND EXPERIENTIAL FOCUSES

There are genuine differences in point of view and in emphasis between trainers. Some regard the emotional-experiential as the primary value in training. Others uphold a more cognitive emphasis, while recognizing that a high degree of emotional engagement is a vital part of training. For their part, participants are, more often than not, so emotionally involved as to be confused about just what it is that they are doing, feeling, or thinking at a given point in time. We know that participants slide back and forth between cognitive and affective experience of training. The participant must partially depend upon external sources for confirmation or disconfirmation. He looks to other members, but most of all to the trainer himself, for clarification. Surely, dependency plays a huge role, but it will not be destroyed by fiat. It is the responsibility of the trainer to make as clear as he can his own activities, his own view of what is significant, and to encourage exchanges of views among participants so that all can have the possibility of differential self-definition and orientation during the training process. This would help prevent a situation where inchoate and inarticulated pressures push individual participants beyond their comprehension.

In training, as in any other society, there are pressures of majority upon minority, of the many upon the one. Scapegoating, where recognized, would be objected to as demeaning whether it occurs as a means of inducing conformity or to build self-esteem. When the focus is upon group processes, it is often brought into the open, discussed, and countered. Where, however, the emphasis is purely on personal expressiveness, the same phenomenon may be used as a pressure rather than exposed. The implicit demand for emotionality and emphasis upon nonverbal communication even makes it more difficult to identify scapegoating when it occurs in such groups.

## ETHICAL ISSUES AND EVALUATIONS

Participants sometimes come to training under "threat" of evaluation. The implications of a refusal to participate by an employee, a subordinate, or a student have not been sufficiently studied. I recall one instance where an employee of a highly sensitive security agency was sent for training. His anxious, conflicted, and disturbed response to training norms of "trust" and "openness" were not only understandable but, in retrospect, predictable. True, the commitment to maintain confidentiality was honored; nevertheless, should his participation have been solicited or even permitted? Evaluation as a participant concern is unavoidable, despite protestations and reassurances to the contrary. Training of trainers should emphasize the professional's ethical responsibility in these matters, but it will not obviate these concerns. The increase in unaccredited and marginally prepared trainers must increase them. It is difficult for most people to monitor their own tendencies to gossip or inform. Especially if the trainer is also an evaluator of participants, he cannot really compartmentalize the impressions he gets of behavior in training, from other data that he has about the participants. Perhaps it would help to make everyone aware of this fact. At least the "risk" then becomes explicit from everyone's point of view.

A diminution of risk was thought to be one of the major advantages of "stranger" groups where time-limited contact was thought to encourage a degree of candor and interpersonal experiment that was nominally proscribed. Obviously, this cannot be the case in groups where participants are related, classmates, or involved in the same company or agency. It should be recognized that it is almost impossible to assure confidentiality under such circumstances or to prevent "out of school" reports. Trainers need to be especially sensitive to this in preparing other trainers. For example, where graduate students are involved in training groups and have social or other connections with one another, or with those they observe, numerous possibilities for teaching the importance of professional detachment present themselves. Trainees should learn how important it is to avoid irresponsible behavior in order to maintain the confidence of participants, how vital it is to inhibit a desire for personal contact when they have a professional role to play. Essentially, they have the same problem that faces the fledgling psychotherapist in inhibiting his own curiosity and social impulse in order to fulfill a professional function. The necessary detachment emphasized here is yet another significant and ethically relevant area that emotional expressiveness as an end in itself does not articulate. Responsibility is taught and modeled. It should be as consciously done in training as in any other helping relationship.

**POSTTRAINING ETHICAL ISSUES**

A strongly positive reaction to training more frequently than not impels the gratified participant to seek further training experiences. Unfortunately, almost as frequently he seeks to do training himself. After all, it appears relatively easy. The apparent power and emotional gratifications of the trainer seem very attractive. If steps in professional preparation in becoming a trainer are not better articulated, and closely wedded to the traditional helping professions, we shall soon have vast numbers of inadequate trainers who practice their newly discovered insights on others, in the naive conviction that they have all but mastered the skills involved in group processes and application to personal and social problems.

A final issue to which I wish to call your attention is that of posttraining contact with the participant. Participants are often dramatically affected by training. In some cases, trainer and group are mutually reluctant to end the group. In a recent case that came to my attention, my view is that the trainer was seduced, as it were, by the group's responsiveness to him. In turn, the participants were delighted by the trainer's continuing interest. Trainers must be aware of the powerful desire to sustain a relationship with them. Therefore, they must be clear at the outset what limits they propose for training. It is as important to be determinate about the termination point of training as about any other aspect of its conduct. Under the conditions of ambiguity and ambivalence of an "indeterminate" relationship, participants appear to be caught, as it were, midstream, uncertain as to the definition or possibilities of a relationship with this presumed expert upon whom they naturally depend for guidance and limit setting.

The questions that I have raised do not admit of a quick solution. They are ethical dilemmas. Steps to eliminate or ameliorate the grossest of them can be taken through awareness and self-monitoring. One practical step that I propose is the immediate creation of a commission by our professional organization to investigate training practices, standards of training preparation, and to recommend a code of ethics for accredited trainers. Research may help, but I doubt that it can come quickly enough to affect the increasing danger of the current and potentially still greater excesses in this area.

Sensitivity training is one of the most compelling and significant psychological experiences and vehicles for learning as well as a promising laboratory for the study of human relationships, dyadic, and group. It may be a superior device for personal and social change, even for amelioration or resolution of social conflict. However, it may also be abused or subverted into an instrument of unwarranted influence and ill-considered, even harmful, practices. The immediate attention of the profession is necessary to maintain its positive potential and correspondingly respectable standards of practice.

**NOTES**

1. This paper was presented at the meeting of the Southeastern Psychological Association, New Orleans, February 1969.

2. Requests for reprints should be sent to Martin Lakin, Department of Psychology, Duke University, Durham, North Carolina 27706.

# 6.
# SPECIALIZED HUMAN RESOURCE DEVELOPMENT: DISADVANTAGED; YOUTH; WOMEN

When considering the specialized human resources of an organization the list that can be compiled is endless. The human resource developer recognizes that employee life styles vary considerably and that different parts of our work population present specific problems. Which ones he needs to study, consider, and give special attention to are partially determined by the needs of the group, the implications for the organization, and the clamorous nature of that specialized group. At this moment in history, three such groups in particular confront the human resource developer: *disadvantaged, youth, and women.*

The attempt in this chapter is not to describe all that is happening but to identify some of the key issues and the direction of current thinking. We first consider the disadvantaged. While some organizations had attempted earlier to tackle this problem, it was not until about 1967 that concentrated attention was focused on the hard core. Few organizations had much experience. The motivations ranged from sentimental and "do-good" to those of capitalizing on a new market for old programs. Most, however, were well-intentioned and did their best to meet the need. Several thrusts emerged:

- Some insisted that hard-core were no different than other employees, and made no changes in their training programs for either the hard-core or the supervisors receiving them.

- Some focused on gimmicks. These included devices to illustrate differences in perception and attempts to utilize some of the "games" from encounter training.

- Some used encounter tapes and texts to force racial minority groups and whites to confront each other. Seldom were the hard-core themselves used, but supervisors might be forced to confront minority-group supervisors in the organization, or minority-group representatives might be brought in to face the supervisors.

- Some employed sensitivity and laboratory training. The pertinent issues and problems normally cannot be reduced in less than a three-day program, however, and qualified trainers are not easily available. This thrust did not gain much momentum.

- Others modified ongoing supervisory programs and focused on critical incident points where the supervision of hard-core might be different from the supervision of regular employees.

For the most part, such programs were developed initially by whites relatively unfamiliar with either the problems of hard-core or of persons from other culturally deprived backgrounds. A great deal of evidence is accumulating that gives us a better "fix" on the problem today.

Theodore Purcell and Rosalind Webster, in "Window on the Hard-Core World," provide a twofold look—at the world of some of the black hard-core as well as at the supervisor, his concerns, and the kind of work situations that trouble him. Their article describes Westinghouse Corporation's experience. In the second selection, "Guidelines for the Employment of the Culturally Disadvantaged," Sidney Fine gives a quick history of our approach to hard-core training and sets out 12 guidelines necessary to conduct a successful program.

Our attention is next drawn to youth. Much, perhaps too much, has been written about the generation gap. Two schools emerge, and one can fairly well predict the stance of each school by knowing the chronological age of the author. Initially, the issue was joined as an "either-or" choice. More understanding and rationality have subsequently emerged, and it is now recognized that at each stage of life one has specific orientations, strengths, and capabilities. Life, society, and the organization need them all. The trick would seem to lie in appreciating this and in using creatively the various contributions men can make within the organization.

Eugene Koprowski's "The Generation Gap, From Both Sides Now" suggests ways that two generations in an organization can interface and form a coalition. In the fourth selection, "How Effective Are Summer Training Programs for Recruiting?", Robert Joseph reports on a study of 62 company programs hiring young people for summer employment. The article is especially interesting for its summarized findings of program characteristics that seemed to work well.

We next turn to women as a specialized group. Little in the past has been written that attempts to understand fully the dynamics of women in work organizations. Any attempt has been met with "Sure. Women are different, and thank God for the difference." Our experience is that few individuals—even women themselves—in organizations are willing to look seriously or creatively at the problem. Most of the literature either describes "how to cope with crying women" or contains masses of employment statistics.

A review of the current literature shows that it is still dominated by these tendencies. This focus is compounded by some in the women's liberation movement who cannot seem to disengage their own personality problems, search for identity, and leadership needs from a more objective look at the problem. Obviously, males have their hang-ups, and this is being well-documented. Undoubtedly the issue of women in organizations will be an arena for much immediate/future research and writing. One of the emerging issues is whether the "identity-search" of women is a legitimate responsibility of organizational training and educational programs.

John Parrish, in "Women's High Level Training and Work: Where To Now?", points out ten lessons learned in the 1960's about the employment of women. He then lists seven basic job needs of women—but most of these would seen to apply to men as well. Finally, he looks at five "social innovations" that may contribute to solving the problem in the 1970's. Theodora Wells' "Women's Self-Concept: Implications for Management Development" is presented as one of the few efforts aimed at getting the subject into the open and out of the realm of techniques and statistics. It opens up some of the implications for organizational training as training attempts to utilize maximally the total work force.

It is extremely difficult to predict future trends. If the three special groups which we have described are successful in gaining some of their demands, it can be expected that other special groups of employees will press for similar consideration. This could lead to a splintering effect and collapse from the sheer futility of such approaches applied with raw force and strained differentiations. We would expect to see this trend emerge.

It is not unrealistic to expect the "silent majority" backlash phenomenon to assert itself at some point. We would predict confusion, if not some chaos, before reason again asserts itself. This is not to say special groups do not have valid causes—rather, it is meant to infer that these will be overgeneralized, over-dramatized; that other special groups will press for attention, and counterforces will assert themselves.

Of course, it is possible that other national and social concerns could emerge and force these issues into the background. Such changes cannot now be predicted; but if they fail to transpire, the human resource developer can expect to deal with a most chaotic mixture of truths, half-truths, generalizations, conflicting goals and voices, militancy, and a general withdrawal of reason, valid research, and creative compromise.

# WINDOW ON
# THE HARD-CORE WORLD

*Theodore V. Purcell and Rosalind Webster*

The white manager, or, for that matter, the black manager living in a middle-class culture, will never understand the rejected hard-core black man merely by reading finely reasoned analyses or executive summaries. He will learn only by confrontation— by hearing these ghetto people out—with an effort at open ears, with neither rebuff nor sentimentality, with enough humility to believe that he has something to learn as well as something to teach.

This article is based on an intensive study of the Westinghouse Electric Corporation's Occupational Training School (OTS), a new and successful "vestibule" training program at the East Pittsburgh plant of the corporation. But it is not a how-to-do-it, or even a how-they-did-it, article.[1]

The primary purpose here is to open a window onto the world of the hard-core ghetto. Middle-class managers, labor leaders, government officers, college professors, and, indeed, white authors—all of us will need to look through windows like this, and try to understand, if we wish to reach the black people of the ghetto, attract them, and help them (as well as ourselves) to build working relationships in the industrial plant.

The secondary purpose is to show how hard it is for local union leaders, white foremen, and white blue-collar workers to look through that window and really understand. They are closer to the window than are the readers of the *Harvard Business Review*. They are much more affected by a sudden influx of hard-core people. Also, they can make or break any hard-core program. So we must also try to understand *them*, and their reactions, if hard-core programs are to succeed and go beyond mere tokenism into a serious war against poverty and discrimination.

## THE OTS PROGRAM

First, a very brief sketch of what the Westinghouse East Pittsburgh vestibule program is all about.

In April 1968, Westinghouse East Pittsburgh negotiated a two-year, $375,691, MA3 contract[2] with the Labor Department to train 196 certified hard-core men from the seething ghettos of the Pittsburgh area for productive jobs in the plant.

Under the resulting OTS program, the trainees start immediately as employees of the company at $2.645 an hour for a month of motivational and sensitivity training. Basic educational instruction in reading, arithmetic, writing, and speaking is provided, rather than formal training in work skills. Central to the training program is instruction in what is to these people the new world of work, represented in this instance by Westinghouse. The trainees begin at once to learn the importance of getting to work on time and not being absent. For the first time in their lives, they are encouraged to talk out their feelings and problems, to exchange ideas and experiences, and to receive a unique type of group support. Gradually a congruence of goals and values is fashioned, and the men are ready for work in the plant.

The majority of the trainees end up in unskilled jobs—i.e., sweepers, supplymen, machine helpers, and janitors. But others also become shearmen, drill press operators, material checkers, and so forth. And *none* of these is a dead-end job; there is true opportunity for promotion in each. Many ex-trainees are going to night school. A number of men with outstanding mental and leadership abilities have been found. There is reason to think that some of these men will advance surprisingly well at Westinghouse.

Who are the OTS trainees? The contract stipulates that funds are to be used to train "hard-core" individuals. The Pennsylvania State Employment Service certifies each candidate; but there is a saying around Pittsburgh that "anyone with a torn shirt" can get certified. OTS Director Richard R. Ross (who is black) goes far beyond such criteria by checking each candidate carefully at his home before admitting him.

The original contract stipulated that no candidate for Westinghouse OTS could be a drug addict or have a felony record. These were viewed as problems too difficult to handle at the outset. Not long after the program was under way, however, Dick Ross felt ready to take on greater risks, and frequent exceptions were made to the initial ruling. And the risks proved to be worthwhile. Ex-convicts and ex-addicts have turned out to be some of his most motivated trainees.

The typical trainee is a young black man about 25 years old. He has been arrested and convicted on charges of anything from petty theft to manslaughter. Although he has had two years of high school education, he has been out of work for a year and a half, or at best has been making, and irregularly at that, only about $1.60 an hour—not enough to support his four dependents. He is an outcast whom the white world hardly knows. He comes from a life of dullness, crime, anger, and, especially, hopelessness.

He now has a job—it is a job that involves a time clock, work on Monday morning, and dealing sometimes with a foreman or fellow worker who dislikes him. But it is also a job that supplies a substantial weekly paycheck, a chance for training and promotion, and, most important, a job that associates him with at least some people at the Westinghouse plant who strongly want him to succeed.

### A BLACK HISTORY

Now come with us, through the rest of these pages, to Pittsburgh's burned Hill District, to Braddock, Homewood, Hazelwood, and Turtle Creek; to the rather dingy meeting rooms on the third floor of the Apprentice Building of the East Pittsburgh works; and finally to the cavernous manufacturing buildings congested with overhead cranes, huge generators in varying stages of construction, coils of cable, welders with torch and mask, drill presses, boxes, and switch gear, where the graduated trainees learn to live and work.

And together let us look at one of the hard-core workers who has been through OTS program—Thomas Mitchell.[3] This man is not typical; rather, he is unusual. Yet most of the problems he has faced, at least taken separately, are the problems any hard-core man has faced. Tom Mitchell is huge, impressive, and intelligent. He used to be a drug pusher—a successful one for a while, too. At one time he was making something like $3,000 a week; he though nothing of "blowing" $500 a day; and he owned 11 suits and 20 pairs of shoes. He would buy a pair of shoes on impulse, and then go buy a $175 suit to match the shoes.

Miraculously, Mitchell cut loose his own drug habit six years ago. Today he is the leader of his entire training group; the trainees listen to him, and many follow his lead. Here is part of his story.

## Early Trouble

*Mitchell*: Like my childhood, it wasn't what you would call bad. My environment was more of a middle-class environment; like I lived in a low-rent housing project. And everybody in there had a sense of pride to an extent, you know. And the children that I grew up with, we were active in sports. In the basketball season we played basketball. And we played football, we swam, we had baseball diamonds. So it was really a real active thing.

Then, I don't know, when I got in grammar school, I started drinking, like my sister. Well, my mother died when I was 2 years old. My father went in the hospital when I was around 13, and he died in the hospital. He never came home again. He had diabetes, tuberculosis—it was a list of things. They had to amputate my father's leg, and he never came home—no more than for a weekend or something, you know. And I stayed with my sister. My sister and her husband reared me. And I got in the habit there; they kept whiskey around the house.

The environment in school—the school was a ghetto school that I went to, an old school that had been there maybe 75 years before I got into the school, you know. It was outdated, and outmoded; and, then, it was in a ghetto neighborhood, and the majority of the pupils were from the ghetto area. And I went to this school. This was where my friends went to school, you know, and we got to where we started drinking in the class.

We'd bring little medicine bottles, like cough syrup, in. It could be wine or whiskey or whatever we could get. We'd drink it in school. It was just a lot of fun—nobody meaning, you know, any harm. And my grades were good. And from this drinking, it led on to where one of our friends had a brother using drugs. He used to steal the caps and bring them to school, and we'd store them, you know, and hide. But it wasn't a thing where anybody got hooked up or anything like this. And then I started into high school.

*Purcell*: Kind of starts off like a little game?

*Mitchell*: Like a game, that's all it was—have some fun. I didn't know. Like Halloween we'd get drunk and go out and mark up the windows. And so I went into high school, and when I went to high school, I went to the Vocational High. This has a very high academic standing, you know. It's aviation mechanic I was studying for, and it was a different environment altogether. This field was away from the ghetto completely; 90% of the students were white, you know. I had a different environment. But even there I had like leadership qualities, you know, like I became a leader in my class. The little white boys, they followed me and they followed my lead, you know. I set the pace, they'd follow my lead.

Then, I don't know, I got involved with the girls—that was another thing. Now this sidetracked me from school again. I'd get out and get running with the girls and everything. And, ah, I wind up knocking a girl up, you know, and we get married. Well, I figure this was a mistake now. I know it was a mistake.

*Purcell*: How old were you then, Tom?

*Mitchell*: I was 17, going on 18. We get married. Then right away we start having differences. I get to messing around again with stuff—narcotics; and I pick up a pistol and I go in and rob a liquor store.

*Purcell*: What were you on? Marijuana? Heroin?

*Mitchell*: Heroin. Marijuana isn't habit forming. This is something that nobody can control, see, and it's something that's hard to explain because if you haven't experienced it, nobody can tell you how bad it is. Like I can know how bad it is in here—I know how bad it is, I know how I did. But if you haven't experienced it, nobody can tell you how bad it is; you can't imagine how bad it is. Well, anyway, I got to messing around again, and I wind up going to jail. I took up a pistol and went in and robbed a liquor store; and I think we got $600—me and two more guys, we got $600, and run through that little $600 in a day or two. And me and my wife were bugging.

*Purcell*: Well, that heroin costs dough.

*Mitchell*: Oh, yeah. Well, then it was only $2.50 a cap. They had little #5 caps—you see them, the smallest caps, #5, $2.50 a cap. And I didn't have no heavy habit then, just a small habit, and then I didn't have the habit long. I went to jail before I really got strung up, before I got a real big habit. I was in jail, so that saved me that time. This was in '53, I went to jail. I come out in '55. Me and my wife, we bug again, we bug again. I wind up going back for parole violation. So now I get out in '58, and I still got these ideas, you know, making the big money, making the fast money. By this time now my sister and her old man, they're into this narcotic traffic too.

**Riding High**

So my wife and I, we go to buggin' again, and I get into a different bag now. I start gambling now. And I was on parole, so I had to work; but I was gambling. I got obsessed with gambling. I started going into crap joints; and a couple times I went in with maybe $10, and 20 minutes later I got $200, you know, and it hooked me up. It was almost as bad as a narcotics addict. And I couldn't stay out of those crap joints, you know, I couldn't wait. Like payday come, I'd get my pay at 12 o'clock, I'm going home at 1 o'clock. Yeah, I'm running the crap game, I'm the big man, and I get a girl. She's giving me $30 or $40, and then the money I'm making from the dope, I'm making money all around. It looked like everything I touched turned to money.

*Purcell*: It seemed like it was going pretty well.

*Mitchell*: Everything was going beautifully. I bought plenty of clothes, a lot of clothes, anything. It was just going real nice. And then one of the guys I had dealin' for me got busted; he got busted with an outfit—that's a spike and a needle—and all this time now, I hadn't been messing around, I had snorted two or three times. But when the stuff would come in, I'd take a little snort to see if it was any good, you know, that's all, but I wasn't messing around myself. I stayed away from it from '53 to about '60, when I came to Pittsburgh.

I came to Pittsburgh in '60, when this guy signed a statement on me. I caught a plane the next day. I left there; I weren't taking no chances on going back to jail there, you know. I say, if they get me, they've got to come and get me wherever they get me. So I went on to Pittsburgh, and right away I got accepted into the same trend, the same vein of life, you know. I got accepted by all the dope pushers, the dope fiends, I got drawn right into that crowd. They looked at me, yeah, well come on. You're accepted right away, you know, and the same thing started in Pittsburgh. I started dealing here. But this time I started messin' around a little more, you know.

I get a girl; she's a dope fiend. And every time I see her, she'd be like save me some, and "Well, baby, I saved you some, come on," and I get to popping in my arm again, popping in my arm again, before you know it, and then I'm dealing too. I got all the stuff that I want, you know. I can get high any time I want to. I've got enough stuff to take care of my habit and her habit and maybe three or four other people, you know, and I suppose I never really realized how bad it was, until I got busted. And after they busted everybody out there, they cut it all off. Then it dawns on me how really strung out I am, you know. Like a bag of stuff ain't nothing now, for me. I've got to have two or three bags, just, just to be all right.

*Purcell*: It's getting bigger and bigger.

## Cutting Loose

*Mitchell*: Yes. So then that's when I decided again that I had to cut this loose. Like it's no place to go if you use the stuff. I see guys now that I know, and see 'em and you can see death on 'em. Maybe, I don't know if you've seen this, but you can see death on 'em. They just have a look like they're dead, like all they got to do is just lie down and die. And you know that drug is doing it to them; they just have that look about 'em.

And this is the way I was getting; I had lost weight. I could take the seat of my pants and grab them like this, and pull the seat of my pants all the way around in front of me—that's how, you know, I'm just melting away to nothing. And I thought, well, this ain't for me, you know. Cut it loose, I'm with that, you know. And from then on, I just started.

*Purcell*: You cut it loose. That was a big move, a big step.

*Mitchell*: This is the only real accomplishment that I feel I've made, you know.

*Purcell*: Well, how did it go after that, then, Tom?

*Mitchell*: Well, I was almost bust; I was on my way to jail when I started to kick. So by the time I got to jail, by the time they got my sentence and everything, I had kicked. And I went on; I went to Lewisburg, and I went in industry there, and saved up some money, you know. And then they sent me and put me in a vocational training program—barbering—I went through there and I came out. And I haven't been into anything since.

I came back, I went to Buffalo, and I decide to come back to Pittsburgh, to come back here. And I went to work in a barbershop down there; and that's where I've been, up until this time, until I got into this program. I've only been back here about a year, a little over a year. I came back, August of last year. So I was looking, like I say, I was looking; I had been down there. I had signed up at a couple of employment offices down on Penn Avenue, down on Fifth, one in Homewood, uh, Oakland, I've been out to American Bridge—every place that I heard that they were doing anything. I would take time off, you know, and go see about it, go put in a application anyway.

*Purcell*: Didn't get anything to go through?

*Mitchell*: No, didn't get anything.

*Purcell*: Why not, do you think, Tom?

*Mitchell*: Well, they'd say they'd take my application. They would get in touch with me if anything comes up. But then, see, I wasn't lying about my record, for one thing, and this was really the handicap.

*Purcell*: That prison record, you mean?

*Mitchell*: Yes, my prison record, and the fact that I, you know, I told the truth . . .

*Purcell*: That you'd been on heroin?

*Mitchell*: . . . about the narcotics thing. Well, that's the worst thing in the world to expose to the public, you know. The first thing they say, "Narcotics, oh, can't be trusted, he's through," you know, so . . . .

*Purcell*: So then you heard about here?

*Mitchell*: One of the fellows, he come by the shop, and he told me he had just got hired; he's starting out here at Westinghouse. He was in this program here, and he told me that Mr. Ross was the man to see, you know. And he told me, "Well, tomorrow morning I'll be out there." And I got in my father-in-law's car the next morning and I come on out here, and talked to Mr. Ross, and he said, well, he's going to give me a chance, you know, and I've done my best ever since then.

*Purcell*: He believed in you.

*Mitchell*: That's the first person—the first person, you know—that just accept me at my word, when I told him about I was hooked, and what I had went through about being in jail, and about my record and everything. And I told him that I hadn't used no stuff in six years and that all I wanted was a chance. Somebody had to give me a chance, somewhere. Yeah, and I told him, "Well, like if you don't give me no job, this doesn't mean that I'm going back to narcotics, you know, because I'm not going to be. I'm not going to let you or nobody turn me around to this point where I go back to this. So if I don't get a job here, well, I'll just go someplace else. I'll just keep on looking."

But he said, "All right, I'll take a chance on you." And he's given me a job, and I intend to do everything I can to prove to him that he didn't make a mistake, and to help the program. Because I know there is a lot of other people out there, you know, that would really appreciate this.

*Purcell*: Why does the program go well?

*Mitchell*: Everybody put a lot of interest in it. See, that's the main thing. He has made everybody realize that this is an opportunity for 'em, you know. This is a one chance in a million, and you have an opportunity, you know. Now it's up to you. If you're not interested in it, why bother with it, why block it for somebody else, keep somebody else out? And everybody has got this interest in it, and that's what makes it good. Everybody wants to succeed in this, and that's the main thing—getting the desire.

Let people know that we do have another chance, you know. See, because it's other guys out there that have records. Maybe not like mine, but they have records. They've been in the penitentiary and they've been slapped down, you know. They go lookin' for a job, and they get slapped down, and get back into the involvement again. And he's shown us that we do have a chance, you know—that we have a chance. And that's what's making it work.

I'm really devoted to the program, and everybody here is devoted, everybody here. Like some of the dudes when they first, when the program first started on, they had, like I said, militant attitudes, you know—attitudes that "if you say something to me, you're picking on me," so. But they're coming out of this, you know; they're all adjusted. And they see the importance of the program, and they're like me and Wayre and the group leaders. We try to talk to the dudes, you know, every chance we get.

And try to make them see that we're older, and the things that these younger boys got to go through, a lot of the things we've been through already, you know. And we try to make them see that if you don't do something now . . . .

## Releasing Tension

*Purcell*: Why does it help?

*Mitchell*: Well, it lets you get some of that inner tension off. And, you see, I feel that anything I've done, I don't have to be ashamed of, because this is something that I've done coming up, this is something. Maybe it was just because I didn't know any better, you know, so why should I be ashamed? So, it eases some of this tension off, to get it out in the open, you know—it does. I know a lot of things that I could talk about here that I couldn't talk about at home, you know, things that I've done.

*Purcell*: Is that so?

*Mitchell*: Sure, at a time, not now, you know. Because now I can talk about anything I want to, you know. I tell my wife what I want to tell her, you know. If she likes it, all right; if she don't, well, "You accept it anyway, because I'm going to be the man in the family."

*Purcell*: So it releases some of the tension—gets it out, outside?

*Mitchell*: It gets it out. But I really feel that this is the best thing that ever happened to me, you know. This is the best thing right here, besides me kicking my habit. Besides that, besides that, this is the best thing that happened to me, you know, to get into this program. And I'm going to do my best at it.

## A BLACK INCIDENT

Here is an incident that happened at work. It illustrates both the kind of problem and the kind of opportunity that these ghetto workers present.

On a certain day last November, one of the hard-core trainees—Roy Sinclair—now working on the night shift, had arrived drunk for work. The rumor was that the foreman had gone over to Sinclair and asked him if he had a problem. Yes, he had a problem. He'd just cracked his wife over the head with a bottle, killing her, and proceeded to shoot another man, apparently his father-in-law.

Donald Heistand, the manager of industrial relations, seemed unworried about the episode. He even quipped, "Well, Dick Ross has really succeeded in getting these people to work on time, no matter what!" The rumor of what had happened had spread throughout the plant like wildfire. There are many nonbelievers just itching to attack the hard-core program, and such incidents add fuel to their fire.

Dick Ross seemed a bit more concerned. He knew that Sinclair had been having severe problems with his wife during training and had once before threatened to kill her. Dick, on the pretext of inviting the trainees' wives in for the day, previously had managed to get the Sinclairs together to talk. They had been reconciled and had returned home together.

We met Mrs. Sinclair that November afternoon. (No, Mrs. Sinclair wasn't dead—the story had been exaggerated!) She was attractive and extremely charming, but the whole left side of her face was cut, bruised, and swollen, and it was stitched together. Ross ignored the wound and proceeded to ask her how she was. A few months before, he had tried to get her a job, and he asked her if she had found work. Then he asked her about her husband, how he liked his work, and what were a wife's duties to her husband. She knew only too well that an unhappy home life affects a man's work life, and that this was especially true for Sinclair, because he always headed for the bar to drown his problems.

Sinclair arrived in the office a while later. He was a wiry little man, probably 40. He loved his wife deeply, and was fiercely jealous of her associations with other men. He had spent years of his life as a sandhog, digging sewers in Washington, Baltimore, and Boston. This was dangerous work, and arriving in the open air at the end of a day was an unexpected pleasure. The sandhogs made good money; but they drank a lot of it away as if there really would be no tomorrow.

Mrs. Sinclair listened attentively as her husband spoke; she was very proud of him. But Mrs. Sinclair loved nice things, a nice home—and, actually, so did Sinclair. These things seemed to be a long time in coming, and it was hard to be patient for so long. Mr. and Mrs. Sinclair left together again, both realizing how important this job was to the future happiness, and how another marital disturbance might jeopardize that future.

## WHITE REACTIONS

At the start of the OTS program in 1968, Local 601 of the International Union of Electrical Workers distributed handbills entitled, "Union Protests 'Dual' Hiring Standards." Like the union leaders, the general work force also resented Westinghouse dropping the high school diploma requirement, entrance aptitude tests, and other criteria just for the new hard-core trainees and not for themselves.

It is not easy for the union leaders, the foremen, and the white blue-collar workers to look through the ghetto window and understand. Their very human reactions come out from some of our foreman interviews.

### Foreman Gillis

This comes from an interview with the foreman of the same hard-core worker that figured in the preceding incident. Foreman Gillis gives *his* view of the Sinclair story.

*Gillis*: Well, I had one incident. One of our boys, Sinclair, from the hard-core program come in here one evening and was visibly under the influence of alcohol or some type of intoxicant; he was very unsteady on his feet. I was notified that he was coming in. And he come in, and he was staggering around. And he took off his clothing, and his clothes was all disarrayed, and there was blood on his shirt.

And I went out, and I said, "Well, Roy, have you been drinking?" And he said, "Well, yes, I have. I have troubles, you know." And I said, "Is there anything I can help you with?" Well, he hesitated about discussing anything with me, because I was right out there with the group. So I took him aside and said, "Look, Roy, if there's anything I can help you with, let's hear." Well, he said he's been having troubles at home; he and his woman weren't getting along. As a matter of fact, he just got done shooting his brother-in-law.

This takes you aback. And, gosh, what is my job? Yes, I'm a foreman. Sure. But I'm not equipped to handle a lot of this when they catch you flat-footed. He went through a story about how he evidently was waving a pistol around at home. And his wife and his brother-in-law took it away from him. And he got a shotgun and shot his brother-in-law and hit his wife with a hammer. I was flabbergasted. What do you do, you know? Is he telling me the truth? Is he fabricating something in his mind because of the condition he's in? I didn't know.

Like I said, he was unfit for work. So I told him I couldn't put him to work in his condition, and advised him that if what he told me was true, he'd better go see a policeman. After some conversation with him, he finally agreed that the best thing he could do was go see a policeman. Well, I tell you, I've only been a supervisor since May of '67, and my training period was approximately six months, so really I've only had a section of my own since last September. And, boy, has it been a broadening experience!

I took him over here to put his outer wraps on, and, gosh, what's he pull out of the top of the locker but a woman's purse! And there's a woman's blond wig in it, falls out on the floor, and he picks it up and shoves it in his pocket. Off we go down the aisle. And he's still talking about shooting somebody. Man, I don't know if this guy's got a revolver on him.

*Webster*: Did a lot of people hear this?

*Gillis*: Unfortunately, evidently on his way up the aisle, he had stopped and talked with several of the other fellows about it and had told them a similar story, not exactly what he told me. Afterwards I went back and tried to piece it together. Here was an unfortunate incident. Although the fellow himself, as far as a worker was concerned, was average, he applied himself. Probably, compared with most of our OTS boys, he was a little better. He wasn't afraid to go in and hustle and sweat a little bit, and get a little bit dirty, do his share of the load and maybe a little bit more.

So, in a way, I was a little sorry to see him go [Sinclair was being transferred, not because of this incident, to another department]. But, unfortunately, when he did come in, he had talked to so many people, the story got around. He was very desirable up until this point. He had missed a couple of days, or was late on occasion with what I felt was good reason. It did create some excitement all over the group. They thought,

"If a guy comes in and is mad at me, he's going to pull out a gun and shoot me or something. All these hard-core guys are the same; they're all a bunch of gangsters."

One of the biggest problems management faces is that it is hard for the foreman to feel that hard-core support is an essential part of his job. A comment Gillis made shows why.

*Gillis*: Unfortunately, from the point of view of a supervisor in the area, my boss says, "How much production did you get out today?" Not, "How many guys did you have in today?" And this is a big drawback for me. This has been my real complaint.

## Foreman Hennessey

Most of the foremen we interviewed feel that they do have to spend more time counseling the hard-core than their regular employees. So it is no wonder that many of them are lukewarm, or even opposed, to the program. On the other hand, a few foremen actually prefer the hard-core trainees, believing that they do twice the work of regular employees. Foreman Tom Hennessey makes the point that, unfortunately, but typically, the trainee's fresh enthusiasm for hard work may soon get dampened by established white employees, who just don't want to be shown up.

*Hennessey*: You have to watch that Carl [a trainee] doesn't get brainwashed by other people that we have, too. ˙

*Webster*: Brainwashed by whom?

*Hennessey*: Other employees. Some of them, you might say they're hard-core . . . .

*Ross* (to Webster): Be sure you get this. This is something that goes all the way.

*Hennessey*: Yes, hard-core, but we've had people in here all along who are in just the same situation, and these people, they've set their standards and so on, and maybe they're a little reluctant to see someone here getting a little better break than they will, you know. There might be a little backlash.

*Webster*: But how would Carl get brainwashed? I don't understand.

*Hennessey*: Well, I say get brainwashed because when Carl first come out here, he went to his machine and he'd go to work. Now, maybe a fellow would say, "Well, look, you're making us look bad. Take a little break now and then." So I just had a talk with Carl, told him he didn't put out quite as much as I thought he should last month; I hadn't said anything to him before—I'd just let him go ahead. But at the end of the month I showed him what he'd done this month and what he'd done last month.

*Webster*: And it was because people had talked to him?

*Hennessey*: I can't say that. But I feel it was. So I told him, "Carl, you're on your own; you know what you can do." This is where one of our big problems is.

*Ross*: If he were on incentive, it would be a different story. I worried about that.

That's one of the major problems of training men. He goes out, he really improves in motivation and wants to work. But there are certain places where you can only do so much. Would you agree?

*Hennessey*: This is true. This is true in the shop.

*Webster*: You've got to get along with your fellow workers as well as your boss.

*Ross*: So, if you work a little bit too hard—you know, this has happened—some of the fellows have told our trainees, "Go, go take a break, go to sleep, you know, go hide." And they don't know how to absorb this.

*Hennessey*: There's a limit to what you can force 'em to do. You can't stand over one man all the time, because the men are not going to stand over him all day. Some of them come along, and to them, you're discriminating. Actually, what I'd be trying to do would be get Carl to do what he's supposed to do and help him. Because if I help him, I'm helping myself. The same thing with Richard. I've put a lot of time into Richard. I've worked hard with him, and I feel like I've accomplished something. Right now, he'll stay away and he'll be visiting. And I'll come up, and what I tell him to do he'll do, regardless whether I tell him to jump off the building.

I don't think Richard ever had anybody in his life who he could put any faith or any trust in. I think from the time that he's been a kid, what he's had he's had to hang onto for himself. I don't think anyone was ever willing to help him or talk to him.

One day, I know he'd come in here, and he said (and I believe he was telling me the truth) he didn't have but about an hour's sleep that whole night because he couldn't get into his bed. He tried to sleep in a chair, and then when he did get to bed, about six o'clock in the morning, he slept in. And, as a result, he was late getting here. And I was giving him heck about coming in late, you know. This is the thing you've got to impress on them—they're never going to get out of the hole, they're never going to better themselves. The only way they're going to get money is by coming in and working.

*Ross*: How about Carl? What's his record? How often has he been late since he's been here?

*Hennessey*: Uh, I'd say about five, six times. And the reason he is late is, he comes from Belchertown, I believe it is. And I don't know, but I think he has to catch two or three buses. This is why he's late. Now, Richard, we had quite an interesting time with him. He comes in, couldn't get here on time, so we even thought we should buy him an alarm clock. This is when I first put my foot down. This is when I first started to have a little faith in Richard. He came in and said to me, he said to me, he'd like to borrow, he'd like to get an alarm clock. I said, "All right, you see me after lunch." Well, he come back in, and he had the alarm clock. I said, "You need the money to get it." "No," he says, "I've got enough money to get it." He bought the alarm clock, and then he brought it in, and he says, "Now, you see if this works."

*Webster*: Did you prepare the rest of the people who work here at all for these people who were coming in?

*Hennessey*: No. No, you can't do that. For the minute you say to the other people, "Now, this is a hard-core fellow that we're bringing in here". . . . The more you can have the other people forget about it and treat him as another employee, another person, the better off . . . .

### Foreman McGuire

Some of the foremen, like Bill McGuire in the Transportation Division, may be dissatisfied with the hard-core trainees that they received, though not dissatisfied with the total program.

*McGuire*: This was the way one of the men started out. He was very slow. If I told him to sweep between those two electric lines down there, and when he was finished, to look across the aisle and see if that needed sweeping, he would sweep between those two lines and take a long time doin' it. And then he'd sort of stand there and look across the aisle and just wouldn't make up his mind whether he even wanted to go over and see if it needed to be swept or not. He had the attitude that he was on a menial task. And apparently this is a prevalent thought, with a few of them anyhow. And in one of our conversations, he remarked to myself and the general foreman, he said, "Well, my friends tell me that I'm on the lowest job in Westinghouse."

McGuire makes the important point that the foremen are not being pressured into giving preferential treatment to their hard-core people.

*McGuire*: This would have really irked me if I said, "Well, look, I want this man fired." He would come to me and say, "Well, now, you don't fire this guy. The government's behind this program, and Mr. Burnham [chairman of Westinghouse] is behind it, and you don't want to get yourself trouble." If they were to try to put me on the spot by saying, "Look, pal, you're going to swing alone on this," I would have been, I would have washed my hands of the whole deal, right then and there!

As it is, I've gone along with them. And I'll say this for Mr. Ross and Mr. Justus, they have been fair with me, in the sense that they told me, "You're the foreman, you're the boss; what you tell us is what we will do. You want the man dismissed from the company, we'll even write the letter for you. You won't have to write it; we'll write it on your recommendation." For this I respect them. At least they're not trying to push something down my throat and make it look to me like, "We're going to put you out on a limb, you know; if the program doesn't work, we're going to say it's guys like you that won't make it work." This I don't think they'll do. . . .

On the other hand, my boss is on me, and the workers are watching this; the old hands, they're watching this like a hawk. They want to see how I'm going to handle this situation, because they have the attitude that these guys are getting preferential treatment, and it's tough to break this notion out of their heads right now.

Preferential treatment in hiring, as McGuire brings out, is hard for the white blue-collar workers to accept.

*McGuire*: So they seem to look at these guys as if the company's just dumped them on them. And they're afraid that they're going to get good jobs one of these days, and knock these old guys out of a job. This is one of their thoughts. One of their prime complaints is that they can't get their sons in here, and I've had this the last couple of days.

Men have come to me and have said, "Is it okay if I go down to the employment office for a couple of minutes?" "Okay, just don't make a day of it." And they come back with a very disgusted look on their face. "What's your problem?" "Well, I went down to employment, I wanted to get an application for my boy, and they tell me they're not hiring. Yet all I see is these hard-cores coming in by the dozen! The company's not hiring? What's the deal? I've been 30 years in this shop. How come I can't get my boy a job? And yet they'll go out and recruit, actually go out on the streets and bring these people in and give them jobs. My boy will push a broom!"

This is their attitude. You know, he isn't proud, he'll push a broom. Give him a chance behind the gate. So, a little bit of resentment from the people. . . .

Also, McGuire brings out an issue that may occur in some plants—the tendency of the blacks to congregate together.

*Purcell*: How do they get along with the whites and both ways, Bill?

*McGuire*: Well, here again is something I don't like, and it's prevalent in the shop. It's that there's definite segregation by choice—by choice—I don't think they make too many attempts to get friendly with the white workers. They'll congregate together. This is the problem which I've had even before the Occupational Training started here. I've had four out of five of my laborers were Negroes, and I was constantly breaking up little conferences. I had a bad egg working for me, a real troublemaker, and he was one of the main causes of these conferences; he was called on the carpet several times.

But they do seem to congregate; I don't think that they make any attempt. And, in the same respect, I don't think the white workers make any attempt. And there'll be six or seven of the blacks, and they'll all be in one little group. And that way you get the feeling, "What are you guys plotting out?" I think there's a natural reaction that's due to the social environment as it is, and the trouble that constantly runs in the cities.

**BLACK & WHITE RESOLUTION**

Problems always show up; successes often slip out of sight. So it is good to get evidence that a foreman who is willing to listen and act fairly, with a trainee who is patient enough to go through the proper channels, can resolve a potentially volcanic situation. Here's what happened to Sam Lucas, another hard-core trainee.

*Lucas*: The first day that I had my interview with him [the foreman], we sit down for approximately an hour to an hour and a half, and discussed things—what he expected of me; if there was anything that I wanted to know, to come to him, if there were problems where the other employees were concerned, to come to him, and that he would iron 'em out, and he would do whatever was necessary to be done for there to be a relationship between me and the other employees.

*Webster*: Did you ever go to him about anything?

*Lucas*: Well, yes, I went to him once, I went to him once. I had a problem. Well, yes, I had a problem with one of the employees. He was a youngster. He did something that I didn't appreciate, but rather than turn to violence or anything of that sort, which the average man would have done, I look down and say, "He's just a kid. For me to protect my job, I'll overlook it; but I'll take the right steps."

So I went to the kid's father—his father's employed here. So I went to his father and discussed the matter with him. And I went to the foreman, and I says to him, "Well, if this happens again, I'm not going to be responsible for my own reactions because I've asked him, I've told him, I've spoke to his father and I'm speaking to you about it."

But it's a funny thing—I haven't had any more trouble. We worked side by side every day after that, and he was a wonderful kid. He turned out to be a wonderful kid. Because I don't know what they told him, but whatever they told him, it stuck in his mind that he shouldn't be doing things of this sort, you understand.

*Webster*: What was he doing?

*Lucas*: Well, he kicked me, yes.

*Webster*: Why? Because you're black or because you're hard-core or . . .

*Lucas*: No, no, I'm not going to accuse the man of reasons why. The only thing, it was wrong, what he did was wrong. Whether it was through play or what his purpose was, it was wrong. He took the side of his foot, and he kicked me on the upper part of my leg. So, any other time I would've made a fuss, you know, but I overlooked it. It turned out to be all for the best, because, you know, I didn't jeopardize my job, which I need. But how much can a man take? You don't expect a man, although it's my livelihood, you don't expect me to just let my pride and dignity go because of things like this, you understand.

Some companies have had success in "sensitizing" their middle managers and supervisors to the ways of black people, especially the hard-core. But it is a task management has hardly begun to tackle. Still more remote is the task of helping the white blue-collar workers to see and understand.

## REASONS FOR SUCCESS

In spite of the opaque windows, the Westinghouse OTS program is succeeding with a 90% to 95% retention rate—better than the National Alliance of Businessmen figure of

67% and the MA3 record of 84%. Further, the OTS graduates are doing about as well in absenteeism and tardiness as the other employees. Five factors appear to us to be the main reasons for this success:

1. *The commitment of management.* Donald Burnham has taken a strong public stand both in theory and in action on the need for business to involve itself in the affairs of the ghetto and the city. His stance has helped to set up an affirmative-action climate among the East Pittsburgh managers that lets foremen, employees, and union representatives know that the company wants the program to work.

2. *The fact of having a certain job now.* No doubt about it, the fact that a man from the ghetto, rejected nearly all of his life, can immediately become a full employee of Westinghouse once he is accepted for the program becomes a strong motivator for the hard-core person to stay and try to succeed. For these people, just having a good job at good pay is the first breakthrough of their entire lives.

3. *Careful and insightful selection.* As we said, Ross carefully screens candidates for the OTS school. In every case he makes a visit to the candidate's home. Placement is never made on the basis of a mere application blank or formal interview. Ross adds the intangible criteria of his own insight into the candidate's potential as a person in his own home. It is true that because of the growing reputation of Westinghouse OTS in the Pittsburgh ghettos, Ross now need only take 14 out of every 100 persons who would like to come. But he does not take just the cream of the crop. He takes risks continually, though not enough to jeopardize the success of the program.

4. *A sensitive program fitted to the trainees' needs.* The Westinghouse Learning Corporation, subcontractor for the OTS, was to supply a curriculum format for the school. But the curriculum format was delayed two months, and meanwhile Ross, by trial and error, devised his own curriculum. It was perhaps a bit disorganized, and broke some of the rules of white academe, but it was sensitized to the needs of the people Ross knows so well. His rather chaotic program developed so successfully that, when the Westinghouse format arrived, its traditional approach seemed too rigid and unrealistic for the situation.

5. *The dedication and ability of the OTS director and staff.* Another important reason for the success of the program is the devoted, intelligent, hard work of Director Richard Ross, his boss, James Higinbotham, and his two staff men. Ross combines the unusual talent of knowing the language and customs both of plant foremen and of the men of the ghetto. Ross and his staff work 15-hour days, far beyond the hours and confines of the OTS itself, following up the trainees in many plant areas, going to the ghettos and the homes of the trainees, securing bail, arranging credit, fixing marriages, persuading, being tough when it is needed, encouraging, supporting, and, more than anything else, believing in the integrity and possibilities of the men they select for the school.

Westinghouse began with some preconceived notions regarding the problems of the hard-core and the best methods of training. As the program developed, the company found many of these assumptions were incorrect and had to be modified. The success of a program like this requires the wisdom to be sensitive to the situation and flexible enough to discard preconceptions. It requires an honest look through the window.

**NOTES**

1. For that kind of article, see Hodgson, James D., and Marshall H. Brenner, Successful experience: training hard-core unemployed, *HBR* (September-October 1968), 148; and Janger, Allen R., "New start"— for the harder hard core, *The National Industrial Conference Board Record* (February 1969), 10.

2. "MA3" signifies a contract supported by the third round of funds allocated under the Manpower Defense and Training Act (1962), and the Economic Opportunities Act (1964), as part of the Job Opportunities in the Business Sector (JOBS) program of the U.S. Department of Labor, Manpower Administration. Since the MA1 and MA2 programs were experimental, the MA3 contracts represent really the first full operational effort on the JOBS program.

3. All names are fictitious, except for the OTS staff and the Westinghouse top management.

---

# GUIDELINES FOR THE EMPLOYMENT OF THE CULTURALLY DISADVANTAGED

*Sidney A. Fine*

### GENERAL CONSIDERATIONS

In 1968, following several years of frustration and failure, some small degree of success began to be experienced in the employment of the culturally disadvantaged. In this brochure an attempt is made to discuss some of the reasons for the previous lack of success and to bring together the know-how derived from the experience of industry and government that appears to have a potential for turning the tide and contributing to more fruitful efforts in the future.

To begin with, the term "culturally disadvantaged" should be placed in proper perspective. Like many labels, "culturally disadvantaged" is not entirely satisfactory

---

This selection originally appeared as a staff paper of the W.E. Upjohn Institute for Employment Research. Reprinted by permission of the W.E. Upjohn Institute for Employment Research. Certain examples and explanatory passages from the original paper are not included here.

because of its denigrating nature, but it is more accurate than such terms as "unskilled," "hard-core unemployed," or "poor people." We have, in fact, a two-sided problem, but it can be overcome by increased understanding obtained through education and training. After all, any person who lacks information or experience required for a specific job may be considered culturally disadvantaged. Employers are also disadvantaged if irrelevant cultural barriers in their personnel systems prevent them from hiring the workers they need.[1] The Peace Corps views its corpsmen as culturally disadvantaged in the countries to which they are sent until they are retrained in the language, technology, and customs of that country. The Peace Corps has found that the effectiveness of the corpsmen is vastly increased by providing them with three months of intensive training at a cost of about $2,500 per trainee, either in the host country or in the United States with instructors from the host country. The cost of training a Peace Corpsman can be compared to the $3,500 cost of training a culturally disadvantaged person in the National Alliance of Businessmen JOBS program.

The "culturally disadvantaged" people referred to in this paper are men and women over the age of 16 who live outside the mainstream of American life in urban ghettos and in isolated rural areas. This group includes both minority group members (Negroes, Mexican-Americans, Indians, etc.) and many whites. They are functionally illiterate people. Their reading ability is rarely above sixth-grade level; if they are hired as workers, they must frequently be provided with basic education by industry. They are people who have not experienced our mainstream culture in terms of buying and maintaining decent housing, eating balanced meals, wearing good clothes, indulging in recreational pursuits such as playing golf or attending the theater, or taking vacations—all goodies that we identify with affluence and well-being in the United States. Instead of being consumers of the American cornucopia, they have been consumers—recently militant consumers—of welfare services. They are people whose family stability is assailed and undermined because the opportunities available to most of white society are not available to them. These people make up several million adults in the United States and are concentrated in the central cities.[2] In the past decade their numbers in urban areas have swelled, especially in the case of Negroes, because of migration from rural areas to the cities. The magnitude of this problem has been especially underscored by the recent *Report of the National Advisory Commission on Civil Disorders.*[3]

Guidelines for the employment of the culturally disadvantaged emerged from the following general observations.

First of all, the time for gimmicks, for stop-gap and crash programs, has run out. Such programs as summer hiring of youngsters will not solve the problem and will not quell unrest; the research data are quite clear on this point. For example, a program formerly in great favor, consisting of training people how to be workers or of orienting them to work, will not by itself prepare the culturally disadvantaged to become workers.[4]

Second, a total approach is needed—an approach incorporating a broad understanding of the problem and the total involvement of every segment of a business or institution. The problem faced today is the problem of workers on every level in management, in the union, and in the rank and file. Each group has a role to play; each in one way or another must be brought into the action if the problem is to be dealt with constructively.

Third, the good intentions and the charitable attitudes that have prevailed in the past are not going to be enough. Definite plans should be made to provide jobs for the culturally disadvantaged. A very deliberate, intensified effort is needed—the same kind of effort that ordinarily would go into reducing a budget if a person suddenly found himself overextended and needed to restore his financial balance. Having good intentions not to spend more or not to charge more would not do it. Setting definite realistic spending limits and giving up certain cherished niceties are the deliberate actions that would be required. Likewise, to employ the culturally disadvantaged, deliberate action must be taken—action such as the reexamination of personnel policies concerned with selection, hiring, placement, and promotion. Some treasured but not necessarily useful stereotypes may be surrendered in the process.

Fourth, discussion of the employment of the culturally disadvantaged sometimes gets bogged down because of the belief of some people that the middle class is trying to impose its values on another culture—be it the Mexican-American, Indian, Negro, or even the Appalachian culture. There seems to be little merit in this attitude. The pertinent survey research indicates that the culturally disadvantaged would like to have the material possessions that affluent Americans have—and why not? Certainly minority groups are entitled to the fruits of technology just as much as anyone else. Thus, the concern represented by the foregoing contention appears to be specious and a rationalization for doing nothing.

The values involved in becoming adjusted to work, and which are involved in the problems experienced by the culturally disadvantaged, have to do largely with the needs and the demands of technology, not with middle-class values. Most middle-class people, whether they realize it or not, have made their peace with technology. They are willing to get up every morning early enough to get to work on time five days a week, to dress appropriately, and to do whatever else is necessary to establish a reputation for dependability. "Middle-class" behavior is very often simply the result of concessions that people make to the production system. These concessions include dressing and behaving in a uniform way and being, in some respects, as regular as a machine. A worker is thus expected to be quite predictable; if he suddenly deviates from the accepted norm for no apparent reason, he is likely to receive a dressing down.

Before the guidelines are presented, it is worth while to note that they are a distillation of the knowledge gained from research, from the experience of private industry, and from the experience of the United States government in administering about $30 million worth of experimental and demonstration programs.

Here is a sample of a research finding. About four or five years ago, it was thought that all we had to do was give the culturally disadvantaged some vocational training in plumbing, welding, food service, or some other trade. And so we went on quite a binge using this approach in the Manpower Development and Training Act (MDTA) program and various other programs. Now we are a lot wiser. Evaluation of those programs that provide primarily vocational training indicates that few such programs have worked for the majority of the culturally disadvantaged. As I look at the findings, I think that the reason was not poor vocational training but rather the single-shot approach of those programs. Today we can see that anything less than a total approach won't work in the majority of cases.

We come now to the guidelines themselves, which are organized as follows. The first several guidelines are concerned with preparing your business or organization for the employment of the culturally disadvantaged. These are followed by some guidelines concerned with the hiring process itself. The concluding guidelines deal with the problems of placement, training, and promotion or mobility. In conclusion, some observations are made concerning the gains you might realize in your total personnel operation as a result of implementing some of the guidelines.

## PREPARING YOUR ORGANIZATION FOR THE EMPLOYMENT OF THE CULTURALLY DISADVANTAGED

### Guideline 1. Make a Total Commitment.

The first step is committing your organization to deal constructively with the problem of employing the culturally disadvantaged rather than merely to comply with contractual or legislative regulations. This is fundamental. Commitment is not the tokenism represented by hiring a few blacks (creaming them off the top of the available labor supply) and putting them in front offices to show compliance with applicable regulations. Commitment requires the decision to employ significant numbers of the culturally disadvantaged and to adjust employment policies to make this possible.

What you are likely to find when you take a hard look at your personnel policies is that they have produced the kind of situation once made famous by a *New Yorker* cartoon which showed the director of personnel welcoming into the company a new employee who could have been his twin brother. In other words, what goes on as a result of existing personnel policies is organizational inbreeding—continually bringing into the organization "our kind of guy." This of course leads to conformity and conventionality. Yet, at the same time that a company is practicing this inbreeding, it is probably demanding creativity and imagination, regardless of the fact that its very operating policies tend to undermine these qualities.

In order to hire the culturally disadvantaged, you may have to give up the requirement for high school graduation and most of your written tests—you may even have to give up testing entirely. You may also have to give up expecting customary levels of performance at first, and allow more time for workers to achieve the required standards for quantity and quality. You are going to have to be patient and be willing to adjust any attitudes that you may have such as, "They don't want to work," or "Well, my grandfather came here an immigrant and he worked his way up and why can't they do the same thing?"

You must learn to accept the fact that the culturally disadvantaged have been consistently pushed further and further away from the mainstream of American society and that very special and costly efforts must now be made to bring them back. That's why it costs about $8,000 per year to send a culturally disadvantaged person to the Job Corps as compared to $4,000 or $5,000 to send somebody to Harvard for the same period of time. In noting the cost of sending someone to Harvard, we ignore completely the social cost of 18 years' cultural preparation of that young person so that he may have a good chance of succeeding in his studies at Harvard.

Thus, commitment means that the first thing to be done is to adjust company behavior, thinking, and expectations to the reality of the situation, which in turn means making various kinds of allowances. We cannot continue to stand by and demand that the culturally disadvantaged must change, knuckle down, and accept the realities of the world of work while we remain adamant in our prejudices and stereotyped thinking. Without commitment it will be difficult if not impossible to make these adjustments and to tolerate some of the problems that are bound to arise as a result of employing the culturally disadvantaged.

### Guideline 2.  Put the Reins in High-Level Hands.

Some high-level company officer must be given responsibility for implementing the effort. He must be someone on a vice-presidential level—someone whose leverage—whose power—means something. He must be able to deal with protests because the flak that he will get from the lower ranks trying to do their jobs in the old traditional way will be loud and threatening. Someone in a high-level position must be available to deal with this reaction in a constructive and effective way. Someone must be able to develop a program which will involve all staff levels within the company—rank and file, first-line supervision, second-line supervision, etc.—particularly first-line supervision.

### Guideline 3.  Organize a Training Program for Company Personnel.

A definite training program must be organized to educate company employees, particularly supervisors, union stewards, and employment office interviewers. (See Guideline 11 for reference to a training program available commercially.) This training should not be merely a pep talk or an exhortation. What is necessary here is a true training program. The employees need to know to what extent the company is committed. They need to hear about the culturally disadvantaged from local leaders of the Urban League, the Congress of Racial Equality (CORE), or the National Association for the Advancement of Colored People (NAACP)—from someone who can give them a real gut-level orientation as to the nature of the problem. They need to hear from someone who can tell it like it is. For example, it was discovered that 25 percent of the culturally disadvantaged surveyed in one study couldn't even tell time; understandably this would contribute to their lack of punctuality.[5] Your present employees need to know facts like these to gain some understanding of the problems to be faced. Perhaps five or six training sessions would be required, and perhaps at some point the company employees could be addressed by a representative of a local community-action group which has been involved in upholding the rights of the disadvantaged—rights to which many of them don't even know they are entitled. Such a speaker could demonstrate the leadership potential that is waiting to be tapped in minority groups.

### Guideline 4. Pinpoint Entry Jobs for the Culturally Disadvantaged.

At the start of your effort, it is probably unwise to get involved with major job or organizational redesign. It is better initially to consider your simplest entry jobs as openings for the culturally disadvantaged. These jobs should become the focus for (a) more extensive on-the-job training and (b) some simplification and redesign if the jobs involve reading, writing, or arithmetic tasks that are beyond the immediate abilities of the new workers.

Many of the culturally disadvantaged are better able to relate to things or to people than to data, particularly since data have played a limited role in their lives. Jobs primarily involved with things are probably to be preferred for the new entrants because things are more tangible, more impersonal, and thus will be less threatening for them. Jobs primarily involving things also have more clearly inherent in them the possibility of learning a craft. Furthermore, on the lower functional levels they tend to pay better than data or people jobs.

Attempts to design jobs which are just tacked onto an existing framework smell of "make-work." It is quickly apparent that they don't lead anywhere, and thus they are rejected both by the disadvantaged workers and the existing employees. Using existing jobs with slight modifications is least disturbing to currently employed staff and most realistic for the new entrants. Entry jobs should not only be pinpointed; they should also be integrated within the organizational job structure so that they lead somewhere. It should be apparent to the worker when he is hired that after three to six months in his entry job some improvement will occur, even if it is only a wage increment for dependable work and/or some additional discretion in his work where this is possible.

To summarize, the four guidelines useful in preparing for the employment of the culturally disadvantaged are: making a total commitment, assigning responsibility to high-level hands, organizing a training program for company personnel to orient them to the problems of the culturally disadvantaged, and pinpointing entry jobs in which the culturally disadvantaged will be placed, including possible lines of advancement. Each of these preparations is important. If you omit any one of them, the consequences of your omission will plague your program later in one way or another.

# HIRING

## Guideline 5.  Interview; Don't Test.

With the possible exception of work-sample tests[6] which are akin to on-the-job tryout, no tests are very useful in hiring the culturally disadvantaged. Whether the tests are nonverbal or matrices tests or so-called "culture-free" tests, they are all unfair. Basically tests show how well, in comparison with peers, the testee has absorbed his culture and education. Obviously, testing individuals who have not really participated in the same culture will merely prove what we already know—that *they are culturally disadvantaged as far as technology and employment are concerned.*

After the culturally disadvantaged are hired, there are some situations in which testing can be of help. For example, coaching the culturally disadvantaged on the very tests that they are going to be given to qualify as apprentices or for promotion (such as those given to qualify for a police force) has been helpful. But this can only be done on a small scale in rather special situations. Those individuals with a little more on the ball, especially if they have seen some of their peers get jobs as a result of tests, can be motivated to go through with a test. But a job must be the definite and automatic result of a successful score on a test.[7]

Fundamentally, tests have a negative effect on the disadvantaged—they demotivate. To the hard-core unemployed, they are the antithesis of commitment, and evidence that the establishment is not sincere as far as hiring them is concerned. They walk out. They walk away. To understand what being tested means to these people, we must keep in mind that to take a test requires skills in self-management acquired as a result of successful experiences in childhood and adolescence. Even in middle-class families, some young people are quite nervous about tests. They may be diligent students, but when tested they don't do very well. They are able to pass tests only after considerable cramming and coaching—and often with a little cheating. Tests reveal not only an individual's knowledge but also his adjustment to the testing situation or his cultural adaptation.

The interview, despite its "unreliability," is nevertheless a more human, less cold, and less impersonal means of selection. It enables you to get your message across in regard to the particular demands of, and necessary qualifications for, the job in question. Above all, it is relevant, and it is a vehicle through which meaningful communication can occur.

If you are going to make any probes at all during the course of the interview, simply check on any experience the individual has had in a frank way, asking him, "What work have you done; what experience have you had that shows you will be able to do the job for us? It doesn't have to be work that you were paid for."

The lowest possible qualifications consistent with safety of the new employee and his coworkers should be set for the entry jobs. Specific decisions should be made as to what criminal record and amount of education will be acceptable—and these decisions will necessitate realistic judgment.

If you feel that you would prefer to hire a culturally disadvantaged person only on a probationary basis, the interview is the time to tell him so. He should be told exactly how long the probationary period will be—for example, eight weeks. He should also be made aware that he will be given a certain time to make his adjustments before the usual quality control standards are applied to his work.

In the case of interviews which are conducted at your plant or place of business, it might be possible for you to show the prospective employee the actual place where he will be working. This kind of communication speaks louder than words.

In conclusion: Interview—don't test. Screen in applicants wherever you can rather than be quick to screen them out. This procedure is in line with your commitment to accept people with the lowest qualifications.


**PLACEMENT**

**Guideline 6.  Place the Applicant on the Job for Which He Is Interviewed.**

The job in which the worker is placed should accord as closely as possible to the job for which he is interviewed. He is entering a new world; everything is more or less unfamiliar. He is on guard and is not sure whether this is going to be another nothing situation like many others he has experienced in the past. Therefore any shift in the beginning is likely to arouse his suspicions and make him wonder if he can rely on the company's word.

It is important for you to keep these considerations in mind, particularly when observing the initial attitudes of the new workers which may suggest passivity, a lack of enthusiasm, or a lack of motivation. An evaluation of MDTA experimental and demonstration projects states: "Disadvantaged youth often look and act unmotivated to work *in the absence of opportunities to work and in the absence of the incentives which work entails.* When the opportunities present themselves, the classical diagnosis of 'unmotivated youth' often turns out to be wrong. In short, what appears to be a lack of motivation is more likely to be a withdrawal from potential or expected failure to gratify one's *motives.*[8] Unfortunately, this describes an all too common situation.

From the start, make clear to the new employee what is expected of him. You must clearly define the basic prescribed and discretionary content of the entry job; that is, what is specified and required and what is up to the judgment of the worker. He should be told, "This is what is expected of you for a few months. You are going to do these specific tasks; you will be a helper [or whatever his position will be]. Later it will be possible for you to work into something that requires the experience you will get on this job, and then you will have your own opportunity to progress and to earn a little more." That's enough for a beginning.

The point is that there must be communicated to the new worker a feeling that his job is not just another nothing (dead-end) job but that he is entering into the mainstream of activity and there is a future to his job. Of course, the wage paid will indicate this, as well as the fringe benefits that go with it.

## TRAINING AND SUPPORT

The next five guidelines are concerned with training and supporting the disadvantaged worker on the job. They involve making conscious efforts to do things for disadvantaged workers which in other ways are already done for advantaged workers and taken for granted by them. The actions recommended can easily be misunderstood as coddling and therefore warrant some prior explanation.

Normally employers expect entry workers whom they employ to be "educated"—that is, to evidence a state of readiness for work which requires only that they be trained in the specific content of their jobs. Selection processes—testing, interviewing, etc.—are designed to screen the qualifications of individuals to determine precisely their state of readiness.

What does this state of readiness consist of and how are the characteristics of readiness usually acquired? One way of determining this is to take a closer look at what effective performance involves. Elsewhere I have suggested that effective performance consists of a blend of three types of skills: *adaptive skills* concerned with management of self in relation to time, space, people, and impulse control, particularly as such management relates to the physical, interpersonal, and organizational conditions of work; *functional skills* concerned with the individual's ability to relate to things, data, and people from simple to complex involvement; and *specific content skills*, which enable an individual to fulfill the requirements and specifications of a particular employer and achieve standards that satisfy the market.[9] That all three types of skills are involved in a balanced way in achieving effective performance becomes evident upon the analysis of various types of ineffective performance.

How are these skills acquired? Normally, adaptive skills that enable one to function in a work situation are acquired in childhood in the environment of family and peers and reinforced in school; functional skills are acquired in play and school experiences and reinforced in various casual work experiences, both in and out of school; specific content skills are typically acquired on the job with training and reinforced by growth in the work situation.

If this analysis is valid (and there is much evidence to suggest that it is), then the problem faced by the culturally disadvantaged worker and the employer becomes quite clear. The family and school situations have not functioned for the culturally disadvantaged worker as they have for the culturally advantaged person—that is, they have not provided him with the adaptive and functional skills that make it possible for him to enter upon work with normal expectations of success. It is likely that the way of life and the inadequate schools in a ghetto or isolated rural area have caused him to develop maladaptive skills, including an antipathy toward school and work.

Thus the job becomes the first real connection of the culturally disadvantaged worker with the mainstream of society. The employer is confronted with a situation in which, instead of just having to train the worker in specific content skills, he must provide the opportunity for the worker to acquire adaptive and functional skills as well, including such basic skills as reading and simple computation.

This is where commitment and initial preparation are put to the real test. The employer must assume an unfamiliar and basically unwanted role. Furthermore, the job itself becomes a sort of crucible where the worker serves instrumentally to produce a product or service and the organization plays a significant role in shaping the worker.

It is with these considerations in mind that we now turn to the guidelines concerned with training, educating, and supporting the disadvantaged worker in his new-found opportunity.

**Guideline 7.  Coach To Teach and Reinforce Adaptive Skills.**

Initially, the job must be considered as a vehicle through which the worker can identify and achieve adaptive skills relevant to technology. The job gives the culturally disadvantaged person the opportunity to respond as a whole person to the range of stimuli in a job situation, and gives the employer the opportunity to reinforce the adaptations that satisfy technological standards. In short, the job initially becomes a means through which communication takes place. The worker's exposure to the job content and tasks is important in this learning situation, but of equal importance are the interactions of the worker with his peers and supervisors and the reinforcement of adaptive skills relevant to punctuality, safety, impulse control, etc. It is in this context that coaching can be tremendously useful.

Here is my definition of what it means to coach: "Befriend and encourage an individual on a personal caring basis by approximating a peer or family-type relationship, either in a one-to-one or small-group situation. Give instruction, advice, and personal assistance concerning behavior, participation in groups, activities of daily living, and various institutional services."

The coaching technique worked in Pontiac, Michigan. With recruiting help from the Urban League, the Pontiac Motor Division of General Motors Corporation hired 281 "unemployables" in the fall of 1967. "Of the 281 hires, 150 (53%) still were on the job after six months and doing satisfactory work. Thirty-nine had been dismissed and the remaining 92 had left of their own accord. 'This record,' the Division's personnel director states, 'exceeded our expectations.' He adds that Pontiac's overall experience with the retention of regular hires is about the same."[10]

One key factor in the success of the Pontiac program was the fact that a coordinator was appointed by the company to work with the new employees. By keeping close tabs on each of the disadvantaged workers, aided by feedback from foremen and supervisors, he was able to deal with most problems before they got out of hand. Working with this coordinator were Urban League volunteers, who took a strong personal interest in helping the workers to succeed. Speaking of these volunteers, a Pontiac executive said, "These volunteers know the 'employables' and the problems they must overcome because they come from similar backgrounds themselves. They feel badly when one of the trainees slips, and they try to make sure he doesn't slip again. They work with him like an A.A. member works with an alcoholic. They keep after him and support him until he is able to make it alone."[11]

The success of Alcoholics Anonymous in rehabilitating "hard-core" drinkers through peer relationships, or coaching techniques, is well known. These techniques can work equally well with the culturally disadvantaged whose problems in adjusting to the demands of a job are deep rooted.

The Neighborhood House in Richmond, California, apparently was the first organization outside industry to use coaching successfully with disadvantaged youth.[12] Coaching is now a major component of the Jobs Now Project in Chicago.[13]

To be culturally disadvantaged is terribly discouraging. The culturally disadvantaged person will make mistake after mistake because that is what he subconsciously expects of himself. He's going to stumble. Who can best help him? It seems natural that it should be someone from his peer group, someone who is on the same social level but making it on the job. Assigning this function to an already employed worker would seem to be an excellent way of involving the rank and file. In some cases, a worker especially suited for this role might be asked to coach more than one person. If it seems desirable, a worker assigned to be a coach could receive a small pay incentive for his additional responsibility.

It is the worker with the coaching assignment who helps the culturally disadvantaged person to tell time and to show up for work in the morning—sometimes by going after him and dragging him out of bed. Maybe he has to be dragged out of bed because that bed was occupied by someone else the first part of the night. Or maybe there was a disturbance going on next door, or maybe any one of a number of different circumstances may have made it difficult for him to get up in the morning, considering the housing conditions under which he probably lives.

The coach may show the new worker how to get around town and may also advise him where to shop or where to get a discount or a bargain. He may discuss the pitfalls of borrowing money at high interest rates or of buying too much on the installment plan. This is coaching, not counseling. It helps to make life tolerable and possible. Coaching provides the kind of information that middle-class individuals exchange in car pools or across backyard fences.

It's important to note also that coaching is not supervising. It is generally unwise for supervisors to try to function as coaches. Supervision is concerned with maintaining job standards, getting the work out on time and in the right quantities, evaluating the worker, and maintaining harmony and smooth working relationships among the workers. The pressures and pushes of supervision are acceptable to the disadvantaged worker and are responded to only if the values reinforced by coaching are common among the workers. Trying to impose supervision on a worker before these values really exist for him is an affront to his dignity and identity. He can't accept it.

Drag someone out of bed in the morning? Yes, that kind of follow-through may be necessary with one who has been out of the mainstream of employment and has developed habits that are maladaptive to ordinary working conditions. It usually takes several weeks to a couple of months for the hard-core individual to get into the swing of things—but he doesn't need coaching forever.

**Guideline 8. Distinguish Between Prescribed and Discretionary Job Content.**

Every single job involves prescribed and discretionary content, embedded in the job instructions and training. Prescribed content refers to those methods, outputs, etc., of the job which are specified and requested. Even the President of the United States has some prescribed content in his job—that which is written into the Constitution. What is not prescribed is necessarily discretionary; that is, up to the judgment of the individual worker. Unfortunately, this area of discretion is rarely defined, especially in low-level jobs. Yet it is in this area especially that the job can be a vehicle for adaptation and growth. It is the place where the culturally disadvantaged person can become aware that whatever has not been specified by the technology of the situation leaves him room to express himself as an individual. He must learn to understand that the inner diameter of a bearing being produced must measure 1.500 inches plus or minus .005 inches for the bearing to fit and function properly, and thus that a foreman's insistence upon strict conformity to specifications is not due to his irascibility or middle-class values.

And so I suggest a training approach in which the instruction is technology-centered and the worker is learning the difference between what is prescribed and what is discretionary. It is particularly important that performance standards associated with prescribed specifications not be arbitrarily carried over into areas where personal discretion is the rule. For example, it may be natural for the worker to dance a few steps while doing his job, because of personal exuberance or because the work itself is not particularly exciting. Now that he has the money, he may dress in colors and styles that are quite different from those of the regular work force. These are matters of his personal discretion; and, if this behavior does not interfere with the achievement of technological standards or anyone else's safety or performance, there is no reason to interfere with it. Remote as it may seem, the tolerance of such personal discretion can lead to relevant innovation on the part of the worker.

**Guideline 9. Teach Specific Content Skills on the Job; Teach Functional Skills off the Job but in the Job Environment.**

As already noted, workers usually acquire their specific content skills on the job. These skills are concerned with mastering the specific requirements and conditions of a job. These requirements and conditions reflect the character of the company and the know-how which the company believes has led to its success. Whether the specific content behavior relates to dress, to safety, to record-keeping, to relations with peers, or to production procedures, it is oriented to a particular establishment and is essentially independent of the worker. It is for this reason that such behavior is best learned from peers, supervisors, and trainers in the immediate job situation.

Schools cannot anticipate all the unique requirements and conditions of different establishments in the same technological field and hence cannot equip the trainee with specific content skills. At best they can reinforce adaptive skills in the individual so that he is prepared to meet those unique situations and can then draw on the functional skills which he has developed at school.

The culturally disadvantaged worker, at least in the beginning, is not about to go back to school to acquire functional skills. Hence, the job environment must substitute for the school if he is to acquire these skills. One approach that has been successful is to provide functional skill training in reading and arithmetic within the plant in an ordinary room equipped to accommodate programmed learning and some variant of teaching machines, such as tape recorders. Professional teachers are not needed; high school graduates have been satisfactorily used for this purpose.[14]

Increased skill in handling tools and machines, whether involving manipulation and adjustment of controls or maintenance and repair of equipment, requires both knowledge and practice. Practically all plants have extensive experience in setting up both types of training in an in-plant environment. The knowledge aspect is usually handled by regular company trainers; the practice, by leadmen and supervisors. The amount and kind of practice assigned the worker is determined according to his performance in class and his lower level functional performance on the job.

Acquiring functional skills requires not only supervised practice but also progressive exercise of one's abilities by undertaking increasingly difficult tasks. Clearly the average job is too specific in expected output—too structured—to serve as a learning situation for functional skills. Perceptive supervisors deal with this situation where the circumstances warrant such flexibility by enlarging a job either through prescription and/or discretion or by lateral transfer of the worker to broaden his experience. Such perception and flexibility on the part of supervisors is even more expedient in working with the culturally disadvantaged because their adaptive skills are likely to be deficient.

### Guideline 10. Keep Counseling in the Background.

The hard-core unemployed have been counseled to death; they've had it. When counseling has worked, it has been embedded in a job situation. What is indicated, therefore, is to have counseling services available if needed—after the disadvantaged worker is on the job and receiving an income.

In some manpower development and training programs, the participants were trained for jobs which were supposed to be awaiting them, but which often did not materialize. And so instead of getting jobs, these people were given counseling. It is obvious how under such circumstances the disadvantaged have come to regard counseling with suspicion if not downright resentment. Evaluative research into many of these training programs provides ample support for the notion that if you are going to use any counseling, let it be unobtrusively embedded in the job situation.[15]

**Guideline 11. Contract Out; Don't Try To Do It All Yourself.**

Private commercial companies have entered the field of training culturally disadvantaged workers. Their adequacy can be judged by the fact that they are carving out a profitable market for themselves by producing results. What distinguishes them are three things: (1) they use modern technology—both hardware and software, (2) they staff to get the job done, which means that they do not depend on certified teachers, and (3) they teach in the job environment, not in school.

MIND, Inc., for example, teaches arithmetic, spelling, vocabulary, and word skills on the basis of programmed lessons recorded on cassettes played by the students on individual portable tape recorders. The monitors (not teachers) are college dropouts, former secretaries, waitresses, airline stewardesses, etc., or merely high school graduates in some cases just one step ahead of the students. Their fundamental role is to provide support and continuity. (In one operation, a monitor with a teaching background who started to use her professional training quickly switched to the more informal approach of the monitors.) In effect, the students teach themselves at their own pace—without grades, without pressure, and without anxiety.

The results are impressive. MIND's basic education courses, in 160 hours of instruction, are designed to raise a trainee's math and literacy skills by three to five grade levels. The tenth grade level is often achieved; in some instances even better results are obtained. As a result of such training in basic education, students have raised their IQ's as much as 10 points. Recently MIND, Inc., has added typing courses designed to train beginners to type 45 to 60 words a minute after 14 hours of instruction.

MIND's basic course varies in length and cost, depending on the needs of the students, the base from which they start, and the achievement level aimed for. Text materials are of a workbook nature and so are not reusable; but there are cassettes which may be used again and again on tape recorders. Hence the more students that are involved, the lower the cost per student.

Another company in the field, United States Research and Development, concurs that only a total approach such as the one described in these guidelines actually works with the culturally disadvantaged. The company says that its training can be accomplished only within a climate of human resources development. A third company, Responsive Environments Corporation, makes use of the "Talking Typewriter." The "Talking Typewriter" is a computer-based, multisensory, multimedia learning environment which directly involves the student's sight, hearing, and touch, and which is especially adapted to the teaching of reading. In a number of studies the company has found that not only do the students acquire basic functional skills, but also, indirectly, their adaptive skills are much improved. Larger companies such as General Learning Corporation, IBM, and Westinghouse Electric are also developing approaches to these problems.

That there is more to training the culturally disadvantaged than equipping them with specific basic functional skills is also evident in the fact that MIND, Inc., has recently undertaken to develop two additional types of training. One is "environmental and interpersonal skills" training (possibly the same as adaptive skills mentioned earlier), which includes impulse control, how to open a checking account and balance bank statements, how to shop, how to get around town, how to get along with supervisors, etc. For this purpose, video tapes are used on which dramatic situations, such as supervisors displaying insensitive behavior toward ethnic minorities, are portrayed. Subsequently these situations and the trainees' reactions undergo roundtable discussion, the object being to develop attitudes that generate effective coping behavior in the trainees.

Another type of training is directed at supervisory personnel for the purpose of improving their communication skills with the hard-core unemployed. Again video and audio tapes are used for demonstration, followed by active involvement in developing and practicing the new skills. With such training, "managers gain as much insight into their own 'blindspots' in interpersonal relationships as they do in what 'bugs' the unemployables now employed by their company. And they learn to understand and *solve* 'people problems' rather than simply *control* people."[16]

For recruiting purposes, outside groups such as the Urban League and the NAACP can be used. Although the branches of such organizations vary in their adequacy, as is to be expected, they are proving helpful in many cities.

## MOBILITY

### Guideline 12. Advance the Worker As Soon As Feasible.

Mobility doesn't necessarily mean that the worker has to be moved up a ladder. It is preferable to think in terms of a lattice with systematic opportunities for the individual worker to move to jobs that suit him and the company mutually. The initial advancement may take place within the framework of the entry job in the form of added responsibility or a salary increment or both. Or he can be told that his work is now ready to be judged according to normal supervisory standards, with a consequent raise in pay. Thus, he is encouraged to feel that he can carry the job by himself, that his production can meet the quality control standards of the company. After six months, he might even be able to function in a coaching role—to do for some new people coming in what was done for him. Who would better know how to coach newcomers than someone who has been helped and is now making it? This function could also entitle the coach to a small pay raise. This is mobility with a career aspect. Later on, once the worker has received additional training, he can, if he wishes, start planning a career in a more extensive sense.

## THE PAYOFF

The above 12 guidelines do not purport to deal with every problem that might be encountered; they do purport to cover most of the important elements of a total personnel program which could lead to success in the employment of the culturally disadvantaged. By success I mean providing the employer with effective manpower and providing the culturally disadvantaged with a handhold on the opportunity system in American life.

There are other possible benefits. It has already been suggested that you might discover more effective methods of recruitment, particularly for certain segments of your work force. The coaching approach might well be applied to your total work force because its humanizing aspects may produce important returns for workers who have disabilities but whom you wish to retain. For example, "Chrysler Corporation recently hired a white alcoholic, 45 years old, who once had been with Studebaker. He has had three 'lost weekends' at Chrysler, each lasting a week, but the company is keeping him in the pre-employment training program. 'I've invested too much time in this guy to lose him,' says his counselor, who ironically, is a Negro."[17]

Another benefit will be your greater, more meaningful involvement with the community. What is essentially proposed in these guidelines is that industry be a key participant in human resources development. Such participation would mean a closer relationship to the schools, to their vocational programs, and to their industry advisory committees.[18] Your experience could well be a resource for showing them how they can do a more efficient job in training and education of the culturally disadvantaged. After all, it is these same schools that have been squeezing out the very people you are now attempting to employ.

I think that the attitudes and feelings toward your company on the part of all your employees will improve—but not at first. You'll have real problems at first. Remember, that's why it is recommended that someone on a vice-presidential level be in charge of the employment of the culturally disadvantaged. It will take powerful leverage to combat those problems. But eventually the process—the activity, the involvement—is going to affect your entire company, even your stockholders. Evidently profound changes are occurring in the United States in the climate in which employment of the culturally disadvantaged is taking place. "Just a few years ago, many companies had to risk irritating stockholders by involving themselves. A reliable poll now shows 65 percent of stockholders feel corporations should participate in the war on poverty. There is of course an element of self-interest about this. 'If we do not act,' said a Chase Manhattan Bank vice president to a business audience this month, 'we must realize that we will undercut the healthy social and economic environment that is so vital to the very existence of our corporation.' "[19]

And as a very personal payoff, perhaps you will feel a lot better about yourself because finally, once and for all, you won't be leading a schizophrenic life with regard to democracy and opportunity in America.

NOTES

1. Cassell, Frank H., The disadvantaged employer, *Personnel Administration* (November-December 1968), 24-29.

2. Sheppard, Harold L., *The Nature of the Job Problem and the Role of New Public Service Employment.* Kalamazoo: The Institute, January 1969.

3. *Report of the National Advisory Commission on Civil Disorders.* New York: Bantam Books, Inc., March 1968.

4. Wellman, David, The wrong way to find jobs for Negroes, *Transaction* (April 1968).

5. Gordon, Jesse E., *Testing, Counseling, and Supportive Services for Disadvantaged Youth.* Ann Arbor: The University of Michigan, 1967, 37.

6. Tests that sharpen work skills, *Business Week* (January 4, 1969), 88-90.

7. For information about the experience of the Workers Defense League in test coaching, see Marshall, F. Ray, and Vernon M. Briggs, Jr., *The Negro and Apprenticeship.* Baltimore: The Johns Hopkins Press, 1967, 72-78.

8. Gordon, *op. cit.*, 67.

9. Nature of skill: implications for education and training, *Proceedings, 75th Annual Convention, American Psychological Association*, 1967.

10. Habbe, Stephen, Hiring the hardcore unemployed, *The Conference Board Record* (June 1968), 20.

11. *Loc. cit.*

12. Hoos, Ida R., *Retraining the Work Force—An Analysis of Current Experience.* Berkeley: University of California Press, 1967, 142-165.

13. Jobs now project, *Jobs Now Project First Year Report, C–Coaching* (Chicago, 1967).

14. Greenleigh Associates, Inc., *Field Test and Evaluation of Selected Adult Basic Education Systems* (New York, September 1966), 93-96.

15. Gordon, *op. cit.*, 169. "One could almost say, the more the program depended on counseling, the poorer it was, or, the less the counseling stood as an activity in its own right, the better was the counseling." See also Gross, Edward, Counselors under fire: youth opportunity centers, *The Personnel and Guidance Journal,* **47**, No. 5 (January 1969), 404-409, for an excellent analysis of false assumptions made in counseling the disadvantaged.

16. Charles F. Adams, president of MIND, Inc., in a talk before the National Laboratory for the Advancement of Education at the Washington Hilton Hotel, Washington, D.C., November 19, 1968.

17. *The Wall Street Journal*, August 12, 1968.

18. See Burt, Samuel M., *Industry and Vocational-Technical Education.* New York: McGraw-Hill, 1967.

19. *The Christian Science Monitor*, November 26, 1968.

## THE GENERATION GAP, FROM BOTH SIDES NOW

*Eugene Koprowski*

In his classic work, *The Golden Bough,* Sir James Frazer tries to broaden our understanding of man's peculiarities and behavior by taking us back to the dawn of civilization when myth fused a fragile web between primitive man's fears, desires and recorded history. A curiously fascinating example is the legend of the King of the Wood who at any hour of the day or night could be found with sword in hand grimly guarding a certain tree that grew in a sacred grove near the calm waters of the Lake of Nemi in the Alban hills. For anyone who sought to take his place would first need to slay him in single combat, and pluck from the tree a golden bough that signified his right to succession.

And so it seems to have been since the beginning of time. Only the names have been changed to confuse the innocent. Now, we call this great primal drama, The Generation Gap, and the King of the Wood is magically transformed into the depersonalized Establishment, while the would-be challenger to his throne becomes the equally depersonalized Younger Generation. The golden bough remains, as always, the powers and privileges of command.

While this scene is dutifully re-enacted by each generation, its practical consequences take on dramatically different forms. So each successive generation must ask the question, "What does the generation gap mean today?", both for those who guard the tree of power and those who would slay the King of the Wood and pluck the golden bough.

To begin with, the current generation gap is complicated by a number of characteristics that make it substantially different from its predecessors. First, there is the awesome arithmetic of it. More than fifty percent of our population is under twenty-five, and the U.S. Bureau of Labor Statistics predicts that by 1975 there will be a thirty percent increase of people fifteen to twenty-four and a forty percent increase of people twenty-five to thirty-four. The elders of the tribe are badly out-numbered. For one of the first times in modern history, the values, manners and morals of the ruling generation are being dominated and dictated by their children.[1]

And a very special breed of children they are. Nutured by the tender loving care of Dr. Spock's permissive child rearing practices, conditioned to action, spontaneity and impulsiveness by the great grey tube, they are ready to take on the whole world and presumably change it for the better. Add to this an unprecedented level of affluence and the stage seems to be set for what many feel is not so much a generation gap as a full blown social revolution with the young people at its cutting edge.

From *Management of Personnel Quarterly*, 8, No. 4 (Winter, 1969). Reprinted by permission of *Management of Personnel Quarterly.*

If this is true, those in positions of power and responsibility must look beyond the level of appearances—beyond the beards, beyond the long hair, beyond the unusual and sometimes bizarre dress, beyond the mind-expanding drugs, beyond the propensity for nudity, and beyond the communal living. They must, instead, search for the meanings in these sometimes perplexing and sometimes annoying patterns of youthful behavior.

In recent months, scores of articles have been written on the subject. Some of these express pro-youth sentiments, some patronizingly chide youth for their shallowness and lack of historical perspective, and others simply report research findings that deal with the attitudes and sentiments of young people. Many of the pro-youth articles are written by those interested in social reform and anti-Viet Nam war sentiments.[2] The gist of their message is that today's youth, freed from the fears and anxieties of making a living, are turning their attentions to more humane and substantive issues like the morality of the war, the problems of human poverty and suffering, the pollution of the environment and the relevance of education to help solve these problems. The majority of these writers hope that the tensions being generated by the activist youths will serve as a catalyst to end the war and to bring about long overdue change in our educational and social institutions.

Writers who fall into the second category take quite a different stance.[3] Their message seems to be that today's youth, despite their exuberance and articulateness, lack historical perspective and are better at calling our attention to broad obvious problems than at analytically probing into the complex range of solutions. They argue that what is happening today between the generations is really nothing new after all—that anyone who is familiar with history would know that youth movements are as old as mankind itself. Perhaps of even greater concern to these writers is the anti-intellectual spirit that pervades so much of modern youth's thinking and behavior. "Doing your own thing" doesn't sit too well with those whose rigorous intellectual training tells them that reason, not feelings, will lead mankind out of the wilderness.

Research studies dealing with the attitudes and sentiments of young people present a little "purer" picture of the precise dimensions of the generation gap. What most of these studies seem to tell us is that there is a generation gap, that it's growing, and that it will continue to have an important impact on our lives.[4] Specifically, these studies show that young people tend to see their elders as provincial in their interests, materialistic, resistant to change, compromising with their values, overly concerned with security, disinterested in the other people's problems, overly respectful of people in authority, and inconsistent in what they practice and what they preach.

They tend to see themselves as basically rejecting the Calvinistic Work Ethic, as being more honest with themselves, more open to new ideas and experimentation, more concerned with beauty, more interested in world events, more self-centered, more optimistic about the future, and less impressed with formal authority.

The kinds of changes they would like to see in society are: more participation in decisions that affect them, less emphasis on material things, more acceptance of other people's peculiarities, more emphasis on work being meaningful in its own right, and more freedom to do their own thing providing it doesn't hurt anybody. Although they feel business makes a major contribution to society and is a key element in the future, they *do not* feel it allows for creativity, individuality, self-development or self-expression.

But the articles that are being written and the research that is being conducted is only part of the story. They provide us with mental maps. This is not the same, however, as a personal tour of the territory. It would be difficult indeed to understand the meaning of a city like Paris by carefully examining a map. I do not suggest by this that you run off and ride an LSD cube into space. I do suggest, though, that you tune up your senses to "read" what is going on through communications media other than articles (like this one) that simply tell about, but are not part of, the youth revolution.

Listen to their music.[5] You'll notice that the animal screams engulfed by pounding rock are on their way out. Poetry set to music is "in." The poetry is about the stupidity of war, about being black, about being poor, about being lonely, about hypocrisy, and about businessmen and politicians. Some of the words don't seem to make sense until you've listened to them a few times. The Beatles will still do fine, but you might try The Cream, The Creedance Clearwater, or the Mothers of Invention. Simon and Garfunckel still sound good, and Bob Dylan still remains the major guru of the tribe. One of the interesting things is that most of the newer white singers sound black. A lot of people say the white kids have found soul in the black music that is lacing in the white suburban society. Other people say it's because the white kids have found in the Civil Rights Movement something worth identifying with.

See a few movies. If you've been putting off seeing *The Graduate*, don't. It tells the story as well as most. *Easy Rider, Alice's Restaurant, Medium Cool* are three fine movies by perceptive young writers and directors who try to tell it like it is. The trend here is toward realism; no phony multi-million dollar chariot races, but relatively low budget semi-documentary themes; small snatches of real life, interspersed with unusual visual effects, to make maximum use of a powerful media. Feeling, not reason, sets the pace. But the influence of the young goes far beyond movies made with youth as the content. Visiting any local theater on any given night you are likely to hear words that once were reserved for the pool hall, and see more of the human body exposed than in most harems. You will see the bad guys become good guys, and the good guys become bad guys. Finally, you will see violence displayed in all of its multi-colored vicissitudes. The message? Movies are the things we want, or the things we are guilty about having.

Visit a few art galleries, or if that doesn't "turn you on," flip to the art section of *Time* or *Newsweek* the next time you're tuning in the world. You'll notice that the newer art forms are trying to break away from the conventional media, such as oil and canvas. The avant-garde young artists of today are combining all sorts of unrelated objects in space, in an attempt to create total involvement on the part of the recipient. One of the latest offshoots is a movement called "fun art."[6] In fun art, the artist creates a combination of objects that people can interact with—almost like a gigantic and mysteriously fascinating toy. Artists seem to be trying to live with technology by incorporating it into their art forms and thus mastering it. The key elements in the developing world of art seem to be "involvement," use of the total environment in exploring artistic possibilities, and an attempt to arrange a shot gun wedding between art and technology.

Read some of the books that seem to be turning the young people on. Something on Eastern thought and Eastern religion is a must. Allan Watt's *The Way of Zen* published in 1957 will still do fine. Equally important is an exposure to Existentialism. Walter Kaufmann's *Existentialism from Dostoevsky to Sartre* is a good primer. Also try to read *Demian* and *Steppenwolf* by Herman Hesse. Among the major themes in these books are: that man is an integral part of nature not its ruler, that values do not exist outside of man but man creates values by his actions, and that reason and logic explain only the superficial and trivial aspects of life.

Looking behind these sometimes gaudy, sometimes morbidly introspective appearances of the youth movement, one can see the vague outlines of its substance. This substance suggests a generation who will have a markedly different set of attitudes toward their jobs, their employers, and their immediate supervisors.

As they approach problems on their jobs they can be expected to look at these problems from a much broader perspective than former generations. They will tend to see the organization set in an international community with compelling social obligations to use their resources to help create an environment that is livable and humane. Although they will understand computer technology, they won't completely trust it. Feelings and intuition will weigh heavily in their decision making. They will be action-oriented and less prone to thought and ponderous reflection. Finally, they will place much more emphasis on the human side of problems than former generations.

From the organizations that employ them, they will expect a genuine sense of social responsibility and the willingness to do something about it. Those who seek careers in business will be especially suspicious about the real intentions of the corporate enterprise. They will seek career paths that give them the greatest degree of mobility and will shy away from jobs that lock them into a particular organization. Most of all, they will expect to be given work to do that utilizes whatever skills, abilities, or knowledge they have to offer. Many will not be willing to move up the ladder in the traditional sense. They will want meaningful work now. As a result, turnover, especially among college trained young people, is likely to be painfully high during the next decade.

Perhaps the toughest job in dealing with the youth will be that of the immediate supervisor. He will be at the interface of the generations, and a difficult place it will be. Most young people will see their supervisors not so much as a person with formal authority who tells them what to do, but as a facilitator who provides them with the things they need to get the job done. This facilitation could be in the form of technical knowledge, physical resources, financial resources, or moral support. The personal attributes young people are likely to react most favorably to in their immediate supervisor are technical competence, honesty, and sensitivity to the feelings of others. Finally, they will expect their immediate supervisor to recognize their individual talents and to challenge these talents in an atmosphere that allows them as much freedom as possible to "do their own thing."

So much for what the youth expects from the world of work. What can the youth be expected to supply in return? To begin with, they will enter their first job with a greater storehouse of knowledge than any previous generation. They will be relatively free from the fears of survival, and as a result will be more honest and open in their dealings with other members of the organization. They will be energetic, action-oriented, and open to change and experimentation. Many of them will be social idealists, who are very sincere in their desire to make this a better world for all of us. They will not require close supervision so long as the work they are doing "turns them on."

All of this points up the fact that there are some rather profound changes occurring in our society, and the youth seem to hold the key to understanding exactly what is happening, particularly to our social values. But, there is more to it than that. To understand the attitudes, opinions, art forms, manners and morals of young people, only gives us part of the picture. For much of their behavior is more a reflection of *reaction against*, rather than *progression toward*, some newly defined set of goals or objectives. They are against the war, they are against racial injustice, they are against poverty, they are against our pollution of their environment, they are against our educational systems, they are against any restrictions on their personal freedom, and most of all, they are against the Establishment that got us into this mess.

And, who is the Establishment? The Establishment are those people in power who run things. People for the most part in their fifties and sixties, who were not reared by Dr. Spock or conditioned by the great grey tube. People who entered the world during the Great Depression, or lived through it as children. People who were thankful to get a job and keep it. People who had to concentrate their energies on such crass considerations as making enough money to keep themselves and their families alive. It is little wonder their vision of the world is a bit different than that of the Electric Generation. In a very real sense the Depression Generation survived by their strict adherence to the Calvinistic Ethic. Loyalty to your employer, respect for authority, even playing politics had a different meaning at that point in time. In this survival type of environment, man's nobler virtues had little room to romp and play. Perhaps it is an unfortunate twist of nature that one tends to carry through his adult life those postures that sustained him early in his development—even when they have apparently outlived their usefulness.

It is one thing to understand the differences between the Electric and the Depression Generation; it is another thing to do something about it. Viewing the generation gap in its broadest context, it would seem that individuals in positions of power and authority are left with three choices: first, they can deny the problem exists; second, they can decide to fight; or third, they can try to form a coalition with the Electric Generation. A good rationalization for those who choose the first alternative is that kids today are no different than they ever were and that once they knock their heads against the "real world" a few times they'll get the message.

For those who decide to fight, cold war tactics may have more merit than all-out war. The first step here is to woo them into your organizations by cleverly designed recruiting campaigns. To do this, you must appeal to their idealistic values. In your advertisements play up to the opportunities for creativity and individuality. Even use their phrases like "doing your own thing." Also emphasize that your organization is interested in its broad social responsibilities and not just making money. When you interview these young people be sure not to emphasize your pension program or other company benefits too much. Remember, they resent materialistic and security-oriented approaches. Your primary goal is to get them into the organization. You are confident that if they are "reasonable" young people, once they begin seeing the world as it really is they will adjust accordingly.

Your third choice is to attempt to form a coalition with the Electric Generation. This alternative is based on the assumption that the young people of today will neither go away nor will they change substantially in the direction of the value posture of the Depression Generation. The hope here is that both generations have something to learn from one another. The reality is that the Electric Generation constitutes the labor pool for the next decade. Any organization considering this approach might seriously experiment with the following strategies.

**Level with one another.**    Don't present your organization as something it is not. Don't advertise opportunities to "do your own thing" or talk about social responsibility, if the candidate you are trying to hire will end up in some plant in Newark, New Jersey, where the plant manager and the immediate supervisor never heard of Abraham Maslow or Eldridge Cleaver, or couldn't care less.

**Be prepared to take risks.**    Perhaps more than anything else, young people today want meaning in their work. They have a low boredom tolerance. If you want to keep them and tap their creative energies, involve them in responsible work as soon as possible. Don't use your own career as a model. You might be a completely different person today if you had been stretched continuously in your career. Job rotation, individualized career development, special assignments, job enrichment, task force projects are all examples of ways of making work meaningful.

**Involve them in the decision-making process.**    It is difficult to play a meaningful role in any organization if all of the decisions are made for you. The youth of today can make a major contribution to the decision-making process by providing a fresh outlook and new frames of reference for viewing old problems. Give them a chance.

**Create a climate of trust.**    You can't take any real risks with young people if your organization doesn't have an atmosphere of trust. While laboratory training methods have been both maligned and praised, they certainly appear consistent in their goals with many of the sentiments being expressed by today's youth. One of the major goals of this movement is to help create an organizational climate where feelings as well as reason are recognized as part of organizational life. To the extent this goal is achieved, trust may come to replace suspicion, fear and organizational paranoia.

It has been said that the youth of a society are its greatest resource. They are also its greatest challenge. For in addition to being a resource, the youth comprise a vast explosive reservoir of energy. Up to this point in history this energy has been kept at a manageable level by draining part of it off through wars, hard physical work, and the taming of a hostile physical environment. So what happens when wars become smaller and less frequent, when work becomes primarily mental, and when the environment is designed to maximize comfort and minimize physical effort? Only time will tell. But unless leaders in all walks of life begin finding ways to constructively tap this youthful exuberance, we are all in serious trouble. For as things now stand, it looks as though our society is being transformed into one gigantic temper tantrum where the dissenting youths kick their feet, pound their heads, and hold their breaths and turn blue, while their elders scamper timidly about trying at almost any cost to restore tranquility and order to the scene. It doesn't have to be that way; but only we can change it.

## NOTES

1. For some interesting parallels between the current generation gap and some of the conditions that preceded the fall of Rome, read Edmund Stillman's, "Before the Fall," *Horizon* (Autumn 1968), 4-15.

2. See Chomsky, Noam, *American Power and The New Mandarins*, Pantheon Books, 1966; Goodman, Paul, *Growing Up Absurd: Problems of Youth in the Organized System*, Random House, 1960; Riesman, David, and Christopher Jencks, *The Academic Revolution*, Doubleday, 1968; Marcuse, Herbert, *An Essay on Liberation*, Beacon Press, 1969.

3. See Aldridge, John W., In the country of the young, *Harpers* (October, 1969), 49; Laquer, Walter, Reflections on youth movements, *Commentary* (June 1969), 33; Lifton, Robert Jay, The young and the old: notes on a new history, *Atlantic* (September, 1969), 47.

4. See *Fortune*, January 1969; *Look Magazine*, May 1969, and *Psychology Today*, October 1969; also, Kappmeyer, Keith Karl, The generation gap—a management problem, unpublished Master's thesis, Alfred P. Sloan School of Management, MIT, June 1969.

5. For a good historical review of the pop-rock movement see Ribakove, Sy, and Barbara Ribakove, *Folk Rock; The Bob Dylan Story*, Dell Press 1966; and Davies, Hunter, *The Beatles: The Authorized Biography*, McGraw-Hill.

6. See Meehan, Thomas, Fun art, *Horizon* (Autumn 1969), 4.

# HOW EFFECTIVE ARE SUMMER TRAINING PROGRAMS FOR RECRUITING?

*F. Robert Joseph*

The centrality of the job is the most distinguishing characteristic of the job economy. Consequently, preparing for a job, getting a job (and) holding a job . . . are crucial matters for the bulk of the labor force.

Daniel H. Kruger, the author of this paragraph,[1] says the job has become "the most important economic activity in the lives of most of the American people." If this statement is true, then the following analogous statement should also be true.

The centrality of an employee is the most distinguishing characteristic of the employee economy. Consequently, recruiting an employee, hiring an employee and holding on to this employee are crucial matters for the bulk of American industry.

The difference between these two short paragraphs is in their outlook. The first defines the employment process from the worker's point of view; the second takes the company's point of view.

Since it has become so crucial for American business firms to recruit, hire and retain qualified new employees, some firms are now using a summer training program in order to attract more and better college graduates for future permanent employment.

The recent growth of formalized summer programs makes it appear that they must be successful as recruiting tools. It might be, however, that some firms have established them because "everyone else has one." The question then is how truly effective are these programs?

In an attempt to answer this question, a twenty-six item questionnaire was sent to sixty-two firms out of the approximately four hundred that recruit at The Graduate School of Business Administration at The University of Michigan. Thirty of the firms were known to have summer programs; the additional thirty-two were selected as those most likely to have summer programs. Sixty percent of the questionnaires were completed and returned. An additional fourteen percent were returned with an explanation that they did not have formalized summer training programs.

The purpose of the study was two-fold. First, it attempted to determine the general characteristics of the programs. Since there is not a great deal of published material available on summer training programs this information will help companies compare their current or anticipated programs with those included in the study. They can look at particulars such as salary, or they may be interested in seeing how well others are doing in their hiring of past summer trainees.

From *Management of Personnel Quarterly*, **8**, No. 1 (Spring, 1969), 18-24. Reprinted by permission of *Management of Personnel Quarterly*.

The second purpose was to find out which program characteristics had the most favorable results as far as future employment is concerned. This information can be useful since it helps to form basic guidelines to follow when setting up a summer program.

The firms included in the survey were divided into nine basic industry categories: manufacturing (11) banking (10) advertising (4) public accounting (4) retailing (2) government (2) public utility (2) publishing (1) and insurance (1).

The sizes of the companies ranged from several hundred employees to over one hundred thousand. Total employment for the thirty-seven respondents was approximately one and one-half million. Each firm was placed into one of six classes depending on its size: less than 1000, three firms; 1000-5000, thirteen firms; 5000-15,000, seven firms; 15,000-25,000, three firms; 25,000-50,000, five firms; over 50,000, six firms.

## PROGRAM CHARACTERISTICS

A few of the important program characteristics found in the surveyed firms are presented below. Although there were wide variations in some, the descriptions are fairly well representative.

**Age.**   Over eighty percent of the programs have been established within the last ten years. The average age of the thirty-five firms responding to this question was seven years. Not all, however, were new since one had been in existence for more than forty years.

**Size.**   The average number of trainees in each program was one hundred fifty-three. This figure, however, includes several firms that employ over one thousand trainees. Eliminating these firms from the calculations yields a more representative twenty-six. This figured out to be one quarter of one percent of total company employment.

**Year of student.**   Most firms hired seniors and graduate students that were one year from completing their education. About one third of the companies would hire students at the junior level, while only three were willing to hire those in any year of school.

**Salaries.**   The range in salaries offered was quite large. Part of this variation was caused by differences in student's year in school. The lowest salary offered was $325; the highest was $825 per month. These figures were for freshmen and graduate students respectively. The average for all firms was $615. Two things must be noted about these figures: first, salaries may represent averages of the figures given by a firm. (For example, if a company answered by saying that they pay their trainees $600 to $700 per month, the amount plotted would be $650); secondly, salary ranges may be set up by the company for students at different class levels (i.e., Senior, Junior, etc.), and a company hiring undergraduate as well as graduate students may have a lower *average* salary than one which hires only graduate students. This company might, however, pay its graduate students more as an individual group.

**Duties.** Forty percent of the firms had their trainees performing duties similar to the regular, permanent workers. The majority, however, were given special projects to perform. The major difficulty in assigning a summer trainee regular work is that he may not know exactly what to do, and may take most of the summer to become acquainted with the company operations. Because of this, most of the firms which put the trainee on regular assignments hire technical-type students (engineering students or business students majoring in accounting). Most of the trainees also reported to a line manager at the middle management level.

## STUDENT PERFORMANCE

The companies were then asked to give information regarding performances by the students, contact made during the school year, and final percent hired. As stated earlier, the summaries given are only generalizations of the firm's answers.

**Performance.** The results in this area should be gratifying to the students who participate in summer programs as well as to the schools that train them. Most firms felt that over ninety percent of the trainees performed their work satisfactorily (the lowest estimate was seventy percent of the students). Three firms felt that *all* of their trainees did *well*. The major reason given for unsatisfactory performance was the student's lack of interest in the work.

**Contact.** All but one of the companies remained in contact with the student after he returned to school. The most common methods were letter, personal contact and company magazine.

**Hired.** On the average, one third of the trainees returned to their company to take permanent positions. Only eleven percent of the firms had more than half returning. The highest in any company was ninety percent, while another had failed to hire a single past trainee (the program, however, is only two years old).

The responding companies were divided into two groups according to the percentage of trainees finally hired for permanent employment. Firms (4) with over fifty percent were categorized as *high*; those (12) with less than twenty-five percent were *low*. Then each of the program's characteristics, as well as the company data, was analyzed to determine which qualities resulted in *high* returns and which in *low*. (See recruitment characteristics table.)

This survey was concerned with the summer training program and its effectiveness as a recruiting tool. Although I believe this to be the major reason why firms establish programs, others must also be considered. It is up to each company, however, to decide what results it expects to accomplish with such a program. Eight advantages that can be offered by summer programs are discussed; the first two are related to the survey quite directly, the others, however, may be more valuable to some firms.

### 1. The Company has an Opportunity to Look at the Student.

The three month program enables a firm to learn a great deal about an individual and see how he is likely to react in situations other than the classroom. This period gives the employer a greater opportunity to make a final decision about future permanent employment. It also reduces the chance of a serious mistake being made to the detriment of both the company and the student.

### 2. The Student has an Opportunity to Look at the Company.

This is the mirror advantage of the one above. A short training period allows the student a chance to determine if his first choice is one that he can enjoy and properly handle. It allows for easier adjustment, if necessary, with the minimum of problems.

### 3. Goodwill for the Company is Created on the Campus.

Aside from the direct advantage of finding qualified workers, a company benefits from the goodwill that is created through the use of a summer training program. Students who participate in them usually spread the word to their classmates who in turn may become interested. This advantage, however, hinges on one thing. In order for the "good word" to spread, a trainee must feel the program is worthwhile. If he does not, then it is very possible the program will have a negative effect upon additional campus recruitment. This is the reason why firms interested in establishing summer programs should use all means available to present one that is both effective and rewarding.

### 4. The Company is Better Able to Learn Student Attitudes.

Summer training programs help the firm's management stay in touch with the campus and the youth of today. The attitudes of students are continually changing. Firms hoping to attract these students must be aware of such changes and make necessary adjustments which may be needed. A summer program is made up of students and not businessmen. As a result, firms are more likely to obtain reliable information about their program and its ability to interest students in permanent employment.

### 5. A Smaller and Less Well Known Firm can Enter the Recruiting Arena.

The use of a summer training program enables a smaller firm to compete with larger, well-known companies. The reason is that summer jobs are relatively scarce. This is especially true for good ones. Firms which offer such programs are likely to become well known on campus. Students who would not normally consider taking a job with this company on a permanent basis will probably jump at a chance to work during the summer months. This is where the advantage lies. Many trainees hopefully will be impressed by what they see and will seriously consider this firm for future employment. Even if they do not return, they will tell others about their experiences and perhaps convince them of the advantages that can be offered by a smaller company.

**Characteristics of Programs with High/Low Recruitment Results**

| Characteristic | High | Low |
|---|---|---|
| Industry | Three industry groupings were represented in this category. They are public accounting, advertising and retailing. Half of the high group was comprised of accounting firms. | Industries represented by governmental agencies and public utilities fell totally within this group. Almost three-quarters of the banks were also low. The remaining companies in this group were manufacturers. |
| Size of firm | Generally, the smaller firms made up this category. Three-fourths of the companies employed less than five thousand workers. No firm over twenty-five thousand is in this group. | Unlike the *high* category, no firm size is outstanding. Small, medium and large firms were divided equally in the low group. |
| Age of program | This group contains the older programs. Fifty percent of these firms have programs that were over ten years old. | The newer programs have had the poorest results. Half of the programs which have been in existence less than six years are in the low group. |
| Salary | Surprisingly, the firms that offered the lowest salaries for summer trainees had the best success. Three-fourths of them had monthly salaries of less than $570. | Over half of the firms with low returns paid their trainees a salary between $570 and $700 per month |
| Type of work | This characteristic gave the most clear-cut results. All of the firms giving their trainees regular work to perform are in this category. | Three-fourths of the firms in this group gave their trainees project type assignments to perform during the summer. |
| Contact made | No one type of contact made with the student after he returned to school seemed to be outstanding. However, those which made several had better results than those making only one contact. | Of the methods used for contact, firms using a letter only had the poorest results. |
| Starting salary | All of the firms in this category said they offered returning trainees a higher salary than other college graduates without this summer experience. | Salary level showed no real difference in this group. |
| Desire to return | The fact that a student (at the end of the summer) expressed a desire to return after graduation seems to be a good indication that he will. All firms which had over three-fourths of the trainees express this were in the *high* category. | Half of the firms which had forty percent or less express desire to return ended up in the *low* group. |

### 6. The Company Can Concentrate Its Efforts on the Exceptional Trainee.

Although most trainees will perform satisfactorily enough to be offered permanent employment, there are a few that will do outstanding work. The summer training program helps a firm pick out these individuals for recognition where it might not have been able to do so by grades alone. A company which finds such a student may be willing to spend a little extra effort and money to convince him to return. This effort might never have been made and a valuable employee might have been lost had it not been for the summer program.

### 7. Students Perform Valuable Services for the Company.

Many students who are hired for the summer can perform important tasks for a firm. Some jobs are continually being put aside because no one wants to be bothered. Many of them, however, are important and should be done. This is where the trainee can be of service. Companies must be careful, though, not to give the trainee "make work" projects that may turn him against the program. They may end up hurting their entire campus relations as well as this one trainee. Some firms can also give the summer employee regular work assignments that will add to his value to the company. Trainees can help replace men who are on vacations, or can handle extra work during busy periods.

### 8. A Company is Likely to Have Lower Turnover Among Returning Trainees.

When a past trainee returns to a firm after graduation he is more likely to stay than a non-trainee graduate. He knows the firm and knows what can be expected. There will probably be no surprises that will cause him to become dissatisfied by his choice. If this trainee came back it is because he was "sold" on the company. His sincere belief in the company may have an influence on other new employees who likewise will be convinced that their company is the best.

### RECOMMENDATION

These advantages may slip by, however, if a company does not have a program that is effective and interesting. Some firms start with a good program, but fail to carry it through to completion. An "Objectives" approach may be very useful in setting up a program that yields the desired results; such an approach should: 1) state program objectives (both the needs of the firm and the needs of the students); 2) train management in program objectives; 3) hire capable students; and 4) compare results with program objectives.

Before a company establishes a summer training program it should first decide what it hopes to accomplish. Without doing this, the likelihood of its success is very dim. Such a program should not be considered lightly because of the expense required in its planning and implementation. Objectives should reflect the goals of the company and be aimed at solving anticipated needs.

In order for a program to meet these objectives, the desires of the student must also be considered. He has established for himself goals to accomplish, is concerned about the social role he must follow, and wonders about his future. Any program must consider these needs in order to properly motivate the student.

After objectives have been established, the next step is training the line managers who will be involved in the project. Since they are in daily contact with the trainee it is up to them to see that the program is a success. Unless their cooperation is gained, no amount of planning will enable the program to succeed. Managers will also be required to evaluate the trainee and the program at the summer's end. They must know the objectives in order to do this.

Some firms might feel that selecting a summer trainee is not as important as selecting a permanent employee since he will be working for only three months. This, however, is not correct. Since the trainee may be a future employee the same care is needed in his selection. In addition, he will be returning to school; an unqualified student will not be able to relate his experiences to fellow classmates.

Finally, a company with a successful program will gather the facts, compare them with the objectives, and attempt to draw conclusions about its effectiveness. Whenever the results are below the expectations, reasons should be found and corrections made. There is great opportunity to learn from past mistakes, but unless a company is willing to make the effort, solutions will remain hidden. Until this final step is completed, the true value of any program will not be realized.

#### NOTES

1. Kruger, Daniel H., Manpower problems and the business community, *Personnel Journal,* **47**, No. 11 (Nov. 1968).

---

## WOMEN'S HIGH LEVEL TRAINING AND WORK: WHERE TO NOW?

*John B. Parrish*

The 1960's saw strenuous and unprecedented efforts by many women's organizations to increase the participation of talented women in high level work. What was accomplished?

The decade can probably best be described in the following capsule summary:

*Many breakthroughs for the few —*
*Few breakthroughs for the many.*

---

From *Training and Development Journal,* **24**, No. 11 (November, 1970), 20-22. Reprinted by permission of the American Society for Training and Development.

The press headlined "new breakthrough careers" for American women. A woman was employed for the first time as a commercial airline pilot. A woman scientist for the first time received the top "Award of Achievement" of the Atomic Energy Commission. The federal government proudly announced the appointment of the first woman tugboat captain under Civil Service. And the first women were photographed huddled around the South Pole in Antarctica.

These and similar "firsts" were real achievements and deserve the applause and commendation which they received. But after one leaves the front pages and the TV cameras, the story is not so exciting. In fact it is disappointing. The truth is, *for the many, there was little or no progress* for American women in the upper echelons of the occupational structure. In some high-level jobs there was decline. Should one conclude, therefore, that the 1960's were "wasted" or at least was a decade in which women's higher level training and work simply marked time? By no means, as will be indicated below.

## SOME LESSONS LEARNED IN THE 1960's

If we grant that no major high level breakthroughs for the many occurred in the 1960's, the decade was not "lost." Many important lessons were learned. Some ten will be briefly cited here.

First, it was learned that chronic shortages of high level personnel would not be sufficient *per se* to attract very many women. At one time it was believed when job opportunities became abundant, employer discrimination would decline, women would respond. The former occurred, the latter did not.

Second, relatively little can be learned from foreign experience. International comparisons showing the high percent of medical, science and engineering personnel who are women in other countries, particularly the Soviet Union, proved interesting, but not really relevant. Conditions here are much too different. Our problems are unique.

Third, the relatively greater expansion of professional and subprofessional occupations will not be followed by automatically being restructured, which will provide easier access, mobility and career ladders for women. The "institutional inheritance" is too great and too heavy for this to happen without planned effort.

Fourth, the enactment of "equal rights" legislation, while attended by much publicity and a few legal successes, did little or nothing to break down the real barriers to women's high-level work. It helped only a few blue collar women workers.

Fifth, the development of women's higher education continuation centers to facilitate comeback by college trained women was a constructive step, but a very, very small one. There was a little feedback to enable more women to obtain and utilize higher training.

Sixth, the publicity given to women in the professions by a continuous series of national and international conferences may have redirected a few young talented college women, but the overall effects were minimal. The "exchange of views" stimulated chiefly the conference participants who were already professionals.

Seventh, the decline of "women's education" and the spread toward coeducation may have promoted "human relations" and "equality" but had no perceptible effect on upgrading women's choice of careers.

Eighth, the increasing participation of women in the labor force at all age levels was reinforced steadily during the decade, but with no gains at higher occupational levels. There was no "spill over" or "pushup" effect.

Ninth, the wastage of women's talents probably increased steadily during the decade as the percent of women obtaining higher education rose, but the participation at higher levels remained stationary or declined.

Tenth, the dissatisfaction of talented women with their societal roles probably increased because of higher educational attainment, greater awareness of professional opportunities and social needs but accompanied by no realistic way in which to break down the barriers.

In sum, the decade of the 1960's tells us much about the complex forces at work influencing the career decisions and achievements of talented women. The decade established the fact that if progress is to be made in this area, in the 1970's, there will have to be major breakthroughs in entirely new directions utilizing new strategies. The old ones didn't work in the 1960's and are not likely to in the 1970's.

## WHAT DO TALENTED WOMEN REALLY WANT?

The decade of the 1960's was not lacking in efforts to find out what talented women really wanted in the way of careers and life roles. The research was unprecedented in variety and formidable in quantity. At the risk of being presumptuous, a very brief summary of the vast literature will be attempted here.

At least seven basic job needs of talented women may be identified. First, is the opportunity to explore and test out a variety of careers during the college years. Curricula are now balkanized. Once one begins study in a given field, it is difficult to change. If change is made, it is limited to one or at the most two options. It is difficult to combine liberal arts studies and pre-professional studies.

Second, is the need for facilities that would permit easier combination of marriage and continued study. The lack of day care centers and reduced registration fees for married women are major barriers to continuance.

Third, is the unitary and sequential nature of present professional training. There are no stages where one may get off the ladder and then return. It is all the way to the M.D. or nothing. A 90 percent M.D. has no value. Even the subprofessions or semi-professions are rigidified.

Fourth, there are few opportunities for continued higher home study for women already trained, or partially trained, in a professional area and who have temporarily dropped out for family responsibilities.

Fifth, there are very limited opportunities for part-time professional work that would facilitate both child raising and work. This despite the fact that the few carefully-planned experiments using part-time women professionals have been uniformly favorable both in the government and private sectors.

Sixth, professional work for wives is often unrewarding because of the regressive nature of the income tax laws. There is no provision for women to offset either the higher costs of working (hiring child care, housekeeping personnel, travel, clothes costs, etc.) or the higher joint income tax payments when the husband is already in a high tax bracket. It not only doesn't pay some women to work at high levels, it actually costs the family in time, money and stress.

Seventh, there are very few sub- or semi-professions which may be practiced and which at the same time provide continuing education and career ladders to higher jobs. Each has its own dead end with no mobility between related professions.

### CAN WE FIND THE BREAKTHROUGHS?

If the foregoing outline is even approximately correct about where we have been and where we are now with women's high level careers, it is evident, if we are to do better in the 1970's, some major breakthroughs will be needed for the many talented women who will be moving through our colleges seeking both higher education and more satisfying life patterns.

The big question is: "Where do we find the breakthroughs?" If there is already a "crisis" for many talented women and if it may get worse in the future, how do we resolve it? Are there any grounds for optimism after the disillusionment of the 1960's?

While caution is always a good attribute, this report suggests that there are grounds for some optimism. There are some new "social innovations" and "technology turns" on the horizon. They hold much promise for the 1970's. This brief report permits discussion of only five.

First, the accelerating interest of the private sector in developing and marketing "learning machines" and accessory educational equipment constitutes a revolution with great potential for women. It will make possible greater variety and flexibility within the colleges. It will make possible study at home. It will facilitate the development of career ladders.

Second, the colleges and universities swept up in the ferment of change which ushered in the 1970's are probably more open to constructive innovation than any time in the postwar period. Preoccupied with the crunch of massive enrollment increases in the 1960's, educational leaders are now searching for ways to make traditional education more meaningful and realistic.

Third, a major, in fact almost unsurmountable handicap, of women's career counselors in the past, has been the lack of current occupational information. The development of job vacancy statistics is finally under way by the U.S. Department of Labor and this development could be promoted more rapidly by pressure from women's groups. Further, the leading federal statistical agencies are now turning to the nation's lack of "social statistics." These will surely be developed in the early 1970's and should be of great help to professional women's organizations.

Fourth, the need to break up professional jobs into levels and stages is now recognized. And the techniques for doing this through restructuring are now available. Job dilution is a very old and useful strategem in manufacturing industries. It has never been applied to the professions largely because there has been no need. The time for the professions has now come.

Fifth, training is itself now a profession. It has developed slowly but steadily and can now stand on its own. Professional training personnel can now develop on-the-job training programs for the high-talented advantaged as well as for the low-education disadvantaged. In-company, college-level courses are growing very rapidly in the private sector. This will give women new options not available in the past.

Sixth, there is plenty of evidence that women's groups have "got the steam up" to seek new breakthroughs in contrast to much apathy and confusion in the past. And how can this steam be directed in such a way as to get results as well as publicity?

## DEMONSTRATION PROJECT AN ANSWER

On this question, this article suggests women's organizations, particularly those concerned with high level careers, take their cue from one of the oldest and most experienced groups of professionals in America—the agricultural educators. Beginning about 1800 they saw the need to transfer scientific knowledge to uneducated "dirt farmers." But how? For three quarters of a century they tried every conceivable technique to put their ideas across. And they failed. The "dirt farmers" wanted no part of "book" farming. In desperation the educators turned not to teaching but to "showing." They began "demonstration" plots and centers. Then when the "demonstration" farmer got 40 bushels of corn per acre to only 20 for everyone else, the farmers got the point—and quick.

There is important need to restructure the curricula in our academic institutions and professional tasks through "demonstration" projects which can then be used as guidelines for others. This can be done. It should be done. We can hope it will be done.

# WOMEN'S SELF-CONCEPT: IMPLICATIONS FOR MANAGEMENT DEVELOPMENT.[1]

*Theodora Wells*

Increasingly, qualified women will be advancing into management development programs to the higher positions in business, industry, government and community organizations. We need to begin *now* to evaluate present programs to see if their design will meet the needs of these women and the men with whom they will be working.

The purpose of this article is to review the current pressures, relevant research and practical problems of placing women in management development programs and subsequently into the network of long-established interrelationships within dominantly male organizational hierarchies.

## PRESSURES FOR MORE WOMEN IN MANAGEMENT TRAINING

Historically, the participation of women in management development programs has been nil or very low. There are a number of forces operating that indicate changes in this pattern in the near future. Let us look at what some of these change pressures are.

There is a continuing need for developing more qualified managers. The supply of potential managers is indeed limited and the prognosis is for a continuing shortage. This was recently confirmed by Assistant Labor Secretary Jerome M. Rosow in a forecast of the 70's based on Bureau of Labor Statistics projections, "The real squeeze in demand will be for managers and supervisors in the 30-45 age range, and their ranks 'show no significant growth in numbers during the 70's.'"[2]

There is a recognition that women are a major under-utilized resource. U.S. Department of Labor figures show that 80% of all women workers are in the lower-paying jobs (compared to 52% of all male workers in the same jobs).[3] Yet, the median educational attainment in all categories is essentially the same for both men and women.[4] In a recent management survey there were almost 50 companies where the workforce was over 50% women, yet in about 40% of these companies there were no women at all in management positions.[5]

Our own past president, Gordon L. Lippitt, recognized the under-utilization of women in his future projections. "Inadequate use of minority group members, such as blacks, Mexicans, Puerto Ricans, *women* (emphasis added), and older workers, will be a constant challenge in an evolving and changing society... This will require an ever-continuing involvement in creating new designs for effectively developing the capabilities of human resources."[6]

New pressures for admission of women into management development programs are coming from the requirements for legal compliance with the Civil Rights Act of

1964. Title VII of this Act specifically prohibits sex discrimination in training programs.[7] Executive Order 11246 extends Title VII provisions to government employment and Executive Order 11375 adds the sex discrimination provisions. New guidelines, effective June 9, 1970, require contractors to be able to demonstrate that both sexes have equal access to all types of training programs. Specifically in reference to management trainee programs, the sex discrimination guidelines state, "Women have not been typically found in significant numbers in management. In many companies management trainee programs are one of the ladders to management positions. Traditionally, few, if any, women have been admitted to these programs. An important element of affirmative action shall be a commitment to include women candidates in such programs."[8]

Another pressure is *The Report of the Presidential Task Force on Women's Rights and Responsibilities: A Matter of Simple Justice.*[9] Many facets of sex discrimination, especially in education and employment, are discussed with accompanying recommendations for changes in the law. Although the effect of these findings in the form of implemented legal actions may be some years away, the extent and pervasiveness of sex discriminations is clearly stated. This information is being widely circulated and is of concern to all managers.

A growing pressure is now coming from the many organizations proliferating in the women's rights movement. These groups are vitally concerned with the bread-and-butter issues of equal pay and benefits for equal work, free child-care centers, maternity leaves without loss of seniority, equal insurance, pension and social security provisions, and other issues deeply affecting the lives of women who work, many of whom are heads of households. Most of these women want the oportunity to produce without being penalized for sex, and seek no special privilege because of their sex.

## WHAT HAPPENS TO POTENTIAL WOMEN MANAGERS?

One major source of potential managers is new graduates from colleges and universities. Women graduates are typically excluded from the avenues to organizational power, influence, responsibility and rewards available to those men who also excel academically. Even women M.B.A.'s from Harvard Business School have had this experience.[10]

Another major source is the women currently employed in company positions that are at the "invisible ceiling" level. Although there may be no *formal* restriction from further advancement, it becomes clear that they will go no higher. There are a number of euphemistic ways of describing the "invisible ceiling." For example, "It's never been done before and now is not a good time to try it." Or, "Our customers wouldn't accept it. They expect to do business with a man." Of the few women now in management, most of them have had to be exceptional in their skills, and exceptional in "bending the stereotypes" in reference to their advancement.

The women at the "invisible ceiling" level may be in executive assistantships, staff or administrative capacities or in various supervisory positions. Many have trained one or more male bosses for the next-level position for which they may be well qualified but somehow are not considered eligible to occupy. Even with temporary occupancy with a performance rating of excellent, permanent promotion usually remains unavailable. Too often, a less qualified man will get the position and the woman will be asked to "show him the ropes." This represents a vast under-utilization of trained, proven management, or potential management talent.

The last source of experienced managers is by recruiting from the external market. Women typically are excluded from this market because almost no management or executive search or placement agency will handle a woman, even though this is a flagrant violation of Title VII mentioned above. A woman may come well-referred by her invaluable "connnections" of people who know her work, but the net result is almost inevitable. "There would be no problem at all, but XYZ Company just won't pay that kind of money to a woman." Or, more deadly, "They *really* like your qualifications, but they want a man."

## RESEARCH RELEVANT TO SEX-ROLES AND EMPLOYMENT

Some notable research is currently being done that bears on the nature and effects of sex-role stereotyping, bringing together related work over the last 20 or more years. Three areas of particular interest to us here.

**1. Sex-role stereotypes and self concepts.**    In seeking to specify the valued characteristics of men and women, Rosenkrantz et al[11] found that traits valued in man (by both men and women) are; being aggressive, independent, unemotional, dominant, competitive, direct, adventurous, skilled in business, able to make decisions easily, a self-confident leader, able to separate feelings from ideas, and that men are superior to women. Traits valued in women (by both men and women) are; being talkative, tactful, gentle, aware of feelings of others, expressive of tender feelings, neat and quiet, interested in own appearance, strong need for security, appreciative of art, literature and religion, and non-use of harsh language. There was general agreement among the men and women subjects (college students) on what the valued traits are, and both sexes agree that the masculine traits are considered to be more socially desirable than the feminine traits.

The self-concepts of both men and women were found to be very similar to the respective stereotypic traits. And the women, presumably, also held a negative valuation of their personal worth relative to men. The implication is that "the factors producing the incorporation of the female stereotype *along with its negative valuation* (emphasis added) into the self-concept of the female subjects, then, must be enormously powerful."[12]

**2. Sex-role stereotypes and mental health.**    A more recent study was made with the subjects being psychiatrists, psychologists and psychiatric social workers. Broverman *et* al[13] showed that a double standard of (mental) health exists, wherein ideal concepts of health for a mature adult (sex unspecified) are meant primarily for men and less so for women.

Their findings indicated a powerful negative assessment of women. The ideal healthy woman differed from the ideal healthy man by being more submissive, less dependent, less adventurous, more easily influenced, less aggressive, less competitive, more excitable in minor crises, having their feelings hurt more easily, being more emotional, more conceited about their appearance, less objective and disliking math and science. The researchers felt compelled to comment, "This constellation seems a most unusual way of describing any mature, healthy individual."[14]

Both men and women clinicians held these different concepts of health for men and women. Further, these concepts were found to parallel the sex-role stereotypes that are prevalent in our society.

The discussion of the researchers made it clear that a women has to decide whether to be a mature, healthy adult—that is, exercising the positive characteristics considered desirable for men—and have her "femininity" questioned; or, she can "behave in the prescribed feminine manner, accept second-class adult status, and possibly live a lie to boot."[15] Even while we emphasize equal opportunity and freedom of choice in American society, the findings indicate that social pressures toward conformity to the sex-role stereotypes tend to restrict the actual career choices open to women and, to a lesser degree, those open to men.

**3. Women's motive to avoid success.**   A new, provocative area of research has been opened up by Matina Horner[16] at Harvard University. She observed that the studies on achievement motivation were on men only. No theories or facts were available about women and their motive to achieve. Her findings show that, for women, the desire to achieve is often contaminated by a *motive to avoid success*. She found that this motive, like the achievement motive, is a stable disposition within the person, acquired early in life along with other sex-role standards. Further, her findings suggest that women with high intellectual ability and histories of academic success will not fully explore their intellectual potential when they have to compete. This seems to be particularly true when these women are competing with men.

It appears, then, that we may socialize women to be in a perpetual double bind: "If she fails, she is not living up to her own standards of performance; if she succeeds she is not living up to the societal expectations about the female role."[17]

As a result, women tend to disguise their abilities, not admit to their successes and otherwise downgrade their strengths. They tend to believe that men are smarter than women, therefore it is important to appear less "smart" to the men from whom they seek self-esteem reinforcement. This circular dependency pattern led Horner to comment that, "unless ways are found to reduce the fear of success, we will continue to waste the vast potential of over one-half of our population."[18]

The general thrust of these studies can be summarized by some conclusions from a study by Clarkson *et al* [19] of the Rosenkrantz-Broverman group. They found that although sex-role stereotypes assign greater competency to the masculine role and lesser to the feminine role, that competency can be more broadly conceived as a human developmental attribute toward which healthy adults of both sexes may aspire. They observed that the items making up the "competency cluster" (the male-valued stereotypic items which include the achievement values) describe a rational, competent, active, mature individual who is capable of functioning effectively in our society. Therefore, they say that "incorporation by women of the male-valued stereotypic items . . implies an enhancement of self-concept along a dimension of mental health, maturity or self-actualization."[20]

## IMPLICATIONS FOR TRAINING

Clearly, then, there will need to be some new aspects to management training programs that include women participants. These aspects are in the area of *self-concept training* in the direction of self-actualizing patterns.

First, women need to deal with a negative valuing of self when (1) they are functioning below their capabilities but are being valued by others (both men and women) in terms of behaving in a more dependent, "feminine" way; or (2) when they are functioning in a more mature, healthy, self-actualizing way but are being valued negatively by others because they differ from expected norms of "feminine" behavior.

In order to sort out this dilemma, it may be necessary to explore what "not losing one's femininity" really means. It may have several aspects of meaning; the sex-role expectations, the "sexiness" of a woman when seen as a sex-object, and a woman's sexuality. When a woman grows beyond the dependent, passive, self-deprecating behavior of the feminine role, she may be less concerned about her "sexiness" as a sex-object. She may even enhance and enjoy her sexuality as a more fully-functioning, self-valuing woman and person (Maslow).[21]

Although this analysis may seem inappropriate for the training of managers, Horner's findings on women's motive to avoid success strongly indicate that (1) the dilemma of social role vs. self-needs, and (2) the need for reinforcement of the social role, especially from men, centrally affects the self-concepts of women. Therefore, self-concept training must be a part of management development training, as applicable to the participants.

Second, others in the management training group, both men and women, may need to see how they maintain their own self-concepts, to what degree it is important to "keep women in their place" and for what reasons. If a person has a need to put others down, it may be important to feel into what that means for him or her. It is suggested that it may be less threatening to work with the more mature, healthy, fully-functioning woman than with a subordinated "feminine" woman who may engage in destructive behavior by projecting alienated parts of herself on others in order to maintain an acceptable self-image (Putney & Putney.)[22] (This dynamic is, of course, not limited to women.)

Third, as changes in self-concepts begin to take place, the established or expected behaviors and relationships will change in ways that, predictably, may have a powerful impact on the participants. People make long-standing personal investments in their conceptual systems, and therefore tend to overlook, rather than understand, variations from these. For example, Harrison[23] describes the usual concept that a woman has qualities of warmth, lovingness and femininity, and that these are incompatible with a ready ability to express anger. Even in the face of ample evidence to the contrary, when a woman shows anger the urge is to pass it off with, "She is not herself," or "She's not really that mad," or other ways to avoid questioning the conceptual system. The *last* alternative considered is, "It is perfectly possible for a woman to express deep anger readily and still be warm, loving and feminine."

Offsetting this defense, Harrison feels that people also have a *need to know*—a drive toward competence—which can operate in a training group where there are relationships of mutual support, respect and trust. Maslow,[24] in terms of his hierarchy of needs and the need to know, indicates that curiosity and exploration are higher needs than safety needs. However, he also notes the conflict that "often it is better not to know, because if you *did* know, then you would *have* to act and stick your neck out" (emphasis his).

The central change that needs to happen is a move away from perceiving men and women in the traditional sex-role patterns in the work environment, as was so well documented by Bowman *et al,*[25] toward perceiving people as human beings first, seeking their own ways of growth, and who are defined only secondarily by their biological sex traits.

Lastly, this kind of change requires an organizational climate where individual growth is valued. Argyris[26] has shown that when managements use *formal* organizational principles the climate breeds individuals who are dependent upon, passive toward, and subordinate to the leader. Consequently, they have little control over their working environment and their time perspective is shortened because they do not control the information needed to predict their future.

Argyris describes these individuals as childlike rather than adult. Such behavior can also be described as female sex-role behavior: passive, dependent, subordinate. Since formal organizational principles tend to be used in authoritarian systems, and there may also be considerable pressure for adherence to traditional sex-roles,[27] a climate for growth is not created. Therefore, the kind of management training being discussed here may not be possible in that climate.

Manager growth programs may be more effective in organizational climates created through the use of consultative and participative systems of management styles described by Likert,[28] provided such training draws on only one system of management style. Fully-functioning adult behaviors imply an interdependence, resulting in ego-building, cooperative efforts which move in the direction of the participative style. Such a climate seems to be needed for the kind of growth programs being discussed here.

## WHAT CAN BE DONE IN THE ABSENCE OF INFORMATION

The silence in research about man-woman working relationships is deafening! The vast bulk of research done in management and all the behavioral sciences is by men who operate from male-oriented frameworks of thinking, which may include the double standard of mental health referred to above. Studies of manager behavior and behavior change are on male managers. Therefore, what is reported is how men researchers frame hypotheses to investigate how men interact with other men. We also know something about men in the superior role to women, but less about the dynamics of women in the subordinate role, as disclosed by Horner above. We know virtually nothing about women in superior roles to men, and relatively little about women in superior roles to women. Peer relationships between man-woman and woman-woman as they operate in economic organizations are also sparsely researched.

So far, we are still operating on long-established stereotypes and assumptions for which there is little evidence except the operation of the self-fulfilling prophecy. The traditional sex-roles are generally held to be an accurate description of what men and women are like. These may be an accurate description of how we *socialize* people on the basis of their biological sex, but as Weisstein[29] points out, until we have similar social expectations for both sexes, we simply do not know what immutable differences exist that would support the biological definitions prevalent today. Broverman, *et al*,[30] also found no evidence that biologically-based behaviors are a basis for stereotypic attributes, and adds that these would be inappropriate because of the large within-sex variability of these characteristics.

Clearly, one of the major actions indicated is to get more information. Research that has already been done could be used as a starting point for formulating additional hypotheses about women subjects, getting new information about man-woman relationships and comparing these with man-man relationships. For example, there is a study, "Change in Self-Identity in a Management Training Conference," (French, Sherwood & Bradford)[31] of the effects of the amount of feedback on various dimensions on self-identity changes. This study *never stated the sex of its subjects*, identifying them only as "20 middle-management employees of a large corporation." Since no between-sex data was given, "middle-management employees" presumably means "men." The same research design using men and women subjects would yield data to compare with the first study. Such data might provide important guidance for the kind of training under discussion here.

Another promising avenue to more information is to reapply knowledge we already have. For example, McClelland[32] found that achievement motivation can be developed in local leaders of an underdeveloped country (India). This less achieve-ment-oriented environment was intentionally chosen to test the effectiveness of their achievement training design. He reports short-term success and speculates that a climate of confidence may also generate longer-lasting effects than when the training occurs in a climate of doubt and pessimism.

Traditional sex-roles are formed in what may amount to two parallel cultures, masculine and feminine, within the American Family, school, and work structures. Achievement expectations are substantially different for men and women, as shown by Maccoby's[33] findings on changes in intellectual functioning of boys and girls over time. We know that there are strong social pressures for women not to achieve if they are to remain "feminine." It is possible that the motive not to succeed could be changed by the training methods found to be effective with others who have acquired low achievement motivation. This could be researched by reapplying McClelland's research design to study achievement training efforts on motivation change in American women.

A well-known avenue to improved relationships is the use of sensitivity methods in management training. We know that self-concept changes occur in these groups. Role expectations vs. full functioning as an evolving person can easily be explored in the context of team tasks and other methods used in task-oriented sensitivity groups, as well as in groups of persons who may have been excellent employees but "didn't use discretion." As long as sex relationships are treated as if they didn't exist, these dynamics will predictably continue.

In order to cope with (1) the sense of appropriateness, (2) all the facets of work life, and (3) the emotional tensions around sex aspects of man-woman relationships, it may be essential to bring in outside consultants, perhaps a man-woman team. Ideally, these dynamics can be openly discussed in a trusting training group, provided that the trainer(s) is comfortable with his or her own sexuality and perceives him/herself as a self-actualizing, growing person first, and a sexual being second. This focus, in the writer's opinion, is essential to keeping the sexual dynamics in appropriate perspective. If this kind of trainer is not available, the content can probably be better discussed in separate-sex sessions, in outside training programs, or in private channels arranged for by the organization.

From the experiences from teaching several courses in management development for women, it has become very evident to the writer that avoidance of this subject will make a mockery of serious efforts to evolve good human working relationships between men and women. The sub-rosa relationships are powerful, the motive to hide them is strong, considerable duplicity may evolve, and many facets of communication and productivity are affected negatively.

These very dynamics may have operated to keep women from participating in management training programs. Not only do some women use their sex unethically, but some men do not know how to handle their sexual reactions when working with women. It may be that the man-woman problem—which calls for self-concept training—has been avoided by keeping women out of management. In the past, this may have been a workable strategy. Today and in the future, avoidance will not suffice.

## CONCLUSION

The movement of women into management positions is in an early stage, but it is clearly on its way. Considerations of resource utilization, compliance with regulations and the law, and simple social justice flow together toward this conclusion. Management development training must adapt to these trends by finding sound means of integrating women into the management team. New research is needed on man-woman relationships in organizational settings, and on effective training methods to make such relationships smooth and productive. Enough is known from past research to indicate that self-concepts are the critical area for training. The training effort must move ahead without waiting for new research results. Training programs will improve by profiting from the experience provided by early training efforts and from concurrent research.

## NOTES

1. I wish to express my appreciation to Lee Christie for his valuable suggestions and contributions to this article.

2. Rising need for better-trained workers—forecast for the seventies, *Training and Development Journal* (Sept. 1970), 11.

3. Based on U.S. Dept. of Labor charts in Rebelling women—the reason, *U.S. News & World Report* (April 13, 1970), 35-37.

4. *Background Facts on Women Workers in the U.S.*, U.S. Dept. of Labor, Women's Bureau, Table 8, 12.

5. *U.S. News & World Report, op. cit.*, 35, referring to a study by the Bureau of National Affairs and the American Society for Personnel Administration.

6. Lippitt, Gordon L., Future trends affecting the training and development profession, *Training and Development Journal* (Dec. 1969), 10.

7. For a full text of Title VII of the Civil Rights Act of 1964, the Equal Pay Act of 1963, other related data, and an excellent discussion, see Kanowitz, Leo, *Women and the Law: The Unfinished Revolution.* Albuquerque: University of New Mexico Press, 1969.

8. *Federal Register*, Doc. 70-7115. Title 41, Sec. 60-20.6, Affirmative action (filed June 8, 1970).

9. *The Report of the Presidential Task Force on Women's Rights and Responsibilities: A Matter of Simple Justice.* Supt. of Documents, U.S. Govt. Printing Office, Washington, D.C.

10. Bird, Caroline. *Born Female: The High Cost of Keeping Women Down.* New York: Pocket Books, 1968, 40-85.

11. Rosenkrantz, P., S. Vogel, H. Bee, I. Broverman, and D. Broverman, Sex-role stereotypes and self-concepts in college students, *Journal of Consulting and Clinical Psychology*, **32**, No. 2 (June 1969), 287-295.

12. *Ibid.*, 293.

13. Broverman, I., D. Broverman, F. Clarkson, P. Rosenkrantz, and S. Vogel, Sex-role stereotypes and clinical judgments of mental health, *Journal of Consulting and Clinical Psychology*, **34**, No. 1 (Feb. 1970), 1-7.

14. *Ibid.*, 5.

15. *Ibid.*, 6.

16. Horner, Matina S., Woman's will to fail, *Psychology Today* (Nov. 1969), 36 ff.

17. *Ibid.* 38.

18. Horner, Matina S., Follow-up studies on the will to fail in women, a paper delivered to the American Psychological Association in Miami Beach, Fla. on Sept. 6, 1970.

19. Clarkson, F., S. Vogel, I. Broverman, D. Broverman and P. Rosenkrantz, Family size and sex-role sterotypes, *Science*, 167 (Jan. 23, 1970), 390-392.

20. *Ibid.*, 391.

21. Maslow, Abraham H., *Motivation and Personality.* New York: Harper & Row, 1950, 245.

22. Putney, S., and G. Putney. *The Adjusted American: Normal Neurosis in the Individual and Society.* New York: Harper & Row, 1964, 23-74.

23. Harrison, Roger, Defenses and the need to know, in Eddy, W., W. Burke, V. Dupre, and O. South (eds.), *Behavioral Science and the Manager's Role.* Washington, D.C.: NTL Institute of Applied Behavioral Science, 1969, 66.

24. Maslow, Abraham H., *Toward a Psychology of Being.* Princeton: Van Nostrand, 1962, 60-63.

25. Bowman, G., B. Worthy, and S. Greyser, Are women executives people? *Harvard Business Review,* July/Aug. 1965, 43:4, 14 ff.

26. Argyris, Chris, *Personality and Organization.* New York: Harper & Row, 1957, 54-75.

27. When adherence to traditional sex-roles is reflected in severe sex-typing of jobs, there will be no women candidates for management training, typically.

28. Likert, Rensis, *The Human Organization.* New York: McGraw-Hill, 1967, Table 3-1, Appendix II; also 47-49, 129.

29. Weisstein, Naomi, Woman as nigger, *Psychology Today* (Oct. 1969), 20 ff. Condensed from Kinder, kuche, kirche as scientific law: psychology constructs the female, *Motive,* **29,** Nos. 6 and 7 (March/April 1969), 78 ff.

30. Broverman, *et al, op. cit.,* 6.

31. French, J., Jr., J. Sherwood, and D. Bradford, Change in self-identity in a management training conference, *Journal of Applied Behavioral Science,* **2,** No. 2 (April/May/June 1968), 210-218.

32. McClelland, David C., Achievement motivation can be developed, *Harvard Business Review,* **43,** No. 6 (Nov./Dec. 1965), 7 ff.

33. Maccoby, Eleanor E., Sex differences in intellectual functioning, in Maccoby, E. (ed.), *The Development of Sex Differences.* Palo Alto: Stanford University Press, 1966, 25-55.

# 7.
# STRUCTURING WORK FOR DEVELOPING PEOPLE

During the late 1960's a major focus of behavioral application in organizations was on the role, function, and work of the individual. The impetus for much of this can be attributed to the concepts of Abraham Maslow and the findings of Frederick Herzberg, whose "job enrichment" offered specific approaches for structuring work to motivate individuals. Herzberg's theory developed into a practical, tangible method of improving work for individuals, increasing their motivation, and presumably resulting in greater output for the organization. While Herzberg's work has received the most attention, other important work has been done that sometimes complements, but sometimes seemingly contradicts, Herzberg's findings.

The four selections in this chapter deal either directly or indirectly with Herzberg's theory and its application. While many benefits have derived from applications of Herzberg's methods, those who apply them often lack the broad perspective necessary to apply them well. The selections in this chapter have been chosen to give this broader perspective and facilitate greater understanding of the nature of man's work.

The first selection, "Motivating People: Money Isn't Everything," from *Newsweek*, serves as an introduction to the increased emphasis on job structure in the late 1960's. "Job Enrichment Pays Off," by William Paul, Jr., Keith B. Robertson, and Frederick Herzberg, describes the application of Herzberg's theories and the present state of job enrichment. It also supplies some basic information on Herzberg's theories and thus, along with the Newsweek article, gives necessary historical background on the subject.

Thomas C. Rodney, in "Can Money Motivate Better Job Performance?", discusses the role of money in motivation to work. According to Rodney, Herzberg's classification of pay as a maintainance factor rather than a motivating one has caused many to underrate it as an incentive. He raises some pointed questions about Herzberg's classification of pay, and his article should provoke thoughtful discussion both among proponents of Herzberg's job enrichment and others who are interested in motivation in the organization.

The final selection gives broad perspectives on jobs and motivation. "Motivation and Job Performance," by Melvin Sorcher and Herbert Meyer, relates job design to the larger organization environment. Sorcher and Meyer do a thorough and thoughtful job of presenting the views of practitioners in organizations.

Job design will continue to be popular in the near future. Unfortunately Herzberg's job enrichment seems to be following the pattern of some earlier popular methods of developing human resources, i.e., rapid popularity, followed by disillusion because the method is not a panacea; then abandonment by many practioners. It requires experimentation plus thorough research in organizational settings, and this does not appear to be forthcoming on any large scale. At the same time, competent practitioners have learned a great deal about job design and will continue to use this valuable new knowledge as an integral part of their art after the current popularity of job-structuring methods has faded.

## MOTIVATING PEOPLE: MONEY ISN'T EVERYTHING

*Newsweek Staff*

**What makes people work?**    At first glance, the question seems easily answered—or downright silly. Yet for U.S. industry continuously searching for new ways to get the most out of payroll dollars hard and fast answers have been elusive since the question was first asked seriously 50 years ago. About the time of World War I, it seemed obvious that people worked solely to feed and clothe themselves, and the way to get more out of them was to put on the screws—perhaps with a sharp tongue-lashing from a tough, dictatorial boss. From the 1930s through most of the 1950s, the feeling was that people worked out of "loyalty" to an organization, and the way to increase productivity was to organize company softball teams, publish chatty house organs, pump in soft music and pour on fringe benefits. But alas, as a personnel man sighed last week, nothing has really worked: "We haven't found the magic motivator—if it exists at all."

Yet a small band of behavioral scientists, most of them from leading U.S. universities, has been insisting for some time that there are better ways to motivate people. They have names little-known outside the bookish world of motivational research: Frederick Herzberg, 44, of Cleveland's Case Western Reserve University, or Rensis Likert, 64, of the University of Michigan. But they are beginning to make an impact on industry, and today perhaps 200 companies are, in varying degrees, following their advice. Says the gangling Herzberg of his packed consulting schedule: "At last we are being heard. Industry is listening."

What Herzberg, Likert and their fellow theorists are saying about motivation is this:

**Companies should stop deluding themselves that more money and more fringe benefits automatically lead to more productivity.** They don't, indeed haven't, and their primary effect is to encourage people to stay on the job, not produce more or be happier. While continuing to provide for the physical needs of employees, companies should begin thinking of ways to satisfy psychological needs, such as feelings of responsibility and accomplishment. These are the things that in the long run make people work harder.

**Companies should stop over-organizing jobs, fragmenting them into meaningless tasks that suppress the real capabilities of employees.** As it is now, the pool typist yawns between assignments that use a tenth of her potential, and the engineer takes to the bottle when he finds himself only a cog in a huge machine. The current widespread practice is to fit people into rigidly designed jobs, then judge capabilities. It should be the other way around: jobs should be fitted to individual talents.

**Companies should recognize that attitudes of managers at all levels can effect productivity.** An employee may be bright and capable, but the chances of these qualities surfacing are slim if the boss is laboring under a Victorian stereotype of workers: that they are lazy, that they crave direction, that they can't make decisions, that they must be coerced into producing. Such a manager must get off his autocratic pedestal and seek advice from employees in running the business, encouraging what the theorists call "participative management."

**In the case of money as a motivating factor, the theorists find no fault with the assumption that people work for money up to a certain level—to provide for their personal conceptions of the good life.** But they say there is considerable evidence that people simply don't view money the same way companies do—as an incentive to production by holding it up as a reward or threatening to withhold it for poor performance. In fact, notes one psychologist, the threat of firing has lost much of its muscle in the current tight labor market, where practically anyone with a marketable skill can find another job.

In Herzberg's jargon, money and fringe benefits are known as "negative motivators"; their absence from a job unquestionably will make people unhappy, but their presence doesn't necessarily make them happier or more productive. From this assumption, management consultant Saul W. Gellerman of Englewood Cliffs, N.J., concludes that more money in routine amounts (such as the annual raise) is largely taken for granted, anticipated before it arrives and viewed as a justly deserved reward for past services, not a stimulus to new effort.

In Gellerman's view, raises genuinely geared to individual performance, such as merit increases and executive-level bonuses, can make a difference—but in practice even these are often handed out for routine performance. Profit sharing, geared directly to productivity and used in various forms by some 125,000 companies, is considered by some as more of a prod to loyalty than increased output. Reasons: most people don't feel their individual jobs have that great an effect on over-all corporate profitability, and full payouts are almost always delayed until after several years' service.

In a new book about working, "Management by Motivation" (to be published in May by the American Management Association), Gellerman suggests that if companies really want to motivate people—and especially top executives—with money, they should give them a lot of it—enough to provide a massive upgrading in office status as well as social level. But Gellerman adds a qualifier for those who would take him too literally: the increases must be given to the "right people"—people who can be trusted by everybody to use their higher status for the benefit of the company, not simply for personal aggrandizement.

**Old Story.** If much of the so-called new theory sounds self-evident, it is nevertheless surprising how widely it has been ignored by U.S. businesses long used to rigid job classifications and pay scales. Indeed, the theorists can get arguments on almost every hand from personnel experts and top executives in business. In the case of money, for example, veteran du Pont personnel man James Sears says simply: "Just take it away and see what happens."

Some businessmen argue that workers themselves are more resistant to change than management, or that unless workers are motivated to begin with, no amount of management tools will help. Many still cling to the old tradition that mollycoddling is nonsense, and it is every worker's duty to put in an honest day's work for an honest day's pay. As a top Chicago manufacturing executive exploded last week: "It's wrong to be permissive with employees, turning them loose like children. The employees have to work to beat hell, do the work right and help turn out quality products. If they don't, out they go!"

Michigan's Likert winces at such bluster, yet concedes that many companies are reluctant to give up the old tried-and-true methods of management. "You can still get increased production by putting the screws on," he agrees. "The trouble is it works for awhile, then breaks down."

But the motivational gospel is spreading, and Herzberg, for one, is on the road 90 days a year consulting with a list of 35 blue-chip clients. More and more companies are beginning to practice the "participative management" technique expounded by Likert, who is director of Michigan's Institute for Social Research. According to Likert, it is quite possible to motivate employees by drawing them into the decision-making process, so they can relate their personal goals to those of the company.

**Incentives:** In practice this means that big Dallas-based Texas Instruments pulls blue-collar production people off the line for troubleshooting conferences with the company's engineers. Says president Mark Shepherd, who reflects TI's breezy informality by wearing short-sleeved sport shirts and eating with the help in the company cafeteria: "We've got to get all our people involved. The girls on the production line may not understand solid-state physics, but they sure as hell do understand the problems of nailing that radar together."

Delta Air Lines in Atlanta has set up a program that gives every employee down to the lowliest baggage clerk a chance to discuss his job with a top executive at least once a year. At Aerojet-General in California, line workers are presented with typical production problems and asked what they would do to solve them; in many cases their suggestions have been applied successfully. Aerojet-General and TRW, Inc., also have tackled the task of improving the skills of their managers in handling people. In conferences lasting three or four days, managers of both companies are required to explain how they do their job, and in the case of Aerojet-General receive written (and anonymous) critiques from their peers. Saga Foods, a big (1967 sales: $86 million) catering firm in California, has carried the management-grooming technique a bit further. Saga unit managers are required to submit a "performance" plan that sets their own goals for the next year, then stand or fall by it. As an incentive, each manager is told where his salary stands in relation to all others in the company.

One of the most literal applications of the new theory is at American Telephone and Telegraph Corp. The giant utility has involved about 3,000 of its 841,000 employees in applying a key conclusion of Herzberg's motivation theory: enlarging jobs to make them meaningful and more interesting in order to increase efficiency.

In Minnesota last week A.T.&T. payroll workers were no longer being hounded by supervisors who check and recheck everything. Instead, they were being told they had first-line accuracy responsibility for entire payrolls. At Illinois Bell in Chicago, service representatives were determining the credit rating of people who wanted phones installed and fixing the amount of deposits—if in their view they were required. In New York, long-lines installation teams were handling everything—from initial order to turning over working circuits to customers. The result, says A.T.&T. personnel executive Robert Ford, has been "better production, less turnover and higher morale."

Herzberg himself worked closely with the company in setting up the projects, including a 1965 test run in A.T.&T.'s troubled department of shareholder relations. There, women—70 percent of them college graduates—were plainly unhappy in their jobs, and with reason. They were second-guessed every step of the way in their handling of correspondence from A.T.&T.'s 3.1 million stockholders. Herzberg's solution: lift supervision, let the girls write and sign their own replies, encourage them to become experts in problems that interested them. "All we did, really, was let them run their own jobs," says Ford. The upshot: turnover dropped, productivity rose to above pre-test levels, and job satisfaction, measured on a scale of 100, soared from 33 to 90 in six months—all without a pay increase.

**Challenge.**   Eventually, A.T.&.T. hopes to apply job enlargement at upper levels of management, but one official believes the best place to start such projects is near the bottom. "That way," he says, "decision-making and planning functions get sucked downward."

Where all the activity and thinking will lead is anybody's guess. Generally, the theorists agree that it is harder to motivate assembly-line workers chained to repetitive jobs. "I just don't know what will happen to the non-elite, the unskilled, many of whom will be Negroes and minority workers," says Gerald Leader of Stanford's Business School. "It frightens me."

But the motivational experts see a fruitful field in the higher job levels. As they envision the future, working hours will tend to become less structured, less bound to the 9-to-5 routine, with employees working longer hours when there is a heavy load and knocking off when work is slack. "Lines between work and leisure will get fuzzy," says one. Similarly, job classifications and pay scales are likely to become unstructured, with employees roaming freely between related jobs and salaries varying widely for the same work, depending upon the employee's ability. Most experts see increasing use of the task-force concept of lifting workers from the rut of their normal jobs to work with others on special projects. In short, what the experts are aiming at is to cultivate a rooting interest that really springs from within. "To do that," says Herzberg, "will be industry's biggest challenge."

## JOB ENRICHMENT PAYS OFF

*William J. Paul, Jr., Keith B. Robertson,*
*and Frederick Herzberg*

In his pioneering article, "One More Time: How Do You Motivate Employees?"[1] Frederick Herzberg put forward some principles of scientific job enrichment and reported a successful application of them involving the stockholder correspondents employed by a large corporation. According to him, job enrichment seeks to improve both task efficiency and human satisfaction by means of building into people's jobs, quite specifically, greater scope for personal achievement and its recognition, more challenging and responsible work, and more opportunity for individual advancement and growth. It is concerned only incidentally with matters such as pay and working conditions, organizational structure, communications, and training, important and necessary though these may be in their own right.

But like a lot of pioneering work, Herzberg's study raised more questions than it answered. Some seemed to us to merit further consideration, particularly those in regard to the (1) generality of the findings, (2) feasibility of making changes, and (3) consequences to be expected. Consider:

*1. Generality.*    Can similarly positive results be obtained elsewhere with other people doing different jobs? How widespread is the scope or need for equivalent

Reprinted with permission from *Harvard Business Review*, **47**, No. 2 (March-April, 1969), 61-78. Copyright 1969 by the President and Fellows of Harvard College; all rights reserved.

change in other jobs? Can meaningful results be obtained only in jobs with large numbers of people all doing the same work and where performance measures are easily available?

*2. Feasibility.*    Are there not situations where the operational risk is so high that it would be foolhardy to attempt to pass responsibility and scope for achievement down the line? Because people's ability and sense of responsibility vary so much, is it not necessary to make changes selectively? Do all employees welcome having their jobs enriched, or are there not some who prefer things to be left as they are? Can one enrich jobs without inevitably facing demands for higher pay or better conditions to match the new responsibilities? And, in any case, is not the best route to motivational change through participation?

*3. Consequences.*    In view of so many possible difficulties in the way, are the gains to be expected from job enrichment significant or only marginal? Do they relate primarily to job satisfaction or to performance? What are the consequences for supervision if jobs are loaded with new tasks taken from above—i.e., does one man's enrichment become another's impoverishment? Finally, what are the consequences for management if motivational change becomes a reality? Is the manager's role affected? If so, how? And what are the implications for management development?

There are undoubtedly more questions that could be raised and investigated. But these seem particularly important from a corporate point of view if job enrichment is to take place on a widespread basis, as part of management practice rather than as a research activity. Accordingly, the purpose of this article is to probe into the complexities of job enrichment in an attempt to shed light on these questions and to determine how the concept may be most effectively applied in furthering the attainment of corporate business objectives.

In order to do this, we shall report in Part I on five studies carried out in Imperial Chemical Industries Limited and other British companies. Two of the studies—covering laboratory technicians in an R&D department and sales representatives in three companies—will be examined in some detail. The other three—encompassing design engineers, production foremen on shift work, and engineering foremen on day work—will be summarized. In Part II, the main conclusions emerging from the studies will be presented in the form of answers to the questions raised at the beginning of this article.

Each study was initiated in response to a particular problem posed by management, and the conclusions drawn from any one can be only tentative. Among them, however, they cover not only widely different business areas and company functions, but also many types and levels of jobs. Collectively, they provide material which adds to our understanding of both theory and practice.

## PART I: THE JOB ENRICHMENT STUDIES

As in all studies on job satisfaction and performance, the need to measure results introduced certain constraints which do not exist in normal managerial situations.

Consequently, three main features were common to the studies we are reporting in this discussion:

*First*, the "hygiene" was held constant. This means that no deliberate changes were made as part of the investigation, in matters such as pay, security, or working conditions. The studies were specifically trying to measure the extent of those gains which could be attributed solely to change in job content.

*Second*, recognition of the normal hygiene changes led to the need to have an "experimental group" for whom the specific changes in job content were made, and a "control group" whose job content remained the same.

*Third*, the studies had to be kept confidential to avoid the well-known tendency of people to behave in an artificial way when they know they are the subject of a controlled study. Naturally, there was no secret about the changes themselves, only about the fact that performance was being measured.

All studies set out to measure job satisfaction and performance for both the experimental and control groups over a trial period following the implementation of the changes. The trial period itself generally lasted a year and was never less than six months. The performance measures always were specific to the group concerned and were determined by local management of the subject company. To measure job satisfaction, we relied throughout on a job reaction survey which measures the degree of people's satisfaction with the motivators in their job as they themselves perceive them.

## Laboratory Technicians

Managers in an industrial research department were concerned about the morale of laboratory technicians, or "experimental officers" (EOs). This group's job was to implement experimental programs devised by scientists. The EOs set up the appropriate apparatus, recorded data, and supervised laboratory assistants, who carried out the simpler operations. The EOs were professionally qualified people, but lacked the honors or doctorate degrees possessed by the scientists.

The average age of the experimental officers was increasing. A quarter of them had reached their salary maximums, and fewer now had the chance to move out of the department. Their normal promotion route into plant management had become blocked as manufacturing processes grew more complex and more highly qualified people filled the available jobs. Management's view of the situation was confirmed by the initial job reaction survey. Not only were the EOs' scores low, but many wrote of their frustration. They felt their technical ability and experience was being wasted by the scientists' refusal to delegate anything but routine work.

Against this background, the research manager's specific objective was to develop the EOs into "better scientists." If job enrichment was to be useful, it would have to contribute to the attainment of that goal.

*Changes and Experimental Design*

Here is the specific program of action devised and implemented for the experimental officers.

*Technical:* EOs were encouraged to write the final report, or "minute," on any research project for which they had been responsible. Such minutes carried the author's name and were issued along with those of the scientists. It was up to each EO to decide for himself whether he wanted the minute checked by his supervisor before issue, but in any case he was fully responsible for answering any query arising from it.

EOs were involved in planning projects and experiments, and were given more chance to assist in work planning and target setting.

They were given time, on request, to follow up their own ideas, even if these went beyond the planned framework of research. Written reports had to be submitted on all such work.

*Financial:* EOs were authorized to requisition materials and equipment, to request analysis, and to order services such as maintenance, all on their own signature.

*Managerial:* Senior EOs were made responsible for devising and implementing a training program for their junior staff. In doing so, they could call on facilities and advice available within the company.

Senior EOs were involved in interviewing candidates for laboratory assistant jobs, and they also acted as first assessor in any staff assessment of their own laboratory assistants.

These changes drew on all the motivators. Each one gave important chances for achievement; together, they were designed to make the work more challenging. Recognition of achievement came in the authorship of reports. Authority to order supplies and services was a responsibility applying to all the EOs involved. The new managerial responsibilities reserved to senior EOs opened up room for advancement within the job, while the technical changes, particularly the opportunity for self-initiated work, gave scope for professional growth.

Some 40 EOs in all were involved in the study. Two sections of the department acted as experimental groups (N = 15) and two as control groups (N = 29). One experimental and one control group worked closely together on the same type of research, and it was anticipated that there would be some interaction between them. The other two groups were separate geographically and engaged on quite different research.

The changes were implemented for the experimental groups during October and November 1966, and the trial period ran for the next twelve months. After six months, the same changes were introduced into one of the control groups, thus converting it into an experimental group (N = 14). This was done to see whether a similar pattern of performance revealed itself, thereby safeguarding against any remote possibility of coincidence in the choice of the original groups.

Research work is notoriously difficult to measure, but as the aim was to encourage more scientific contribution from EOs, this was what had to be judged in as objective a way as possible. All EOs were asked to write monthly progress reports of work done. Those written by experimental and control group EOs were assessed by a panel of three managers, not members of the department, who were familiar with the research work concerned.

Reports were scored against eight specifically defined criteria thought to reflect the kind of growth being sought: *knowledge, comprehension, synthesis, evaluation, original thought, practical initiative, industry, and skill in report writing.* Whenever the assessor found particular evidence of one of these qualities in a report, he would award it one mark, the total score for a report being simply the sum of these marks.

In order to establish a baseline for clarifying standards and testing the assessors' consistency of marking, reports were collected for three months prior to the introduction of any job enrichment changes. The very high consistency found between the marking of the three assessors encouraged confidence in the system. The assessors, naturally, were never told which were the experimental and control groups, though it became easy for them to guess as the trial period went on.

The other main measure was to use the same system to assess research minutes written by the EOs. These were compared against an equivalent sample of minutes written by scientists over the same period, which were submitted to the panel for assessment, again without identification.

*Motivational Results*

The assessment of monthly reports written by the experimental officers is given in *Exhibit I*, which compares the mean score achieved by all experimental group EOs each month with that achieved by all control group EOs. On occasions when a monthly report had obviously suffered because of the attention devoted to writing a research minute covering much the same ground, a marginal weighting factor was added to the score depending on the quality of the minute concerned. Both experimental and control groups improved their monthly report scores at about the same rate during the first five months. There is no doubt that with practice all were getting better at report writing, and it may be that the mere fact of being asked to write monthly reports itself acted as a motivator for both groups.

Once the changes had been fully implemented in the experimental groups, however, performance began to diverge. Although the reports of the control groups continued to improve for a time, they were far outpaced by those of the experimental groups. With some fluctuations, this performance differential was maintained throughout the rest of the trial period. When, after six months, the motivators were fed into one of the two control groups, its performance improved dramatically,

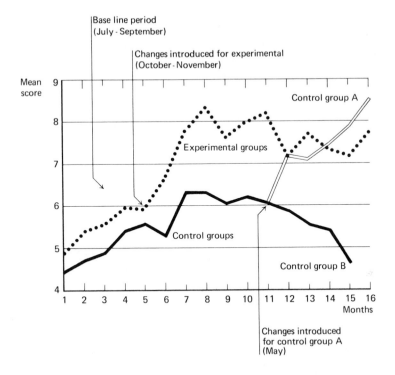

**Exhibit I.**   Assessment of EOs' monthly reports

following the pattern achieved by the original experimental groups. Meanwhile, the performance of the other control group, unaffected by what was happening elsewhere, began to slip back toward its original starting point.

During the 12 months of the trial period, a total of 34 research minutes were written by EOs, all from the experimental groups, compared with 2 from the department as a whole during the previous 12-month period. There were also a number of minutes jointly authored by scientists and EOs, which are excluded from this analysis. Of the 34 being considered, 9 were written by EOs in the control group which was converted into an experimental group, but all came from the time after the changes had been introduced.

It is one thing for laboratory technicians to write research minutes, but whether the minutes they write are any good or not is a different matter. *Exhibit II* shows the quality of the EOs' minutes compared with that of the scientists'. The EOs' mean score was 8.7; the scientists' 9.8. All EO scores except three fell within the range of scores obtained by the scientists; the three exceptions were written by one man. Three

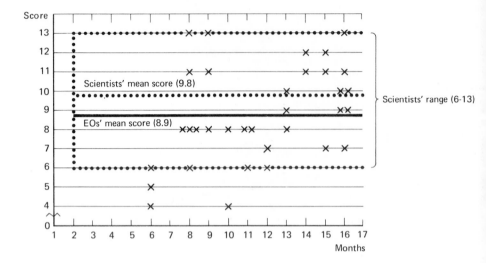

**Exhibit II.**   Assessment of EOs' research minutes

of the EOs' minutes, one in fact written by a laboratory assistant with guidance from an EO, were judged to be as good as the best of the scientists' minutes.

Encouraged by the success of a training scheme designed for laboratory assistants, the EOs initiated one for themselves. It aimed to give them the opportunity to come to terms with the ideas and terminology of chemical engineering. Managers judged it to have been of considerable value, and one EO summed it up by saying, "A couple of pages of chemical engineering calculations and formulas won't frighten us off now."

One original idea followed up, as the changes now permitted, by an EO from an experimental group resulted in an important discovery with possible applications in certain kinds of national emergency. The idea was investigated further by a government department, which described it as the most promising of some 200 ideas submitted on that topic.

Three staff assessments on EOs were carried out—at the beginning, middle, and end of the trial period. Each followed the normal company procedure. The only group which showed a consistent improvement was one of the experimental groups.

The job reaction survey was given both before and after the trial period. In the initial survey, experimental and control group EOs could not be specifically identified, and so an exact comparison of the before and after scores of each group cannot be made. The overall mean score attained by all EOs in the department was no higher at the end of the trial period than it had been at the beginning. Although managers believed there had been a positive change in job satisfaction, that is not a conclusion which can be supported with data.

An internal company report, written by the personnel officer who managed and coordinated the study throughout, concluded that there had been definite evidence of growth among the EOs, particularly in one group, and that much useful work had been accomplished during the exercise. One of the experimental groups had been able to keep abreast of its commitments even though it lost the services of two of its six scientists during the trial period and functioned without a manager for the last five months of the study. There can be little doubt that job enrichment in this case helped to further the research manager's objective of tackling a morale problem by getting at the root of the matter and developing experimental officers as scientists in their own right.

## Sales Representatives

To investigate the potential of job enrichment in the sales field, work has been done in three British companies dealing with quite different products and markets, both wholesale and retail. In only one study, however, were experimental conditions strictly observed.

The company concerned had long enjoyed a healthy share of the domestic market in one particular product range, but its position was threatened by competition. A decline in market share had been stabilized before the study began, but 1967 sales still showed no improvement over those of 1966. So far as could be judged, the company's products were fully competitive in both price and quality. The critical factor in the situation appeared to be sales representatives' effort.

The representatives' salaries—they were not paid a commission—and conditions of employment were known to compare well with the average for the industry. Their mean score in the job reaction survey, like that of other groups of salesmen, was higher than most employees of equivalent seniority, which suggested that they enjoyed considerable job satisfaction.

The problem in this case, therefore, was that for the vital business objective of regaining the initiative in an important market, sustained extra effort was needed from a group of people already comparatively well treated and reasonably satisfied with their jobs. Here, job enrichment would stand or fall by the sales figures achieved.

### Changes and Experimental Design

Here is the specific program of action devised and implemented for the sales representatives.

*Technical:*    Sales representatives were no longer obliged to write reports on every customer call. They were asked simply to pass on information when they thought it appropriate or request action as they thought it was required.

Responsibility for determining calling frequencies was put wholly with the representatives themselves, who kept the only records for purposes such as staff reviews.

The technical service department agreed to provide service "on demand" from the representatives; nominated technicians regarded such calls as their first priority. Communication was by direct contact, paperwork being cleared after the event.

*Financial:*    In cases of customer complaint about product performance, representatives were authorized to make immediate settlements of up to $250 if they were satisfied that consequential liability would not be prejudiced.

If faulty material had been delivered or if the customer was holding material for which he had no further use, the representative now had complete authority, with no upper limit in sales value, to decide how best to deal with the matter. He could buy back unwanted stock even it it was no longer on the company's selling range.

Representatives were given a discretionary range of about 10% on the prices of most products, especially those considered to be critical from the point of view of market potential. The lower limit given was often below any price previously quoted by the company. All quotations other than at list price had to be reported by the representative.

The theme of all the changes was to build the sales representative's job so that it became more complete in its own right. Instead of always having to refer back to headquarters, the representative now had the authority to make decisions on his own—he was someone the customer could really do business with. Every change implied a greater responsibility; together they gave the freedom and challenge necessary for self-development.

The company sold to many different industries, or "trades." In view of the initial effort needed to determine limit prices and to make the technical service arrangements, it was decided that the study should concentrate on three trades chosen to be typical of the business as a whole. These three trades gave a good geographical spread and covered many types of customers; each had an annual sales turnover of about $1 million.

The experimental group ($N = 15$) was selected to be representative of the sales force as a whole in age range, experience, and ability. An important part of each member's selling responsibility lay within the nominated trades. The rest of the sales force ($N = 23$) acted as the control group. The changes were introduced during December 1967, and the trial period ran from January 1 to September 30, 1968.

The background of static sales and the objective of recapturing the market initiative dictated that sales turnover would be the critical measure, checked by gross margin. The difficulties of comparing unequal sales values and allowing for monthly fluctuations and seasonal trends were overcome by making all comparisons on a cumulative basis in terms of the percentage gain or loss for each group against the equivalent period of the previous year.

Since they were selling in the same trades in the same parts of the country, the performance of all the representatives was presumably influenced by the same broad economic and commercial factors. In two of the trades, the experimental group had the bigger share of the business and tended to sell to the larger customers. In these cases it may be surmised that prevailing market conditions affected the experimental

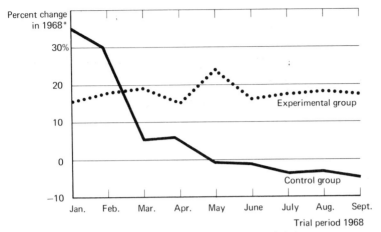

*Against corresponding 1967 period, plotted cumulatively.

**Exhibit III.**    Sales turnover within trades chosen as typical of the business as a whole

group's performance, favorably or unfavorably, more than the control group's. As it happened, in one of these trades commercial trends were favorable, while in the other they were distinctly unfavorable. In the third trade, the experimental and control groups were evenly matched. Taken together, then, the three trades give as fair a comparison as can be obtained between the performances of sales representatives under those two sets of conditions.

### Motivational Results

During the trial period the experimental group increased its sales by almost 19% over the same period of the previous year, a gain of over $300,000 in sales value. The control group's sales in the meantime declined by 5%. The equivalent change for both groups the previous year had been a decline of 3%. The difference in performance between the two groups is statistically significant at the 0.01 level of confidence.

Exhibit III shows the month-to-month performance of the two groups, plotted cumulatively. It can be seen that the control group in fact started the year extremely well, with January/February sales in the region of 30% above the equivalent 1967 figures. This improvement was not sustained, however, and by May cumulative sales had dropped below their 1967 level. By the last five months of the trial period, performance was running true to the previous year's form, showing a decline of about 3%.

The experimental group, on the other hand, started more modestly, not exceeding a 20% improvement during the first quarter. During the second quarter, outstanding results in May compensated for poorer figures in April and June. The third quarter showed a steady, if slight, rise in the rate of improvement over 1967. This sustained increase of just under 20% was in marked contrast to the previously declining performance of the trades as a whole.

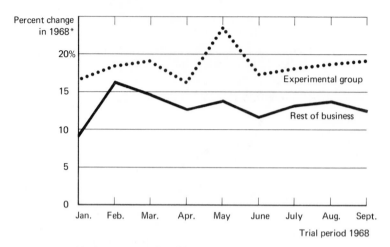

**Exhibit IV.**   Sales turnover: experimental group and rest of business

Comparisons with other trades suffer from the disadvantage that different economic and commercial factors affect the various parts of the business. Nevertheless, the experimental group's performance was consistently between 6% and 7% better than that for the rest of the business. *Exhibit IV* shows the month-to-month picture. It can be seen not only that the experimental group maintained a higher rate of improvement than the rest of the business throughout the trial period, but that the gap widened if anything as time went on. At the 1967 rates of turnover, this performance differential in all trades would be worth $1.5 million in sales value in a full year.

In view of the greater negotiating authority granted to the experimental group representatives, it is important to check whether their substantial increase in turnover was achieved at the expense of profit. As all quotations other than at list price were reported by the representatives, it was possible to analyze the gross margin achieved by both groups. The analysis showed without doubt that the gross margin of the experimental group's sales was proportionally as high, if not higher, than that of the control group's sales.

Managers had the impression that representatives actually used their price discretion less often than they had previously asked for special prices to be quoted by the sales office. Also, in the sales manager's view, once the representatives were given real negotiating authority, they discovered that price was not the obstacle to sales which they had always imagined it to be. Under the new arrangements, they were able to assess more completely what the true obstacles to sales were in each individual case.

Over the trial period the control group's mean score in the job reaction survey remained static. In contrast, the experimental group's score rose by 11%.

**Design Engineers**

The engineering director of one of the divisions of ICI wanted to see whether the job of design engineer might lend itself to motivational change. His design department faced an increasing work load as more design work for the division's plants was being done internally. The situation was exacerbated by difficulties in recruiting qualified design engineers. People at all levels in the department were being overloaded and development work was suffering.

*Changes and Experimental Design*

Here is the specific program of action devised and implemented for the design engineers.

*Technical:*   Experienced engineers were given a completely independent role in running their projects; the less experienced technical men were given as much independence as possible. Occasions on which reference to supervision remained obligatory were reduced to an absolute minimum. The aim was that each engineer should judge for himself when and to what extent he should seek advice.

Group managers sponsored occasional investigatory jobs, and engineers were encouraged to become departmental experts in particular fields. They were expected to follow up completed projects as they thought appropriate.

When authority to allocate work to outside consultants was given, the engineers were to have the responsibility for making the choice of consultants.

*Financial:*   Within a sanctioned project with a budget already agreed on, all arbitrary limits on engineers' authority to spend money were removed. They themselves had to ensure that each "physical intent" was adequately defined and that an appropriate sum was allocated for it in the project budget. That done, no financial ceiling limited their authority to place orders.

*Managerial:*   Engineers were involved in the selection and placing of designers (drawing office staff). They manned selection panels, and a recruit would only be allocated to a particular engineer if the latter agreed to accept him.

Experienced engineers were asked to make the initial salary recommendations for all their junior staff members.

Engineers were allowed to authorize overtime, cash advances, and traveling expenses for staff.

*Motivational Results*

In summary fashion, these are the deductions that can be drawn from this study:

- Senior managers saw a change in both the amount and the kind of consultation between experimental group design engineers and their immediate supervisors. The supervisors' routine involvement in projects was much reduced, and they were able to give more emphasis in tneir work to technical development. Some engineers still needed frequent guidance; others operated independently with confidence. The point is that not all were restricted for the benefit of some; those who could were allowed to find their own feet.

- The encouragement of specialist expertise among design engineers was a long-term proposition, but progress was made during the trial period.

- The removal of any financial ceiling on engineers' authority to place orders within an approved project with an agreed budget proved entirely effective. Whereas before the design engineers had to seek approval from as many as three higher levels of management for any expenditure over $5,000—a time-consuming process for all concerned—now they could, and did, place orders for as much as $500,000 worth of equipment on their own authority.

- There is no evidence of any poor decision having been taken as a result of the new arrangements. In fact, at the end of the trial period, none of the senior managers concerned wanted to revert to the old system.

- The changes involving the engineers in supervisory roles were thought by the senior managers to be at least as important as the other changes, possibly more so in the long term.

- There was no doubt about the design engineers' greater involvement in the selection process, which they fully accepted and appreciated. Significantly, they began to show a greater feel for the constraints involved in selection.

- The responsibility for overtime and travel claims was fully effective and taken in people's stride. There was no adverse effect from a budgetary control point of view.

- The involvement of design engineers in making salary recommendations for their staff was considered by the senior managers to have been a major improvement. If anything, engineers tended to be "tighter" in their salary recommendations than more senior management. There was general agreement that the effectiveness of this change would increase over time.

- Senior managers felt that none of the changes of its own accord had had an overriding effect, nor had all problems been solved. But there was no doubt that the cumulative effect of the changes had been significant and that the direction of solutions to some important problems had been indicated.

The changes may have been effective, but in this particular study the important question was whether they had a significant impact on job satisfaction. Some of the motivators introduced into the experimental groups had been in operation in the control group for some time; others—because of the specialist nature of the control group's work—were not as important to it as to the experimental groups. The control group had scored high in the initial job reaction survey, while the experimental groups had both achieved very low scores. If the experimental groups' scores did not improve, doubt would inevitably be cast on the relationship between job content and job satisfaction. As it turned out, comparison results of the before and after job reaction surveys revealed that the mean scores of the two experimental groups had increased by 21% and 16%, while those of the control group and all other design engineers in the department had remained static.

## Factory Supervisors

The final two studies, one in ICI and one in another British company, concerned factory supervisors: production foremen on shift work fabricating nonferrous metals, and engineering foremen on day work providing maintenance services. As the two studies seem to be complementary, they are considered jointly.

In both cases management was concerned about the degree to which the traditional role of the foreman had been eroded in recent years. The increasing complexity of organizational structures, plant and equipment, and industrial relations had left the foreman isolated. Decisions in the areas of planning, technical control, and discipline—originally in his province—were now passed up the line or turned over to a specialist staff. Many managers believed that as a consequence small problems too often escalated unnecessarily, managers were being overloaded, and day-to-day relationships between the foreman and his men had been weakened.

### Changes and Experimental Design

Here is the specific program of action devised and implemented for the production and engineering foremen.

*Technical:*    Foremen were involved more in planning. Production foremen were authorized to modify schedules for loading and sequencing; engineering foremen were consulted more about organizational developments, given more responsibility for preventive maintenance, and encouraged to comment on design.

All were assigned projects on specific problems such as quality control, and could draw on the necessary resources for their implementation.

Other changes included giving foremen more "on the spot" responsibility, official deputizing for engineers, the writing of monthly reports, and more recognition of foremen's achievement of plans.

*Financial:*    Engineering foremen were given complete control of certain "on cost" budgets. Production foremen were encouraged to make all decisions on nonstandard payments.

*Managerial:*    Production foremen were given the authority to hire labor against agreed manning targets. They interviewed candidates for jobs and made the decisions on their selection.

All the foremen were given complete disciplinary authority, except for dismissal. They decided what disciplinary action to take, consulted the personnel department if they thought it necessary, conducted the interviews, and kept the records.

All were given formal responsibility for the assessment, training, and development of their subordinates, and in some cases for the appointment of their own deputies. On the production side, a newly appointed training officer acted as a resource person for the foremen. Engineering foremen were involved more in the application of a job appraisement scheme and in joint consultation and negotiation with union officials.

The objective of integrating the foremen more fully into the managerial team dictated that responsibility should be the motivator chiefly concerned in these changes. Control of his own labor force, backed up by more technical and financial responsibility, was designed to give the foreman more opportunities for achievement and personal growth in the job. The main issue in these studies was whether foremen would prove themselves capable of carrying the increased responsibility. Thus, in monitoring the effectiveness of the changes, the aim was primarily to detect any instability or shortcomings in performance.

*Motivational Results*

In summary fashion, these are the deductions that can be drawn from this study:

- In six months the production foremen recruited nearly 100 men, and were judged by the personnel officer to be "hiring a better caliber of man at an improved rate." Their immediate supervisors were categorical in their approval and noted that the foremen were taking special care to "design their own shifts." Recruitment interviews were said to have improved the foremen's ability to handle encounters with existing staff and shop stewards.

- Training was handled equally successfully by the production foremen. For each job it was specified that there should be a certain number of men trained to take over in an emergency. During the trial period, the margin by which the target number was missed was reduced from 94 to 55; the number of operators unable to do another's job fell by 12%, and the number of assistants unable to do the job of the man they assisted fell by 37%. No comparable improvement was achieved in the control group.

- It became clear from both studies that foremen were fully capable of carrying disciplinary responsibility. An analysis of all cases arising during the trial year showed that there had been a reduction in the number of "repeat offenses" among employees with poor disciplinary records and a substantial reduction in short-term work stoppages. The analysis concluded that foremen were not prone to take one kind of action rather than another, they had developed a purposeful approach to such problems, and there had been no adverse union reaction.

- About 50% of the engineering foremen's monthly reports during the trial year referred to consultation and negotiation with union officials—this on a site not noted for its harmonious industrial relations. Topics included demarcation, special payments, and the easing of bans imposed on "call outs." The incidence of such reports was spread evenly throughout the experimental group; their frequency increased during the trial period as the foremen became more confident of their abilities. All such matters appear to have been handled capably.

- From both studies came evidence, confirming what has long been demonstrated in training courses, that special investigatory projects give foremen much needed opportunity to contribute their experience and expertise to the solution of long-standing technical and organizational problems. In only three cases where financial evaluation was possible, the estimated annual savings totaled more than $125,000.

- Regarding the engineering foremen's control of budgets, in some cases the aim was to meet the target exactly; in others it was to reduce costs as much as possible. Both aims were achieved by the foremen at least as well as they had been by the managers. There is no evidence that plant efficiency or work effectiveness suffered in any way as a result of cost savings achieved by the foremen.

- In the case of the engineering foremen, the experimental group's staff assessments at the end of the trial year were markedly better than those of the control groups. Despite the attempt made in the initial selection of experimental and control groups to achieve as good a balance as possible in ability and experience, there can be little doubt that the experimental group did in any case contain some more able men. But no one anticipated that such a large difference would show itself at the end of the trial period. As evidence of development, 45% of the experimental group's assessments referred to significant improvements in performance during the year, and 36% made particular mention of how effectively the foremen had dealt with increased responsibility received during the year. These assessments were written by managers who were not party to the study.

- In the production foremen's study, superintendents reported that the new conditions were "separating the wheat from the chaff "; some of those who had previously been thought to be among the best of the foremen had not lived up to their reputations in a situation which placed little value on compliance, while others had improved enormously.

- The production foremen's job reaction survey scores showed no particular improvement over the trial period. In the case of the engineering foremen, the experimental group's mean score showed a 12% increase, while the control group's had only risen by 3%.

## PART II: THE MAIN CONCLUSIONS

What has been described in the first part of this article is the consistent application of theory in an area where custom and practice are normally only challenged by individual hunch or intuition. As we have seen, each study posed a separate problem concerning a different group of employees; the only common element among them was the conceptual framework brought to bear on the problem, enabling a specific program of action to be devised and implemented. Much was learned in the process, by ourselves and managers alike.

Now in Part II, the main conclusions which emerged from the job enrichment studies are presented in the form of answers to the questions raised at the beginning of this article.

### Generality of Findings

*Can similarly positive results be obtained elsewhere with other people doing different jobs?*

Yes. The studies reflect a diversity of type and level of job in several company functions in more than one industry. From the evidence now available, it is clear that results are not dependent on any particular set of circumstances at the place of study. Our investigation has highlighted one important aspect of the process of management and has shown that disciplined attention to it brings results. The findings are relevant wherever people are being managed.

*How widespread is the scope or need for equivalent change in other jobs?*

The scope seems enormous. In brainstorming sessions held to generate ideas for change in the jobs covered by the studies, it was not uncommon for over a hundred suggestions to be entertained. The process of change in these particular jobs has started, not finished. In many places it has not even started. Though there probably are jobs which do not lend themselves to enrichment, we have never encountered a level or a function where some change has not seemed possible. It is difficult to say in advance what jobs are going to offer the most scope; the most unlikely sometimes turn out to have important possibilities. We have certainly not been able to conclude that any area of work can safely be left out of consideration.

The need is as deep as the scope is wide. The responsiveness of so many people to changes with a common theme suggests that an important and widespread human need has indeed been identified in the motivators. Moreover, it would seem to be a need which manifests itself in a variety of ways. If, from a company point of view, a gain once demonstrated to be possible is accepted as a need, then the performance improvements registered in these studies would seem to betray an organizational need which is far from fully recognized as yet.

*Can meaningful results be obtained only in jobs with large numbers of people all doing the same work, and where performance measures are easily available?*

No. Meaningful results can be obtained in situations very far from the experimental ideal. Indeed, the very awkwardness of many "real-life" situations leads to perceptions which could not come from a laboratory experiment.

Organizational changes are made, work loads fluctuate, people fall sick, managers are moved, emergencies have to be dealt with. The amount of attention which can be given to managing changes designed to enrich people's jobs is often slight. When a man's immediate supervisor does not even know that a study is taking place, there is no vested interest in its success. In circumstances such as these, whatever is done stands or falls by its own merits.

In few of the studies could members of the experimental groups be said to be doing exactly the same work. Changes sometimes had to be tailor-made to suit specific individual jobs. Yet from the diversity of application came an understanding of the commonality of the process. Although laboratory technicians were engaged in quite different kinds of research, they were all doing research work; although foremen were looking after radically different operations, they were all supervising.

The changes that seemed to have the most impact were precisely those which related to the common heart and substance of the role played by people whose jobs differed in many important details. More than this, it became clear that all of them—the laboratory technician following up an original idea, the design engineer buying equipment, the foreman taking disciplinary action, the sales representative negotiating in the customer's office—are essentially in the same situation, the crux of which is the private encounter between an individual and his task. Only a change which impacts on this central relationship, we believe, can be truly effective in a motivational sense.

Real-life conditions not only give an investigation authenticity; they highlight the problem of measurement. What is most meaningful to a manager, of course—a foreman's proprietary attitude toward his shift, for example—is not always quantifiable. An important discovery, however, was that the better the motivator, the more likely it was to provide its own measure. Employees' "sense of responsibility," judged in a vacuum, is a matter of speculation; but the exercise of a specific responsibility, once given, is usually capable of meaningful analysis. Laboratory technicians may or may not be thought to have innate potential; the number and quality of their research minutes can be measured. Several times managers commented that job enrichment had opened up measurement opportunities which not only allowed a more accurate assessment of individual performance, but often led to a better diagnosis of technical problems as well.

## Feasibility of Change

*Are there not situations where the operational risk is so high that it would be foolhardy to attempt to pass responsibility and scope for achievement down the line?*

Probably there are, but we have not encountered one. The risks attached to some of the changes in the sales representatives' study seemed frightening at the time. Few managers who have not tried it can accept with equanimity the thought of their subordinates placing orders for $500,000 worth of equipment on their own authority, even within a sanctioned project. The research manager in the laboratory technicians' study concluded that a change was only likely to be motivational for his subordinates if it made him lose sleep at nights.

Yet in no case did disaster result. In reviewing the results of the studies with the managers concerned, it was difficult in fact for us as outsiders not to have a sense of anticlimax. By the end of the trial period, the nerve-racking gambles of a few months before were hardly worth a mention. The new conditions seemed perfectly ordinary. Managers had completely revised their probability judgments in the light of experience.

Theory provides an explanation for the remarkable absence of disaster experienced in practice. Bad hygiene, such as oppressive supervision and ineffectual control systems, constrains and limits performance, and may even lead to sabotage. Administrative procedures that guard against hypothetical errors and imaginary irresponsibility breed the very carelessness and apathy which result in inefficiency. With too many controls, responsibility becomes so divided that it gets lost. Hygiene improvements at best lift the constraints.

The motivators, on the other hand, make it possible for the individual to advance the base line of his performance. The road is open for improvement, while present standards remain available as a reference point and guide. When a man is given the chance to achieve more, he may not take that chance, but he has no reason to achieve less. The message of both theory and practice is that people respond cautiously to new responsibility; they feel their way and seek advice. When responsibility is put squarely with the person doing a job, he is the one who wants and needs feedback in order to do his job. His use of the motivators, not our use of hygiene, is what really controls performance standards.

As managers, we start having positive control of the job only when we stop concentrating on trying to control people. Mistakes are less likely, not more likely, than before; those which do occur are more likely to be turned to account, learned from, and prevented in the future, for they are seen to matter. Monitoring continues, but its purpose has changed. Now it provides the jobholder with necessary information and enables management to see how much more can be added to a job rather than how much should be subtracted from it. That way, continual improvement, while not being guaranteed, at least becomes possible as the scope for the motivators is extended. It is the nearest thing to a performance insurance policy that management can have.

Such is the theory, and from the evidence of the studies, practice bears it out. If the studies show anything, they show that it pays to experiment. No one is being asked to accept anything on faith; what is required is the courage to put old assumptions and old fears to the test. For the manager, the process is like learning to swim: it may not be necessary to jump in at the deep end, but it surely is necessary to leave the shallow end. Only those who have done so are able to conquer the fear which perverts our whole diagnosis of the problem of managing people.

*Because people's ability and sense of responsibility vary so much, is it not necessary to make changes selectively?*

No. To make changes selectively is never to leave the shallow end of the pool. We are in no position to decide, before the event, who deserves to have his job enriched and who does not. In almost every study managers were surprised by the response of individuals, which varied certainly, but not always in the way that would have been forecast. As the job changed, so did the criteria of successful performance change. Some people who had been thought to be sound and responsible under the old conditions turned out merely to have been yes-men once those conditions were changed; their performance was the same as it had always been, but now compliance was no longer valued so highly. At the other extreme was one classic example of an awkward employee, about to be sacked, who turned out to be unusually inventive and responsible when he has given the opportunity to be so.

In one study, not reported, a promising set of changes brought relatively disappointing results—the changes had been implemented selectively. When pressed to explain the grounds on which people had been chosen, the manager quoted as an example someone who had already carried similar responsibility in a previous job. It is exactly this kind of vicious circle that job enrichment seeks to break.

When changes are made unselectively, the genuinely good performers get better. Some poor performers remain poor, but nothing is lost. Because the changes are opportunities and not demands, all that happens is that the less able ignore them and go on as before. Some people, however, develop as they never could under the old conditions, and do better than others originally rated much higher. This is the bonus from job enrichment. Not only is overall performance improved, but a clearer picture emerges of individual differences and potential.

So long as a foundation of new job opportunities available to all is firmly established, there is no harm in restricting certain changes to the more senior of the jobholders. Such changes can be seen in both the laboratory technicians' and the design engineers' studies. This is a very different matter from introducing changes selectively in the first place. It is a way of providing scope for personal advancement within the job and recognizing the achievements of those who build well on the foundation of opportunity already provided.

*Do all employees welcome having their jobs enriched, or are there not some who prefer things to be left as they are?*

Individual reaction to job enrichment is as difficult to forecast in terms of attitudes as it is in terms of performance. Those already genuinely interested in their work develop real enthusiasm. Not all people welcome having their jobs enriched, certainly, but so long as the changes are opportunities rather than demands, there is no reason to fear an adverse reaction. If someone prefers things the way they are, he merely keeps them the way they are, by continuing to refer matters to his supervisor, for example. Again, there is nothing lost.

On the other hand, some of the very people whom one might expect to duck their chance seize it with both hands, developing a keenness one would never have anticipated. In attitudes as well as in performance, the existence of individual differences is no bar to investigating the possibilities of job enrichment.

*Can you enrich jobs without inevitably facing demands for higher pay or better conditions to match the new responsibilities?*

Yes. In no instance did management face a demand of this kind as a result of changes made in the studies. It would seem that changes in working practice can be made without always having a price tag attached.

Here, as in the matter of operational risk, what is surprising in practice is easily explicable in terms of theory. The motivators and the hygiene factors may not be separate dimensions in a manager's analysis of a situation, but they are in people's experience. It is time that our diagnosis of problems took more account of people's experience. The studies demonstrate again that, when presented with an opportunity for achievement, people either achieve something or they do not; when allowed to develop, they either respond or stay as they are. Whatever the result, it is a self-contained experience, a private encounter between a person and his task.

It is something quite separate when the same person becomes annoyed by his poor working conditions, worries about his status or security, or sees his neighbors enjoying a higher standard of living. The cause-effect relationship between hygiene and motivation scarcely exists. Motivation is not the product of good hygiene, even if bad hygiene sometimes leads to sabotage. Higher pay may temporarily buy more work, but it does not buy commitment. Nor does commitment to a task, by itself, bring demand for better hygiene.

Managers often complain of their lack of room for maneuver. In doing so, they are generalizing from the rules of the hygiene game to the total management situation. There is little evidence that the workforce in fact prostitutes its commitment to a task, although incentive bonus schemes, productivity bargaining, and the like assiduously encourage such prostitution. Before the process goes too far, it seems worth exploring more fully the room for maneuver freely available on the motivator dimension.

This is not to say, however, that the motivators should be used as an alibi for the neglect of hygiene. If people genuinely are achieving more, taking more responsibility, and developing greater competence, that is no reason to take advantage of them for a short-term profit. Any tendency to exploitation on management's part could destroy the whole process.

*Is not the best route to motivational change through participation?*

Yes and no. We have to define our terms. So far as the process of job enrichment itself is concerned, experimental constraints in the studies dictated that there could be no participation by jobholders themselves in deciding what changes were to be made in their jobs. The changes nevertheless seemed to be effective. On the other hand, when people were invited to participate—not in any of the reported studies—results were disappointing. In one case, for example, a group of personnel specialists suggested fewer than 30 fairly minor changes in their jobs, whereas their managers had compiled a list of over 100 much more substantial possibilities.

It seems that employees themselves are not in a good position to test out the validity of the boundaries of their jobs. So long as the aim is not to measure experimentally the effects of job enrichment alone, there is undoubtedly benefit in the sharing of ideas. Our experience merely suggests that it would be unwise to pin too many hopes to it—or the wrong hopes.

Participation is sometimes held, consciously or unconsciously, to be an alternative to job enrichment. Instead of passing responsibility down the line and possibly losing control, the manager can consult his subordinates before making a decision, involve them, make them feel part of the team. It all seems to be a matter of degree, after all. Participation, in this sense of consultation, is seen as a safe halfway house to job enrichment, productive and satisfying to all concerned.

A multitude of techniques are available to help the manager be more effective in consultation: he can be trained to be more sensitive to interpersonal conflict, more sophisticated in his handling of groups, more ready to listen, more oriented toward valuing others' contributions. Better decisions result, especially in problem-solving meetings that bring together colleagues or opponents in different roles or functions.

But in the specific context of the management of subordinates, it is worth asking who is motivated in this kind of participation. The answer would seem to be the person who needs a second opinion to make sure he comes to the right decision—the manager in fact. The subordinate does not have the same professional or work-inspired need for the encounter, for he is not the one who has to live with responsibility for the decision. It is doubtful whether his "sense of involvement" even makes him feel good for long, for an appeal to personal vanity wears thin without more substance. However well-intentioned, this halfway-house kind of participative management smacks of conscience money; and receivers of charity are notoriously ungrateful. In the case of professional staff it is downright patronizing, for the subordinate is paid to offer his opinion anyway.

Theory clarifies the position. It is not a matter of degree at all. The difference between consultation and enrichment is a difference in kind. Consultation does not give a subordinate the chance for personal achievement which he can recognize; through involvement, it subtly denies him the exercise of responsibility which would lead to his development, however humbly, as an executive in his own right. Far from being the best route to motivational change, this kind of participation is a red herring. It is hygiene masquerading as a motivator, diverting attention from the real problem. It may help to prevent dissatisfaction, but it does not motivate.

The laboratory technicians, sales representatives, design engineers, and foremen did indeed participate, but not in a consultative exercise designed to keep them happy or to help their managers reach better decisions. Nor was it participation in ambiguity—an all too common occurrence in which, although no one quite knows where he stands or what may happen, the mere fact of participation is supposed to bring success. The participation of employees involved in the studies consisted of doing things which had always previously been done by more senior people. In all cases consultation continued, but now it was consultation upward. In consultation upward there is no ambiguity; tasks and roles are clear. Both parties are motivated, the subordinate by the need to make the best decision, to satisfy himself, to justify the trust placed in him, to enhance his professional reputation; the manager by the need to develop his staff.

When design engineers consulted their more senior colleagues, it was on questions of technical difficulty, commercial delicacy, or professional integrity—all more to the point than the mere price of a piece of equipment. Foremen consulted their managers on unusual budgetary worries, or the personnel department on tricky disciplinary problems. Sales representatives consulted headquarters on matters such as the stock position on a certain product before negotiating special terms with a customer.

Participation is indeed the best route to motivational change, but only when it is participation in the act of management, no matter at what level it takes place. And the test of the genuineness of that participation is simple—it must be left to the subordinate to be the prime mover in consultation on those topics where he carries personal responsibility. For the manager, as for the subordinate, the right to be consulted must be earned by competence in giving help. Therein lies the only authority worth having.

**Expected Consequences**

*In view of so many possible difficulties in the way, are the gains to be expected from job enrichment significant or only marginal?*

We believe the gains are significant, but the evidence must speak for itself. In all, 100 people were in the experimental groups in the studies described. A conservative reckoning of the financial benefit achieved, arrived at by halving all estimated annual gains or savings, would still be over $200,000 per year. Cost was measurable in a few days of managers' time at each place.

*Do the gains relate primarily to job satisfaction or to performance?*

Contrary to expectation, the gains, initially at least, seem to relate primarily to performance. Wherever a direct measure of performance was possible, an immediate gain was registered. In one or two instances, performance seemed to peak and then drop back somewhat, though it stayed well above its starting point and well above the control group's performance. Elsewhere there seemed to be a more gradual improvement; if anything it gained momentum through the trial period. We have no evidence to suggest that performance gains, once firmly established, are not capable of being sustained.

In the short term, gains in job satisfaction would seem to be less spectacular. Attitudes do not change overnight. Satisfaction is the result of performance, not vice versa, and there is a long history of frustration to be overcome. When direct measurement of job satisfaction was possible, the most significant gains seemed to come when the trial period was longest. There is every reason to think that in the long term attitudes catch up with performance and that job enrichment initiates a steady and prolonged improvement in both.

*What are the consequences for supervision if jobs are loaded with new tasks taken from above—i.e., does one man's enrichment become another's impoverishment?*

The more subordinates' jobs are enriched, the more superfluous does supervision, in its old sense, become. Several of the studies showed that short-term absences of the experimental groups' supervisors could be coped with more easily as day-to-day concern for operational problems shifted downward. The need for the supervisor to be always "on the job" diminished; greater organizational flexibility was gained.

But though supervision may become redundant, supervisors do not. Fears of loss of authority or prestige were never realized. Far from their jobs being impoverished, supervisors now found that they had time available to do more important work. Design engineers' supervisors were able to devote more effort to technical development; production foremen's supervisors found themselves playing a fuller managerial role.

The enrichment of lower-level jobs seems to set up a chain reaction resulting in the enrichment of supervisors' jobs as well. Fears that the supervisor may somehow miss out are based on the premise that there is a finite pool of responsibility in the organization which is shared among its members. In practice new higher-order responsibilities are born.

Even when subordinates are given responsibilities not previously held by their own supervisors, as happened in the sales representatives' study and to a lesser extent in some of the others, there is no evidence that supervisors feel bypassed or deprived, except perhaps very temporarily. It soon becomes apparent to all concerned that to supervise people with authority of their own is a more demanding, rewarding, and enjoyable task than to rule over a bunch of automatons, checking their every move.

*Finally, what are the consequences for management if motivational change becomes a reality? Is the manager's role affected? If so, how? And what are the implications for management development?*

The main consequence is that management becomes a service, its purpose to enable, encourage, assist, and reinforce achievement by employees. Task organization and task support are the central features of the manager's new role. In task *organization* two complementary criteria emerge: (1) tasks have to be authentic—i.e., the more opportunity they give employees to contribute to business objectives, the more effective they are likely to be motivationally; (2) tasks have to be motivational—

i.e., the more they draw upon the motivators, the more likely they are to produce an effective contribution to business objectives. In task *support*, factors such as company policy and administration, technical supervision, interpersonal relations, and working conditions all have to be pressed into the service of the motivators. Control of the job is achieved by providing people with the tools of their trade, with the information they require, with training as appropriate, and with advice when sought.

The job itself becomes the prime vehicle of all individual development, of which management development is only one kind. In aiding the process of development, our starting point, as always, is problem diagnosis—in this case, assessment of individual abilities, potentials, and needs. When people are underemployed, we have no way of distinguishing between those who are near the limit of their abilities and those who have a great deal more to contribute. All too often, potential has to be inferred from risky and subjective judgments about personality. Such judgments, once made, tend to be static; people become categorized. The studies show that when tasks are organized to be as authentic and motivational as possible, management receives a more accurate and a continuing feedback on individual strengths and weaknesses, ability, and potential. Task support becomes a flexible instrument of management, responsive to feedback.

If the job itself is the prime vehicle of individual development, task support is the means by which management can influence it. We still think of individual development, especially management development, far too much as something which can be imposed from outside. We pay lip service to on-the-job training but go on running courses as a refuge. We speak of self-development, but we are at a loss to know how to encourage it. Now, however, we can postulate a criterion: self-development is likely to be most effective when the task a person is engaged in is authentic and motivational and when in doing it he receives understanding, imaginative, and capable support. When these conditions are met, the job itself becomes a true learning situation, its ingredients the motivators.

Though only one study set out specifically to measure individual development, the most pervasive impression from all was one of development and personal growth achieved. The latent inspirational value of the jobs appeared to have been released. People were able to demonstrate and utilize skills they already possessed, and go on to learn new ones. Each new facet of the task required a response in terms of individual development, and results suggest that that response was seldom lacking.

The best evidence of development came, however, not from the experimental groups in the studies, but from the managers who put the studies into effect. It is sometimes said that attitude change is the key to success. But in seeking to improve the performance of our business, perhaps we rely too much on efforts to change managers' attitudes. These studies went ahead without waiting for miracles of conversion first. Just as the experimental groups in the studies represented a cross section of employees engaged on those jobs, so the managers who put the studies into effect represented a cross section of managers. Enthusiasts and skeptics alike agreed to judge the studies by their results. They did, and the effect was clear for the observer to see. Success proved to be the key to attitude change. In retrospect, who would want it otherwise?

NOTES

1. *Harvard Business Review* (January-February, 1968), 53.

---

# CAN MONEY MOTIVATE BETTER JOB PERFORMANCE?

*Thomas C. Rodney*

Throughout its history as a branch of personnel administration, wage and salary administration has proceeded on the assumption that money, properly administered, can motivate people to improve job performance, and that money poorly administered can be a powerful influence leading to lowered job performance. Money, however, in the practical industrial environment, does not exist in a vacuum. It is generally the symbol of something more than its own inherent value, i.e., it is generally the medium by which good performance is recognized. Arch Patton, a pioneer in the field of executive compensation, expresses this point of view:

Financial motivation is the final item on this brief motivational agenda. This is not to minimize its importance but rather is an acknowledgment of the complexity of the "money motive" and the fact that its administration is so closely interrelated with the other key executive motivations.

The psychologists tell us that money is not the most potent motivation on the industrial scene. More often than not, they nominate "the approval of associates" as the number-one motivation. . . .

Important as group approval is as a motivation, the psychologists frequently overlook the fact that money is the generally recognized yardstick by which this approval is expressed. In other words, money is a motivation that has many facets and means many things to its recipient. . . . The man who has done outstanding work expects to be financially rewarded. Poor work—lack of approval—is penalized by fewer and smaller merit increases and smaller bonuses. To be sure, promotion is an important measure of "approval"—the most important, because of its status implications—but it occurs infrequently compared with merit increases or bonus payments, hence it is not so readily available as a measure of approval. . . .

---

Reprinted from Volume 30, No. 2 (March-April, 1967), pages 23–29 of *Personnel Administration,* Copyright 1967, by permission from the Society for Personnel Administration, 485-87 National Press Building, 14th and F Streets, N.W., Washington, D.C. 20004.

But the greatest impact of the money motivation on the executive group results from consistent administration of promotion, salary, and bonus to reflect the performance of individuals. If this is done effectively . . . compensation administration becomes an instrument for targeting the efforts of individual executives on the objectives of the business, as well as a stout ally in the executive development process.[1]

In September of 1964, Dr. David W. Belcher, one of the accepted academic leaders in the field of wage and salary administration,[2] startled the world of wage and salary practitioners by publishing an article extremely critical of current practices.[3] In his article, Professor Belcher asserted that certain ominous trends, if not reversed soon, would lead to disappearance of the wage and salary administration function, or to a decrease in its importance of such magnitude that the function would become sufficiently routine to be taken over by one of the smaller computers. First among these ominous trends, according to Belcher, is the growing acceptance of Frederick Herzberg's satisfiers-dissatisfiers theory of motivation, which, according to Belcher, appears to destroy the concept of pay as a motivation.[4] Belcher then proceeds, however, to assert that the acceptance of Herzberg's theory as disproving pay as a motivator may be something of a misinterpretation of the theory itself, and that if pay is geared to achievement and serves as recognition of achievement, it may really be a motivator, after all.

If Belcher's qualifying statement is true, the argument has come full circle to the position articulated by Arch Patton.[5]

In two recent wage and salary administration courses held by the American Management Association in New York City, in which the author was privileged to participate as both chairman and lecturer, Belcher's article and the real meaning of Herzberg's theory were debated warmly. At both meetings, much heat but little light was shed upon the real meaning of Herzberg's theory, and especially upon the implications of that meaning for practicing wage and salary administrators.

**THE PROBLEM DEFINED**

In view of the ambiguity introduced by Belcher's article and the seeming lack of information possessed by practicing wage and salary administrators regarding Herzberg's real position on the role of salary as either a satisfier or dissatisfier, the purpose of this article will be:

1. To examine the Herzberg theory of satisifiers-dissatisifiers to analyze the role which Herzberg assigns to money as a motivator of improved job performance, and,

2. To develop the practical implications of that role for day-to-day wage and salary administration applications.

**THE HERZBERG STUDY—ITS NATURE**

The Herzberg study referred to by Prof. David W. Belcher was published in 1959, under the title, *The Motivation to Work.*[6] The study was made as a result of a grant from the Buhl Foundation, supported by matching funds from a number of industrial firms in the Pittsburgh area. The work was essentially a study of job attitudes, and was expected to be beneficial from three different viewpoints:

1.  The potential payoff to industry might be increased productivity, decreased absenteeism, and smoother work relations.

2.  The community might profit from a decreased bill for psychological casualties, an increase in over-all productive capacity of the industrial plant, and better utilization of human resources.

3.  Individuals might gain a better understanding of the forces that lead to improved morale, greater happiness, and greater self-realization.

At the time the study was undertaken, there was no dearth of research in the field of job attitudes and their effects on work performance. Herzberg and some of his earlier associates had already done an extensive review of the research available and had evaluated several thousand articles and books on the subject.[7] The real problem lay in the apparent disagreement and confusion in the field. There was evidently little or no agreement on results obtained—due in no small part to the unstable nature of the subjective data on which studies in the field were typically based.[8] However, one dramatic finding that emerged from the review of the literature was the fact that there was a difference in the primacy of factors in job attitudes, depending upon whether the investigator was looking for things the worker liked about his job or things he disliked. The concept, later adopted by Herzberg, that there were some factors that were "satisfiers" and others that were "dissatisfiers" was suggested by this finding.[9]

The basic new approach to the study of job attitudes undertaken by Herzberg and his associates was that job attitudes in total (i.e., factors, attitudes, and effects) should be investigated simultaneously. Herzberg believed that the factors-attitudes-effects complex should be studied as a unit. In order to undertake this, he decided to question some 200 professional engineers and accountants working in nine widely varying organizations within the greater Pittsburgh industrial complex regarding times when they felt exceptionally good or bad about their jobs. From the data revealed, Herzberg hoped to develop a coherent picture of the factors responsible for the interviewees' job attitudes and the effects of these attitudes on their job performances.[10]

## THE HERZBERG STUDY—ITS FINDINGS

Herzberg's most pressing and immediate objective was to develop an answer to the question, "What do people want from their jobs?" He had already determined from his review of the previous literature that different answers to that question were derived when the study design was concerned with what made people happy with their jobs as opposed to those studies directed toward discovering the factors that led to job dissatisfaction. The results accruing to his investigation reported in 1959 substantiated this fact rather conclusively. In order to better understand Herzberg's findings, we need, at this point, insight into his basic definitions of "satisfiers" and "dissatisifiers":

One of the basic habits of scientific thinking is to conceive of variables as operating on a continuum. According to this, a factor that influences job attitudes should influence them in such a way that the positive or negative impact of the same factor should lead to a corresponding increase or decrease in morale. Perhaps some of the confusion as to what workers want from their jobs stems from the habit of thinking that factors influencing job attitudes operate along such a continuum. But what if they don't? What if there are some factors that affect job attitudes only in a positive direction? If so, the presence of these factors would act to increase the individual's job satisfaction, but the failure of these factors to occur would not necessarily give rise to job dissatisfaction. Theoretically, given an individual operating from a neutral point, with neither positive nor negative attitudes toward his job, the satisfaction of these factors, which we may call the "satisfiers," would increase his job satisfaction beyond the neutral point. The absence of satisfaction to these factors would merely drop him back to this neutral level but would not turn him into a dissatisified employee. Contrariwise, there should be a group of factors that would act as "dissatisfiers." Existence of these factors would lead to an unhappy employee. The satisfying of these factors, however, would not create a happy employee. This basic difference between "satisfiers" and "dissatisfiers" which operate in only one direction in determining the job attitudes of workers, was one of the hypotheses of our study. In our own data, of course, we found that this unidirectional effect was truer of dissatisfiers than satisfiers.[11]

As his "satisfiers," Herzberg lists achievement, recognition, work itself, responsibility, and advancement. These are the things, which, when improved, can materially elicit positive increases in job attitude and performance. Among his "dissatisfiers" Herzberg lists company policy and administration, supervision (technical and human relations), and working conditions. Note that his job satisfiers deal with factors involved with *doing the job*, while his job dissatisfiers deal with the factors that *define the job context*. Poor working conditions, bad company policies and administration, and bad supervision will lead to job dissatisfaction. Good company policies, good administration, good supervision, and good working conditions will not necessarily lead to positive job attitudes. In opposition to this, recognition, achievement, interesting work, responsibility, and advancement all lead to positive job attitudes. Their absence will much less frequently lead to job dissatisfaction.

Herzberg treats the subject of salary as a "satisfier-dissatisfier" in a separate way:

It would seem that as an affector of job attitudes salary has *more potency* [12] as a job dissatisfier than as a job satisfier. . . . To be more specific, when salary occurred as a factor of the lows (low job attitude sequence), it revolved around the unfairness of the wage system within the company, and this almost always referred to increases in salaries rather than the absolute levels. It was the system of salary administration that was being described, a system in which wage increases were obtained grudgingly, or given too late, or in which the differentials between newly hired employees and those with years of experience on the job were too small. Occasionally, it concerned an advancement that was not accompanied by a salary increase. In contrast to this, salary was mentioned in the high (high job attitude sequence) stories as something that went along with a person's achievement on the job. It was a form of recognition; it meant more than money; it meant a job well-done; it meant that the individual was progressing in his work. Viewed within the context of the sequences of events, salary as a factor *belongs more in the group* [13] that defines the job situation and is *primarily* [14] a dissatisfier. [15]

To stop with the above observations would be to perform an intellectual disservice to Herzberg's theory. He is very careful to further distinguish the role of money as a motivator:

The failure to get positive returns in both job attitudes and job performance from rewarding the avoidance needs of the individual is most clearly seen in the use of monetary incentives. We have listed salary among the factors of hygiene, [16] and as such it meets two kinds of avoidance needs of the employee. First is the avoidance of the economic deprivation that is felt when actual income is insufficient. Second, and generally of more significance in the times and for the kind of people covered by our study, is the need to avoid feelings of being treated unfairly. . . .

Where morale surveys have differentiated between dissatisfaction with amount of salary as opposed to the equity of salary, the latter looms as the more important source of dissatisfaction. . . .

How then can we explain the success of the many employee motivational schemes that seem to rely directly on the use of wage incentives and bonuses? . . . .

Money thus earned as a direct reward for outstanding individual performance is a reinforcement of the motivators of *recognition* and *achievement*. It is not hygiene as is the money given in across-the-board wage increases. [17]

Thus, when we view Herzberg's work objectively, we see that money can really play two separate and distinct roles in affecting job attitudes. First, when salaries are either too low, or when salary inequities exist as a result of the administrative system in use, money operates as an absolute "dissatisfier" according to Herzberg's use of the term. Secondly, money which is given in recognition of outstanding performance, in reinforcing the positive "satisfiers" of achievement and recognition, must be viewed in itself, as a "satisfier." These are precisely the points which Belcher makes when he says:

To regard Herzberg's theory as disproving pay as a motivator may be something of a misinterpretation of the theory itself. Rather, it can be argued that whether pay is an achievement or a maintenance factor depends on how pay is determined. If pay is geared to achievement and serves as a recognition of achievement, it would seem to be an achievement factor and thus a motivator. It is when pay is unrelated to performance that it serves purely as a maintenance factor. [18]

## THE HERZBERG STUDY—IMPLICATIONS FOR
## WAGE AND SALARY ADMINISTRATORS

No implications may be drawn for practitioners of wage and salary administration that do not take into account certain inherent limitations of the Herzberg study. The principal limitations of the study are really threefold:

1. The study was limited to professional engineers and accountants.

2. A very small sample (200) of these professionals was interviewed, and the sample may not have been representative of all industrial engineers and accountants.

3. All of the engineers and accountants interviewed in the study worked within a 35-mile radius of the center of Pittsburgh.

Nevertheless, to the extent that generalizations may be drawn from the study, and within the universe represented by the limited sample, certain interesting conclusions may be derived. Among these conclusions are the following:

1. Such monetary rewards as automatic increases, cost-of-living increases, economic adjustment increases, market-value increases, and across-the-board type general increases will only serve to prevent dissatisfaction among employees. These increases will work as "dissatisfiers," i.e., their absence will help generate bad job attitudes, but their presence will not motivate increased job productivity. Included among such monetary rewards must be all financial adjustments based on individual relationships to maturity curves. Such increases, in effect, amount to longevity increases and must be classified as maintenance factors, and therefore, as non-motivators.

2. Promotion and merit increases and bonuses which can be directly related to outstanding performance will act to reinforce the "satisfiers," achievement and recognition. Such increases must, therefore, be considered to be motivators.

3. Wise company managements will clearly distinguish between the type of financial rewards represented by (1) and (2) above and will not make the error inherent in believing that monetary rewards are always positive motivators. Such managements will also do well to recognize that lack of such rewards can work as negative motivators.

4. Distinction between maintenance monetary rewards and motivational monetary rewards must be clearly communicated to affected employees. If this is not done, the improved motivating effect of rewards linked to outstanding performance will be lost to the employer.

5. Better ways must be developed to measure performance in terms of job requirements. To the extent that this is accomplished, monetary rewards for outstanding performance will become more effective motivators.

6. Care must be taken to fault poor performers through lack of merit increases. If a distinction is not clearly made among degrees of performance, monetary rewards

attached to outstanding performance will become meaningless, and the potential motivating factor of a salary increase in such cases will be converted into a maintenance factor.

## NOTES

1. Patton, Arch, *Men, Money, and Motivation*. New York: McGraw-Hill, 1961, 33-35. For a similar viewpoint, see Whyte, William Foote, *Money and Motivation*. New York; Harper Brothers, 1955.

2. David W. Belcher is a professor of management at the San Diego State College School of Business Administration. He is widely experienced in industry and is the author of one of the most widely accepted textbooks in the field, *Wage and Salary Administration* (Englewood Cliffs, N.J.: Prentice-Hall, 1962). Professor Belcher earned his Ph.D. in economics at the University of Minnesota.

3. Belcher, David W., Ominous trends in wage and salary administration, *Personnel*, **41**, No. 5 (September-October, 1964), 42-50.

4. Belcher, *op. cit.*

5. *Infra*, p. 2.

6. Herzberg, Frederick, Bernard Mausner, and Barbara Bloch Snyderman, *The Motivation To Work*. New York: Wiley, 1959.

7. Herzberg, Frederick, Bernard Mausner, Richard O. Peterson, and Dora F. Capwell, *Job Attitudes: Review of Research and Opinion*. Pittsburgh: Psychological Service of Pittsburgh, 1957.

8. Herzberg, *et al, The Motivation To Work*, vii.

9. *Ibid.*, 7.

10. For a detailed explanation of the techniques used to perform the interviews as well as to analyze the data, see Herzberg, *et al, The Motivation To Work*, 1-52.

11. *Ibid.*, 111-112.

12. Italics mine.

13. Italics mine.

14. Italics mine.

15. Herzberg, *et al, The Motivation To Work*, 82-83.

16. Herzberg uses the words "factor of hygiene" synonymously with the term "dissatisfier."

17. Herzberg, *et al, The Motivation To Work*, 116-117.

18. Belcher, Ominous trends . . . , 44.

## MOTIVATION AND JOB PERFORMANCE

*Melvin Sorcher and Herbert H. Meyer*

### DOES THE FACTORY EMPLOYEE REALLY CARE IF HE TURNS OUT A GOOD PRODUCT? CAN CHANGES IN THE WORK ENVIRONMENT IMPROVE THE CHANCES THAT HE WILL CARE?

These are questions that we have sought to answer through controlled experiments in the shop. We have taken a look at the human side of factory work, without losing sight of the fact that the production system must be efficient from the technical standpoint.

The most common way to design factory jobs has always been to simplify them. The object is to permit the hiring of minimally qualified employees at lower rates; and also to reduce the chance of errors. In recent years, however, such simplification has tended to backfire. It has smothered any interest or challenge in the jobs of many workers. It generates boredom, apathy, fatigue—and worse, resentment and active resistance. Far from eliminating errors, simplification has diminished workmanship, made employee turnover a serious problem, and left production even more vulnerable to disruption by work stoppages, slowdowns, and strikes.

**Why is this a recent problem? Why have we experienced increasing signs of resistance over the last twenty years—increased turnover, work stoppages, industrial sabotage?** Partly because of prosperity. Jobs are plentiful. The worker doesn't have to put up with an undesirable situation. Unions have also contributed to the problem for management. But the problem also stems in large part from significant changes taking place in our culture that must be considered when jobs are designed for workers in the shop.

The trend toward increased education, for example, means that members of our work force are better educated, on the average, with each passing year. Better educated people, it seems logical to suppose, want more meaningful and challenging jobs. Second, changing attitudes toward authority in our culture leave people less inclined than they were in years past to follow orders blindly. American industry has been very fortunate over past generations to have a steady supply of immigrant labor to man its shops. Most of these people came from European countries where they not only were accustomed to an authoritarian environment but they also had strong moral values instilled in them from childhood. They believed that you must give a good day's work if you were to take a day's pay.

Unfortunately, this desirable source of labor has run dry for us. The worker of today is likely to be much less responsible and conscientious. He is less inclined to respect authority as the legitimate source of power and to take for granted that work must often be unpleasant and uninteresting. Nowadays workers not only want some say in determining what they do and how they do it, but they are also more inclined to question the directions handed down from their superiors. Furthermore, to an increasing extent, whether we like the thought or not, people have an alternative to accepting work that is dull and unattractive to them: they can participate in public welfare programs instead.

Against this background, some managers have begun to question whether the negative effects of job simplification on employee motivation do not actually outweigh, in the long run, the cost savings that supposedly result. Attention begins to be focused on job design in relation to productive motivation. Some reports of studies of job design conducted in manufacturing plants have begun to appear in the literature. Up to now, such studies have emphasized factors like cycle time or the number of operations performed by one individual. Several studies have reported instances in which jobs were changed so that one operator could assemble a complete unit instead of one part of it. Such studies are actually experiments in "job enlargement." The present research differs from these in that it is not confined to evaluations of job enlargement. Rather, it is a basic premise that there are a number of actions open to management—other than or in addition to job enlargement—which directly influence motivation and performance.

## Possible Areas of Change

Management might move, for example, in the direction of *discretionary variables*. Usually the chance for an employee to exercise his own discretion (latitude for making decisions about his work) is ignored in job design. If we think of job content as on a continuum running from completely prescribed to completely discretionary, most assembly line jobs would without question fall near the prescribed end. In prescribed jobs, let us remember, the processes are mandatory; the content is specifically determined by management. Therefore, even though the number of operations performed by an employee might be increased (job enlargement), the work would still be prescribed. There would be, in short, no leeway for individual judgment or discretion. Of course, many jobs just do not permit the incorporation of individual judgment; the operation of a simple press, for example, is one.

Another job factor open to change is *participation in work planning and decision-making*. Two kinds of participation are possible. The first involves merely the exercise of some discretion by the employee in the day-to-day performance of his work, as described above. The second, however, refers to participation with management in the over-all design of a job. It might include, for example, establishing work methods and performance goals. This kind of participation differs from the first in that it takes place not during the performance of the job, but prior to the start of the actual work. Both kinds build self-esteem and open up the possibility of finding satisfaction in one's work.

Certain other variables can be grouped under the heading of increased job understanding or *role-training*. Here we mean the opportunity for people to see how their own jobs fit into the entire operation, and what bearing their own performance has on the task of others at subsequent work stations. Are they working on a TV camera for the Rose Bowl? Tell them! Instead of putting a new employee to work as soon as he learns the motions, and with no thought to other aspects of the job situation, role-training brings in such activities as plant tours, talks by managers and specialists, voluntary take-home reading relevant to the work and the final product, vestibule training to increase proficiency in a particular operation, and formal in-plant training programs. A frequent comment by the girls in one such program was, "Now I can tell people what I do!"

## Productive Motivation

Our studies have focused on improving the *productive motivation* of workers. We use this term to refer to a relatively restricted aspect of the concept of motivation in industrial situations: making an employee really care about how well he does his job. The problem at issue is whether the redesign of a job, or an alteration in the conditions surrounding it, or the building of an increased understanding of the job can bring about enough change of attitude (i.e., productive motivation) to result in a favorable effect on job performance.

The specific attitudes, identified as components of productive motivation, we have dealt with in our studies are:

*Attitudes or Feelings About the Work Itself (Job Content):*

- Enjoyment versus boredom
- Pride in workmanship
- Sense of accomplishment (or achievement)

*Attitudes or Feelings About the Work Environment (Job Context):*

- Perceived relationship between personal needs and department or company goals
- Identification with the department or company products
- Perception of general management
- Perception of immediate supervisor

These are attitudes which merit the closest attention from management, for they exert a direct influence on three critical areas:

1. Productivity—quantity to meet customer demand.
2. Quality of work—workmanship to keep customer satisfaction.
3. Labor (employee-management) relations—a working environment which minimizes income loss to employee and company.

Figure 1 depicts this relationship between attitudes and work.

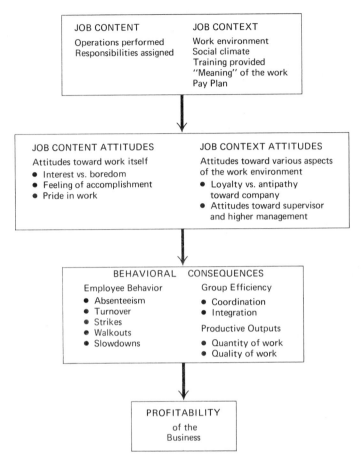

**JOB CONTENT**

Operations performed
Responsibilities assigned

**JOB CONTEXT**

Work environment
Social climate
Training provided
"Meaning" of the work
Pay Plan

**JOB CONTENT ATTITUDES**

Attitudes toward work itself

- Interest vs. boredom
- Feeling of accomplishment
- Pride in work

**JOB CONTEXT ATTITUDES**

Attitudes toward various aspects
of the work environment

- Loyalty vs. antipathy
  toward company
- Attitudes toward supervisor
  and higher management

**BEHAVIORAL   CONSEQUENCES**

Employee Behavior

- Absenteeism
- Turnover
- Strikes
- Walkouts
- Slowdowns

Group Efficiency

- Coordination
- Integration

Productive Outputs

- Quantity of work
- Quality of work

**PROFITABILITY**
of the
Business

**Figure 1.**   Research model for study of job design

## Explorations

A small exploratory study prepared the way for deeper probing and a program on a larger scale. What one needed first was to find out which job-related factors—e.g., cycle time, size of work group, training, repetitiveness—seemed to have a significant effect on motivation and quality of work. Two measures were used to gauge effectiveness of job design: (1) employees' attitudes about their jobs; (2) quality of workmanship.

The procedure was simple. Five departments at General Electric were asked to identify work groups that were consistently very high or very low in quality of output. Twenty-five work groups at the high end and 25 at the low end made up the study. The foreman of each group was interviewed for factual information such as cycle time, group size, and the like. In addition, a few employees from each group, randomly selected by the researcher, were asked to fill out a questionnaire dealing with pride in work, job meaningfulness, sense of accomplishment, monotony, identification with the product and the company, and attitudes toward management.

Certain practical suggestions emerged from this study, along with certain questions which seemed to warrant further attack .

- Establish a formal training program for hourly employees beyond the required minimum.

- Create subgoals to measure accomplishment in repetitive jobs where workers do not see the finished product.

- Let employees know regularly how they are doing—with recognition for good work given just as much emphasis as is notification of errors.

- Maintain an orderly work area.

- Provide for occasional physical activity—by job rotation, by letting workers fetch their own supplies, or by adding operations.

### Widening the Field

With the handle provided by this exploration, researchers went further into the matter of how one makes a job meaningful to an employee. Out of the pilot study they selected the elements that dealt with the meaningfulness of tasks. The assumption behind the research is simple. The better one understands the motivation of employees the more one can:

- Attract new people to work in one's factories in a competitive labor market;

- Minimize costly turnover;

- Maintain a highly effective work force, marked by high quality of workmanship, good productivity, minimum labor problems.

In this later research, departments in seven General Electric plants at widely scattered locations were involved, representing both geographical dispersion and product differences. They were singled out partly for the opportunities they provided to test specific hypotheses and partly because their local managers offered to support the research. In all, about 700 direct-labor hourly employees from these departments served as subjects. They constituted about 80 functionally different work groups ranging in size from 3 to 40.

### Making the Study

From the exploratory study, eight job-related variables were chosen:

1. Responsibility for own work; that is, the extent to which an individual is permitted to use his own discretion;

2. Shift worked;

3. Repetitiveness of the work—a function of cycle time *and* the number of operations;

4. Physical activity; that is, whether the work is sedentary or not, how much physical energy is required, and so on;

5. Rotation between work stations;

6. Goals, in terms of eventual use of the product, the logical number of units to produce;

7. Group structures, whether small groups working together or individuals at work stations more or less independent of each other;

8. Role-training, involving any informal or formal program promoting insight into the importance of a job and psychological investment in the work.

To these variables, then, two types of study were applied. (1) "Natural" experiments; that is, observations and comparisons between existing work groups where operations performed were similar but individual jobs were designed differently or the job environments differed in some significant way. (2) Controlled experiments, where changes were made and effects upon motivation and performance studied.

Three kinds of results measures were taken in the situations studied: (1) Data on attitudes, in response to a 21-item questionnaire completed anonymously and identifiable only by work groups; (2) Estimates of quality of workmanship, typically measured by the number of rejects and/or waste due to breakage (periodic quality control reports were normally the source here, or, where not available, a report from the foreman); (3) Measures of quantity where possible—though not so important as quality, since the former is often machine-controlled, the latter directly under the control of the worker.

### Effects of Responsibility

Work groups performing similar operations were classified as to the amount of responsibility workers had in carrying out their own work. Various comparisons were then possible between groups low or high in this regard. We wanted to find out if the groups with a relatively high degree of responsibility would also turn out to have a higher degree of productive motivation. Quite definitely they did. Attitudes toward job content were unmistakably higher among the more responsible. Workers assigned more responsibility get less bored, they take more pride in their work, they feel they have accomplished something. Attitudes toward the job, such as toward the company or supervision, were also more favorable for high responsibility groups, but the differences were not as clear-cut as for job content attitudes. Interestingly enough, the reverse of the coin confirms the message: there was no instance of a low responsibility group having significantly more favorable attitudes than a high responsibility group.

Could differences in foremen account for differences in attitudes? Perhaps work groups assigned more responsibility also had more sophisticated and considerate foremen. One department offered a good test of this possibility. Here, two work groups each had a "twin"—a group about the same in every way except for having a different degree of responsibility and a different foreman. Since each foreman supervised other groups as well where amount of responsibility assigned did not differ, it was possible to determine that differences in motivation were not a function of the foreman but, one must conclude, of the amount of responsibility.

### Work Shift a Factor

Differences between shifts also offered a good opportunity to study effects of responsibility on motivation. In several departments, identical operations were performed on first and second shifts, but second shift groups had less supervision and greater latitude on how to perform work. Past surveys had shown that attitudes of second shift workers are usually less favorable than first shift workers because of the unfavorable hours and the fact that employees on second shift are usually younger and newer—typically less satisfied with their work than older employees. Despite these facts, motivation was significantly higher on second shift where these groups had more discretionary responsibility. In no case was over-all motivation higher for the day-shift workers with less responsibility.

As an additional check here, several work groups were found where the amount of responsibility was the same for both shifts. In comparisons of these groups, no differences in motivation were found. We are led to suppose, therefore, that greater responsibility leads to better motivation—even to the extent of overcoming the negative effects of less popular working hours.

### Repetitiveness

Defined as a function of cycle time and the number of steps performed, repetitiveness provides another case in which preconceptions come in for adjustment. A comparison of groups similar in every way except the repetitiveness of their tasks showed that over-all productive motivation was lower in three of five departments for workers engaged in very repetitive work. Once again, too, we can say that in no department was productive motivation greater for the highly repetitive group.

On the other hand, one must also take account of the fact that there were many cases where groups with less repetitive work failed to show better attitudes toward their work. Other factors, such as cultural differences, predominant sex of employees in the work group, and type of manufacturing process involved have weight here. In short, repetitiveness has to be put in context. It is reasonable to suppose, for instance, that older women in a factory town, accustomed to performing light, relatively pleasant even though repetitive jobs, may not particulalry mind that aspect of their tasks and may actually have rather favorable attitudes toward the work.

## Rotation, Scheduled and Casual

The matter of rotation—an occasional change in work station or task—brings us to another surprise. One would be inclined to take it for granted that any rotation of jobs would be desirable, with regular rotation probably being best, but failing that, at least *some* change. But this seems not to be so. Higher motivation comes with regular rotation, yes; but no rotation turns out to be better than occasional rotating. In short, the poorest motivation was found with casual rotation.

A possible explanation runs like this; call it the "ray of light" hypothesis. People who perform dull work for long periods of time often come to expect just that and nothing more. Attitudes go hand in hand with expectations. If they have come to expect to continue in their routine, their attitudes toward it and their motivation to do it have probably become fixed at a certain, almost inevitably low, level. If, however, a respite from routine is offered by an occasional change in work station or task rotation, it is no longer possible to take for granted the old acceptance of how dull a job should be. A ray of light has pierced the gloom, bringing with it the expectation and desire for more and brighter light. If these new hopes are thwarted (for instance, by the nature of the work itself, if it allows only minimal rotation), then the disappointment may result in a depression of attitudes ending in even worse motivation than at the start. The casual rotation is not enough to change the job, but more than enough to upset the adjustment.

## Physical Activity and Social Interaction

Where physical activity is possible—walking, lifting, changing position—it is linked with higher motivation. In one of the departments studied, this relationship was especially striking; it held in three of the five departments; it was reversed in none. Physical activity builds up a sense of "doing," which may carry over into greater involvement with "doing one's work"—an involvement which in turn might well result in feelings of accomplishment and self-importance.

This being so, it would be natural to assume that increased social interaction would have the same beneficial effect as physical activity. Conversation, for instance, might lessen drudgery. To this end, we compared the motivation of employees whose work stations were grouped around a table or machine with those who were strung out in a row along a bench. But the results turned out to be puzzling. Some workers seemed to show significantly better motivation at relatively isolated stations; in some other comparisons the results are inconsistent. Additional research must be done before the situation here becomes clear.

## Participation and Role-Training

Several experiments were carried out specifically in connection with techniques designed to increase one's psychological involvement in work. Some of the specific approaches tried were:

a)    Participation in the establishment of meaningful work goals;

b)    Participation in the actual implementation of goals;

c)    Better orientation about the significance of any job in its larger setting;

d)    Formal job training.

On this topic there is already a good background of research. In the first place, the positive effect of giving workers a voice in the how and when of the work process is well known. Studies have shown, for example, that workers want a voice in decisions about the way their own work shall be organized and evaluated. Such an opportunity to participate would be expected to raise self-esteem and along with it productive motivation and general performance.

Second, one knows that seemingly endless routine is often marked by a decay in motivation. Why should anyone care about monotonously inserting screws into parts whose final destiny he never knows? If, however, a worker can be somehow provided with successive goals, meaningful and logical *to him*, he has the possibility of regarding his arrival at each such landmark as a criterion of accomplishment and success. And once he experiences a sense of accomplishment, he is on his way to a source of higher motivation and hence higher performance.

*What Sorts of Specific Goals are Possible? What Constitutes a Reasonable and Meaningful Goal?*

Though each goal must be worked out for its own unique situation, here are a few possibilities. Employees can be told the destination and use of the total equipment which they are building–a TV camera for the Rose Bowl, a sonar for a particular submarine. Or they can learn the eventual impact of their product; for instance, a transformer order which will give power to 800 new homes in a recently developed part of California. Or there can be logical units of production within which it is possible to reach milestones, such as the 50 dip-solder boards or 1,057 transistors which are needed to build a radar receiver. Such an imaginative use of goals, adapted to particular work situations, can go far to combat the feelings of futility that come with seemingly endless and unaccented routine.

Finally, our past research has revealed–in every plant and for virtually every factory employee–that most workers are aware neither of their personal role in the manufacturing process of their own importance or individual contribution to the business. Indeed, one can carry this a step further. They are ignorant of how their own work affects the work of others in the same plant, and in general even of what those other processes in the same plant are. It is against this background that we speak of role-training.

By role-training is meant seeing how one's job fits into an entire operation. It embraces a good many activities–plant tours to see how one group's work affects the work of other groups; voluntary take-home reading about an individual's own work and the product manufactured; talks by managers and specialists; vestibule training to increase proficiency in a given operation; and formal in-plant training programs. In short, role-training puts the employee psychologically in a spot where he has perspective on his own job in its total context.

All of this is a startling departure from the old notion of putting someone to work as soon as he has mastered the required motions. In the present case, hourly employees are not only allowed, but actively encouraged, to become involved in their work. Are motivation and performance then enhanced, as one would expect? Let us take a look at the experiments.

### Experimental Plan

One of the departments participating in the research program provided an opportunity to study the effects of role-training in two types of job situation:

- *Area A*, containing eight work groups in which employees had an unusually high amount of responsibility, discretion, variety, and physical movement in their job content in comparison with other assembly line jobs.

- *Area B*, containing six work groups in which the jobs were more typical for assembly work; employees moved around very little, and there was little variety in the work.

Approximately parallel experiments were conducted simultaneously in this department. The employees, however, were not aware of the fact that an experiment was taking place.

In general, the experimental treatments were aimed at obtaining greater behavioral involvement from all groups, whether in Area A or B. But in addition we were particularly interested in any differences in response among the groups. The various activities included discussion meetings with foremen and a tour of their manufacturing operation. The discussion meetings were held separately for each of the small functional work groups (none for large combinations of groups), and emphasis was on the part each girl and her particular job played in the business of that department. The groups also learned how their work affected that of subsequent work stations; and to sharpen this awareness, they were taken on a tour of other work stations to establish a more personal—and perhaps a more meaningful—relationship between their own work and that of others. They were also asked, group by group, to set quality goals for themselves and to discuss feasible ways of meeting such goals.

### Over-all Productive Motivation

Over-all productive motivation improved in both Areas A and B. To no one's surprise, it improved more in Area B. Since the Area A groups already were permitted a certain amount of responsibility, the experimental program meant less change in ordinary procedure. In both groups, however, employees' opinion of the foreman went up; and in Area B there was especially a heightening of pride in workmanship and a sense of accomplishment.

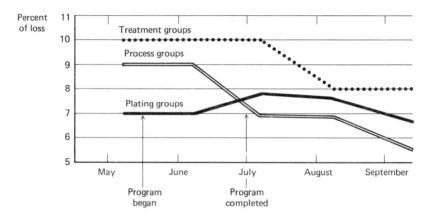

**Figure 2.**   Effects of role training on quality in area A

## Improvement in Quality

The effects of role-training on quality of output were rather striking. In Area A, which has a very long product cycle time, the manufacturing engineers anticipated that no measurable improvement would be possible until at least three months after the beginning of the program. Well under that time, however, there had been substantial improvement in two of the three sets of groups in Area A—a decrease in percentage of loss of 20 percent for one group, 33.3 percent for the other. (See Figure 2.) The lack of improvement in the third set of groups, the plating area, was attributed by the manager of shop operations to the nature of the process—it permitted little opportunity for improvement.

In Area B the figures are even more telling. There, quality was measured at three control points, the results being shown in Figure 3. Notice that for the 8 weeks preceding the program the average acceptance was 57.9 percent and 66 percent at two different control points, while tac-probe machine down-time averaged some 3.3 percent for the same period. For the 9 weeks following the program, however, acceptance percentages rose to 69.2 and 92.1, with tac-probe machine down-time more than cut in half. In addition, foremen in Area B reported a significant speeding-up of cycle time, so that improvements of about 20 percent in productivity were also chalked up. Since these groups had already been producing at standard task rate, the gain represented a substantial contribution to the reduction of manufacturing costs.

## Engineer's Report

An engineer who conducted experimental role-training activities for Area A, but who was not part of the research staff, wrote a report for his own manager which bears further witness to the value of the program. Foremen, he said, were now better able to

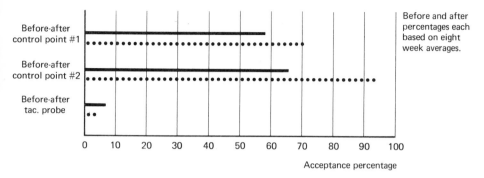

**Figure 3.** Effects of training on quality in area B

understand and interpret to the operators their engineering instructions. He pointed out that operators had set a goal for themselves to reduce wafer loss from 26 percent to 15 percent by the end of the month—and they bettered this goal. He listed 72 good, directly applicable suggestions contributed by employees during group meetings. These were objective facts. On the subjective side he could say that employees in both areas had expressed great satisfaction at having the chance to see how their work fitted into the business as a whole—so much so that a number of them had remained after work on their own time to ask many questions about the manufacturing process. New girls had subsequently come around to ask when the program would be repeated so that they too might participate.

Finally, he quoted one of the girls in his program, who after the plant tour had summarized her experience in these words:

I started in Product Classification and I couldn't understand why people sent me devices with bent leads. I moved to the Device Assembly area and understood bent leads but now couldn't understand why I got bad pellets. I moved to Pellet Processing and I saw how the bad ones got out but didn't appreciate why we got all the bad wafers. I moved to Wafer Processing and now I've got the whole picture. I think I can do my job better now that I know what problems I'm giving those other girls.

### Defects Reduced

In still another department there was a chance to make comparisons of motivation and performance before and after brief training courses to increase job understanding. These were one-day courses covering the hows and whys of the work procedures. In two of the five groups it was possible to measure attitudes only—not quality or quantity of the product—since the work was such as to make the latter checks impossible. But measurements of attitudes, taken shortly before the training program and again 4 weeks after its completion, demonstrated that over-all productive motivation, and especially enjoyment of the work itself, had increased significantly.

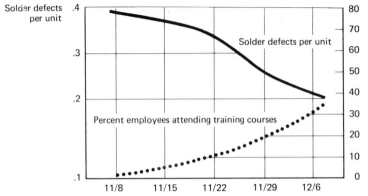

**Figure 4.**   Reduction in defects after training

In the other three groups measures of quality, in the form of number of defects per unit, were available. Figure 4 presents a composite of the results achieved in the three groups. The magnitude of improvements in quality surprised the managers. Reductions in defects were directly proportionate to the percentage of employees in a group who had attended the training course. The resulting cost savings far outweighed the cost of the training itself.

In another large group (about 120 workers) where role-training activities were introduced precise measures of outputs and costs were possible. The training costs in lost production due to time off the job were computed to be approximately $1,000. The savings due to reductions in rejects were over $1,000 per week! And these results were sustained and even improved upon over time. Thus, over a year, the return on the investment in role-training was about 50 to 1.

### In Summary

The design of factory jobs has come a long way since the early stages of the industrial revolution, when the primary aim was to simplify manual operations. Presumably this permitted the employment of minimally qualified people; teach them one motion, one operation, and they were in business. Presumably also it reduced the chance of making errors and hence the number of rejects. Hence—presumably, again—it saved money.

These are practices and tenets, however, which in days of better education, greater leisure and higher aspirations have begun to backfire. Simplification brought disadvantages along with its hoped-for advantages: it brought boredom, meaningless-ness; it removed challenge and any sense of individual commitment. Not only does simplification carried to its limits do damage to the worker's self-esteem and motivation, but repetitiveness, when it entails boredom and lack of goals, also increases poor quality work rather than decreasing it.

So from every point of view, from considerations of humanity to those of profit, it now becomes the task of industry to engage the employee in a more meaningful role. It is with preliminary research in this direction that the present article has been concerned. Our findings have tended to convince us that both the hazards of oversimplication—lack of motivation and the high costs of rejects and labor turnover—can be attacked by the various methods of deeper involvement.

Needless to say, the first requisite in any efficient operation is technological know-how; without a technically sound and efficient system, nothing is possible— neither a satisfactory and profitable product not a satisfied and motivated worker. This we take for granted as prerequisite and background. But the point is that nowadays we *cannot* take it for granted that against such a background there will always be properly motivated people. And since manufacturing operations are not completely automated, their smooth and efficient conduct still rests upon the efforts of properly motivated workers.

Convincing proof is beginning to pile up to the effect that the direct-labor employee can be motivated to become more involved in his work. We have presented some of the methods: the use of goals, the provision of more than minimum training for assembly line tasks, the encouragement of employee participation in goal-setting. Our research has also suggested that productive motivation can be improved by broadening the worker's responsibility, by reducing repetitiveness, and by introducing variety in the work.

In short, one sentence can sum up what we have been saying. In the design of jobs, attention should be given not merely to the prescribed tasks to be performed, but also to those factors which enhance the self-esteem and thus heighten the motivation of the operator.

# 8.
# EVALUATION AND FOLLOW-UP OF TRAINING AND DEVELOPMENT

For two reasons the selections in this chapter form a less cohesive package than is found in the preceding chapters. First, the art of evaluating development is not highly advanced, and most work in evaluation has been done with individuals or individual training courses. Second, the subject of evaluation has been covered in parts of the selections in other chapters.

There are presently two trends toward greater emphasis on evaluation of human development in organizations. Systems approaches to developing human resources emphasize better evaluation and planning. As planning improves so will evaluation, and vice versa, since the one depends upon the other. Also, as the study of organizations and their development becomes more sophisticated, management and organizations will become better understood, planned, and evaluated.

"Putting Judgment Back Into Decisions," by Larry Greiner, D. Paul Leitch, and Louis B. Barnes, reports a recent large-scale evaluation of a Federal Government organization and has strong implications for future evaluation of organization and management development. In it the authors found substantially more agreement among managers making subjective appraisals of performance than among those making quantitative appraisals.

The second article deals with the evaluation of training on a large scale. Warren H. Schmidt's "How to Evaluate a Company's Training Efforts" gives a remarkably comprehensive macroapproach to evaluating training programs and relating their evaluation to organizational needs.

The evaluation of human resource development will become more sophisticated in the future, but progress will be slow. The Greiner/Leitch/Barnes study is a significant development, but it took an immense amount of time and manpower.

Similar progress will require further great efforts and will consequently be painstakingly slow. Useful practical application is likely to take even longer, not only because practice follows theory, but also because meaningful criteria for evaluating individual, group, and organization development must evolve before effective evaluation can take place.

# PUTTING JUDGMENT BACK INTO DECISIONS

*Larry E. Greiner, D. Paul Leitch, and Louis B. Barnes*

Top managers are currently inundated with reams of information concerning the performance of organizational units under their supervision. Behind this information explosion lies a seemingly logical assumption made by information specialists and frequently accepted by line managers: if top management can be supplied with more "objective" and "accurate" *quantified* information, they will make "better" judgments about the performance of their operating units.

But how valid is this assumption? A research study we have recently completed indicates that quantified performance information may have a more limited role than is currently assumed or envisioned; in fact, managers rely more on subjective information than they do on so-called "objective" statistics in assessing the overall performance of lower level units.

## THE HUMAN FACTOR

Despite the increasing desire for and trend toward the quantification of performance results, most managers are the first to admit that their performance assessments begin and end with human judgment. Managers determine what kinds of performance information to collect; and later, when this information is in front of them, they study the data, make up their minds, and decide what to do. For example, here is how a vice president of finance in a large steel company describes the importance of human judgment in assessing organization performance:

"We have capital budgets, we have fixed budgets, we have variable budgets, we have standard costs. We have the full assortment. None of our controls is 100% effective. None replaces subjective judgment."[1]

There are several reasons why managerial judgment is critical in evaluating the performance of lower level units in today's organizations:

- Organizations are becoming so large and complex that, as yet, no universal mathematical formulas exist for encompassing all of the variables that reflect the total performance of a particular subunit.

- Events within and around an organization change so rapidly that indicators of "good" performance last year may not be appropriate this year.

Reprinted with permission from *Harvard Business Review*, **48**, No. 2 (March-April, 1970), 59-67. Copyright 1970 by the President and Fellows of Harvard College; all rights reserved.

*Authors' note*: We are grateful to the Internal Revenue Service and the Division of Research, Harvard Business School, for supporting this study.

- Managers are frequently aware of nonquantifiable factors which information specialists don't usually hear about or record on their standard forms.

- Ultimately, it is managers, not computers, that must make decisions based on their assessments of performance. If a manager makes a "biased" judgment of performance, then his actions are also likely to be "biased."

In this article, we shall describe the purpose and methods of our study. Then we will present the major findings, which at times are coupled with some broad implications for management. Finally, we shall conclude with more specific suggestions for improving the quality of performance judgments in organizations.

In particular, we shall consider these important questions that bear on the judgmental process:

- How important relatively are quantitative and qualitative criteria to managers in making judgments of performance? (If quantitative criteria are less important than assumed, then the organization may be able to redirect the activities of computers and staff analysts to use them more efficiently.)

- Are managers consistent from one day to the next in their judgments?

- Do managers agree more on current effectiveness than they do on changes in effectiveness over time?

- Can managers actually agree with each other in assessing the performance of organizational units beneath them? (If they can't, then they are likely to give off conflicting signals to lower levels.)

- Must managers agree on specific criteria if they are to agree in their overall judgments about performance?

- Does a manager's position in the organization affect his judgements of performance? (If it does, misunderstandings among managerial levels are likely to ensue.)

## HOW THE STUDY WAS MADE

We conducted our investigation in a large government agency, the Internal Revenue Service. Although the IRS is not a business organization, it does contain many elements common to most large, complex organizations. More than 60,000 people are employed by the IRS in either the national office headquarters or the 7 regional and 58 district offices, or the 7 computer service centers. The IRS organization is also divided functionally into several major divisions, with each division having a representative group at all regional and most district offices. The measurement of performance is a key concern of IRS managers; many statistical indicators of performance are regularly collected, including indexes of costs, output, and morale.

Top management in the IRS became interested in having a study made partly out of curiosity about the reliability of their performance assessments of district

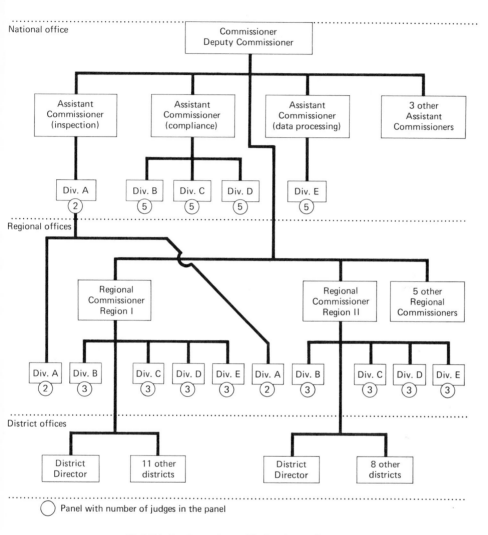

**Exhibit I.**  Location of judges' panels

operations. Despite their access to many quantitative performance measures, they readily acknowledged that their overall assessments of district performance depended, in the final analysis, on subjective judgment. At the national office level, managers were interested in knowing if they agreed with their counterparts at the regional level, and vice versa. In addition, managers at all levels were curious about the degree to which they relied on quantitative versus qualitative information in forming their judgments.

The study focused on three types of performance evaluation mentioned most frequently in initial interviews with IRS managers at the national and regional levels:

1. The current effectiveness of divisional subunits within a district. (This is important because it provides early signs of problems in the making.)

2. The performance improvement of these units over the preceding 18 months. (This adds perspective to the judgments of current effectiveness, especially when a currently high-performing unit is slipping or a low-performing unit is improving.)

3. Specific reasons for a unit's performance improvement, or lack of it. (This provides more precise clues for taking corrective action. For example, corrective action might be quite different if the reason were judged to be an uncontrollable "natural disaster" rather than a "lack of leadership.")

**The Judging Procedure**

To investigate how the IRS top managers evaluated these three performance dimensions, we formed 15 panels, representing 5 headquarters divisions and 10 regional divisions; see *Exhibit I*. Each panel consisted of 2 to 5 managers acting as judges. Insofar as possible, judges were selected for their familiarity with the performance of their particular divisions at the district level and for their reputed "objectivity" in assessing subunit performance.

The procedure we used to study the performance judgments of these 15 panels is described in *Exhibit II*. We have covered this method in some detail because, as we shall suggest later, other organizations may be interested in undertaking similar studies. (This is the first study, as far as we know, that has designed and utilized a methodology for systematically examining managerial judgments of subunit performance.)

**Exhibit II.**   Steps in the judging procedure

---

*Step 1:* Each judge received a folder containing a range of performance information on each unit to be evaluated. This was done to provide a common starting point. The information covered an 18-month time period. Some of it was statistical (for example, productivity indexes), and some was more subjective (such as "personnel management" conditions). Each judge was asked to study this information thoroughly for two days, then put it away and not look at it again.

*Step 2:* Each judge received two identical decks of cards. One deck was to be used for judging overall current effectiveness, while the other was for judging overall performance improvement over 18 months. Each card within a deck listed a pair of comparable divisional units from two different district offices (for example, Division A from District 1 as compared with Division A, District 2). All possible combinations of district pairs were covered in each deck. Numerous precautions were taken in the construction of each deck to prevent bias. For example, the order in which pairs were presented was determined by a random number table so as to delete any effects due to order of presentation. Also, each unit appeared the same number of times on the left side as it did on the right side of each card so as to cancel effects of placement.

*Steps 3 and 4:* Each judge was instructed to circle the unit on each card which had the higher performance, using one deck for judging current effectiveness and the second deck for evaluating improvement. Half the judges were asked to make their effectiveness judgments first, while the other half made their improvement judgments first. This was done to counter any biasing effects arising from making one type of judgment before the other. In addition, judges were asked not to confer with other judges, so as to ensure that each judge was making an independent assessment.

*Steps 5 and 6:* Three days after Steps 3 and 4 were completed, each judge was given two more decks of cards, both identical in format to the first two decks. His instructions were to repeat exactly the procedure followed in making the first judgments. Our intent here was to find out if judgments were stable from one time period to the next.

*Step 7:* As a final step, each judge was asked to write three reasons on the back of each card in the improvement deck to explain why he had picked one unit over another. From this information, we hoped to learn more about the specific criteria that each judge was using.

---

When each judge had completed the procedure described in *Exhibit II*, he sent his data cards directly to us for analysis. Our analytical procedure was based largely on a mathematical technique called correlation analysis. First, we totaled the number of times that each judge chose one unit over another. From these totals we computed for each judge a rank order of those units evaluated by him; the unit chosen most over other units received a rank of "1," and so forth down the list. Then this rank order was correlated against the rank orders for the other judges in each panel. This produced a "level of agreement" *within* each of the 15 panels.

Additional correlations were also computed *between* panels by comparing an overall rank order for each panel (based on an average of individual rank orders) with the overall rank order for other panels. Perfect agreement between rank orders, as measured by a statistical correlation, was +1.00, while perfect disagreement was –1.00. There is no fixed rule for determining an "acceptable" correlation of agreement, although the following guideline tends to be commonly used in research:

+.9 or –.9 = high correlation.
+.7 or –.7 = substantial correlation.
+.5 or –.5 = moderate correlation.
+.3 or –.3 = low correlation.

## AGREEMENT AMONG MANAGERS

A basic and critical question for any management is: Can our managers agree with one another about the performance of units under their supervision? Pessimists contend that managers cannot mentally assimilate and agree on all the complex performance data available, or that managers are such an idiosyncratic lot psychologically that it is impossible for them to agree with one another. On the other hand, optimists argue that managers are quite adept at simplifying complex information, being far more logical and objective than the pessimists might believe.

Our findings strongly support the optimists. While we cannot answer the agreement question for *all* organizations, *Exhibit III* does reveal that the particular managers we studied were, in general, able to reach a substantial level of agreement in their overall judgments of *both* current effectiveness and performance improvement. There was also a high correlation between their first-day and third-day judgments on both performance measurements.

**Exhibit III.**   Level of overall agreement

|  | Current effectiveness | Performance improvement over 18 months |
|---|---|---|
| Average correlation of agreement within 15 panels | +.76 | +.71 |
| Average correlation of agreement between Day I and Day 3 judgments for 50 judges | +.90 | +.83 |

The critical reader should ask, of course, if high agreement was merely a product of common "bias" among the judges within each panel. If such a bias did exist, this would be disturbing because IRS managers, while in overall agreement, could be making inaccurate assessments. One check on the amount of bias was to examine the extent of agreement between each divisional panel at the regional level and its counterpart panel at the national office. These panels all reported to different bosses and were separated by large physical distances. Under these conditions of limited authority and interaction we felt that high agreement between national and regional office panels could not be explained in terms of a commonly shared bias.

The findings indeed revealed considerable agreement between regional and national office panels from each of the five divisions: an average of +.75 for their current effectiveness judgments and +.65 for their performance improvement judgments. Therefore, we think it reasonable to infer that common bias was not a strong contributing factor toward high agreement.

The improvement evaluation is obviously a complex assessment which includes many subjective considerations and also requires a longer time perspective. Yet IRS managers seemed to find themselves on relatively the same historical wavelength. This finding is important because a manager's awareness of performance trends is often what tempers his action-taking plans. Lack of agreement about trends could produce not only inappropriate actions, but also conflicting decisions from different managers.

At the same time, we should point out that a considerable range existed between panels with the lowest and highest levels of internal agreement. For current-effectiveness judgments, the lowest agreement panel had an internal correlation of +.16 while the highest agreement panel had +.99. For performance-improvement judgments, the internal correlation was +.10 for the lowest agreement panel and +1.00 for the highest panel. Thus, a large majority of panels revealed substantial internal agreement, while a few panels revealed much disagreement. This suggests the importance of discovering the factors that block agreement on some panels and the factors that cause high agreement on others.

## Effect of Distance

We found two important organizational variables which seemed to distinguish between high- and low-agreement panels. The most potent variable appeared to be "organizational distance." *Exhibit IV* shows not only that members of national office panels (two levels removed from districts) agreed less with one another in comparison with judges on regional office panels (one level removed), but also that their judgments were less stable from Day 1 to Day 3.

**Exhibit IV.**  Relationship between organizational distance and level of overall agreement

|  | Current effectiveness | Performance improvement over 18 months |
|---|---|---|
| Average correlation of agreement within: |  |  |
| 5 national office panels | +.53 | +.41 |
| 10 regional office panels | +.84 | +.81 |
| Average correlation of agreement between Day 1 and Day 3 judgments for: |  |  |
| 22 national judges | +.80 | +.71 |
| 28 regional office judges | +.93 | +.87 |

We prefer the term "organizational distance" to "physical distance" because the Region I office and its 12 districts were located within 600 miles of Washington, while the Region II office and its 9 districts were situated more than 1,300 miles away. Yet national office panels did not reach any more agreement about the closer Region I districts than they did about the more remote Region II districts. It appears that sitting close to the top of the organizational pyramid is not necessarily the easiest or best vantage point for assessing field unit performance. Undoubtedly, certain information disappears in the gap between levels, never reaching the top.

For us, these findings raise doubts about concentrating too much decision-making power at the top of large organizations when the decision to be made is based on the evaluation of performance. They also cause one to question an overreliance on centralized information systems. Centralized systems, because of their remoteness and need for uniformity, may be particularly insensitive to what is happening in each field unit.

### The Effect of Size

A second important, but less pronounced, organizational variable was the size of functional divisions. *Exhibit V* reveals that panels from the two largest agency divisions (A and B), each of which employed more than twice as many people as any other division, reached lower levels of agreement. These large division panels, regardless of their level in the organization, seemed to have particular difficulty in assessing performance improvement over time.

**Exhibit V.**   Relationship between organization size and level of overall agreement

|  | Current effectiveness | Performance improvement over 18 months |
| --- | --- | --- |
| Average correlation of agreement within: | | |
| 6 large division panels | +.73 | +.48 |
| 9 small division panels | +.82 | +.86 |
| Average correlation of agreement between Day 1 and Day 3 judgments for: | | |
| 22 large division judges | +.83 | +.73 |
| 28 small division judges | +.92 | +.89 |

Managers in large divisions are often physically and organizationally separated; they also become more specialized in their job functions. As a result, their communications are likely to be less frequent and conducted from narrower frames of reference. Further evidence of this communications breakdown was found in the fact that large division panels from the national office agreed with their counterpart panels at the regional offices only at the level of +.46 when judging performance improvement, while national and regional panels from small divisions agreed with each other at a much higher level, +.83, in judging improvement. Apparently, the communications pipeline between national and regional levels was more open in small divisions.

Both *Exhibit IV* and *Exhibit V* make clear that the performance judgments of IRS managers are affected by their positions in the organizations. We suspect that the same findings apply to other large organizations as well. If a manager is located at headquarters, he is less likely to agree with his colleagues. In addition, if he is in a large division, he is less likely to agree not only with his peers at headquarters but also with managers at the next lower level in his division. Judgments of current effectiveness probably will not be as strongly affected by these organizational forces as are judgments of performance improvement.

Lower level managers, because they can agree more with each other, may be able to teach higher level managers a few of their trade secrets. Some clues to these trade secrets became more obvious when we focused on the specific criteria used by high-agreement panels.

## CRITERIA FOR JUDGMENT

While broader organizational forces (distance and size) produced variations in judgment, the specific criteria used by judges also contributed to differences in agreement. An analysis was made of the criteria filled out by judges on the reverse sides of their "performance improvement" cards.

As a first step, we arranged for an independent group of IRS analysts in Washington to categorize the criteria reported by the 50 judges. This group of analysts individually rated each of the reasons given by the judges on a 5-point scale: a rating of 4 or 5 was given to highly qualitative criteria, a 3 to mixed qualitative and quantitative criteria, and a 1 or 2 to highly quantitative criteria. One example of a qualitative criterion was "management is setting challenging goals," while a quantitative one was "time spent per average case."

*Exhibit VI* shows the ranking of the 10 most frequently mentioned criteria. The phrasing of these criteria was done by the IRS national office analysts, who inferred the categories from a variety of specific phrases found on the judges' cards. Some categories are unique to IRS operations, but they indicate general types of criteria that could apply to other organizations as well. Important here is the fact that a large majority of items (7 of 10) are qualitative (rated 4 or 5 on the rating scale), although two strongly quantitative criteria (rated 1) were also mentioned by the judges. The most important criterion was "quality and effectiveness of management"; it was used by judges in 13 of the 15 panels.

**Exhibit VI.**   Most frequently mentioned criteria

| Rank | | Rating on 5-point scale* |
|------|------|:---:|
| 1 | Quality of effectiveness of management | 4 |
| 2. | Productivity measurements | 1 |
| 3. | Manpower utilization | 4 |
| 4. | Overall improvement, status quo, or decline | 3 |
| 5. | Inventory level of uncollected TDAs (taxpayer delinquent accounts) | 1 |
| 6. | Progress and achievement of established objectives and planned programs | 4 |
| 7. | Morale | 4 |
| 8. | Management participation and concern in local problem solving | 5 |
| 9. | Potential available and use to which potential is put | 4 |
| 10. | Improved quality and composition and balance of fieldwork | 5 |

*1 = highly quantitative; 2 = more quantitative than qualitative;
3 = mixed quantitative and qualitative; 4 = more qualitative than
quantitative; and 5 = highly qualitative.

From this initial categorizing process, we found that 92 different criteria were used by the entire group of judges. These criteria divided themselves into 39% qualitative, 22% mixed, and 39% quantitative, based on the ratings assigned by the IRS analysts. Of significant interest here is the fact that such a high percentage of qualitative criteria were used. The IRS devotes considerable manpower and money to quantifying performance results; yet these numerical results played a more limited role than we suspected.

**Number of Factors**

Next we compared the criteria used by four high-agreement panels (those panels with an internal correlation of +.84 or better) with the criteria used by four low-agreement panels (those with an internal correlation of +.30 or lower). Here we did not find any significant difference in the total number of criteria used; that is, low-agreement panels did not appear to be confusing themselves with too many criteria. High-agreement panels averaged 11.8 different criteria per panel, and low-agreement panels, 12.8. One high-agreement panel used as few as 7 criteria, while another used 20. Approximately the same range of total criteria (6 to 20) was found among low-agreement panels.

### Points of Agreement

An important distinction was discovered in the extent of *common* criteria used by high-agreement panels. *Exhibit VII* reveals that 44% of the criteria used in each high-agreement panel were commonly used by *every* judge within that panel. Only 12% of the criteria used in low-agreement panels were common to every judge.

We conclude from *Exhibit VII* that lack of agreement about specific criteria probably results in lack of agreement about the overall performance of a unit. At the same time, we should point out that "perfect" agreement on specific criteria is not essential; a high percentage of criteria (41%) were unique to individual judges in high-agreement panels. Apparently, many judges took somewhat different reasoning paths to arrive at essentially the same end result.

A broad implication here is that, while managements should work toward agreement on criteria for evaluating overall performance, they should also leave some latitude for each manager to select his own reasons. All too many managements spend endless meeting hours trying to agree on a limited number of criteria. According to our findings, this costly and often frustrating task may not be necessary.

**Exhibit VII.** Consensus about criteria

|  | Used by all members | Used by some but not all members | Used by only one member |
|---|---|---|---|
| Four high-agreement panels | 44% | 15% | 41% |
| Four low-agreement panels | 12 | 17 | 71 |

### Qualitative Criteria

One very significant finding was that high-agreement panels used considerably more qualitative than quantitative criteria in making their decisions. *Exhibit VIII* shows that 69% of the criteria used by high-agreement panels were qualitative, compared to only 20% for low-agreement panels. Low-agreement panels used 68% quantitative criteria yet could reach only an overall agreement level of no better than + .31. Furthermore, we found that the only criteria which low-agreement panels could completely agree on were *quantitative* criteria; there was far less agreement on qualitative criteria. This suggests that if managers want to be more in line with their colleagues in assessing total performance, they need to use not only *a greater proportion of qualitative criteria, but also develop more consensus on the specific qualitative criteria to be used.*

**Exhibit VIII.**  Type of criteria and level of overall agreement

|  | Types of criteria used | | |
|---|---|---|---|
|  | Quantitative | Mixed | Qualitative |
| Four high-agreement panels | 17% | 14% | 69% |
| Four low-agreement panels | 68 | 12 | 20 |

Why would qualitative evidence be relied on so heavily by high-agreement panels, and why might these criteria lead them to greater overall agreement? As we interpret our findings, there are at least three reasons:

1.  Qualitative factors probably give more *concrete, more sensitive,* and *more current* clues to the underlying strengths of a unit; whereas statistics, despite their apparent preciseness, are usually averages or aggregates that fail to portray the complex events behind them.

2.  Qualitative criteria present clearer leads for required corrective action; whereas statistical results may give little indication of *why* events happened as they did.

3.  Qualitative criteria tend to be broader because they are not tied to particular measurable points; whereas quantitative criteria, just because they have to be particularized to certain narrow segments of field operations in order to be measured, may result in very diverse inferences being drawn from them in judging overall performance.

### APPLYING THE RESULTS

Up to this point, we have mentioned some general implications of our findings; now we would like to draw them together and offer some specific suggestions for action:

- Most important is the need to recognize that managers—not computers, numbers, or information systems—are the critical element in the assessment of subunit performance.

  Statistical reports have increasingly taken on the revered status of "objectivity," while managerial judgments have too often been sidetracked as overly "subjective" or "opinionated." Thus we find organizations building larger headquarters staffs to process ever larger amounts of statistical performance information, much of which is never used.

- All organizations ought to be vitally concerned with studying how their managers actually assess subunit performance. While organizations frequently spend large sums of money generating more and more information about subunit performance, they seldom consider what information is actually used or needed by their managers. Nor do they always recognize the importance of achieving a high level of agreement among top managers about subunit performance. If managers cannot agree, there is something amiss, either with the company's information system or with the managers and their organizational environment.

We therefore suggest that organizations take periodic "X rays" of their judgmental process. The study methodology used in the IRS is one useful approach. The findings can be used both for training managers to reach more informed judgments about subunit performance, and for designing information systems which will provide more help to managers in making their judgments.

- Management training should use research findings derived from the actual company environment to design programs that fit the needs of its particular management group. To do this, the key management group participating in the study could be brought together to hear and discuss the significant findings.

The critical questions before these managers should be: (a) Why do we have these results? (b) What do we do about them? The answers, of course, will vary with each organization and its unique findings. But the general thrust of actions afterward should be more informed and constructive.

For example, a top management group may decide to pay greater attention to the judgments of its field managers. Or agreement may be reached to place greater and more explicit emphasis on qualitative criteria. Or the present information system may be altered to provide data on those criteria which are most frequently used, while eliminating data on those which are not heavily used.

The next step would be to discuss the findings within smaller functional groupings. It would be useful for those groups in lowest agreement to sit down and discuss why they see subunits from such different perspectives. They may discover, in the process of this examination, that they fail to discuss their observations sufficiently with each other. Or they may find that each is using too diverse a set of criteria, and that more consensus needs to be reached on particular criteria.

- The formal information system must be designed to complement these changes if they are to be put into practice. For instance, it makes little sense for a company computer to continue providing data on 50 variables when its managers are in substantial agreement after using data on only 15 variables.

A real challenge for some organizations is to build more qualitative information into their formal systems. One method used in some companies is to request a written narrative with each submission of statistics from the field. Another method is to hold periodic, in-depth discussions involving several managers from different levels so that each can contribute whatever qualitative data are available to him.

Organizations might also consider the possibility of incorporating a judgmental procedure, such as the one used in this study, into an organization's on-going process of performance assessment. Managements need to consider the challenge of systematically recording managerial judgments as much as they systematize statistical results. Lower level managers can attest to their feelings of frustration when one upper level manager tells one of them that he is doing a "good" job while another upper level manager downgrades him. On the other hand, if this same manager knows that five upper level managers systematically agree in ranking his unit at the "tail-end" of the pack, he cannot as easily rationalize his position.

Our suggestion at this early state, however, is to experiment with, but not institutionalize, a more systematic judging procedure, perhaps in only one division of a large company. Every formal system, if taken too seriously and rigidly, can become more of a hindrance than a help. There are always bugs to be worked out of these systems before giving them wider application.

**CONCLUSION**

A major task of any management is to know what is *actually* taking place within its organization. One critical, but seldom examined, function is the manner in which key managers assess the performance of units under their supervision. In the absence of knowledge, numerous myths and assumptions have abounded. Particularly noticeable is a growing mistrust of the reliability of managerial judgments. Signs of this mistrust are reflected in current trends toward more statistics, more computers, more information specialists, and more centralized information systems—the IRS, where this study was conducted, being no exception.

Yet the findings of this study seriously dispute many of these newer trends and assumptions. Notably:

1. Managers can generally agree with each other about the current effectiveness and performance trends of subunits under them.

2. Their judgments seem to be quite stable from one day to the next.

3. Managers who agree most with their colleagues tend to come from levels closest to the field; work in smaller divisions; use more commonly shared criteria; and rely more on qualitative than on quantitative criteria.

These conclusions must be qualified to the extent that they are based on *one study in a single nonbusiness organization*. Therefore, we should treat them more as propositions to be tested further, rather than as final answers.

However, we believe these findings place a new challenge before every management: to seek new ways of studying, assisting, and restoring confidence in the performance judgments of their managers. This will not occur magically. First, a concerned management will have to investigate and identify its current practices for judging performance. Then, it will have to use the study findings to train its managers in improving their judgmental practices. Finally, it will have to strive to make its information system a more helpful servant rather than an irrelevant master.

**NOTES**

1.  Letter from Robert Jacobs, From the thoughtful businessman, *Harvard Business Review* (January-February 1967), 48.

# HOW TO EVALUATE A COMPANY'S TRAINING EFFORTS

*Warren H. Schmidt*

Every year American companies spend millions of dollars for training. This money is used for company training staffs to conduct in-house programs, programs conducted by outside agencies, and a variety of materials, films, and consultation. Most organizations regard their training effort as an investment in people and in the future.

This is one investment, however, which usually escapes careful and systematic scrutiny. Training budgets tend to expand in periods of company prosperity and to shrink dramatically in periods of low profits. Many training directors complain that "when things get tough, training is the first place they cut." Such decisions tend to be made more on the basis of a nebulous "feeling" about training's value than on the basis of any hard data about what trade-offs are being made.

In many companies training is given much lip service, but is treated as a second-class activity whenever it competes for recognition, representation, and status. At least part of this inconsistency stems from the fact that no key executive can actually tell you how effectively his company's training dollars are being spent. If such an executive knew more precisely the cost of training—and knew the cost of *not* training—he could make more consistent decisions and statements.

But how do you undertake a process of realistic and meaningful evaluation—particularly in a large, sprawling organization where "training" covers a wide range of activities and programs?

A large national airline recently confronted and successfully dealt with just this question. This article describes and analyzes how the President of United Air Lines (UAL) initiated a process of inquiry which stimulated and continues to strengthen training efforts throughout the entire organization.

In early 1967, President George E. Keck appointed a committee to review all nonpilot, nonmanagement training being done within United Air Lines. Training activities involved in the study required an annual expenditure of about $14,000,000. Most intense attention was given to training programs for stewardesses, ticket agents, maintenance personnel, and cargo and ramp personnel. President Keck instructed this committee to make a comprehensive study:

to ascertain that the company's money is being well spent, that we are receiving value for the expenditure, that we are using the best methods and techniques to accomplish good results, that we do not have duplication of efforts or expenditures, and that we have a need for the training being done.

**Figure 1.** Design of United Air Lines training study project

| Phases | Objectives | Methods and Activities |
|---|---|---|
| *I. Mapping the field* | 1. To get over-view of training activities and costs in all non-pilot areas.<br>2. To determine which areas should be reviewed in depth.<br>3. To develop initial impressions to be tested in later phases of the study. | — 900 Questionnaires to instructors, administrators, managers.<br>— Work Team interviews of more than 400 selected instructors, administrators, managers.<br>— Analysis of data to determine areas and issues to study in greater depth. |
| *II. Identification and study of training strengths, weaknesses and new approaches by United personnel* | 1. To bring into focus training practices, problems and possibilities as seen by key personnel within the UAL system— managers, training administrators, program developers and instructors.<br>2. To stimulate UAL personnel to diagnose training problems and take action to resolve these problems. | — Six 2-day residential Training Seminars involving more than 200 managers, training administrators, program developers and instructors.<br>— Analysis and Synthesis of seminar data into draft report.<br>— Report critique seminar with key United training specialists. |

**Figure 1.** Design of United Air Lines training study project (continued)

| Phases | Objectives | Methods and Activities |
|---|---|---|
| | 3. To develop better communication and understanding among different groups related to the training function.<br>4. To develop interest and involvement in the Training Study Project. | |
| *III. Critique and expansion of findings and recommendations by outside experts: preparation of final report* | 1. To test preliminary UAL Committee findings by submitting them to a panel of outside training specialists.<br>2. To fill any existing gaps in study.<br>3. To prepare a summary report and proposal for its utilization to affect desired changes. | — Two and a half day seminar with panel of outside training specialists.<br>— Follow-up contact with UAL seminar participants to fill gaps.<br>— Preparation of report to President.<br>— Summary session with President and key advisors. |
| *IV. Implementation and follow-up* | 1. To insure understanding and utilization of study findings and recommendations. | — Report review meetings with President and Senior Officers.<br>— Distribution of parts of report and other appropriate communications within UAL System.<br>— Creation of Corporate Training Implementation Committee to coordinate recommended actions. |

To insure as objective an approach as possible, this five-man Training Study Committee was composed of executives (including two vice presidents) who had no direct relationship to existing training programs in the company. A full-time Work Team, made up of nontraining personnel from various departments of United Air Lines, was assigned to gather data and perform other staff functions for the Committee. An outside behavioral science consultant was engaged by the Committee to assist in designing and carrying out the study.

The Committee approached its task in a four-phase operation (see Figure 1).

- Phase 1 Mapping the field
- Phase 2 In-depth study of training strengths, weaknesses, and opportunities by United Air Lines personnel

- Phase 3 Critique and expansion of findings and recommendations by outside training experts
- Phase 4 Implementation of recommendations

The total effort resulted in (1) documented answers to the President's initial questions; (2) nearly eighty recommendations for improved training practices; (3) a definitive policy statement on Corporate Training and Development; (4) appointment of a Corporate Training Implementation Committee; and (5) numerous new approaches to training initiated throughout the United system. Another subtle—but perhaps most powerful—result was the increased awareness and interest on the part of key executives and managers in training as an investment in future service and efficiency.

## ISSUES AND PROBLEMS

When a key executive wants to find out how effectively training is being done in his organization, he must be prepared to face a number of issues and problems. Evaluation almost always carries some degree of threat—often to the very people who must be asked for dependable data. Some of the more critical issues involved in a study of training are identified and commented on in this section.

### 1. How to Initiate a Study of Training

When a training study is announced, the most critical question likely to arise in the minds of those personnel concerned is, *"Who wants to know—and for what purpose?"* Those responsible for training may be particularly concerned about whether the study implies dissatisfaction with the job they are doing.

The second question is likely to be, "Who will conduct the study; what are their competencies and biases?" If training personnel initiate the study themselves, their motives will be suspect in some companies. They may be seen as trying to gather evidence to support a larger training budget or to forestall impending cuts. On the other hand, if the study is initiated by the comptroller's office, the anxiety among training personnel is likely to soar markedly. They will wonder whether accountants who live in a world of numbers will ever be able to understand the subtle and often intangible results of training.

The president of the company is probably the ideal person to initiate a training study. He personifies the overall concern for the company's present operation and future success. His "vested interest" is in the health of the *total* organization, not of one department or division. Moreover, his active involvement and support underscore the significance of the study effort and pave the way for various data-collection processes.

## 2. How to Develop a Systematic Plan

This is not an easy task. Its difficulty leads some companies to engage an outside consulting firm to take the responsibility. An "inside group" requires a certain amount of "tooling up" time to enter a somewhat vague and complex enterprise. This moving into new and uncharted waters can produce high anxiety among the study-group members. They begin to realize that much of their reputation and future may be affected by the quality of their findings and recommendations. The questions of how to get started, what kind of time schedule to set, what priorities to adopt, how to use available staff help—and many others—flood in on them.

Several factors can help a committee to develop a sense of direction and overall plan of operation:

**1. Good relations among committee members.**    A high level of trust is tremendously important during the anxious period of trying to understand the task and appreciate its complexity.

**2. Large blocks of time for planning.**    One- and two-hour meetings are of little use at this point. More progress can be made if full days—or at least half days—can be set aside for planning.

**3. An outside consultant with planning skills.**    This makes expertise available, but keeps control of the planning in the hands of the responsible "inside" group. The consultant can question assumptions and develop alternative approaches; the internal study group can tailor these approaches to the company. The consultant can also add some element of authority and objectivity to the study group's image among their colleagues.

In the UAL case the Study Committee, using an outside behavioral science consultant, approached its task in phases (see Figure 1). After the completion of Phase 1, enough information was available to determine where priority attention should be given and the approximate amount of time required.

## 3. How to Get the Full Cooperation of Training Specialists in the Company

Any active internal study requires cooperation from those closest to the activity under study. The kind of data provided by experts is likely to be determined by the confidence these experts have in the study group's integrity and influence. Can they be trusted, and will their report have any real impact? If the study group is seen as a threat, many sources of data will dry up. Even worse, data may be distorted. On the other hand, if the study group is seen as ineffectual, it is likely to get only minimal cooperation.

In the UAL case the Training Study Committee did several things to gain the confidence of colleagues:

1. It adopted as its name "The President's Training Study Committee." This identified it as a group with some influence. By using the word "Study" rather than "Evaluation" or "Assessment," it sought to reduce some of the threat to training personnel.

2. It sought to make clear that the study would be based on

"...the experience and best thinking about training by United personnel"

—and—

"...experience and the best thinking available from personnel *outside* the United system."

In effect, the Committee viewed itself as a stimulator and focuser of thinking—rather than as an investigating body.

Training personnel throughout United soon came to view the Study Project not as a threat, but as an opportunity to get a hearing for their views at the highest level in the organization.

### 4. How to Remain Open to Influence Without Losing Independence of Judgment

Good recommendations depend on good inputs. To control inputs of influence too rigorously may eliminate the most creative insights and ideas. To open the door wide, however, may invite those with vested interests to dominate the direction of the study group—particularly if it is composed of "non-experts" in the area of investigation.

The dilemma is, therefore, how to invite, listen, and understand without becoming a "captive" of any single point of view prematurely.

In the UAL case the Training Study Committee clearly separated—psychologically and in time— the process of collecting ideas from the process of sifting ideas. It designated Phase 2 of the Project (see Figure 1) as the period for gathering information, opinions, analyses, and proposals from the entire system. Two-day residential seminars were convened to provide occasions for such inputs. Committee members always listened, raised questions to probe and clarify—but *never evaluated ideas in public.*

### 5. How to Process Masses of Data, Analyses, and Proposals into Succinct Statements of Problems and Recommendations

Unstructured data are always difficult to process. They are easier to produce because they fit the frame of reference of the producer rather than the researcher. Unless a careful distillation process is developed, however, the resulting report will be either too bulky, detailed, and chaotic to use, or too abstract and general to make an impact.

Most executives want findings and recommendations to be concise, with details and supporting data available, but not in the foreground. Arriving at this point, however, requires a dogged process of reading, grouping, regrouping, writing, and rewriting. At every point there is the gnawing question, "Are we losing a key point—are we watering down the spirit of what we have found?"

In the UAL case the four-man work team took major *responsibility* for organizing synthesizing, and condensing data, sharpening issues, and drafting alternative courses of action (see Figure 2). Periodic meetings of Work Team Committee members and the consultant further distilled and sharpened the statements of problems and recommendations. Each of these meetings was designed in advance by the consultant to make productive use of the group's working time. Some issues were handled by subgroups; others by combined committee and work team. (One of the most valuable features of the committee's operation was the quality of the relationship between committee members—all senior executives in the company—and work team members—with much lower status and seniority. In joint sessions these status differences were completely ignored and the group functioned as a single unified policy-making body.)

**Figure 2.**   Data Flow in United Air Lines training study project

---

Facts, Observations, Opinions, Proposals from groups and individuals throughout Organization

(Raw Data)

---

↓

---

This Raw Data grouped by Work Team into "spread sheets" with these categories:

Problem| Contributing Causes| Consequences |Ideas for Solving Problem

---

↓

---

Categories reduced by Committee and Work Team into the following:

Problem | Analysis | Draft Recommendations

---

↓

---

Statements of Problems and recommendations reviewed, critiqued by select panel of UAL professional training personnel to examine impact of recommendations.

---

↓

---

Tentative Agreement on problems and recommendations by Study Committee and Work Team.

---

↓

---

Review and critique of major problems and issues by Outside Review Panel (non-UAL training specialists and educators).

---

↓

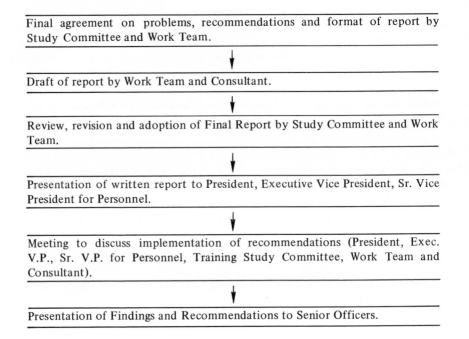

Final agreement on problems, recommendations and format of report by Study Committee and Work Team.

Draft of report by Work Team and Consultant.

Review, revision and adoption of Final Report by Study Committee and Work Team.

Presentation of written report to President, Executive Vice President, Sr. Vice President for Personnel.

Meeting to discuss implementation of recommendations (President, Exec. V.P., Sr. V.P. for Personnel, Training Study Committee, Work Team and Consultant).

Presentation of Findings and Recommendations to Senior Officers.

### 6. How to Determine Realistic and Appropriate Boundaries for the Study

Training effectiveness in a company may be affected by many factors, including organizational arrangements and personalities. Are these factors "fair game" for investigation by a training study team? Should such a team confine its attention solely to matters involving training personnel, materials, and methodology? Should the study group develop its recommendations on the assumption that the present personnel and organizational structure will be retained? Should it push for reorganization of the company to facilitate better training?

In the UAL case the committee noted in its findings that some blocks to effective inter-departmental cooperation on training were due to personality factors and departmental rivalries. Rather than proposing drastic organizational changes, however, it recommended new coordinating mechanisms for by-passing existing obstacles and establishing a climate in which rivalries became less necessary. By its process of study, the committee also provided settings in which key personnel from "competing" departments confronted and resolved some of their misunderstandings and sources of tension.

### 7. How to Avoid Setting Unrealistic Expectations

When a study is launched, expectations begin to develop among those who may be affected by the results. If these people are asked for data and opinions, their expectations will be further heightened and crystallized. If the group conducting the study operates on a very open basis—providing feedback on its findings as it goes along—the expectations become even more firmly fixed. Some people begin to anticipate the direction of the report's recommendations and begin to make decisions based on those assumptions. The result can be that if the final report differs from these expectations, some will be highly critical and feel "let down."

In the UAL case the Study Committee recognized this hazard and decided to risk the consequences. At every point possible, committee members underscored the fact that they were listening to conflicting points of view and that in the final analysis their report could not encompass every proposal. . . .Even with this risk, the committee felt that the possibility of unrealistic expectations was a small price to pay for the high level of interest and involvement they had stimulated.

## 8. How to Increase the Chances of Impact

Many carefully-designed studies come to an end with a report that is filed away. Others influence policy decisions which somehow are never implemented. People in large organizations often develop ingenious ways of rejecting changes while seemingly acquiescing to them. The sequence and fate of many study efforts might be depicted as follows:

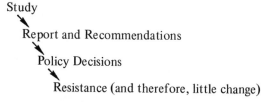

Study
    Report and Recommendations
        Policy Decisions
            Resistance (and therefore, little change)

When this pattern occurs, all of the study effort and expense is relatively useless. Even worse, it tends to discourage or undermine future studies—which also must begin under a cloud of cynicism. ("Here we go again. When we don't know what else to do we start a study.")

In the UAL case the Study Committee used as its basic procedural model the following sequence:

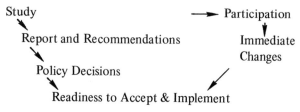

Study                        Participation
    Report and Recommendations       Immediate
                                     Changes
        Policy Decisions
           Readiness to Accept & Implement

Some specific strategies and procedures that proved to be particularly effective were the following:

- Naming the project a training *study* project, rather than an *evaluation* or *assessment* project. (Less threat)

- Distributing questionnaires by work team members at the various stations, rather than mailing them. (A personal touch)

- Using residential seminars to gather in-depth information, analysis, and proposals from the field people. (Rather than doing this through individual interviews)

- Giving prompt post-seminar reports to all participants. (Within one week of the seminar)

- Encouraging colleagues to initiate training improvements without waiting for the study to be completed.

- Sending follow-up requests for "second thoughts" and actions taken by study seminar participants. (One month after each seminar)

- Giving visibility to changes being undertaken by various people throughout the company. (And thus encouraging others to do likewise)

- Keeping the President informed of developments and involving him at strategic points in the process. (At points where he could make a unique contribution)

- Testing draft recommendations with key training personnel to understand the consequences better

- Involving an outside review panel of training specialists and educators to test and enrich the findings. (And to lend another stamp of authority to the study)

- Giving careful attention to the format of the report. (So that various parts of it could be self-contained guides for various departments in the organization)

### 9. How to Communicate Study Results and Implement Recommendations

After the data are all in, the analyses made, and the recommendations formulated, a bulky document comes into existence. What happens next may well determine whether significant improvements will occur or whether things will go on as usual.

Here is a critical point for clear leadership by the one who initiated the effort. He must—in consultation with his colleagues—determine what actions are required, who should take those actions, and how he can support their efforts. If changes are to be implemented over a long period of time, he may want to set up some mechanism or procedure for systematic follow-up. To do less is to emasculate the work of the study group (and to reduce the credibility of any future studies).

In the UAL case the President, Executive Vice-President, and Senior Vice-President for Personnel studied the report individually, then met with the Study Committee to clarify some findings and review possible courses of implementing action. The following first action steps then took place:

- The President issued a statement of Corporate Policy on Training and Development (Figure 3), thus implementing the first recommendation of the Study Committee.

## UNITED AIR LINES STATEMENT OF
## CORPORATE TRAINING AND DEVELOPMENT POLICY

United Air Lines is a service organization. Our value to customers and our success as a business depends on how effectively and efficiently the people of United carry out their responsibilities.

A people-centered organization like United must also be a people-developing organization. Management at every level must understand clearly that time and money spent wisely in training our personnel is an investment in the most crucial part of our system.

Each person in United is ultimately responsible for his own development to become an increasingly effective member of the United team.

Each manager and supervisor is responsible for providing the climate, conditions and direction for the job-related development of his subordinates. (This responsibility cannot be delegated, since the most consistent training occurs day by day in the work situation.)

Each training specialist or training administrator is responsible for working with managers and supervisors to improve consistently the conditions and opportunities for developing subordinates' skills, knowledge and attitudes.

United's operations must be flexible and adaptive to the increased tempo of change. This flexibility is directly dependent on our ability to train people promptly and effectively. It is therefore our policy to maintain a group of training specialists to insure that the training is well-planned, well-coordinated, well-conducted and utilizes the most appropriate methodology available.

Training is a costly investment and must be planned, budgeted and evaluated with care. The importance of this must be recognized at all levels of the company.

To insure that the training function is carried on effectively, we shall strive to develop within United Air Lines the following:

1. A corporate training policy that is understood throughout the system.

2. Managers and supervisors who understand, accept and know how to fulfill their basic responsibility to train subordinates.

3. An approach to training which begins with clearly identified needs and ends with the measurable achievement of practical training objectives.

4. A clearly understood procedure which budgets, accounts for, and reports the cost of all training.

5. Systematic methods for assessing job performance and the effectiveness of training in improving that performance.

6. An organizational climate that encourages, recognizes and rewards inter-administration and inter-departmental planning and implementation of training programs.

7. Maintenance of a professional training unit responsible for the qualifications of training personnel, technology, methodology, and media to keep United current with new developments in the training field.

8. Organizational mechanisms and procedures for effective inter-administration and inter-departmental planning of training programs and use of specialized training capabilities.

9. A system of recognition and rewards which attracts competent personnel to training positions and encourages them to develop their capability for a professional training career.

10. The early involvement of training personnel in planning those changes which have training implications.

**Figure 3.** Corporate training policy statement resulting from study project

- The Senior Vice-President for Personnel was designated as the key executive to guide the process of implementing recommendations.

- A Corporate Training Implementation Committee, consisting of the top training specialists from every administrative department in the UAL system, was appointed to plan specific ways to carry forward the study results.

- The Study Committee Chairman and consultant were invited to present the study results to the senior officers of the company at their annual retreat. Here the President stressed the importance of their understanding the final report and supporting the recommendations.

In reviewing the United Air Lines effort, it is possible to identify a number of critical factors which contributed significantly to its success. Some of these may also be appropriate for other companies undertaking a similar study:

1. Initiation, support, and continuing involvement of the president of the company.

2. Selection of a Study Committee of high-level corporate executives having no direct connection with training operations.

3. Selection of a full-time working team to perform staff functions for the committee.

4. Selection of an outside behavioral science consultant to work with both the committee and the working team.

5. Development of close relations among committee members, working team, and consultant so that the group could function as a unified problem-solving body. (Some sessions devoted to group process issues facilitated development of relations.)

6. Maintaining the view that the study report was a means toward increasing training effectiveness, not an end in itself. (This action-orientation influenced greatly the processes used in the study, and even the language employed.)

7. High commitment to the study by committee, work team, and consultant. (This commitment showed itself in willingness to entail large blocks of time and late hours when necessary.)

8. Confidence in the Study Committee and support of the study project by key training personnel in the company.

9. Adequate financial and personnel support of the study efforts, and Committee authority to command resources and assistance.

Training is an essential and expensive process. Many organizations treat it more casually than its importance warrants. There is considerable evidence that this will become an increasingly critical function in organizations in the future.

Training effectiveness is difficult to assess. Many of its results are subtle, and even some of these may be attributed to other processes and factors. However, a systematic assessment and analysis is likely to reveal strengths which should be reinforced and problems which can be handled more effectively. Improvements have great implications for company profits and effective people.

Whether a training study will be significant or "just another study" depends on how it is initiated, who conducts the study, and how that study group develops its relationships within the organization.

This article reports some of the principal learnings from one study in a company which has a multi-million dollar training operation. This study was exciting and carried great impact. Therefore, it suggests procedures and approaches which may be of general value to both large and small organizations.

# 9.

# EMERGING ROLES AND RESPONSIBILITIES OF THE SPECIALIST IN HUMAN RESOURCE DEVELOPMENT

In this final chapter, the authors examine the responsibilities, roles, and qualifications of those designing and implementing training and development.

While this chapter seems to put emphasis on the professionalization of the human resource development function, the authors have real questions about whether any confirming list of knowledges, skills, or degrees can adequately deal with the need for creativity and flexibility in the ever-widening field of human resource development.

The first article in this chapter, written by two of the editors of this volume, raises the question, "Is Training a Profession?". Gordon Lippitt and Leslie This conclude that the field has not yet reached this status, but they identify some of the areas which can contribute to professionalism.

Frank Goodell's "Reflections of a Training Director" puts the question of professional development on the doorstep of the individual. He indicates that a test of whether we have standards in the manpower planning and development field is necessary to examine the people we hire and promote in the field.

Julius Eitington uses some picturesque nouns to present several different typologies or roles in trainer behavior, in "Which Role for Today's Trainer?". He questions whether some of these roles are fitting for the mature manpower-development specialist.

The last article in this chapter is "Looking at the Role and Behavior of the Training Professional," by Gordon Lippitt, who looks at four key roles of the training specialist. He examines the learning specialist, administrator, information coordinator, and consultant functions of the human resource development person. In the latter part of this article he sets out the pro-active—as opposed to reactive—responsibility of the learning planner.

If we are to take seriously the challenge of the future, the ideas in this chapter will need to be discussed, argued, questioned, and thoughtfully considered by training, personnel, and adult-education associations, along with other professional groups. Most important, however, these points of view must penetrate the mind and heart of the individual practitioner in today's schools, churches, industry, government, community organizations, and all those who are seeking to more effectively perform their responsibilities.

Human resource development will seek multidimensional persons who are willing to take off their blinders and enlarge the scope of their lives. It will require a person who is receptive to new learnings through his own experience as well as through the experience of others.

## IS TRAINING A PROFESSION?

*Gordon L. Lippitt and Leslie This*

The literature in the field of training repeatedly gives evidence of the yearning of training personnel for professional status. Statements, ranging from the "Wouldn't it be nice to wear a gold pin indicating membership in the 'Association of Mystic Professional Training'" to impassioned, learned pleas, can be found in the pages of this *Journal*, books on training, resolutions from chapters, various study groups and committees, and convention speeches.

Some of the critics of training and education have made jibes at such a yearning:

"Educationists are morbidly self-conscious about the standing of their profession. They exhort one another to be 'professional minded' and each feels his pulse from time to time to make sure it has the right professional beat. Beneath it all, however, is a frightened uncertainty concerning the exact nature of a profession, and a desperate longing for palpable tokens of salvation."[1]

Part of this mutual exhortation, of course, comes from three usually unspoken motivations:

1. The desire for financial security which professional standing bids to enhance.

2. Recognition and status.

3. The lack of acceptance of the training director and his job by "outsiders" and the necessity to find solace, compassion, understanding, and assurance of his worth from fellow-sufferers.

Unfortunately, too often there seems to exist some sort of naive faith among training personnel that a cataclysmic change in public opinion, an enlightened act of

From *The Journal of the American Society of Training Directors*, **14**, No. 4 (April, 1960). Reprinted by permission of the American Society for Training and Development.

legislation, or a scrooge-like change in the vice-president to whom training reports, will miraculously create a professional status for them. If there is action, it usually is in the form of passing a resolution along the lines "These are desired personal characteristics, knowledges, skills, and attitudes in a Training Director. This group affirms we believe in them—have them—and with their passage management and the public will hereafter treat us with dignity and respect and raise our salaries."

This phenomenon, of course, is not peculiar to training directors; it is the problem of every new profession. Recently we saw a group of credit managers, striving for professional recognition, who drew up a list of desired qualities, skills, and knowledges for a credit manager, and honestly believed when they submitted the statement to their company presidents it would make the president accept them as professionals. Somewhere, at this writing, there is undoubtedly a group of 25 sadly disillusioned and frustrated credit managers.

Training people, fortunately, are now beginning to realize that they will have professional status only to the extent that they create it themselves—and it is so recognized by those who employ them and use their services.

### CRITERIA FOR A PROFESSION

As we review many professions, we find that professional recognition frequently stems from four sources:

1. Persons in the profession having skills and/or knowledges that take years to acquire, are recognized by the population as being highly desirable and needed, and are possessed by few in the population. Examples are the lawyer, doctor, civil engineer.

2. Persons in the profession having skills and/or knowledges that are in short supply, with the numbers coming into the profession rigidly guarded. Certain crafts and unions are examples.

3. Persons in a field with a long history of being called a profession. The auctioneer, chimney-sweep and circus barker are examples.

4. Persons who are especially good in any field—who excel—such as football and baseball players, sports specialists of all kinds, jugglers, salesmen, car workers, garbage collectors, well diggers, yoyo twirlers.

Such definitions, however, hardly serve us in trying to answer our question, "What is a Profession?" The National Education Association's Division of Field Service has suggested eight criteria as follows: "A profession

1. Involves activities essentially intellectual

2. Commands a body of specialized knowledge

3. Requires extended professional preparation

4. Demands continuous in service growth

5. Affords a life career and permanent membership

6. Sets up its own standards

7. Exalts service above personal gain

8. Has a strong, closely-knit professional organization."[2]

Another attempt to appraise the characteristics of a profession lists these criteria:

1. Does the profession have a well-defined function, the nature scope of which can be identified?

2. Does the profession have a philosophy, code of ethics, and other means of self-regulation which assure that its practice transcends the bounds of political, sectarian, and economic self-interest?

3. Does the profession have a unified pattern of organization that can speak for it with one voice?

4. Does the compensation received by the professional practitioners indicate that the public is willing to pay them as skilled and responsible professional workers?

5. Is the practice of the profession limited, or tending to be limited, to persons with approved general and professional preparation?

6. Is there, in fact, a recognized systematic body of knowledge, skills, and attitudes which can be identified and transmitted as a regimen of professional preparation?

7. Is the regimen of professional education recognized as a quality appropriate for inclusion in the graduate and professional offerings of a university?"[3]

Flexner[4] suggests that professions have still other criteria:

1. They involve essentially intellectual operations

2. They derive their raw material from science and learning

3. They work up this material to a practical and definite end

4. They possess an educationally-communicable technique

5. They tend to self-organization

6. They are becoming increasingly altruistic in motivation.[4]

One other resource, our last, to which we might turn to help us identify the criteria of a profession is to define it. One dictionary offers the following:

"The occupation, if not commercial, mechanical, agricultural, or the like, to which one devotes oneself; a calling; as, the *profession* of arms, of teaching; the *three professions*, or the *learned professions*, of theology, law, and medicine."[5]

Other criteria may need to be added to meet the peculiarities of the training profession, for example, some criteria to demonstrate conclusively that training does have a very real dollars-and-cents and quality pay-off. As noted earlier, this is an area in which the training field is trying many approaches to reach a demonstrable conclusion. Another example might be tangible demonstration that a person trained by recômmended professional standards does a better training job than does the employee selected because of pragmatic reasons whose skills are mainly in his technical field, not in training. One of the difficulties we face is that training deals in large part with human relationships and other intangibles, and everyone in the organization considers himself an expert in these fields. Opposing concepts are difficult to prove or disprove—since trainees have a way of learning even in dramatically opposite training settings.

It is well known that a dictionary, however, is but a history of words. Current usage of the term "professional" seems to be quite casual. Anyone who specializes in a job and does it better than anyone else today seems to be entitled to use the term, but such usage does not have the element frequently mentioned in our quote, "activities essentially intellectual."[6] Accordingly, we speak of professional football players, professional baseball players, professional rug cleaners, professional cesspool cleaners.

The problem becomes even more frustrating when we find much evidence that employers follow this same pattern. When a training job opens, employers reach down into supervisor ranks and come up with an employee who seems to be able to do an ambiguous something better than any other supervisor—and we have a training director or training assistant. What it is this supervisor can do better than any other supervisor no one really can identify.

Unfortunately, as one of the criteria suggests, "Does the compensation received by the professional practitioners indicate that the public is willing to pay them as skilled and professional workers?," the customers who control our destiny are not the public.[7] We have to sell vice-presidents, company chairmen, and company presidents. What we possess must be seen and recognized by them as being something unique and worthwhile, and in this selling we probably have a long way to go, as witness much of our activity to prove that training results can be measured and proved to be cost-reducing. Too often our employers see us only as good presenters of material, often not even as good teachers.

The field of social work has had a similar problem. Recently the professional workers in the field established a deadline date after which entrance to the professional society would be limited, among other requirements, to persons who had completed two years of graduate work in the field. Such a step connotes, among other things, (1) that the bulk of recognized leaders in the profession are in the professional society; and (2) that those who identify themselves as professionals with the professional society perform a job that is recognizably superior to the job of those not so identified.

It is interesting to note, from these limited definitions, the criteria that appear at least twice in the quoted material. Arranged in order of frequency mentioned, they are:

1. The profession has a body of specialized knowledge.
2. The profession sets its own standards.
3. Its activities are essentially intellectual.
4. The profession requires extensive preparation.
5. The needed body of specialized knowledge is communicable.
6. The profession places service above personal gain.
7. The profession has a strong professional organization.

These criteria might serve as a beginning effort to outline the directions in which training directors must channel their efforts in fashioning a profession that will be recognized by those in the field who are the recipients of our training programs.

## BODY OF SPECIALIZED TRAINING KNOWLEDGE

We should like to address ourselves now to the one criterion that appears in each of the definitions quoted: "The profession has a body of specialized knowledge." It is our feeling that training directors have had too limited a concept of the content encompassed in an adequate training position. Many of us remember the time when mastery of the "Phillips 66" method and JIT was considered pretty adequate background for a training director. Although the profession has come a long way from those early days, it has not yet come up with an acceptable outline of educational content. We suggest the following as essential areas of professional competence for training personnel:

1. The ability to utilize appropriate findings from the social sciences.
2. The development of a working theory about personality growth and development.
3. The development of concepts of learning based on research findings.
4. The ability to design growth–learning experiences.
5. The ability to accomplish further research on the training process.
6. The development of a philosophy of training related to our present knowledge of the individual, the group, the organization, and the community in which people live.
7. The development of progressive, planned in service growth opportunities for the individual training director.

8. A good working knowledge of accepted training methods, techniques, and visual aids, and the ability to utilize them effectively in the design of training programs.

9. The ability to sell to, plan with, and work with, the operating people on effective immediate and long-range training programs.

10. The ability to do—to teach—to train—to lead workshops. There is a difference of opinion on this area. To some it is the paramount skill; to others it is seen as of waning importance in the skill areas of the training director of the future.

If these areas are accepted as being some of the major essential ones of desired professional competency, we ought to take a look at some of the social sciences with significant contributions to make to these content areas. Following is a listing and an indication of major contributions each could make:

1. *Psychiatry*—an understanding of individual dynamics—derivations—the limits of training for the "average" and "normal."

2. *General Psychology*—an understanding of personality growth and development.

3. *Social Psychology*—an understanding of interpersonal relationships.

4. *Educational Psychology*—an understanding of learning research, method, and theory.

5. *Business and Public Administration*—an understanding of the dynamics of organizations.

6. *Political Science*—an analysis of social systems.

7. *Sociology*—an understanding of the forces in the community and their implications for training.

8. *Anthropology*—an understanding of the function of a culture and the role of training in it.

This may strike some training directors as being unrealistic and too broad an educational background. However, there is much evidence to indicate that most of management's disenchantment with training has been created by training operators who turn knobs and pull controls without adequate understanding of the forces and factors they are trying to manipulate. We see the training personnel of the future, the training directors, as being *learning theorists* rather than merely training methodologists. The latter can be bought much more cheaply and should not be placed in strategic, top training roles. The learning theorist will be both comfortable in and familiar with such learning content as:

1. *The nature and scope of the learning process.* It is much larger than we usually assume—considerably larger than the organizational formal training. It embraces formal education, other job experiences, supervisory training on the job, the job experience itself, reading, family living, other life experiences.

2. *The factors that condition learning.* The individual's dissatisfaction with his own existing behavior, readiness for learning, supportive learning atmosphere, opportunities to get "feedback" of a personal nature in learning, opportunities to practice new learning, cognitive material, and transfer of learning of all factors which affect the learning process. A training director needs to be aware of factors as they relate to the designing of a learning experience, whether of a two-hour nature or a two-year plan.

3. *The factors affecting resistance to learning.* Threat to the individual's self-perception, individual's being defensive about present job performance, cultural inhibition about "exposing inadequacies," need for emotional support during learning, and numerous other factors give meaningful diagnostic dimensions for persons planning training to take into account.

As can be seen from the field of learning alone, we must bring members up to date on the recent studies of learning, effects of group size in training, concepts of mental health for the individual and the organization, and numerous other aspects of behavioral science research that affect this important field of training.

In all our endeavors we must become *professional* in our ability before we can achieve, if possible, the status of a profession.

To act as a professional demands some standards.

## TRAINER CHARACTERISTICS

While there is no clear-cut set of standards for trainers, experience indicates that successful trainers will have some of the following characteristics. (It should be kept in mind that this is a series of proposed guideposts and not an inflexible yardstick to be applied to all training staff personnel.)

1. *Professional background.* Often people with professional preparation in one of the following fields will have attained insights helpful in preparing for the role of trainer: sociology, psychology, social work, educational psychology, psychiatry, personnel, administration. However, because of the wide variance of training, even within a given field, professional preparation does not guarantee competence, and, conversely, people can be competent without such conventional academic training. Nonetheless, knowledge in these fields is essential to a well-rounded training program, whether self-taught or in the academic situation.

2. *Group experience.* In addition to a professional background of some kind, training personnel should have met the practical problems of learning to work as group leaders. Experience with groups might simply have firmed up old habits of authority-wielding and afforded practice in ineffective work habits. Experience, then, can be helpful or harmful for a trainer, depending on its quality.

3.  *Self-understanding.* This is an absolute essential in the trainer's role. The trainer must have sufficient understanding of his own motivations and sufficient control of his own mechanisms of defense to (a) prevent his own needs from interfering with the training process and (b) enable him to empathize with the interpersonal problems of others in the training process.

4.  *Personal security.* Along with his training experience, a trainer must have sufficient personal security to permit him to take a relatively nonpunitive role in the training, to be warm and accepting in his relations with others, to have a genuine respect for them, to have a willingness to share leadership roles, and to relinquish authority as training proceeds. In fact, sufficient personal security to allow the trainer to participate adequately in a rather wide range of interpersonal situations is indispensable.

5.  *Training skills.* With the proper background and maturity, one probably can learn enough of the training skills necessary in modern training designs to become an effective member of a training staff, assuming, of course, that in his professional background the person has acquired a working knowledge of the process of scientific problem-solving and social change. These skills can be acquired. Obviously, the wider his range of skills, the more effective the trainer can be in applying them appropriately in the training design.

6.  *Democratic philosophy.* If a person can meet to a modest degree each of the above criteria, he will probably have as part of his behavior a democratic philosophy of leadership and work so that he can encourage learning situations in which persons learn for themselves.

Such standards, as general as they are, may not be agreed upon by the majority of persons in the training field.

## TRAINING NOT YET A PROFESSION

In summary, training has not yet reached professional status. Some of the questions it must ask, and reach consensus upon among its own practicing members, are:

1.  What is the real purpose of training? Within which specific projects, courses, and programs can it be fitted?

2.  What are the roles of the training office and the training director?

3.  What are the appropriate and agreed-upon criteria for professional development which are likely to determine whether or not training will be accepted as a profession?

4.  How can practicing members best go about implementing these criteria?

There is ample indication that training, ill-defined as it is, has good acceptance in many organizations. Sometimes training is basically accepted. More frequently, however, it resembles a company activity we visited recently which featured a display not only of the company's manufactured items, but also those of its competitors. The rationale was that by featuring the industry all individual manufacturers gained. We asked whether there were evidence of the validity of this rationale. "Oh," was the reply, "we don't know. Frankly, we're afraid to curtail the activity because we might find out it is valid."

We in the training field cannot rest too long our professional case on this sort of evidence. Out of our huddling together, mumbling training ritualistic lingo in one another's ears, and stoutly maintaining in a blunt tone, "We *are* a profession," must come some beginnings, some actions, some planned changing, that will advance our efforts to professional status.

## NOTES

1. Bestor, Authur, *The Restoration of Learning.* New York: Alfred A. Knopf, 1955, 269.

2. National Education Association, Division of Field Service, The yardstick of a profession. Institutes On Professional And Public Relations, 1938-1947. Washington, D.C. *The Association*, 1948, p. 8.

3. Hollis, Ernest V., and Alice L. Taylor, Social work education in the United States; report of a study made for The National Council on Social Work Education. New York: Columbia University Press, 1951, 109-110.

4. Flexner, Abraham, What are the earmarks of a profession? As quoted in *Readings in the Social Aspects of Education* (compiled by Smith, B. Othanel, *et al*). Danville, Illinois: Interstate Printers and Publishers, Inc., 1951, 553-556.

5. *Webster's New Collegiate Dictionary*, 1959.

6. National Education Association, *op. cit.*, 3, 5.

7. Flexner, Abraham, *op. cit.*, 4.

# REFLECTIONS OF A TRAINING DIRECTOR

*Frank C. Goodell*

The January-February issue of *Personnel Administration* contains an article by Mr. Nicholas J. Oganovic captioned, "Improving the Breed,"[1] which has prompted my rumination on the application of this theme to all of us who are engaged in the professional/occupational field of training, development, and adult education.

From *Adult Leadership* (September, 1968), 109-110, 150. Reprinted by permission of *Adult Leadership*.

I would like to offer some constructive criticisms and then pose some areas for improved personal performance. I will conclude this essay with the construction of a model of an effective training director.

These observations which follow are addressed to all who have significant responsibilities for the training and development function of management, whether we call ourselves Training Directors, Employee Development Officers, Directors of Education, Coordinators of Education/Training, Management Development Directors, Instructors, or the like. The objective that we share in common—the very purpose for our professional and occupational existence—is the changing of adult behavior through the dynamic processes of education, training and development.

## LACK OF AN OCCUPATIONAL OBJECTIVE

My first criticism, then, is that too many of us who labor in this vineyard have quite forgotten, or never realized, what it is that we are trying to accomplish. The fundamental concept of our mission—the development of those human resources with which we are working is all too frequently lost in the labyrinth of pursuing daily habit patterns.

We are so eternally busy organizing a program or course or class, meeting it ourselves or lining up the available resources (in most instances following without deviation the routine established on the very first offering of the course), that we never really determine if all this daily effort has resulted in the only really important consideration, namely, the development of certain specified behaviors in those human beings so lately charged to our care.

## LACK OF A CRITICAL ATTITUDE

We educators and training directors so commonly live in a world of our own making. We want to rely on a graduate degree or academic tenure or organizational title to render us immune from any necessity of reviewing our own handiwork.

At times, we may sense that our students/trainees/course participants are puzzled, confused, and quite muddled in grasping significant subject-matter concepts, but how often do we actually reflect on this experience and restructure the approach? Be honest, now, and recall when you last made a genuine change in course content or personal performance in response to a post-course evaluation study.

And what of those in our field who are not even going through the formality of soliciting evaluations? These, I submit, are the worst of our breed. These are our colleagues who don't know that they don't know, and what a disservice they do themselves and the field of training and development by their insulation from the world of reality.

The most charitable view to entertain with respect to this group is that their own careers are at stake and the general trend toward greater sophistication and excellence in management will serve to identify and ferret out these types who refuse to assess and continuously upgrade their own performance.

## LACK OF SELF–DEVELOPMENT

The next area I want to touch on is the frequency with which we seem to meet colleagues in our field who give no evidences of efforts directed toward their own continuous self-development.

Amazing as this paradox is, in view of their working in the very field that is identified with the necessity for continuing education, these unfortunates labor under the notion that they can intelligently diagnose, guide, counsel, and instruct others while not having to expose themselves to the burdens of carrying additional course work, expanding their professional reading, and critiquing their own performance on a continuing basis.

Here we find the employee development officer and the professor alike, whose platform communications are poor and ineffective, and who are taking no steps, developing no plan, to improve their performance. Here we find the training directors and coordinators who know little of their organizations' functional operations and less about the findings of learning theory.

Here we find those in our midst who attempt to communicate with no utilization of audio-visual aids, along with those who ineptly attempt to devise courses and programs around a meaningless montage of training films.

I submit that it is not uncommon in our field to encounter those education/training personnel who are administering tuition refund programs and who haven't availed themselves of this self-development resource to advance their own knowledge of management and educational research.

Here we also find the employee development officers, the training directors and coordinators, and the professors of management-oriented subjects who don't hold memberships in the major personnel, training and development, and adult education societies that are dedicated to making these professional and occupational fields more significant in modern management. But does my observation parallel yours in this respect: how often do you hear this "non-joiner" type disparage the value of these societies while his very conversation soon reflects how poorly informed he is in many areas of behavioral research as well as in the hard management sciences?

## LACK OF A LEADERSHIP ROLE

This logically follows on a base of inadequate matriculation through adult education and management subject matter, overlaid by a lack of motivation for professional development.

The leadership role is there to play, I submit, but the colleague I've been describing can't possibly fill it. Invariably this is sensed by the individual and he reacts by further insulating himself from his more knowledgeable and professional colleagues. He comes in the course of time to the acquisition of a very parochial view of his function in the organization. "What do I do? It's right here in my job description," he says defensively, and then strikes out for another subject for conversation.

## PROPOSALS FOR CORRECTIVE ACTION

In order for the function of training and development to measure up to the heavy responsibility that is being laid upon it for the effective development of human resources, we must develop a many-facted approach to "improve the breed," to borrow again Mr. Oganovic's phrase.

We might begin by frankly recognizing that there are a lot of rather unproductive, unimaginative, uninspired and uninspiring people who are working in this field and carrying around the titles I referred to in the opening paragraphs of this essay.

What can we do about them? Several things, I believe. We can discreetly focus attention upon their unwillingness to conduct meaningful evaluations which will measure not only the attainment of course objectives but the effectiveness of the administrator/instructor/coordinator role as well. We can work to devise systems that will bring these performance appraisals to the attention of higher management.

We can work toward the development of higher professional performance standards and seek to gain recognition for an upgrading of the training and development function in position management. However, great care must be taken to discriminate between training and development administrative levels in recognition that the lower levels do not require an upgrading in relationship to the professional standards that must be written for the higher management functions.

This is a challenging but not overly-difficult task in position management, and it will certainly redress in time the present situation of broad classifications of "Training Directors," "Employee Development Officers," etc. which do not adequately reflect the high performance levels and the broad (as well as specific) knowledges required in the *effective* performance of these higher grade positions.

We must identify, in short, our personnel who work in the training and development function for the knowledges, skills, and attitudes that they *actually* possess. We've got to interrupt this system, now so common in all sectors of management, that sees a "Training Specialist" or an "Employee Development Officer" automatically promoted to the higher grades when, for instance,

... he lacks a genuine ability for conference leadership

... he has a poor platform ability

... he has completed no course work in educational methods, administration, and research; advanced educational psychology, statistics, human relations

... he reflects no command of the principles of business and government organizations; of operations research, automatic data processing, and the currents of behavioral research

... he holds no memberships in the professional/occupational societies in this field and/or does not participate in the local chapters' affairs

... he plays no leadership role in the organization

... he does not personally instruct a course and gives little evidence of having achieved a competence in a pertinent subject area

... he is not locally regarded as an effective and informed speaker; he does not involve himself in the training and development aspects of community-oriented programs

... and–hallmark of hallmarks–he has no discernible enthusiasm for his work and his organization.

Do you recognize him? This is the person who is keeping us from achieving our vital mission. It's up to all of us who are striving for excellence in management and professional development to exercise our influence and do what we can individually and collectively to "improve the breed." It might help to consider a model.

## A MODEL OF A TRAINING DIRECTOR

He is a senior staff member of his organization's personnel management and plays a strong leadership role. He works with those in position management to identify jobs requiring higher and different knowledges, attitudes, and skills. He works with top management in organizational planning, management development, and manpower utilization. He maintains a very close rapport with department and agency heads in order to respond to their needs with programs of interdepartmental and interagency training significance.

He is constantly evolving systems of development for the personnel identified as having higher management potential. He formally conducts (or informally through this leadership role) educational guidance and counseling in the organization.

He is an innovator, an adapter, a visionary. He reads widely in the area of changing patterns of intergovernmental relationships. He is knowledgeable with the major outline and philosophy of the anti-poverty and equal opportunity legislation. He knows that the implementation of these programs of such dynamic sociological significance has both short and long range impacts upon his organization and his future work.

He is conversant with the major management theories and syntheses currently being researched and developed. He can intelligently discuss the rationale of management theories X, Y, and Z; the organizational grid; the functional Planning-Programming-Budget System; the extent of automatic data processing and operations research utilization in his organization.

His background includes an M.A./M.B.A. degree with graduate-level work in educational research and administration, the behavioral sciences, ADP and OR. He is a student of management and is familiar with the chief exponents and classic treatises in this field. He has a solid grounding in personnel management, incorporating both academic and work experience.

He not only administers and coordinates programs of management development drawing upon external resources, but he has a competency to personally instruct in major subject areas.

He is intuitively adept at conference leadership and has extensive classroom experience in the role of discussion leader and course instructor. He has completed an intensive training course and has acquired an expertise and sophistication with all major training formats and program devices. He has at least a seminar knowledge, if not workshop experience, in programmed instruction and CCTV.

He is familiar with the names and product lines of all the major A-V equipment manufacturers. He is conversant with the titles of, perhaps, three dozen management training films produced in the last ten years (he has personally previewed the majority of these).

He knows through personal contact the administrators of the major adult education programs in the community. He welcomes the contacts initiated by representatives of training-service organizations and regards these men and their organizations as valuable resources.

He is a member of national training and development, personnel, and adult education societies. He plays a leadership role in these organizations through his attendance and participation in the local chapters' affairs. He is an effective and willing speaker in the community. He works vigorously both on the job and off to promote greater excellence and sophistication in management.

He closely monitors all programs under his jurisdiction and views his own performance in a very critical light.

He looks to the career growth of his own training staff, taking great care to develop his subordinates to the limits of their capabilities.

And, finally, he looks to his own growth and self-development through wide reading, programmed instruction courses, graduate-level course work, participation in retreat seminars, and assumption of heavier training and development responsibilities.

Perhaps the exemplar doesn't exist in reality. But no matter. If you agree that this is a valid model, then we must bend every effort to approximate the ideal within the limits of our individual abilities. Out of this will emerge a profession.

In the meantime, we will comfort ourselves in the knowledge that we are making a major contribution toward that which is so sorely needed in our time: excellence in management. And management will reward us for our unremitting efforts.

**NOTES**

1.  Oganovic, Nicholas J., Improving the breed, *Personnel Administration*, The Journal of the Society for Personnel Administration (Jan.-Feb., 1966).

# WHICH ROLE FOR TODAY'S TRAINER?

*Julius E. Eitington*

The training literature is full of articles which discuss, debate and delineate the roles of the training man. Similarly, rare is the conference for training people which overlooks this topic. The roles are described variously as "new," "emerging," "broadened," "challenging," "changing," "demanding" and "urgent."

While the concept of the changing role of the training man is a valid one, what may be overlooked in these discussions is that the trainer may, in practice, be saddled or enamored with a plethora of other less attractive and less effective roles. This concept had been brought home to me very poignantly while conducting (four times in the last two years) a course for the Graduate School, U. S. Department of Agriculture entitled "Seminar for Employee Development Officers." Some of these roles reflect attitudes and practices of members of those seminars; some were suggested by seminar members as role descriptions of other trainers they had seen in action. In any case, a number of these roles are discussed below. They are merely meant to be suggestive. The reader will readily call to mind a number of other roles which he has encountered in his training experience. Hopefully, he will use the "mirror technique" to ascertain whether he is filling one or more roles which is vitiating his effectiveness; if so, perhaps he can take appropriate action to assume other more meaningful and productive roles.

## THE REHABILITATION OFFICER

One of the more demanding roles which the training man often rallies to fill is that of the Rehabilitation Officer. The opportunity arises when management presents the trainer with this kind of challenge: "Les Wurk has been aboard 14 years now and in this period of time he hasn't done anything for us except produce delays, consternation and embarrassment. We've tried everything, so now it's your turn. How about sending him off to a year of advanced study at Retread U? It may do him some good, and even if it doesn't, we will have him out of our hair for 10 or 12 months." So the university catalogs are dusted off and a suitable academic tour, or possibly a series of short courses, is found for Les.

A variation on the Rehabilitation role is that of Morale Building. Thus, employees may be generously included in training courses because they are unhappy over a promotion which they didn't receive, or because long-service should be rewarded, or

From *Training and Development Journal*, **24**, No. 2 (February, 1970) 9-11. Reprinted by permission of the American Society for Training and Development.

because they are members of a minority group, or because they haven't had any training for a good while, or because they are in grades or types of jobs which don't ordinarily receive training opportunities. The Morale Officer role can be rationalized away, of course, as a means of "improving relations with management." Conveniently ignored are the facts that employees quite often see through these devices or that the shot in the arm is of very short duration at best.

Oddly enough, employees also may be sent off for training, not as a bonus or reward, but as a punitive or disciplinary kind of thing. Thus, in the Employee Development Seminar cited above, one participant cited a case of a West Coast manager who had been requested in writing twice to attend a two-week leadership course, but which he assiduously avoided over a two-year period. When the organization head learned that his training instruction has been skillfully ignored, he ordered the man to attend an eight-week (!) course in the East (!).

### THE TOURIST REPRESENTATIVE

The training department is in a unique position to aid or frustrate the vacation plans of management and its employees. Thus, with a cooperative attitude it can send staff members to training courses to Florida in the winter and to Maine in the summer. Or, as a special kind of case in point, if Electrical Engineer Short has a daughter in college in Texas, there is no good reason why Short shouldn't take in a training institute in the Southwest rather than in Philadelphia where he is located. The fact that Engineer Short has been dodging training courses for years is not particularly significant for we, as trainers, do want to capitalize on this new-found motivation.

### THE STATISTICIAN

Collecting training statistics was, in years past, a very minor sideline for the trainer. This collecting urge, if unfulfilled, often produced great frustration. But now that the computer is so readily available, the statistically oriented trainer is really in his element. The assumptions now are that (1) we must program everything for "you'll never know when it may be needed" and (2) "since management is footing the bills it is entitled to know" (or is it snow?).

Thus a great deal of energy and ingenuity is devoted to producing tons of printouts which can advise management of vital quantitative tidbits such as:

- The number of middle-level managers between 30-33 years of age in Kansas City who have had training in high school algebra but not in sociology. This datum obviously can be compared with other age groups, with other levels of management, with those at other geographical locations, with height, weight and family size, and with almost anything else.

- The annual cost of all training in Better Report Writing since 1960 compared to the annual cost of carbon paper for the same period.

• The number of man-hours spent in formal training programs, broken down (unimaginatively) by department served, types of training provided, cost per trainee.

However, collection data is only half the task. Additional energies also must be devoted to the production of eye-catching graphic presentations in multi-color, all designed to prove to one's superiors that "training is really paying off."

In general, data such as the number of heads in the classroom may be of interest to management. More significant, of course, is the number of management problems solved.

## THE CHAPLAIN

Although effective training ordinarily relates to fairly concrete end-results, the training man may find that his occasional successes and apparent general expertise push him into the added but less precise role of the Chaplain. This develops since he often is presumed to be an "expert" in human relations (at least he teaches the stuff). Thus, people may gravitate to him with their troubles. The trainer obviously doesn't want to appear aloof or to be a possessor of tunnel vision, so he may readily fall into the trap of serving as a wailing wall. Thus the disgruntled, the disenchanted and the part-time workers (paid full-time, of course) may come around for all kinds of advice or to present criticisms of management operations, or more precisely, to achieve some kind of a catharsis for themselves. At the outset this role may have some ego-gratifying value for the trainer. But as more important chores are left undone, he may develop some awareness that he's caught in a bind. He thus may have to rationalize this and say to himself after a 50-minute listening bout: "Wonder why he wanted to tell *me* about this? Oh, well, I suppose it gives one some added insight into the climate of the organization."

## THE INSTRUCTOR

Confusion between the role of instructor and trainer is hardly a new problem. Stated simply, the Instructor is the chap who is concerned with "giving people the word." He operates, as he sees it, from the vantage point of his accumulated knowledge.

He thus has a compulsive need to share (transmit) this knowledge to others. He thinks in terms of lectures, blackboards, slide talks, overhead transparencies, formal classrooms, detailed agendas, and handouts in support of lectures. Conversely, he is less likely to think in terms of trainee involvement, trainee responsibility and trainee growth. Learning as a shared process would hardly be a key concept to the Instructor. There is also a good likelihood that evaluation of end results and the use of varied methodology, with a heavy emphasis on group work, would not loom very significantly in the Instructor's approach to training. Since the Instructor's needs are best met by a highly-structured program and by personally functioning from the lectern, his potential for growth is limited. A reassessment of this role, although vital, all too often doesn't take place. Instead, energies are directed to "pepping up" lectures or disguising them by terming them "talks" or "lecturettes."

## THE ELECTRONICS SPECIALIST

One of the hazards of the training business is that the trainer may become overly intrigued with the electronic hardware available so abundantly today. Thus, he may become an expert on video tape units, transparencies, film strips, tape recorders, projectors, carousels, teaching machines, tachistoscopes, electronic lecterns, microphones, speakers and the latest marvel, the compact, complete, self-contained, multi-purpose mobile, electronic training unit.

There's nothing wrong, obviously, with using up-to-date audio-visual equipment where appropriate. But what may well be overlooked is that the bright, dazzling and costly gadgetry are essentially devices for one-way communication. In fact, if I had my "druthers" I would opt for trainee-involving methodologies such as buzz groups, role playing, dyads, triads, in-baskets, exercises, games, the laboratory method, etc. and wager that adequately respectable end results would ensue with a minimum of paraphernalia.

## THE EVANGELIST

Another role which the trainer may assume is that of Evangelist or Preacher. His function, as he seems to see it, is to uplift the organization via a lofty doctrine or philosophy which he is quick to expound in depth. The exact nature of the dogma is not significant, so we'll let you, the reader, call on your own experience to cite a specific example. What *is* important is that it has (presumed) high moralistic, ethical and/or quasi-religious overtones.

Remember the old definition of a zealot? Well, it's simply the guy who increases his enthusiasm as he loses sight of his objectives. Nuf said?

## THE PROFESSIONAL

A role which some trainers endeavor to fill is that of the "professional." This role encompasses much verbal obeisance to the "Professional" nature of the work. With great flourish, the professional presents at every opportunity his impeccable (to whom?) credentials of an academic, experiential and/or literary character. Memberships in numerous organizations of a management and academic sort are touted to the impressionable. Attendance at conferences, courses and workshops is exploited to the extent that the budget will bear. Approaches to problems are presented with such opening gambits as "from a professional training standpoint . . ." or "it is widely recognized in professional circles . . ."

In general, the hallmark of the professional is a high concern with image development, all too often forgetting that one is evaluated essentially by what works, not by the ruffles and the flourishes.

## THE INTELLECTUAL

The knowledge explosion in the behavioral and management sciences since World War II has provided the trainer with new concepts, new language and new goals. All of this is helpful to the Intellectual to enable him to present an image of knowledgeability, currency and professionalism.

It thus is not unusual to hear the trainer talking glibly in terms of models, behavioral objectives, systems, real time, operational definitions, self-perceptions, other-directedness, O.R., 9-1, Theory Y, encounter groups, cognitive needs, role theory and the like. And when in doubt, one can always name-drop Likert, Herzberg, McGregor, Bradford, Argyris, McClelland and Maslow. Unfortunately, confusion on the part of line managers, who may be subject to this vague verbiage, will probably be regarded as proof to the Intellectual of the dated character of the line managers, rather than as cues or vital feedback for the communicator to soft pedal his pontifications.

## THE VENDOR

All of us have encountered the trainer who is enamored by the new. He thus is constantly "selling" his training wares on the basis of "this is the latest thing." He thus rides one band wagon after another, constantly hawking the virtues of the new, the novel, the latest, the most promising.

He readily rationalizes this approach by using cliches such as "shopping the competition," "adjusting to change" and "functioning on the frontier." His highest skill is quietly burying yesterday's fad for the enthusiasm of the moment.

## THE "HOBBY HORSE" RIDER

All of us, as trainers, have preferences as to what courses to teach and what programs to emphasize to the organization. However, not uncommon is the trainer who rides with a vengeance a particular training hobby horse. This is not to say the training being favored is not useful. But what goes awry is a sense of balance. Thus, in adopting a molecular rather than a molar view, the overall needs of the organization tend to suffer. In time, operating officials realize that they are dealing with a "specialist's specialist" and comments may be made such as: "There's no point talking to Carrithers about any training programs unless you're willing to settle for his help on his own hobby horse."

## THE BROKER IN COURSES

Our roles gallery would not be complete without at least a brief reference to the chap who serves as a broker or middleman in training courses. He thus can quickly provide the line man with course brochures from the AMA, NTL, and many colleges and universities and allied institutions. His only hangups are that:

1.  He doesn't have a real fix on the merits of one course versus another.

2.  Or for that matter, he doesn't know what the course will really do (end results), nor does he know what past attendees think of the course.

3.  He thus cannot assess for the organization the value, dollars-wise or in any other way, of the course.

4.  He also ignores the possibility of doing some of the training in-house for more measurable results at lesser cost.

Our discussion of roles is hardly complete. In fact, it is intended to be suggestive rather than encyclopedic lest the author find himself unwittingly in the role of the Hypercritic. But if we, as trainers, can't step back on occasion and look somewhat detachedly at ourselves, even if it pains a bit, can we in good conscience encourage the people we train to assume the vital role of Self-evaluator?

---

# LOOKING AT THE ROLE AND BEHAVIOR OF THE TRAINING PROFESSIONAL

*Gordon L. Lippitt*

In the first two sections of this booklet, the author has pictured the *trends* impinging on training and development and the means we use in our field to cope with these trends. Now we come to the most important link—the person who is carrying out the training and development function and role. The increased need of society is producing an enlarged role and increased responsibility for training directors skilled in individual and organizational development. This section will attempt to examine the various roles a professional training person is required to perform in meeting the complex need of organizational management. I see four major roles to be performed by training and development departments or offices in modern organizations:

---

From *Leadership for Learning: Training and Development in the 70's*, American Society for Training and Development (1970), 18-24. Reprinted by permission of the American Society for Training and Development. Portions of this section were excerpted from an article by the author and Leonard Nadler in the August, 1967 issue of the ASTD *Journal*.

Role No. 1: As a learning specialist and instructor.

Role No. 2: As administrator of training and development staff and programs.

Role No. 3: As an information coordinator.

Role No. 4: As a consultant to the management of the organization.

It is my feeling that each of these four roles or functions requires different skills and abilities. In a small organization, the training director may perform all four functions, whereas in a larger organization the "head of a department" might well be the consultant to management for problem solving while those on his staff administer, design and conduct training and educational programs.

## THE HISTORY

It is probable that the roles usually emerge in a sequence. Historically, this can be seen by reviewing the development of training in the United States. The earliest training activities were conducted by those who were concerned with serving as learning specialists and who were recruited out of the classrooms by industry during World War II. As we moved towards a peacetime economy, the tendency was for some of the trainers to return to the classroom. Those who stayed in business, industry, and government found themselves slowly moving towards administrative roles. As a result, management, in selecting people to direct the training function, discovered it had good administrators but weak learning specialists. In recent years it has been felt that some training problems require for their solution a broader attack than that furnished by the usual learning techniques. At that point, the third and fourth role—that of contributing to organizational problem solving—has emerged.

It is quite likely that within a given organization, the role of the training director has emerged in somewhat the same way. The emergence of this role does not mean, however, that the training director has developed the necessary skills to meet the change.

It is my feeling that a training director should be taking the initiative and be professionally prepared in *all four* areas.

## TRAINING PROFESSIONAL AS A LEARNING SPECIALIST

An important aspect of a training director's role is that of a learning specialist skilled in the ability to use learning theory and methods to meet training needs.

In a recent paper about this need for sophistication about learning, it was stated as follows:

Since the training director is concerned with learning, it follows that he should be concerned with learning theory. Training directors often talk about the learning theory that underlies their training. However, most of us do not have a good understanding of learning theories and their application to our training efforts.[1]

The behavioral sciences in the last two decades have made major contributions in the area of learning theory, methods, and skills.

"Research by the behavioral sciences in the learning process is also contributing to the successful practice of management. Recognizing that people come into a learning situation with an image of themselves as self-directing and responsible persons—not as dependent individuals—is one of the important realities to a superior trying to develop his subordinates. Also we know from behavioral science research that there are different levels of change in the development process. We know that people can increase their knowledge, insight, understanding, skills, attitudes, values, and interests; and we know that different methods are involved in developing different levels of these skills or knowledge."[2]

The responsibility of an enlightened and effective training department is to assure itself that one or more persons in the training department should be knowledgeable in the field of learning principles and practices. This could be a prerequisite for effective training designs as well as effective application in individual group learning situations. In the large training operation, the administrator of training may not have the time, inclination, or experience to be an active educator or learning theorist.

In such a case, he will delegate this function to an appropriate person on his staff. As This and Lippitt put it:

The sophistication needed to understand and utilize the implications of learning theory have much to say about the kinds of qualifications and skills a training director should bring to the job.[3]

One of the great challenges, therefore, to the training function is the increased sophistication required of appropriate training personnel in making use of the rapidly growing knowledge about how people learn and change.

## TRAINING PROFESSIONAL AS AN ADMINISTRATOR

As training programs have enlarged in organizations, the administrative role of the training director has begun to demand a major portion of his time, skill, and energy.

One professional practitioner explains it:

And now the training officer has become a training administrator, and his primary interest is the training office. He is more interested in its growth and efficiency than in actually teaching the latest in supervisory development or electronic wizardry. It is through the organization that he can do things, and it is only rarely that he will teach himself. Like college presidents and high school principals, he will direct and coordinate the efforts of those who do. Nor will he be apprehensive if the mission of the entire organization changes; he will adapt the training office to the change.[4]

In this role the training director must apply the skills of administration. He will need to recruit, select, and develop his staff team; plan programs; set up the process of coordination and communication; carry out financial planning of the training effort and all of the other administrative steps of leading a staff function in the organization.

The training director should know the principles and practices used in the administration of training programs. He should also know the concepts of management principles, including areas such as problem solving, the dynamics of organization, controls, and reporting procedures.[5]

The administrative function is a growing one in large organizational systems.

## TRAINING PROFESSIONAL AS AN INFORMATION COORDINATOR

In this function, the training person in an organization or community must serve as a seeker of information, clarifier of information, synthesizer of information, reality-tester of information, provider of information and as a communications "link" in the organization.

Let us examine these functions in more detail:

— As a seeker of information, the training professional must discover the goals and expectations of his organization for the training to be planned. He must learn from those in management what objectives and results are desired and who is to participate. He will want to request certain information from those who will guide the follow-up of training and development services. He will need to seek out information from those who know about the goals to be achieved, and whether other input-output information is necessary so that the training can serve the proper function. This might be symbolized as follows:

— As a clarifier of information, the training man will impart to the involved people, the multiplicity of ideas and information he has collected. Training and development in which there is no common understanding of intentions, plans and objectives is doomed to failure.

— As a synthesizer of information, the training professional will put into a proper frame of reference the different ideas and information which he obtains, bringing it all into focus so that the training activity is not a hodge podge of conflicting ideas and parts, but becomes an integrated learning experience with a proper sequence of events around a basic theme.

— As a reality-tester of information and communication, the training director should always help his superiors, or sponsoring organization, to see that the plans they approve are feasible, workable and realistic. The desires of management may not always be realistic in light of the allocated budget. The number of persons invited may not make possible the necessary learning goals; the facilities may not accommodate the necessary equipment. A professional must assume responsibility for bringing reality into the planning process.

— As a provider of information, the training professional will give proper information and communication to those in the organization from his own experience. He should present ideas, opinions and concepts that will be helpful in planning a successful learning experience. If he cannot do this, he is a "functionnaire", and not a professional member of the management team.

— As a communications link in the organization, the training and development person is the pivot for management, departmental and technical personnel, the meeting presenter and all others participating in the training. Obviously, he must be an effective communicator. To be effective he will need to:

- Be accessible to those who are working on training; or who will participate in it;

- Develop trust between himself and all others concerned;

- Level with people on plans and problems;

- Keep the goals clearly in mind, and help others to do the same;

- Define the responsibilities of others;

- Develop his listening skills.

In this way he will find this not only to be an essential role, but one which is seen as contributing to the greater assurance of a highly successful contribution of individual and organization development efforts to the process of effective change.


## TRAINING PROFESSIONAL AS A CONSULTANT TO MANAGEMENT

We come now to the function the author feels is the most important one in the training portfolio—serving as a problem-solving consultant to the management of an organization.

We have always recognized the need for management to *support* the training effort. The relationship of management to training has been explained in the following way:

The reporting relationship of the person responsible for the formulation of training plans and programs is particularly important, for if the job is to be done with optimum efficiency, he must be able to present his ideas and plans to people in the management who recognize the value of such plans and who are able to act on them with a minimum of discussion and other time-consuming maneuvers.

It is not, however, the support of training by management that is the major need. The major need is for training to be recognized and used as a valuable tool for management problem solving.

Effective training is helping people "learn how to learn" from every aspect of our life. Most problems faced by organizations can be solved by effective application of problem solving, which is itself a *learning process.*

The training office should serve as an example and a resource to management in the *solution of problems*:

Earlier theorists of organization were content to talk of measuring effectiveness in terms of adequate profits, efficient service, good productivity, or effective employee morale. These are not adequate in and of themselves.

Managers of an organizational system need to define its effectiveness in terms of its capacity to survive, maintain itself, adapt, and to develop toward its own goals and in the performance of multiple functions that also affect society.

## AN INCREASING ROLE

The new challenge, then, for a training director and department is to develop their skills and role in the organization as *internal organizational consultants* on problem solving, change, and organizational development.

This "internal consultant" role of the training man is important for the changing organizations of today's society. This role will require increased professionalization and skills in the training field.

"In a sense everyone is a consultant. Everyone has impulses to give advice, information, or help. Teachers, parents, and friends are consultants. Specialists in management, human relations, or finance are consultants. Also, everyone at times feels the need for help. In order that the consultantship between the helper and the recipient optimally meets the needs of both parties, appropriate relationships must be built. It is necessary that both parties have certain kinds of skills, knowledge, and awareness in order to establish these relationships."[8]

It is the feeling of this author that more attention needs to be given by the American Society for Training and Development, universities, and other professional organizations to providing the skills necessary for an effective consultant.

As Beckhard put it:

The consultant (or person in a helping role) always enters such a relationship as a person with authority—achieved either through position or role in the organization or through the possession of specialized knowledge.

To achieve an effective consultative relationship, it is essential that he understand the nature of this power and develop skills to use it in a way which will be viewed as helpful by the person receiving the help.

A person entering a consulting or helping relationship must have the ability to diagnose the problem and goals of the person being helped, and be able to assess realistically his own motivations for giving the help. He must also recognize the limits of his own resources to help in the particular situation.

In carrying out a "helping" relationship to management, a training director will find himself operating along a continuum of consulting roles. In Figure 1, we have

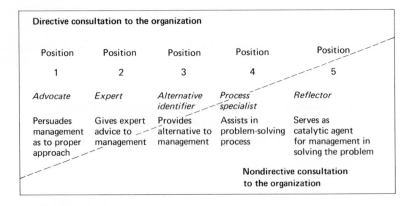

**Figure 1.**  Multiple consulting approaches of the training director

illustrated some of these major helping relationships from directive to primarily non-directive consultations.

## ROLE CHOICES

Let us examine these different choices in response to management need:

### Position 1: Persuades Management as to a Proper Approach

In certain circumstances the management of the organization may be attempting to solve a problem by using a medium or a method which the training man, from his professional experience, feels will not work. The training director may need to use the best of his persuasive skills, especially if time is short, to persuade management not to use that particular approach.

### Position 2: Gives Expert Advice to Management

There will be numerous occasions when management will expect the training director to give an answer when asked about a technical question, for example, about the value of a certain kind of training and its utilization in the organization.

### Position 3: Provides Alternatives to Management

In these circumstances we find that the training director may offer alternatives to management in the solution of a problem. The problem is not one in which the training director is the implementer of a solution, but one where he recognizes the values of identifying alternatives for management in confronting the learning aspect of a problem.

## Position 4: Assist in Problem-Solving Process

In this situation the training man serves as a process observer and consultant to management. He does not get involved in the "content" of the problem, which may be outside his area of competence. Rather, he helps management maintain the quality of its problem solving, through his skill as a specialist in this field.

## Position 5: Serves as Catalyst for Management Problem Solving

In this last category, the training man may only ask questions for management to take into account as it considers a certain direction or action.

What kind of a person is able to perform these four roles appropriately? Whether it is a line manager or a staff person who carries the training and development portfolio, it will require the proper knowledge, skill and attitude.

The effective development of the manpower resources of an organization is essential to its continued growth and viability. In most organizations someone with a training or development responsibility is expected to assist the organization in this respect.

What qualifications does this kind of person need to have? Must he be a behavioral scientist? Does he need to be an expert on communication systems? Does he have to be so courageous or personally active in initiating change, at a risk to his own job, that unusual psychological maturity is required?

Whoever is responsible for initiating manpower development will need to manifest *professional* behavior and leadership. Let me point out a distinction between a profession and professional behavior. In a pamphlet issued by the Society for *Personnel Administration*, this difference is elaborated by two definitions:

*Professional:* A person who is in an occupation requiring a high level of training and proficiency. This person has high standards of achievement with respect to acquiring unique knowledge and skills. A person who is committed to continued study, growth, and improvement for the purpose of rendering the most effective service. The level of training, proficiency, and ethical standards are controlled by a society or association of self-governing members. These people maintain and improve standards and criteria for entrance and performance in the field of work or occupation.

*Professionalism:* High level competence exhibited in action by people in a field of work. This behavior stems from an effective integration of a person's knowledge, skills, and attitudes which are derived from high standard education and experience.

It is a prerequisite for effective manpower development that those giving it leadership manifest professional behavior.

While ASTD is striving to be an organization which furthers the concept of a profession, the primary need is for those of us in the field to manifest professional behavior. This cannot be merely an outgrowth of the acquisition of degrees. It must be a manifestation of appropriate knowledge, skills, and attitudes in our day-by-day work in and for organizations. In this sense, I have found the following guidelines helpful:

- Focus on the problem-solving approach to learning and change; use data, not just hunches.
- Develop inter-dependence with others, not dependency.
- Practice what we preach in the field of our specialized knowledges.
- Diagnose situations, rather than merely treating symptoms.
- Understand ourselves so thoroughly that we do not let our personal needs get in the way of helping people and organizations to develop.
- Communicate on a reality level in an "open" fashion.
- Admit mistakes and learn from failure.
- Develop interests and skills so as to be able to work with people in a non-controlling manner.
- Be willing to experiment and innovate.
- Develop a personal philosophy about working and developing people and organizations.
- Capable of saying, "I don't know".
- Be willing to learn and change.

These criteria may not be the most important or only criteria for professional behavior, but they are some I have valued highly. Unfortunately, I find I am unable to achieve these standards as consistently as I wish. Suffice it to say, that while we want to increase the professionalization of the field of training and development through ASTD, the real goal is not some acquisition of certain areas of knowledge, but the professional styles of behavior each of us demonstrates in our manpower development responsibility.

In addition, I think we need to perform our task with a clear understanding of the ethical questions related to anyone who is involved in planned change through learning.

The professional trainer is a person who has responsibility for initiating, designing, and implementing learning efforts that will hopefully change individual, group, organizational, or community performance and behavior. What right does the training and development professional have to try to make others grow, develop and change? On what grounds does he base his values as the professional training and development person tries to influence others to change in one direction or another?

Recognizing that many words have achieved evaluative weight, it might be well to divorce, for the moment, our necessary value judgments from the processes these words describe. Manipulate, for instance, means the arrangement of conditions so that change in a certain direction may or will take place. The training director who arranges his classroom setting, provides certain selected skill practice sessions, asks certain questions, demands certain self-directed learning experiences, and creates certain motivational drives. He is "manipulating," whether he is teaching supervisory skills, technical expertise, or interpersonal effectiveness. From this point of view, each training professional, acting or refusing to act as a learning influence, is under judgment in accord with his basic beliefs and, stemming from those beliefs, his ethical system.

If we accept this line of reasoning, if we recognize that our commitment to a specific training and development responsibility in the organization often makes us potential renewal agents, then I submit that the question usually asked, "What right have I to try to make persons, groups and organizations different than they are?" must be reversed. The basic question which we cannot avoid is "What right have I to withhold myself, my skills and my convictions in a changing situation from helping that change to take place in a direction consistent with my convictions?"

In other words, the training and development professional should be *pro-active* and not just *re-active* in the way he demonstrates certain beliefs and values about the way people learn and change.

Our culture is based upon a system of values which embraces both individual and social ethics. To apply these ethical standards to the organization, the group, and one's self is an essential undertaking. As I point out in the book, *Organization Renewal*, it is an even greater challenge to relate these ethical values to individual and organization development. It is also important, I think, to clearly understand that there are some underlying assumptions supporting the need for individual and organization renewal:

1. In today's organizations there are unavoidable human problems which involve varying degrees of interpersonal and intergroup tension and conflict that keep the organization from functioning most effectively.

2. It is better that such human problems be solved than remain unsolved.

3. Deliberate planning of solutions to these problems, which necessarily involve changes in the people, the groups, and institutions concerned, is necessary to a degree that it has not been in the past. Trial and error processes of historical accommodation are no longer adequate to the organizational needs of today.

4. The most promising source from which to derive principles of ethical control in the planning of the changes that we must make is in our system of democratic and scientific values. These values can be translated into norms or principles of *method* which can be used in the guidance and direction of the learning and development process, of deciding what changes are needed, and in evaluating the changes that are produced. The alternatives are to identify "democracy" or "scientific" with one substantive solution or another. Some people who favor decentralization will argue for it as "democratic management"—others will identify centralization with the "democratic" way. Let us translate these values into norms of method acceptable to both sides. Through conflict they may work out a solution which may not be what either held in the first place, but which hopefully will be mutually satisfactory to both.

Let me identify some guidelines that I feel might be helpful to the training and development professional.

The first guideline concerns one-way motivation. A trainer can be motivated, in part, by such individual needs as status, security, and prestige. One's own awareness of these motivations may clearly demonstrate the professional aspect of his role. The approach to problem solving should be *task-oriented* rather than prestige-oriented. The essential concern should be that the new condition achieved is better than the first, not that the person initiating change should receive credit or have an enhanced standing in the eyes of others in the organization.

Secondly, the processes by which individual or organization development is planned should be *collaborative*, it should involve appropriately the persons affected by the change.

Thirdly, in order for training specialists to conform to democratic and scientific values, the methods of problem-solving should be *experimental*. Though this norm may be most difficult to derive from basic democratic values, it is still very important. The opposite tends to be a kind of absolutist conviction that your present views are right beyond question. An experimental attitude means giving any reasonable but novel plan a try; it also means building into the learning and training methods of evaluation which will reveal whether the altered practices approach the desired change goals.

Fourth, the method used for individual and organization development, if it is to be democratic and scientific, must be *educational and/or therapeutic* for the people involved, leaving them better able to face and control future situations. We are not trying to only solve present problems, but rather to know better how to deal with future problems as they arise. The idea is not to get away from problems, which is to get away from reality, but rather to help people know better how to confront, diagnose, and solve problems.

Finally, it is my feeling that those of us who are initiating planned educational change must always be aware that we are *accountable*. In the first place, we are accountable to ourselves. The responsibility rests with us to examine our motivation, the results we desire and the methods we employ, and to see how consistently they correspond with the value response required of a professional. And we are accountable to those who are affected by our efforts. In this it is a help, and further guide, to accept the fact that the training and development specialist is always involved in and affected by the change he produces. He does not stand over and above—a little God who calls the shots and determines the destiny of others. He, too, is involved and affected, whether he be an outside consultant or a part of the organization system. He can never disassociate himself from the profoundly inextricable relationship he has with his fellow men in the learning, training and development process.

In this relationship, this author feels the training and development professionals should manifest *leadership*.

We talk a lot about leadership and leaders but the nature of leadership in our society is misunderstood. We recognize that leadership is dispersed in many groups and fragmented among many people. No one person is powerful in all ways. A leader in one field often does not know leaders in other fields. Thus, the important issues and problems of our nation are settled, not by one leader or one power group, but by a balance of power.

What makes a good leader? There is no one answer. The nature of leadership changes constantly. We have tried to identify leaders in various ways, tried to determine what makes a man a leader and not a follower. The behavioral scientists have at least four different views about leadership.

**Great Man Theory** — We used to hold to the theory that a leader is a great man, that leadership qualities are in-born, that people naturally follow the individuals who have these qualities. In this theory the great man is responsible for history; rather than history responsible for the great man.

**Trait Approach** — In this theory we try to identify the traits of a great leader that make him different from the rest of us. Are leaders taller, fatter? Is there any established body type for the great leader? No. Does he have a higher intelligence than the rest of us? No, great leaders come from all groups of citizens. Does he inherit an ability to lead? No. Are chromosomes and genes related to leadership? Many studies have compared the physical, intellectual, and personality traits of leaders, but there are no conclusive findings.

**Behavioral Approach** — Is a leader determined by what he does when in a position of leadership? He may be a symbolic leader, such as a royal personage. He may perform primarily a problem-solving or decision-making leadership function. He may perform an advisory or information giving function. He may function primarily as an initiator or as an advocate of some plan or proposition.

**Situational Approach** — This approach to leadership assumes that there are certain traits and capacities that are crucial for effective leadership in one situation and not in another. Studies in this area indicate that there is a need for flexibility in the selection and training of leaders for different situations.

There are at least three fairly well defined styles of leadership—autocratic, laissez-faire, democratic. In the autocratic style, the decision-making function resides in the leader; in the laissez-faire, it resides in the individual; in the democratic, it resides in the group.

Which kind of leadership style is best? Which style should be developed for leadership in an organization, professional association, or community? It is not that simple. In some situations, autocratic leadership is best. In some, democratic leadership is more effective. And in some situations the laissez-faire style does the best job. There can be no one set style of leadership which we can develop in ourselves or teach to others. Leadership must be flexible in style to meet the need of a particular situation which involves an individual, a group, an organization, or a nation.

Leadership is the effective meeting of the existential situation—whatever the situation is. And this effective meeting comes through confrontation, search and coping.

**Confrontation** — The effective leader does not run away from involvement. He confronts people and situations. He takes the initiative, does not pussyfoot, does not play games. He does not just react to a situation. He acts. He is able to face up to issues and problems.

The effective leader understands himself. The person who best understands himself is best able to confront situations and lead others. In growing into leadership, a man needs to understand himself, to be himself, not try to be someone else. A leader acts as himself, not as a copy of someone else. He does not put on the role of leadership. He is just himself, a person, a leader.

The effective leader must confront the needs of people in the situation. He must be able to understand the people's goal, his own goal, the company's goal. Effective leadership means good communications. It is hard to communicate between the generations, among friends, between management and labor, within a town or metropolitan area. But without confrontation and adequate communication, a man cannot be an effective leader.

**Search** – Effective leadership depends on search. The leader searches for understanding of the people, the situation, the causes and treats them. He knows that symptoms are only shadows cast by causes. The good leader, like the good doctor, looks beyond superficial symptoms to deep-seated causes. But in management we find many leaders who never search beyond the symptoms. They are busy on the surface, but never penetrate beyond the surface.

The effective leader uses the delicate radar of his five senses. He is tuned into others. His sensitivity has not become dulled.

The effective leader searches for empathy. He is "with" the other person. He is living in the situation. He can put himself in another's place.

The effective leader searches for data. We can get all the information we want or need today. The leader knows the importance of facts and data and knows how to use this material to help him make decisions.

The effective leader establishes trust with those with whom he works. He is trusted by the group. He may not be educated or mannerly or smooth or well-dressed, but the group trusts him and has confidence in his leadership and decisions.

**Coping**– The effective leader can cope with problems and situations. The best kind of coping is a minimum attempt to control other people, a minimum pulling of strings. People like to be told honestly what to do, but they do not like to be controlled. They like realistic leadership.

Managers often ask themselves: How can I motivate my subordinates? The question should be: How do I help people release their motivation?

The effective leader copes. He does not clobber people or manipulate them. He uses the problem-solving approach to situations. He knows that an organization is not one big happy family. There are frictions and disagreements which can often be saved if they are brought out and looked at and played out.

The effective leader copes through his ability to experiment, to be flexible, and to be open to change. He knows there is no easy answer, no one right answer to any problem. He is willing to take risks. He is not afraid to rock the boat. He does not fear failure.

The effective leader can cope because he has a good relationship between his philosophy of life and his philosophy of management. The attitudes and values he holds condition the way he manages. He is sure that people want to do a good job, want to change, and want to better themselves so this is the way he manages people. He gets much from them because he expects much and is sure they can do all he expects. He realizes their worth and potential.

The quest for leadership is not a choice we make. It is a responsibility. We are leaders only as we give ourselves to the task of leadership in the exciting, challenging, and demanding field of training and development.

## NOTES

1. This, Leslie E., and Gordon L. Lippitt, Learning theories and training, *Training and Development Journal*, (Apr. and May 1966). Reprint Series, Leadership Resources, Inc., Washington, D.C.

2. Lippitt, Gordon L., Implications of the behavioral sciences for management, *Public Personnel Review* (July 1966).

3. This, Leslie E., and Gordon L. Lippitt, Learning theories and training, *Training and Development Journal* (Apr. and May 1966). Reprint Series, Leadership Resources, Inc., Washington, D.C.

4. Gill, Thomas W., The trainer as an administrator, *Training and Development Journal* (Mar. 1967).

5. Nadler, Leonard, Training directors and professional education institutions, *Adult Leadership* (Jan. 1955). Reprint Series, Leadership Resources, Inc.

6. DePhillips, Frank A., William M. Berliner and James J. Cribbin, *Management of Training Programs*. Richard D. Irwin, Inc., 235-236.

7. Lippitt, Gordon L., Implications of the behavioral sciences for management, *Public Personnel Review* (July 1966).

8. Gibb, Jack R., The role of the consultant, *The Journal of Social Issues,* **15**, No. 2 (1959).

9. Beckhard, Richard, *The Leader Looks at the Consultative Process*. Leadership Resources, Inc., 1961.